Hypnosis, Compliance and Belief

Hypnosis, Compliance and Belief

GRAHAM F. WAGSTAFF

Lecturer in Psychology,
University of Liverpool

THE HARVESTER PRESS

First published in Great Britain in 1981 by
THE HARVESTER PRESS LIMITED
Publisher: John Spiers
16 Ship Street, Brighton, Sussex

British Library Cataloguing in Publication Data

Wagstaff, Graham F
  Hypnosis, compliance and belief.
  1. Hypnotism
  I. Title
  154.7   BF1141

  ISBN 0-7108-0017-7

Typeset in 9 on 11 Times by Inforum Ltd, Portsmouth
Printed in Great Britain by
The Thetford Press Ltd., Thetford, Norfolk

To my mother and father
Martin, Peter and Jan

Contents

Preface

EXPLAINING HYPNOTIC BEHAVIOURS

The major task of the behavioural scientist is to try to describe and explain behaviour, and normally this is accomplished by generating and testing hypotheses that account for the previously inexplicable in terms of what is understood. However, a very curious feature of hypnotic behaviours has been their resistance to explanations in terms of knowledge that is already available; indeed, many scientists and clinicians continue to devise very elaborate experimental procedures to demonstrate that hypnotic phenomena cannot be accounted for in terms of more familiar psychological concepts such as obedience, belief, deception and relaxation, but by a mysterious, illusive 'something else' or 'essence', unique to hypnosis, which generally defies explanation.

Having spent some years studying the literature on hypnosis, I had to admit that no single 'mundane' concept seemed capable of explaining *all* hypnotic effects. In fact, it appeared doubtful whether any single concept could account for the multitude of contradictions and anomalies to be found in this area. For instance, it seemed most odd that people supposedly able to tolerate surgery under hypnosis were not necessarily the same people who were 'hypnotically susceptible' by other criteria, that some subjects judged by a hypnotist to be in a 'deep somnambulistic trance' strongly denied feeling the slightest bit 'hypnotised', and that some 'hypnotised' subjects reported they were 'hypnotised' because they felt lethargic and drowsy, whilst others given similar suggestions were quite alert and managed to lift enormous weights, did complex tests, and acted like buffoons. After puzzling over these problems for some time it occurred to me that perhaps the reason why no investigator has been able to find an acceptable solution to this mystery is that there is no central mystery to solve. Instead, we might have a collection of phenomena, bound together in name only by the term 'hypnosis', but which demand a number of different explanations. My conclusion seemed similar to that arrived at by Kusche (1975) following his investigations of the infamous 'Bermuda Triangle'. He says:

> My research, which began as an attempt to find as much information as possible about the Bermuda Triangle, had an unexpected result. After examining all the evidence I have reached the following conclusion: *there is no theory that solves the mystery*. It is no more logical to try to find a common cause for all the disappearances in the Triangle than, for

example, to try to find one cause for all automobile accidents in Arizona. By abandoning the search for an overall theory and investigating each incident independently, the mystery began to unravel (p.251)

Given this impression, I wondered whether many of the mysteries of hypnosis might be, at least partially, unravelled by reference to a number of possibly related areas of mainstream psychology; and this book represents my attempt to find commonalities between the phenomena subsumed under the term 'hypnosis' and other phenomena more familiar to psychologists and physicians, and hopefully, the layman. Fortunately, much groundwork for this task has been done for me by investigators such as T.X. Barber, T.R. Sarbin and M.T. Orne, who have already applied some social psychological concepts to their investigations of hypnosis. Their work provides a valuable contribution towards the creation of links between hypnotic situations and analogous contexts, and forms an integral part of the analysis used in this book. However, I have not adhered to any one of the particular approaches proffered by these investigators; instead I have attempted to integrate, update, extend, and often reinterpret the empirical data derived from many different approaches.

I can hardly claim that the resulting analysis can adequately account for all hypnotic phenomena in down-to-earth terms, and many intriguing problems remain, but I hope this book will be of interest to anyone who is growing rather weary of the old defeatist cliché that 'nobody knows what hypnosis is, but it works!'

I would like to thank all the staff of the Department of Psychology at Liverpool for their encouragement and their fortitude in putting up with their daily dose of hypnosis, and I would like to express a very special 'thank you' to Van Thompson, Jean Williamson and Dorothy Foulds for their secretarial expertise.

1. Hypnosis Past and Present

Though many scientists and clinicians would object to hypnosis being included within the category of paranormal phenomena along with psychic surgery, spoonbending, and mental telepathy, many of the traditional claims for hypnosis seem no less incredible. Under the influence of hypnosis the most ordinary person is supposedly invested with powers verging on the superhuman; these include regressing to childhood with uncanny accuracy, doing amazing impressions of chickens and zombies, turning on hallucinations, raising blisters, losing warts, becoming deaf, dumb, blind and amnesic and being able to survive attacks by pins, ice cold water and the surgeon's knife without flinching. More recently, it has been claimed 'hypnotised' subjects can recall as much in three minutes as a 'waking' person can in ten minutes (Krauss, Katzell and Krauss, 1974), and are able to show a definite improvement in visual acuity without spectacles (Graham and Leibowitz, 1972). Possibly of even more interest is the demonstration of the capacity for 'automatic' writing and talking (Knox, Morgan and Hilgard, 1974; Stevenson, 1976). According to the proponents of 'neodissociation theory' it is possible to get a hypnotic subject to perform a task with one of his hands, or talk, but he will be unaware this is happening. If given as a post-hypnotic suggestion, it is even possible for automatic handwriting to take place whilst the subject is wide awake; the hand is placed inside a box and writes away, apparently of its own accord, responding to the commands of the hypnotist.

The notion that so many remarkable effects can be embraced by the term 'hypnosis' might remind the more suspicious reader of the old patent remedies guaranteed to cure anything from haemorrhoids to ingrowing toenails. However, anyone who has seen a good hypnotist at work will be impressed by the authenticity of the demonstrations. The fact that these 'look' so good has probably played a major part in maintaining the belief that 'hypnotised' subjects must be in a special 'trance' state in order to manifest these amazing effects. This belief is probably very widely shared by the lay-public. In 1975 I administered a questionnaire on paranormal phenomena to a small sample of the general public attending an open day at the University of Salford. One of the questions concerned the extent to which they believed in hypnosis, 'as a special trance state in which you do things that a person in a "normal" state *cannot* do'. Of the forty-six who answered the questionnaire, 11 per cent said they did not believe in hypnosis as defined by the statement, 11 per cent said they were not sure, and 78 per cent said they did believe hypnosis was a unique trance condition in which one could perform in a way not possible in a 'normal' state.

In order to understand how this belief came about, and how so many apparently disparate phenomena managed to become subsumed under the term 'hypnosis', it may help to look briefly at accounts of some rather colourful characters. Anyone who wishes to read more about them should consult historical reviews of hypnosis by writers such as Mackay (1869), Binet and Féré (1901), Podmore (1964), Ellenberger (1970), Sarbin and Coe (1972), Sheehan and Perry (1976), and Thornton (1976).

MAGNETIC MARVELS

The discovery of hypnosis is generally attributed to Franz Anton Mesmer, whose theory of animal magnetism came to the fore during the 1770s; however, Mesmer himself modified the theory of magnetism communicated to him by one Father Hell, a Jesuit professor of astronomy at the University of Vienna. According to this theory, all bodies were pervaded by a universal magnetic fluid which was influenced by the planets. In human beings the planetary influences created two states, 'intensions' and 'remissions' which, when in magnetic disharmony, produced maladies. Mesmer maintained that if harmony could be restored to the magnetic fluids of the afflicted individuals they would be cured. He attempted to do this by fixing metallic plates or 'tractors' to his patients, and apparently achieved some success (Mackay, 1869). At first he thought the efficacy of the plates depended on their metallic qualities and form, but he subsequently found that he could achieve equally effective results without using them at all by merely passing his hands downwards towards the feet of the patient. Hence the famous 'mesmeric passes' were born. When Mesmer moved from Vienna to Switzerland his reputation grew. 'At his approach, delicate girls fell into convulsions, and hypochondriacs fancied themselves cured. His house was daily besieged by the lame, the blind, and the hysteric' (Mackay, 1869, p.277). Moving on to Paris in 1778 he set himself up in a spacious house. His mode of operation at this time was to seat his patients round an oval vessel, or 'baquet' filled with water and iron filings; the patients sat round it holding each other by the hands and pressing their knees together to facilitate the passage of 'fluid' from one to the other. From the baquet issued long iron rods which the patients applied to the afflicted parts of their bodies. According to Mackay (1869) Mesmer employed young and virile assistant mesmerisers whose job it was to pour streams of magnetic fluid over the patients, and to apply various therapeutic techniques such as embracing them between the knees, rubbing them down the spine, and 'using gentle pressure upon the breasts of the ladies' (p.279). All this was often done to the accompaniment of the piano or harmonica, or the voice of a hidden opera singer. The result of this seemed to be that some of the patients (mainly ladies) went off, one after the other, into convulsions, or 'crises'. During these 'crises' Mesmer would appear wearing a long robe of lilac coloured silk embroidered with gold flowers, and bearing a white magnetic rod. He stroked them over their eyebrows and down the spine and artistically traced figures upon their breasts and abdomens with his white wand until calm was restored. Many seemed to receive great pleasure from Mesmer's back and abdominal message. 'Young women were so much gratified by the crisis, that they begged to be thrown into it anew; they followed Mesmer through the hall, and confessed that it was impossible not to be warmly attached to the magnetizer's person' (Binet and Féré, 1901, p.11).

On 12 March 1784, the King of France appointed two commissions to investigate Mesmer's activities. The commissions included eminent men such as Benjamin Franklin, Lavoisier, and Bailly the astronomer. Bailly noted that the magnetiser achieved most success by the application of his hands and the pressure of his fingers on the abdomen, 'an application often continued for a long time — sometimes for several hours' (Mackay, 1869, p.281). Bailly also noted the individual differences in responses; some were calm and tranquil, exhibiting no effect, others coughed, spat, and sweated profusely, others were agitated and tormented with convulsions, and some rushed around hugging and kissing each other. The report of the commissioners concluded that it was imagination, and not magnetism, that accounted for the phenomena, and Mesmer's reputation in France was ruined; however, magnetism was far from dead and continued to flourish under a number of different guises.

The ecstatic outbursts of Mesmer's ladies seem a far cry from the modern hypnotic subject quietly doing his automatic handwriting or being operated upon. Some of the 'quietening down' can probably be attributed to a French landowner and devotee of Mesmer, the Marquis de Puységur. One day in 1784 Puységur 'magnetised' one of his peasants, one Victor Race. Young Victor, instead of falling into convulsions, appeared to dose off; however, Puységur found he could still communicate with him. He termed this state 'artificial somnambulism' because of its similarity to that of a sleepwalker. Two features of the peasant's behaviour particularly intrigued Puységur; firstly, Victor spoke to his master as an equal, instead of adopting his usual humble and subordinate manner; and secondly, he was unable to recall having done this when he 'awoke' (which was rather convenient!). After further experiments Puységur eventually claimed that he could communicate, soul to soul, with Victor without any physical means whatever. There was then no stopping Puységur; having magnetised an elm tree, he went on to put other patients into a magnetic state, characterised by the appearance of a deep sleep followed by amnesia. By now, the supernatural powers of the patients had surpassed telepathy; according to Puységur not only could they detect the diseased parts of the body of another patient by merely passing their hands over his clothes, but they could also see into the interior of his stomach.

Whilst Puységur was producing these wonders round his magnetised elm tree, another famous magnetiser appeared in Lyons, the Chevalier de

Barbarin. Barbarin managed to send his patients off into the now familiar sleep-like state of artificial somnambulism by sitting at their bedsides and praying that they might be magnetised. Barbarin's followers claimed that a good magnetiser could communicate with his patient from any distance, as well as being able to effect dramatic cures for almost any disease. To the sceptical, these clairvoyant powers would seem to be of dubious validity; however, the competent magnetiser of people did seem to have a genuine ability to relieve a variety of ailments. For example, in 1798, an American surgeon named Benjamin Perkins, a master of the celebrated 'metallic tractors', was so successful in helping the afflicted that a benevolent society built a hospital, called the 'Perkinean Institution', so that all comers could be magnetised for free, instead of the basic fee of five guineas. Unfortunately, Perkins fell into disrepute when it was found that wooden tractors painted silver were equally efficacious (Mackay, 1869). Perhaps Perkins should not have been so committed to the use of metallic plates; Mesmer, Puységur and Barbarin had all recognised that magnets were in fact unnecessary to produce the effects.

Much of the credit for ridding mesmerism of its magnetic origins is due to the influence of a Portuguese priest, the Abbé José Custodio di Faria. In 1819 Faria rejected the concept of a magnetic fluid as absurd, and proposed that the 'magnetised' person was in a state of 'lucid sleep' brought about by 'concentration'. He referred to those in this state as 'époptes'. Faria would induce the state of lucid sleep by simply asking his patients to sit down, close their eyes, and focus their attention on sleep. To terminate lucid sleep he would tell the person to wake up. Faria's observations show interesting insights into the nature of the behaviour; he says 'the sleep that results from the presentation of the concentrator's hand is only an effect of the épopte's concentration. At the sight of this behaviour, the époptes see what is required from them and they immediately lend themselves to fulfilling these demands, and sometimes even in spite of themselves, by the power of conviction' (Faria, 1819, p.356). Faria believed that people were differentially susceptible to 'concentration'; it was ineffective 'in people lacking the necessary disposition' and could only be used 'with particular illnesses and by people who are familiar with it' (p.276). He was aware that the 'cures' claimed by magnetism and concentration, when valid, were the result of the effects of suggestion rather than magnetic forces, and frequently used suggestions in his treatments noting, for instance, that 'a glass of water swallowed with the notion that it is eau-de-vie completely intoxicates' (p.6).

In spite of Faria's influence and the negative findings of a commission in 1837, the amazing powers of Mesmer's followers continued to draw patients and money. Some Mesmerists still claimed to be able to produce visionless sight, precognition and clairvoyance and there were also reports of painless surgery under magnetism. However, the form of induction had changed, most magnetists had abandoned their baquets and metallic tractors; no expensive props were necessary, just a paralysing stare, agile hands, and a monotonous voice.

It was not until the early 1840s that the term 'hypnosis' was introduced. In 1841 a Manchester surgeon James Braid, after witnessing some demonstrations of magnetism, believed that the subject was in a state of nervous sleep, and subsequently coined the term 'hypnosis' from the Greek 'hypnos', to sleep (Sheehan and Perry, 1976). Braid went on to argue that hypnosis is a sleep-like state of heightened concentration, in which imagination, belief and expectancy are more intense than in the 'waking' state. However, Braid's subjects did not lapse into violent convulsions and ecstatic behaviour, or claim paranormal capacities, though the occasional subject did groan a little and show slight convulsions of the limbs (Braid, 1899).

These early years laid the foundations for the common idea of the hypnotic subject as someone in a sleep-like state, controlled by the hypnotist, capable of superhuman feats, and often amnesic about the whole proceedings. However, there were a few more characteristics to be added, largely due to the influence of the celebrated French neurologist Jean-Martin Charcot. In 1878 Charcot set out to demonstrate that hypnosis was a condition related to neuropathology. Like Mesmer he worked mainly with female hysterics, and using these carefully selected individuals he noted three morbid syndromes of reaction or 'stages of hypnosis'. These could be produced by various combinations of Mesmeric 'passes' over the body, presenting unexpected stimuli, such as lights or noise or prolonged fixation of the eyes on a given object. In the first stage the subject was rendered cataleptic, the eyes were open, there was insensibility to pain, the limbs maintained the position in which they were placed, even when this position was rather difficult to maintain, and the hypnotist could instruct the subject to hallucinate. In the second and third stages, the lethargic state, and the state of artificial somnambulism, the eyes were generally closed and the subject appeared to be asleep. The skin was again insensitive to pain, but, especially in the state of artificial somnambulism, this was combined with hyperaesthesia of the senses of sight, hearing and smell (Binet and Féré, 1901). There are a number of important features here which are still evident in demonstrations by some hypnotists; the subject can be in a cataleptic trance with his eyes open, remaining in awkward positions for a considerable length of time and he can be 'hypnotised' by fixating an object (such as a watch), by being touched on the head, or by any other cue, providing he believes that this is an appropriate signal. The ability to freeze in an awkward position is a useful stage demonstration of the 'hypnotised' subject's unusual physical capacities.

The final touches were probably added by Hippolyte Bernheim, a medical professor at Nancy. In 1884 and 1886 Bernheim published works disconfirming Charcot's observation that somnambulism was confined to hysterics, and that it was not necessary to use various specific combinations of induction procedures; rubbing the scalp, fixation, passes, vocal suggestion, and simple closure of the eyelids all produced the same effect.

FROM MAGNETS TO METAPHORS

Sarbin and Coe (1972) have pointed out how the various exponents of magnetism and later hypnosis managed to produce the responses according to their theoretical viewpoints. Thus Mesmer, who believed that he was transmitting an invisible fluid into his patients which would excite them, managed to send a lot of them into a crisis. On the other hand, Braid believed that the power resided in the patient and was not expecting hypnosis to produce some dramatic spectacle, and his subjects were far more quiet and well-behaved. Charcot, looking for morbid symptoms, produced stages of catalepsy, lethargy and somnambulism in his patients, who incidentally, like Mesmer's, were specially 'prepared' by assistants before the master arrived. Bernheim, rejecting Charcot's claims, observed Charcot's three stages in one in several thousand patients, and this single instance was found in one of Charcot's former patients. However, what is also important is that so many of these ideas and effects have merged to produce popular assumptions about hypnosis, and the concept which seems to bind these elements is that of the hypnotic 'trance'.

As 'trance' generally refers to a state of insensibility in which a person appears to be in a profound sleep, it was ideally suited to describe the appearance of the 'hypnotised' subject as produced by people such as Puységur, Braid and Charcot. Some of the popular assumptions relating to the trance concept of hypnosis have been noted in particular by Barber and his associates (Barber 1969b, 1972; Barber, Spanos and Chaves, 1974). These include:

1. There is a special sleep-like state, or trance, which is qualitatively different from the normal waking state, and ordinary sleep. This is generally called a 'hypnotic trance'.
2. This state can be produced by a variety of 'induction' procedures. These include eye fixations, rubbing the scalp and various other parts of the body, making passes over the body, giving vocal suggestions for sleep and relaxation, and introducing miscellaneous auditory and visual stimuli.
3. When a person is in this state he can do remarkable things that are often impossible in a waking state, e.g. show enhanced physical capacities, produce amnesia and hallucinations on command, show insensitivity to pain, be cured of a variety of ailments, and experience strange sensations.
4. 'Hypnosis' is not a momentary condition, but lasts for a period of time. The subject is typically brought out of it by a command from the hypnotist such as 'wake up!', or a predetermined signal such as clicking the fingers, or counting down from 20 to 1. Even then, if he has been given a post-hypnotic suggestion he may still, without awareness, respond to the commands of the hypnotist.

5. There are levels or depths of 'hypnosis'; the deeper the level achieved the more responsive to suggestions the subject will be.

Although a number of present-day theorists continues to employ the term 'trance' in relation to hypnotic behaviour, a definitive account of its characteristics seems to have been rather elusive. The assumption that hypnosis possesses certain levels or depths largely stems from the idea of trance as a special form of somnambulism. However, the assumption that the 'hypnotised' subject is similar to a somnambulist or sleepwalker seems ill-founded. Barber, Spanos and Chaves (1974) point out that the sleep-walker differs from the 'hypnotised' subject in a number of important respects. For instance, the EEG brain wave pattern of the sleepwalker is that of a person in actual stage 3 or 4 sleep, whereas the EEG of a 'hypnotised' individual is that of an awake person, changing according to particular situations. Also, the sleepwalker does not respond to suggestions to be alert; in fact, it is usually difficult to wake him, whereas the 'hypnot-ised' subject usually responds readily when given the cue to wake up.

In spite of the lack of objective correspondence between the 'hypnotised' subject and the sleepwalker, the idea that hypnosis involves some kind of sleep-like state is prevalent in the continued use of terms such as 'somnam-bulistic' and trance 'depth' in the description of hypnotic behaviour (see Wolberg, 1972). Although many argue that hypnosis is not sleep, there seems to be agreement by some that hypnosis does involve some unique altered state. For instance, Bowers (1966) states that: 'Most investigators interested in hypnosis believe that there is an altered state which fundamen-tally differs from the waking state' (p.42), and Orne (1959) makes a similar proposal: 'hypnosis is evidently characterised by the ability of the subject in this special state to experience changes that are not normally found in response to similar cues in everyday life' (p.278). However, it is not clear how many writers who employ the terms 'trance' or 'state' are using them in a descriptive way rather than as explanatory constructs. Hilgard (1975), for example, has rejected these terms as explanatory constructs, and proposes that they are used only as metaphors to categorise hypnotic behaviours.

According to some investigators an important justification for continuing to employ the concepts of trance and altered state is that the terms corres-pond to the subjective experiences of hypnotised subjects. For instance, Sheehan and Perry (1976) state: 'The main reason for considering hypnosis as an altered state stems almost exclusively from the reports of subjects that, while "hypnotised", they experienced reality in an uncustomary fash-ion' (p.271). They go on to say that it is justifiable to postulate an altered state concept if the subjects' reports of depth of trance or state correlate positively with their responsiveness to suggestions. They claim there is merit in Orne's notion that 'whatever hypnosis is, there will be more of it in people who show more effects of hypnotism' (Orne 1972), p.430). Unfor-tunately, not all proponents of trances and states agree as to the utility of using verbal reports as indicators of these concepts. Wolberg (1972) seems quite emphatic about this: 'Asking a subject if he has been hypnotised is of little help. Generally, the subject will deny having been in a hypnotic state, even when he has achieved the deepest somnambulistic trance' (p.49). Furthermore, Spanos and Barber (1976) comment that subjects' reports of having been 'hypnotised' and their responsiveness to hypnotic suggestions can vary independently; subjects may report that they were 'hypnotised' but fail to respond to suggestions, or conversely, they may respond well to suggestions but state that they were not 'hypnotised'.

Several points seem relevant here. Firstly, if the term 'trance' is being used only as a metaphor, it may still be worth considering whether it is an inappropriate and misleading one. But secondly, can we really conclude that *most* people who use the trance concept really use it only metaphorically? The hypnosis literature continues to be dominated by studies either purporting or attempting to demonstrate that 'hypnotised' subjects behave differently from subjects who are 'awake', and that their behaviour is assumed to be a consequence of not just something 'ordinary' like obedience, or motivation or relaxation, either individually or in combination, but something 'extra', a special state that comes about when you are given a hypnotic induction procedure. For example, Evans and Orne (1971) argue that data from their experiments 'are more congruent with the view that hypnosis involves as yet unspecified alterations in the S's state of consciousness' (p.295). Elsewhere we are told that hypnosis is *more* than just a response to suggestion (Hilgard, 1973b), that it is *more* than a placebo (McGlashan, Evans and Orne, 1969), that it is *more* than sham behaviour and *more* than simply changes in motivation (Orne, 1966a, 1970). Whether 'trance' is being used as a metaphor or not, we still seem to be left with the problem of accounting for the 'mores'. Thus if *most* investigators are using the term 'trance' metaphorically, it still seems to refer to some unique property of hypnosis, which now unfortunately does not have a literal name. This really does seem to be a quibble over terminology, and does not detract from what I would consider to be a widely held assumption that hypnotic behaviour possesses a common, essentially 'hypnotic' property or ingredient not present in other behaviours. Whether this ingredient is termed a 'trance', and 'altered state of consciousness', a state of 'dissociation' or 'Big X' seems immaterial to this assumption. It is therefore not really surprising that despite the new, restricted usage of terms such as 'trance' by some academics, little seems to have been achieved in curbing the adherence of some writers to the original conception of hypnosis as a technique for producing some kind of zombie-like state of automatism. For instance, the back cover of a recent book on hypnosis by Hall and Grant (1978) informs us that the contents of the book 'break away from the superstition and mumbo-jumbo that have surrounded it [hypnosis] for so long'. Yet in the book we are still told of how hypnosis is dangerous because some people can be 'hypnotised' in a flash, without their volition, and have suggestions fed in the unconscious (p.51), and also how 'Gimmicky inductions can be·dangerous. For example, a subject can be told to go into a trance when he hears a particular piece of music; but if he is driving his car when the tune comes over his radio, he will probably be hypnotised' (p.52). Unfortunately, we are given no substantive evidence for these claims, but clearly such notions persist.

One way round this problem of definition is to avoid completely the concept of a hypnotic trance or state, and to try and incorporate hypnotic phenomena within the framework of other psychological processes. There have been two major recent attempts to do this. The first is the role-enactment approach of Sarbin and his associates (Sarbin and Anderson, 1967; Sarbin and Coe, 1972). According to this view hypnotic behaviours are manifested when the subject strives to take the role of the 'hypnotised' person. If he becomes very involved in the role, he may actually lose self-awareness or self-consciousness. The second approach is the cognitive-behavioural view of Barber and his associates (Barber, Spanos and Chaves, 1974). They summarise this as follows: 'subjects carry out so-called "hypnotic" behaviours when they have positive attitudes, motivations, and expectations toward the test situation which lead to a willingness to think and imagine with the themes that are suggested' (p.5).

RECENT DEVELOPMENTS AND PROBLEMS

In spite of the fact that 'non-state' theories such as these of Barber, Sarbin and their associates question the utility of the concepts of trance and altered states in relation to hypnotic behaviour, there seems to have been some convergence of views between the state and non-state positions with regard to the role of imaginative processes. Thus in his 1975 review Hilgard concludes: 'there is a convergence of all investigators upon the role played by the subject's imaginative and fantasy reproductions' (p.19). Also, Spanos and Barber (1974) have suggested that the major theoreticians are converging on the conclusion that hypnotic behaviour involves two factors, a willingness to cooperate with the suggestions, and a shift in cognitive orientation to one of imaginative involvement.

Although it is normally encouraging when investigators with different theoretical standpoints can achieve some harmony of views, in the case of hypnosis it also is important to be aware of the possible dangers of assuming agreement when many of the terms that are employed can be interpreted in different ways. For instance, different theorists have referred to 'role-playing' and 'willingness to cooperate with the experimenter' as important factors in hypnotic behaviour. At first, it may seem that implicit in these terms is the capacity for sham behaviour, i.e. the subject fakes 'hypnosis' to please the hypnotist or experimenter. However, they can also be used to cover a variety of other viewpoints. For example, Hilgard makes the following statements about Sarbin's role-enactment theory of hypnosis:

'The expressions he uses [role-enactment] give the impression that he thinks of hypnosis as some sort of sham behaviour. Actually, Sarbin does not believe this' (Hilgard, Atkinson and Atkinson, 1971, p.177). 'The current theory of Sarbin and Coe (1972) is elaborated as a social communications interpretation, one in which a person adopts a role suited to the other and behaves accordingly. He may become very deeply engrossed in a role (that is, he may show organismic involvement in it) even to the degree that it becomes irreversible. Because such organismic involvement is accepted, there is little difference to be detected between this position and the state-theories to which it is set as an alternative' (Hilgard, 1975, p.23). In this context role-playing is clearly not synonymous with sham behaviour. According to Hilgard (1975) the role-playing aspect of Shor's theory of hypnosis (1962b; 1970) involves the concept of 'organismic involvement' (a high degree of role involvement), so according to Hilgard's interpretation, Shor's concept of role-playing is not synonymous with sham behaviour either. Similarly, White's (1941) description of hypnotic behaviour as 'meaningful goal-directed striving' at first gives the impression of a capacity for faked behaviour when he says the most general goal is: 'To behave like a hypnotised person as this is continually defined by the operator and understood by the subject' (p.503). However, he also argues that this behaviour will only be manifested when the goal-directed striving occur within the context of an altered state of consciousness (Spanos and Barber, 1974).

These are interesting developments, for although investigators such as Barber and Sarbin pioneered the way for analysing hypnotic behaviour in terms of a number of more general psychological processes, including sham behaviour, the emphasis on imaginative and fantasy activities has allowed hypnotic behaviours to be reincorporated within the conceptual boundaries of trance and altered states, which can now continue to be put forward as common factors relating all hypnotic behaviours, which in turn, as sham behaviour seems to have lost emphasis on the way, can be pronounced as in some sense 'genuine'. The 'genuine' nature of hypnotic behaviour is clearly emphasised in Sheehan and Perry's (1976) conclusions that 'the problem of sham behaviour no longer constitutes a serious issue in the hypnosis literature' (p.271), and 'no present day theory which conceives of hypnotic behaviour as in some way fraudulent or as sham behaviour can expect to be taken seriously' (p.2).

Unfortunately, the desire to rid hypnosis of the embarrassment of sham behaviour, and to parsimoniously subsume all hypnotic behaviours under a convenient schema such as 'trance' or 'imaginative involvement' may lead us to a premature de-emphasis of the diversity of processes which could contribute to different hypnotic behaviours. Certainly, one of the main problems with attempts to explain hypnotic phenomena in terms of other psychological processes, without positing anything that is unique to hypnosis, is that no single 'ordinary' process is sufficient to explain *all* effects.

One will be hard pressed to explain wart involution in terms of faking, or extraordinary strengths in terms of relaxation. However, as Hilgard (1975) has pointed out, we should not be misled into believing that the postulation of an all-embracing trance or altered state actually explains anything. The trance or 'essence' of hypnosis has only really remained successful in subsuming all hypnotic phenomena because it has remained undefined and it may, in fact, be very misleading to assume that there is some basic hypnotic property common to all hypnotic situations. For instance, to what extent can we justifiably assert that a person undergoing an operation with hypnotic suggestions for analgesia is always in the same 'state', or doing the same 'thing', as a person who engages in automatic handwriting, or shows post-hypnotic amnesia, or regresses back to childhood? An unqualified assumption that there are important commonalities between diverse hypnotic behaviours can lead to rather dangerous sweeping generalisations from one category of responses to another; one argument I have frequently come across goes something like this: 'We know that people don't "fake" hallucinations or amnesia, because people can undergo operations under hypnosis without feeling pain'. As Chapter 8 will show, it may indeed be possible for some people to undergo operations with hypnotic suggestions for analgesia with apparently little or no pain, but perhaps we should be very wary of equating this with someone doing a fair impression of a chicken.

One way of avoiding this problem and elucidating these issues might be to employ a more eclectic approach, and to start from a more general assumption. We could assume that although many hypnotic behaviours may share commonalities, others may be influenced by somewhat different processes, and also different processes may produce similar behaviour in different individuals. In order to determine the plausibility of any particular process being responsible or at least partly influential in determining a particular hypnotic behaviour, it should be possible to look outside the immediate domain of hypnosis to other contexts which share commonalities with the hypnosis situation. For instance, by looking at other contexts in which people can be induced to behave in a bizarre manner and give false statements we may be in a better position to argue whether there is anything unique about the production of bizarre behaviour in hypnosis, and whether there is a strong case for saying some subjects may be exercising deceit. Similarly, if we wish to elucidate the problem of how a person can be induced to genuinely experience changes in feelings, which he may label as being 'hypnotised' or in a 'trance', it may be useful to look at other situations in which people are induced to change their feelings and label their subjective experiences.

In the following chapters an attempt is made to begin such an analysis. However, firstly it may be useful to introduce some of the measures and terms which will be employed.

MEASURING HYPNOTIC BEHAVIOUR

The modern measurement of hypnotic susceptibility has been greatly aided by the development of standardised scales of hypnosis and suggestibility which are widely used in experimental and clinical work. As these scales will be referred to frequently throughout the text it may be worthwhile to give a brief description of the kinds of procedures and contents found in them. Probably the most commonly used are the Stanford Scale of Hypnotic Susceptibility (SHSS) and the Barber Suggestibility Scale (BSS). The SHSS comes in three forms, A, B and C (Weitzenhoffer and Hilgard, 1959, 1962). Forms A and B contain an induction procedure which gives instructions for relaxation and suggests to the subject that he is falling into a sleep-like hypnotic state. This is followed in each scale by twelve items or suggestions. Most are motor suggestions such as eye-closure, hand lowering ('your hand is heavy and falling'), arm immobilisation ('your hand is too heavy to lift'), finger lock ('you cannot pull your hands apart'), and verbal inhibition ('you cannot say your name'). Some require distortions of cognitive functions like post-hypnotic amnesia ('when you wake up you will find it difficult to remember what has happened to you') and hallucinations ('there is a fly buzzing round your head'). The SHSS form C contains a similar induction procedure but contains less motor items and more items requiring cognitive distortion, for example, being unable to smell ammonia.

For group administration, the Harvard Group Scale of Hypnotic Susceptibility (HGSHS) has been developed (Shor and Orne, 1962). This is a translation of the SHSS:A, but subjects score their own responses.

The BSS (Barber, 1969b) is an eight item scale which can be used with or without a prior hypnotic induction procedure and contains both motor and cognitive items, such as arm lowering, arm levitation ('your arm is rising'), hand lock, hallucination of thirst and selective amnesia ('when you wake up you will forget one of the tests').

It should be noted that these scales do not contain items relating to some of the more dramatic hypnotic effects such as insensitivity to pain, increased muscular performance, supernormal feats of memory, or the raising of blisters. Rather they are used as a quantitative preliminary measure of hypnotic susceptibility useful for classifying individuals as 'good' or 'bad' hypnotic subjects. Having established susceptibility in this way subjects of high and low susceptibility can be compared in terms of their performances on the more dramatic tasks. The use of these scales epitomises the modern experimental work on hypnosis. Hypnotists can either read out the detailed instructions to the subjects 'live', or they can be administered on tape. Swinging watches, Svengali gazes and body massages are deemed unnecessary for the manifestation of hypnotic effects.

The distributions of responses to these scales indicate that only a few subjects pass most of the items on the scales. For example, the distribution of the SHSS:C (which has a maximum score of 12), indicates, on a sample of undergraduate students, that 6 per cent score 11–12 (very high susceptibility), 18 per cent score 8–10 (high), 30 per cent score 5–7 (intermediate), but the majority, 46 per cent, score 0–4 (low). Moreover, when all subjects in the sample are considered, some items are passed more frequently than others. For example, on the SHSS:C, 92 per cent of subjects pass the 'arm lowering' item (indicating that even low susceptibility subjects are likely to pass this item), 88 per cent pass the 'hands moving apart' item, 27 per cent pass the item requiring them to forget (amnesia), whilst only 9 per cent state that they are unable to see an object which is placed in front of them (negative visual hallucination).

DEFINITION OF TERMS

Hypnosis as an area seems full of apparent paradoxes and confusions and the task of teasing out the many variables which may contribute to hypnotic behaviour is severely hampered by problems of a semantic nature. Although most people have some knowledge of the general concept of 'hypnosis' when finer definitions are required people's conceptions may differ; in fact, a central thesis of this book is that these very differences in preconceptions and expectations can account for a good deal of the variability in hypnotic responses. Probably the most difficult conceptual difference for many people is that between 'hypnosis' and 'suggestibility'. According to the *Encyclopaedia of Psychology* (Eysenck, Arnold and Meili, 1975), a 'suggestion' is 'A process of communication during which one or more persons cause one or more individuals to change (without critical response) their judgments, opinions, attitudes etc., or patterns of behaviour' (p.1077). The encyclopaedia also notes that 'non-hypnotic differs from hypnotic suggestion by being practised in a waking state' (p.1077). According to this kind of definition suggestions can be given both to people in a hypnotic situation and in a non-hypnotic situation, and 'suggestibility' can thus be defined as 'the individual degree of susceptibility to influence by suggestion and hypnosis' (p.1076). Although it is extraordinarily difficult to clarify the meaning of the very global term of 'suggestibility', perhaps one or two examples of phenomena which are often used as illustrative of suggestibility may be helpful. For example, 'suggestibility' may refer to the uncritical acceptance of ideas in situations where people are subjected to political and commercial propaganda (Eysenck, Arnold and Meili, 1975). Thus, if you uncritically accept what a politician or a salesman tells you, you have succumbed to 'suggestion'. If a person uncritically accepts that a treatment will cure him, he has also been influenced by a suggestion, and when this is combined with the uncritical acceptance of superstitious concepts, 'faith cures' may result (Eysenck, Arnold and Meili, 1975).

It thus seems useful to assume that the term suggestibility can be applied to a number of other contexts besides hypnosis. We would not normally say that a person who sleeps better as a result of taking a sugar pill has been 'hypnotised' by his doctor. If the doctor 'suggested' to his patient that the sugar pill was a potent drug this would constitute a 'waking' suggestion as it would be assumed that the patient was not in a trance or special state of 'hypnosis' when he received the treatment. Consider another example: If a friend came up to you in the street, told you to put your hand out and said, 'your arm is getting very heavy, it's moving down', this would be a 'waking suggestion'. It would be termed so because even if you responded to it, and your arm did feel heavy and moved down, neither you nor he would be likely to consider that you were 'hypnotised' or in a special trance state at the time. Although we will return to the concept of suggestibility in more detail in Chapter 7, some quotes from some eminent writers in the field of hypnosis should illustrate that suggestibility and hypnosis are not usually accepted as synonymous concepts:

> The hypnotic trance is more than just a state of heightened suggestibility (Gibson, 1977, p.24);
>
> Although the link between hypnosis and suggestibility is an important one ... the two concepts are not to be identified ... reports from subjects about their experience of trance forbid the simple equation of suggestibility and hypnosis (Sheehan and Perry, 1976, pp.46–7);
>
> Not all instances of heightened responsiveness to suggestion are properly conceived of as hypnotic in nature (Bowers, 1976, p.86);
>
> Waking and hypnotic suggestibility are conceptually, and quite probably empirically distinct (Evans, 1967, p.144);
>
> Hypnotic behaviour cannot be defined simply as response to suggestion ... the phenomena of hypnosis involve more than specific responses to suggestion (Hilgard, 1973b, p.973).

Even though the concepts may overlap, clearly these writers do not consider suggestibility and hypnosis to be the same thing.

In view of the complex nature of some of the experiments to be discussed, and some of the rather difficult semantic problems that are involved in their interpretation, it may be useful to define some other relevant terms *as they will be used in this book*.

1. *Hypnotic induction*. This refers to any procedure which explicitly or implicitly suggests to the subject that he is entering a special sleep-like state called 'hypnosis'. In most instances, this will be a standardised procedure which involves giving the subject instructions for relaxation and drowsiness and suggestions that he is entering a sleep-like state called 'hypnosis' in which he will be able to experience and perform interesting things. The induction is usually concluded by a statement or signal indicating to the subject to 'wake up'.

2. *Hypnotic suggestions*. These are delivered during or after the initial part of the induction procedure and involve instructions to the subject suggest-

ing to him that he will respond in a certain way, for example, his arm will feel heavy and move down. They *always* occur whilst the subject is assumed to be under the influence of induction, i.e. hypnotic suggestions are given *before* the subject is told to 'wake up'. Any behaviour which occurs as a result of the hypnotic induction or hypnotic suggestions, or during the administration of hypnotic induction or hypnotic suggestions, may be termed a 'hypnotic behaviour'.

3. *Waking suggestions*. These are instructions given to the subject suggesting to him that he will respond in a certain way, for example, his arm will feel heavy and move down, but they are *not* either preceded or accompanied at any stage by instructions suggesting to the subject that he is entering a special state of 'hypnosis', i.e. they are neither preceded nor accompanied by hypnotic induction.

4. *Post-hypnotic suggestions*. These are hypnotic suggestions (i.e. given before the subject is told to 'wake up') that result in responses given *after* the subject has been told to 'wake'. For example, if a subject is given an induction procedure, and it is suggested to him that when he 'wakes' he will remember nothing, the response of recalling nothing *after* waking would constitute a post-hypnotic response.

5. *Hypnotic condition or treatment*. This is to a situation in which subjects are submitted to a hypnotic induction procedure.

6. *Non-hypnotic or waking treatment*. This is a situation in which no hypnotic induction procedure is given, and it is thus never suggested to subjects that they are entering a sleep-like state called 'hypnosis'.

7. *Hypnotic subjects*. These are individuals who have received a hypnotic induction procedure and have *not* been given instructions to fake. (In some experiments some subjects are asked to 'fake' or fool the hypnotist when he gives them an induction procedure. These are not strictly 'hypnotic' subjects.)

8. *Non-hypnotic or waking subjects*. These are individuals who have not received a hypnotic induction procedure.

9. *Hypnotically susceptible subjects*. These are individuals who when given hypnotic suggestions, respond positively, giving the appropriate suggested responses. Thus when the subject is told that he cannot unclasp his hands, he fails to unclasp his hands. Hypnotically 'insusceptible' subjects do not respond positively to any of the hypnotic suggestions, or only very few. Sometimes hypnotically susceptible subjects who respond positively to all or nearly all of the hypnotic suggestions given to them are classed as 'good' hypnotic subjects.

10. *Hypnotised subjects*. These are subjects who have been submitted to a hypnotic induction procedure, and have responded positively to many or most of the suggestions. Whenever the term 'hypnotised' is used in this book, it will be in this operational way, i.e. it will not be implicitly assumed that a 'hypnotised' individual is either in, or experiencing, a special trance state of consciousness.

11. *Hypnosis*. As it is the nature of this term which is under scrutiny no adequate definition can really be put forward, though traditionally hypnosis has been referred to as some kind of special hypothetical sleep-like state, brought about by various induction procedures, which can result in the manifestation of a number of unique experiences and behavioural effects. Throughout this book, when the term 'hypnosis' is employed the reader may assume that it is presented parenthetically, to denote the general area of investigation, without the assumption that it refers to any unified state or entity.

I appreciate that some readers might disagree with these definitions, but as far as the basic view in this book is concerned, the difficulties in finding appropriate definitions may actually stem from the fact that we have terminology in need of distinctions rather than distinctions in need of terminology.

2. Sham Behaviour and Compliance

The most simple theory that could be put forward to explain hypnotic behaviours is that the subject consciously pretends or shams various effects. There seem to be three popular arguments against this proposal. The first involves the generalisation from one category of behaviour to another. For example, we know people do not fake because others can undergo operations under hypnosis, and you cannot fake an absence of pain when somebody is cutting your insides to pieces. The second argument is that most hypnotic effects 'look' so incredible that it would be virtually impossible for a graduate of R.A.D.A. to act them out, let alone an introverted friend or relative. The third is that it seems implausible that anyone should want to fake even if they could. Why should someone sit there and have pins stuck in them and pretend that it does not hurt? Why should anyone make a complete idiot of himself gurgling and babbling like a baby, or brushing away imaginary flies? In the following chapters I hope to show that none of these arguments is sufficiently potent to lead to a rejection of sham behaviour as an important determinant of some hypnotic phenomena. It is important to note that I am not suggesting *all* hypnotic behaviours are faked, but I am attempting to demonstrate that it would be very unwise to preclude the very real possibility that sham behaviour may be an important element in the manifestation of some hypnotic phenomena.

HYPNOSIS FOR FUN

When one of the champions of hypnotic surgery, J. Esdaile, was asked to account for the increased number of patients coming to him at the hospital where he worked, he replied:

> I see two ways only of accounting for it; my patients on returning home either say to their friends similarly afflicted 'What a soft man the doctor is! He cut me to pieces for twenty minutes and I made him believe that I did not feel it. Isn't it a capital joke? Do go on and play him the same trick'. Or they may say . . . 'I am restored to the use of my body and can work for my bread. This I assure you the doctor did while I was asleep, and I knew nothing of it' (Marcuse, 1976, p.49).

The statement reflects an unfortunate and misleading view that the only reasonable motive for faking hypnotic behaviours is that of trying to play tricks and jokes and having a good laugh at the hypnotist's expense. Whilst, as the following chapters will show, this is a gross misrepresentation of the variety of social influence processes which might be operating to produce sham behaviour, we should not perhaps disregard the possibility that some people may indeed be motivated to sham hypnotic behaviours for pure entertainment. It is quite possible that many seemingly ludicrous anecdotes concerning hypnosis are accepted by large numbers of people because of a very charitable, but unfortunately not always accurate, belief that people do not tell lies for 'fun'. For instance, recently after I had delivered a talk on hypnosis a questioner related to me a story of how her boyfriend had been given a post-hypnotic suggestion that on awakening from his trance he would see all those immediately around him naked. According to her, he was apparently able to identify the colour and size of the undergarments of those around him in spite of the fact that the individuals were supposed to be naked. Apparently, she was convinced of the validity of her boyfriend's testimony and remarked that his observations concerning the undergarments of those around him were accurate in every detail. Of interest was the fact that many other members of the audience seemed to think this was a reasonable story— after all, people can undergo operations under hypnosis and regress to childhood — until it was pointed out that what was really being proffered was a highly sophisticated form of post-hypnotic X-ray vision which would better even Puységur's claims. Of course, it is possible that hypnotism may embrace X-ray vision along with its other various extraordinary effects, but it does not seem to be too unreasonable to suggest that some people are also prone to slight exaggerations when reporting their experiences. Supporting examples from outside the field of hypnosis are not difficult to find. Buckhout (1974) has drawn attention to the tendency for people to maintain they were present when a significant historical event took place near where they live even though they were not there at all. In one instance, a story was fabricated about a naked woman stuck to a newly painted toilet seat in a small town. The story was distributed by newspaper and wire services and subsequently citizens of the towns were interviewed. Some claimed to have witnessed and even taken part in the totally fictitious event.

As has been noted, during the days of magnetism some patients, even of some notoriety, admitted to outright deception (Sheehan and Perry, 1976); of course we cannot be sure of the particular social pressures these people may have been subjected to, but if people can lie about seeing nudes in lavatories, it's not too far-fetched to assume some will lie about being 'hypnotised' for no other reason than that exaggerations make good conversation pieces at parties, and most people benefit from a little bit of extra attention now and again.

Sometimes the motives for chicanery are a little more explicit. A famous case in point is that of Smith and Blackburn who purported to demonstrate telepathic powers in a number of experiments which included work on hypnosis. Seventeen years after the last reported experiment Blackburn made this statement:

> I am the sole survivor of the group of experimentalists, as no harm can be done to anyone, but possible good to the cause of truth, I, with mingled feelings of regret and satisfaction now declare that the whole of those alleged experiments were bogus, and originated from the honest desire of two youths to show how easily men of scientific mind and training could be deceived when seeking for evidence in support of a theory they were wishful to establish (Hansel, 1966, p.31).

For the stage hypnotist the rewards for entertainment can sometimes be measured more objectively in financial terms rather than intrinsic satisfaction. As has been noted elsewhere (Barber, 1972; Barber, Spanos and Chaves, 1974) some stage hypnotists are not beyond using some rather devious methods such as employing specially trained stooges, but keeping this information from the audience. They may also produce various effects with a few hidden props. One of these effects is 'stopping the blood flow', which looks quite dramatic as the subject's arm goes pale and the pulse stops on the command of the hypnotist. To achieve this effect, the hypnotist may fasten a golfball under the armpit of the subject, and when it is suggested that the blood is leaving the arm, the stooge simply presses his arm against the ball, thus temporarily stopping the circulation and pulse. Should the hypnotist be confronted with a particularly obnoxious subject determined to demonstrate iron will-power, according to the manuals of stage hypnosis the hypnotist may employ the 'carotid' trick. This involves exerting pressure on the baroreceptors at the carotid sinus, which then produces hypotension and fainting. The manuals instruct the hypnotist to make passes over the subject with his free hand so that the audience is led to believe that the subject has not passed out, but entered a hypnotic trance. Nelson (1965) sums up one view of stage hypnosis with this poignant remark: 'The successful hypnotic entertainer is actually not interested whether or not the subjects are really hypnotised. He is interested in his ability to *con* his subjects into a pseudo performance that appears as hypnotism — to get laughs and to entertain his audience' (Barber, 1972, p.139).

Sham hypnotic behaviour can be fun, it seems, but if it is only confined to enterprising pranksters then it is little wonder that it has been disregarded by many as a serious influence on hypnotic performances. If the concepts of faking or sham behaviour are to be seriously applied to hypnosis then a rather different perspective has to be adopted.

SHAM, FAKED, OR FRAUDULENT BEHAVIOUR

The assumption that any 'hypnotised' subject, if shamming, is in some way using dishonest trickery, in part stems from the inappropriate negative emotional connotations of the words 'sham', 'faked' and 'fraudulent'. For example, supposing you wake up with a splitting headache, a monstrous electricity bill has arrived in the post, and you feel utterly miserable; however, it is your child's birthday, and you do not want to spoil her day, so you put on a brave front, pretend your head does not hurt, and hide your true feelings about the impending overdraft. According to the factual meaning of the words, you would indeed be a sham and a fake, but in this context the emotional connotation of the words would seem rather inappropriate.

The findings described in the next few chapters suggest that the terms such as 'sham', 'fake' and 'fraud' may be equally emotionally inappropriate when applied to hypnotic behaviour. In order to avoid this problem it would be better to employ a term which possesses a similar factual meaning, but a fairly neutral emotional tone. The term 'compliance' as used in social psychology seems to possess these attributes.

THE NATURE OF COMPLIANCE

Social psychologists use the term 'conformity' to refer to a change in behaviour or belief towards a group or person as a result of real or imagined pressure from the group or person (Kiesler and Kiesler, 1970; Aronson, 1977). Two types of conformity have been distinguished, 'compliance' and 'private acceptance'. Compliance refers to overt behaviour which becomes like the behaviour that a group or person expects or wishes an individual to show. The term refers solely to outward actions and does not consider the private convictions of the actor. When the term 'compliance' is used, it can refer to the situation in which a person is behaving as others wish him to but he does not really believe in what he is doing. On the other hand, 'private acceptance' refers to change in private attitude or belief in the direction of those of others (Kiesler and Kiesler, 1970).

Put in this context, the hypnotic subject can be viewed as using 'compliance' when he publically responds 'as if' experiencing what is explicitly or implicitly demanded in a hypnotic suggestion, without the private subjective experience.

Orne (1966) has emphasised that an essential feature of compliance as applied to hypnosis is its volitional quality, i.e. the individual makes a conscious decision to carry out the behaviour; whereas a traditional feature of much hypnotic behaviour is its assumed non-volitional quality. He gives the example of the sway test where it is suggested to the subject that he is falling backward. Orne notes: 'The response is defined as positive by the extent to which the subject actually falls, but it is implicitly assumed that he is to fall because *he feels himself drawn backward* rather than because of the conscious volitional decision: "I will fall backward". To the degree that the actual falling depends on a volitional decision, it has failed to measure an ideomotor response' (p.724). Similarly, he states that an essential feature of a genuine hypnotic response to a challenge suggestion such as: 'Your eyes are tightly glued together; you cannot open them; try to open them', should be that the subject *cannot* comply even when he is challenged to do so.

Thus we can distinguish two categories of responses to hypnotic suggestions which would constitute 'compliance only':

1. Where a volitional act is supposed to reflect an underlying subjective experience but this is not the case, for example, in response to a pain stimulus the subject *says* he is not feeling pain, when privately he feels pain, or he moves his hand as if brushing away a fly, but does not subjectively experience an hallucinated fly at all.
2. Where an act explicitly or implicitly is supposed to be performed nonvolitionally, but the subject consciously decides to perform the act. For example he deliberately raises his hand in response to an arm levitation suggestion without feeling that the arm 'rises by itself'.

There are many historical examples of compliance outside the hypnosis situation. One of the most famous is that of Galileo, who in 1632, in response to threats from the Inquisition in Rome, renounced his heliocentric theory of the universe (i.e. that the earth moves and is not the centre of the universe). It is clear Galileo's renunciation was compliance, he continued to hold his 'heretical' ideas, and according to the well-known story, is reputed to have muttered afterwards: 'Eppur si moore' — it (the earth) still moves. However, hypnotic subjects are generally pressured by a hypnotist, not the Inquisition, so the motivation for compliance seems rather less. The only motive we have discussed so far is trickery or 'fun'. According to this analysis the subject complies to the expectations of the hypnotist because of the satisfaction that can be accrued from putting one over on the hypnotist. Although this possibility could be dismissed as a major determinant of compliance in hypnosis, it does illustrate the fact that behaving in accordance with 'pressure' from others does not necessarily result from the desire to avoid physical coercion or an ignominious fate; the motives for submitting to social pressure may include gains in terms of positive rewards rather than simply the avoidance of punishment.

To illustrate these influences in rather more detail, I have selected three main areas from outside hypnosis for examination: obedience, demand characteristics, and the classic conformity studies. It is hoped that these will set an appropriate context in which to view the influence of compliance in the area of hypnosis.

STUDIES OF OBEDIENCE

One of the most consistent findings in social psychology is that what people say they will do, and what they actually do, often have surprisingly little correspondence. Presumably because most of us consider ourselves to be autonomous individuals who will stick up for our principles and beliefs, it is easy to underestimate the power of quite subtle forms of social influence in producing compliant behaviour. Probably nowhere is this more apparent than in Milgram's classic studies of obedience. The details of the basic set-up are now very familiar to most students of psychology. Milgram (1974) used subjects from a variety of occupations, ranging from unskilled workers to professionals, who volunteered to participate in any experiment ostensibly concerned with the effects of punishment on memory. On arriving at the laboratory each subject met the experimenter, who was dressed in a drab grey technician's coat, and another subject, a forty-seven-year-old accountant, who most observers found 'mild-mannered and likeable' (p.16). The accountant was in fact a specially trained confederate. Using a rigged draw, the real subject was drawn as the 'teacher' and the confederate as the 'learner'. During the preliminary introduction the teacher was informed that the learner had a heart condition. The learner was taken into an adjacent room and strapped into an electric chair and the teacher was seated in front of an impressive electric shock generator. On the generator were thirty switches supposedly capable of delivering shocks from 15 volts to 450 volts in 15 volt increments. The generator also bore verbal labels ranging from 'SLIGHT SHOCK' to 'DANGER: SEVERE SHOCK'. The teacher was given a sample shock of 45 volts, which was usually strong enough to produce expressions of discomfort. The teacher was instructed to administer a memory task and to deliver a shock each time the learner gave an incorrect response. However, the most important instruction to the teacher was that he should move one level higher on the shock generator each time the learner gave a wrong answer. The main response measure in the experiment was the maximum level of shock the teacher would be prepared to give if the learner continued to make errors. In reality no actual electric shocks were given.

The results were rather surprising. In the condition where the subjects could not see their 'victim' or hear his voice, twenty-six of the forty subjects obeyed the orders of the experimenter to the end, punishing the victim right up to the 450 volt shock level. This was in spite of the fact that at 300 volts the laboratory walls resounded as the victim pounded in protest. Not one subject delivered a shock of less than 300 volts. In another condition, twenty-five subjects administered the 450 volt shock even though they would hear the victim screaming to be let out, and shrieking with agony.

It is important to note that some critics (Orne and Holland 1968; Mixon, 1972) have argued that the implications of Milgram's findings are limited because there may have been cues in the situation which indicated to the subjects that the victim was not actually receiving dangerous shocks. The basis of this argument seems to be that the experimenter, by remaining cool, calm, and collected, was indicating that the situation was a 'safe one'. Milgram has replied to these criticisms (1972, 1974) and has provided counter evidence supporting the argument that the subjects did actually believe they were administering very painful shocks. Of particular importance was the occurrence of tension in some of the obedient subjects; they sweated, trembled, stuttered, bit their lips, and many had seizures of nervous laughter. An observer in the laboratory reported, 'I observed a mature and initially poised businessman enter the laboratory smiling and confident. Within 20 minutes he was reduced to a twitching, stuttering wreck, who was rapidly approaching a point of nervous collapse' (Milgram, 1963, p.377). Nevertheless, the criticisms of Orne and Holland and Mixon may be significant in other social influence contexts, a view to be discussed shortly. When Milgram described the experiment to a group of college students, psychiatrists and middle-class adults, not one said he would fully obey the experimenter. When asked how they thought others would perform, a similar group predicted that only a pathological fringe of 1 or 2 per cent would proceed to the 450 volt switch (Milgram, 1974).

A most significant point to be derived from Milgram's research is that the volunteer experimental subject seems willing to obey the experimenter's demands even when these demands involve behaviours that appear to be intensely anti-social. In the case of Milgram's subjects, the motivation for delivering the shocks was unlikely to have been money; they were paid only $4.50 for participating. According to Milgram the obedience was due to the subject assuming an 'agentic state', which he defines as follows: 'From a subjective standpoint, a person is in a state of agency when he defines himself in a social situation in a manner that renders him open to regulation by a person of higher status. In this condition the individual no longer views himself as responsible for his own actions but defines himself as an instrument for carrying out the wishes of others' (p.134). Milgram suggests that one of the most important binding factors that keeps the subject in the agentic state is the etiquette of the particular social situation. He quotes Goffman concerning this point:

> society is organised on the principle that any individual who possesses certain social characteristics has a moral right to expect that others will value and treat him in a correspondingly appropriate way. . . . When an individual projects a definition of the situation and then makes an implicit or explicit claim to be a person of a particular kind, he automatically exerts a moral demand upon the others, obliging them to value and treat him in the manner that persons of his kind have a right to expect (Goffman, 1959, p.185).

Milgram concludes that a refusal to obey would be a rejection of the experimenter's claim to competence and authority in this situation, and thus a severe social impropriety would be necessarily involved. The experimenter-subject relationship can be seen as a hierarchical one, and according to Milgram, 'any attempt to alter the defined structure will be experienced as a moral transgression and will evoke anxiety, shame, embarrassment, and diminished feelings of self-worth' (p.152). It should be noted that the subject does not necessarily carry out the orders of the experimenter because of some altruistic motive to refrain from hurting the experimenter's feelings; it is closely bound with his desire to look good; he does not wish to give the impression of being untoward or rude; and also he may fear the embarrassment of a reprimand. The importance of these factors was given further emphasis by the finding of Sheridan and King (1972) that subjects obeyed the experimenter's request to deliver actual electric shocks to a genuine victim, a puppy. In fact all female subjects obeyed and shocked the puppy with maximum shock.

According to Kiesler and Kiesler (1970) the obedience studies represent a clear case of compliance without private acceptance, as the reactions of the subjects indicated that they were experiencing a conflict between their overt behaviour, as dictated by the comands of the experimenter, and their privately held moral attitudes or beliefs about delivering painful shocks to a victim with a heart condition.

Studies of obedience have not been limited to the laboratory. Bickman (1974) has shown some important effects of social influence in relation to his work on personal appearance. In one study he used forty-eight adult pedestrians in a section of Brooklyn, New York. In this experiment the experimenter, dressed either as a guard in uniform or a civilian, stopped a passerby, pointed to a confederate standing beside a car parked at a parking meter and said: 'This fellow is overparked at the meter but doesn't have any change. Give him a dime!' This was the 'surveillance' condition as the whole scene took place in front of the meter so that the subject was aware that the 'authority' could see if he obeyed. In another condition of 'nonsurveillance', the experimenter simply pointed to the confederate and said to the pedestrian walking towards the car, 'You see that guy over there by the meter? He's overparked but doesn't have any change. Give him a dime!' By the time the subject had reached the car the experimenter was out of sight. Overall, 83 per cent of the pedestrians obeyed the guard, 46 per cent obeyed the civilian, and interestingly, there was no difference between the two surveillance conditions. These studies also indicate the powerful influence a perceived authority figure, or even peer, can have over an individual's behaviour if directives are issued.

STUDIES OF CONFORMITY

If subjects can be induced to carry out socially immoral acts and do ridiculous tasks in situations where no physical coercion is involved, it is not surprising that they can also be induced by social pressures to make grossly erroneous statements which contradict their own private convictions. Some of the most dramatic instances of this are evident in the classic conformity studies.

In the famous experiments by Asch (1951, 1952, 1956), groups of subjects were required to match a single standard line with three comparison lines differing in length, though only one of three comparison lines was actually equal in length to the standard line. In fact, only one of the subjects was naive, the others were confederates briefed to give incorrect judgments on most of the trials. The naive subject thus found himself in a situation where the correct answer on the critical trials was in opposition to those given by a unanimous majority. In Asch's first experiments he found that of the total number of judgments given, 37 per cent were in error, i.e. they were in accordance with those of the unanimous majority. The conflict felt by the subjects is clear in the following report by Asch:

> Most subjects miss the feeling of being at one with the group. In addition, there is frequent reference to the concern they feel that they might appear strange to the majority. One of the strongest (independent non-yielding) subjects reported: 'Despite everything there was a lurking fear that in some way I did not understand I might be wrong; fear of exposing myself as inferior in some way. It is more pleasant if one is really in agreement' (Kretch, Crutchfield and Ballachey, 1962, p.508).

This stress associated with non-compliance is also evident when physiological measures are taken. Bogdanoff, Klein, Estes, Shaw and Back (1961) found that the plasma, free-fatty acid level of subjects increased (a sign of stress) when they were confronted with an incorrect majority in the Asch line-judgment situation. Subsequently, subjects who yielded to the majority showed a reduction of arousal, those who did not comply continued to show a high level of arousal. The fact that in a subsequent experiment (Asch, 1956) conformity was significantly reduced when subjects were allowed to respond privately rather than publicly, indicates that compliance was a key element.

In order to overcome some inconvenient features of the Asch procedure, Crutchfield (1955) devised an apparatus in which five subjects could be run at once without the use of any confederates. Subjects were seated side by side in groups of five in front of five electrical panels and partitioned off from each other. The responses of all subjects were supposedly displayed on each panel. However, the experimenter actually controlled the information on the panels. Crutchfield found that in a sample of fifty military officers 46 per cent expressed agreement with the bogus group that a star was larger than a circle, when in actuality the circle was one third larger in area than the star (Kretch, Crutchfield and Ballachey, 1962). Using an adapted form of the Crutchfield technique, Tuddenham and Macbride (1959) found that some college students would agree to statements such as: 'The United States is largely populated by old people, 60 to 70 per cent being over 65 years of age', and 'These oldsters must be almost all women, since male babies have a life expectancy of only 25 years'.

The studies of Asch and Crutchfield were concerned with conformity due to group pressure, rather than pressure from an individual in authority, yet in both cases similar factors seem to operate. Kiesler and Kiesler (1970) define group pressure as 'a psychological force operating upon a person to fulfil others' expectations of him, including especially those expectations of others relating to the person's "roles" or to behaviours specified or implied by the "norms" of the group to which he belongs' (p.31).

They further consider that two important motives for attending to group expectations are: 1. the desire to be liked and accepted, and not rejected, and 2. the desire to successfully attain the group goal. These factors clearly correspond to those stated earlier in relation to compliance to an authority figure, i.e. the need to fulfil role obligations and expectations, the promotion and defence of the self-image, and the desire to see the goal of the encounter successfully concluded.

STUDIES OF DEMAND CHARACTERISTICS

In the obedience studies the behaviour of the subject is usually directed by an explicit direct command from the authority figure. However, the social rules which govern the experimenter–subject relationship may also effectively evoke behaviours in the subject which are implicitly demanded by the experimental situation. The idea that experiments can be biased by the subject's desire to appear to be a 'good' subject, is certainly not a recent one. As early as 1908 Pierce had made this comment: 'It is to the highest degree probable that the subject('s) . . . general attitude of mind is that of ready complacency and cheerful willingness to assist the investigator in every possible way by reporting to him those very things that he is most eager to find, and that the very questions of the experimenter . . . suggest the shade of reply expected'.

Orne (1962) uses the term 'demand characteristics' to refer to those cues which influence the subject's behaviour in this way and emphasises that part of the role of a 'good' subject is to validate the experimental hypothesis in accordance with the experimenter's expectations. According to Orne (1969) the desire to validate the experimental hypothesis stems not only from an altruistic intent to please the experimenter, but also, if the subject sees himself as being evaluated, he will tend to behave so as to make himself look good. Orne provides a variety of evidence to illustrate how easy it is to get people to comply to ridiculous requests when the context is appropriate. Thus he notes that if people are requested to perform push-ups outside the experimental situation they typically reply: 'Why?' When the same request is given within the experimental situation they are more likely to change their reply to 'Where?' He also points out how, as a lecturer, he can readily get students to acquiesce without question to absurd and meaningless requests such as taking off one shoe, or exchanging ties (Orne, 1959, 1966a). 'The ready complacency and cheerful willingness to assist the investigator' is convincingly shown in his report of a study by Menaker in which subjects were required to perform serial additions on sheets filled with random digits. This required 224 additions per sheet, and subjects were given 2,000 sheets to complete. Each subject's watch was taken away and he was told 'Continue to work: I will return eventually'. The result of this impossible task was that: 'Five and half hours later, the experimenter gave up' (Orne, 1962)! Orne (1962) points out that his observations are consistent with those of Frank (1944) who failed to find resistance to disagreeable or nonsensical tasks. Frank accounts for this 'primarily by subjects' unwillingness to break the tacit agreement he had made when he volunteered to take part in the experiment, namely, to do whatever the experiment required of him' (p.24). This comment corresponds well to the points made by Milgram concerning the social rules governing the experimental situation.

Apart from the promotion of the self-image and the desire to please the experimenter, subjects also seem concerned about the utility of their performances. Orne (1959) suggests that statements made by subjects following the conclusions of experiments, such as 'Did I ruin the experiment?', commonly mean: 'Did my behaviour demonstrate that which the experiment is designed to show?' In practice, 'progress in science' may well be equated with 'making the experiment work' (p.281). This factor again corresponds with the desire to achieve a goal at the end of the session noted in the obedience and group conformity studies.

Other investigators have emphasised that whether a subject will comply in an experiment may depend on an interaction between his desire to confirm the experimenter's hypothesis and his desire to be seen generally in a good light. Sometimes these two desires may conflict; for instance, if a subject knows that the experimenter's hypothesis requires him to be easily persuaded, confirming the hypothesis may result in the subject feeling that he has revealed himself in an unfavourable way. This general apprehension about the image the subject feels he is projecting has been termed 'evaluation apprehension' (Rosenberg, 1969; Weber and Cook, 1972). In the Milgram studies it seems that any apprehension the subjects may have had about appearing to be callous or sadistic were overcome by much stronger apprehensions about committing a severe social impropriety and ruining the experimenter's research programme. If they had actually been told what the experimenter was really testing, they would have been far less likely to have complied, in the same way as when subjects in the Asch-type conformity situation are told of the details of the experimenter's hypothesis they conform considerably less (Horowitz and Rothschild, 1970). It is very important to note that the concept of evaluation apprehensive relates to how the subject perceives he will be evaluated even if he fails to confirm the experimenter's hypothesis; if the subject believes that he will be seen *more* favourably by *not* confirming the hypothesis, then obviously his best strategy is not to confirm the hypothesis. For instance, if you were asked by an experimenter to do a number of puzzles and were told that 'only very exceptional people can do these puzzles, and I predict you will not be able to do them', then you would probably do your very best to prove the experimenter wrong! On the other hand, if you were told 'only obsessive people can do these puzzles', the situation might be rather different. This kind of effect was illustrated in a study by Sigall, Aronson and Van Hoose (1970) in which subjects were required to copy out telephone numbers. In one condition they were told that a low number was expected, in another condition they were told that copying out many numbers would indicate obsessive-compulsiveness. As one might predict, in the first condition the subjects disconfirmed the experimenter's hypothesis, in the second condition they did not. However, in both conditions they seemed to be behaving so that they could be seen in the most favourable light by the experimenter.

The work on demand characteristics and evaluation apprehension has provided serious cause to be cautious about uncritically accepting the validity of subjects' verbal reports in the experimental situation. Giving the experimenter what he wants, making the experiment work, and 'looking good' may result in the subject exercising some deceit to these ends. Thus, Orne (1959) mentions that subjects are usually very reticent about revealing their ideas about the purpose of the experiment (after all, having such knowledge may often ruin an experiment). He says, 'When asked "What do you think this is about?", they tend to reply "I don't know". However, when a clinical approach is used and the subject is pressed, a very different picture is revealed, one may be amazed — horrified — by the subject's ability to formulate one's hypothesis in a lucid and at times highly sophisticated fashion' (p.282).

CONCLUSION

A variety of evidence has now been presented which illustrates the significance of social influence from authority figures and peers in directing behaviour, even when such influence is not supported by formal threats such as corporal punishment, or incarceration. This evidence is crucial in emphasising that, in order to exhibit compliant or fake behaviour, the subject does not have to be a professional con-man, circus clown or psychopath, but an ordinary individual who responds to expectations and social obligations.

3. Compliance and Hypnosis

In many investigations into hypnosis the hypnotist is literally the experimenter, and in a sense every session of hypnosis is an 'experiment' or trial to see what happens; in fact, some hypnotists refer to the most informal demonstration as 'an experiment'. As the hypnotist may be seen as the authority figure or experimenter in his own domain, and the client or patient as the subject, we can now, perhaps, begin to see how the same factors that have operated in studies of obedience, conformity and demand characteristics may apply to hypnosis situations.

HYPNOSIS AS OBEDIENCE

Hunt (1979) has taken the concept of hypnosis as a form of obedience behaviour and formulated in a systematic manner how subjects in some hypnotic situations may respond according to the main factors in Milgram's model of obedience. According to Milgram's (1974) model, when a person is placed in a position where he is subordinate to some authority he shifts to an 'agentic state' in which he comes to see himself as an agent for carrying out the wishes of another person. Hunt (1979) proposes that there are certain features of the hypnotic situation which create conditions ripe for the movement of the subject from the autonomous to the agentic state, for example, the subject fits into the system voluntarily and is confronted by a figure more knowledgeable than himself. When the subject shifts to the agentic state he duly concentrates on the task, pays attention to the instructions, and tries to to what the hypnotist asks. In this situation the subject may thus give up some responsibility for his actions to the hypnotist, and as in Milgram's study he may possibly perform anti-social acts on the grounds that the authority figure will take responsibility. Hunt suggests that once the subject has committed himself to the situation he develops situational obligations so that disruption of the situation could be embarrassing or anxiety provoking. Related to this, Hunt mentions Nelson's (1965) remark that in stage hypnosis it is more embarrassing for a volunteer to refuse to cooperate than to agree to go along with the show. These factors 'bind' the subject to the situation, making him continue regardless of whether he is genuinely experiencing the effects.

Milgram (1974) also suggests that there may be certain 'strain' factors in the obedience situation which pressure the subject not to obey; in his studies the strain sources were the vigorous protests of the victim, and the feelings of guilt that might accrue from harming the victim. Thus whether the subject obeys, and to what extent he obeys depends on the balance of the two sets of factors. If the binding factors are stronger than the strain factors the subject will obey, if the strain factors outweigh the binding factors, then he will not, with various degrees in between. Hunt (1979) has suggested how this analysis might also apply to the hypnotic situation. The strain factors might include finding the hypnotic suggestions trivial or ridiculous or embarrassing, or alternatively disappointment that the experiences are not of a more 'mystical' nature. One could add that the experience that the suggestions simply experimentally 'don't work', or a desire not to fake might be other important strain factors. According to Hunt (1979) the conflict between the binding and strain factors would show itself ultimately, if the strain factors were sufficient, in the subject engaging in a physical exit from the situation. However, she remarks that it is rare for subjects, *after starting with the induction*, to refuse to carry on; instead the balance of the strain and binding factors may be more likely to show themselves to various degrees in the different 'depths' of hypnosis. The subject may refuse to carry out the one or more suggestions which he finds too ridiculous or embarrassing. This is a useful formulation as it not only accounts for why some hypnotic subjects appear to be 'good' (very obedient), and some 'poor' (not obedient), but the particular pattern of strain and binding factors may also account for the varying degrees of susceptibility between the 'good' and 'poor' extremes.

In order to test some of these proposals Hunt conducted an experiment employing forty hypnotically susceptible subjects. Although subjects were treated in pairs, only one was a real subject, the other was a stooge who had previously been briefed by the experimenter. In one condition, a straightforward testing of hypnotic susceptibility occurred. In a second condition, the testing went on as usual until the subjects reached the point on the SHSS which required them to have a 'dream'. At this point the stooge replied, 'Oh, this is so ridiculous, I just can't go on'. The experimenter responded by asking him to sit quietly, but the stooge replied, 'No, I'm sorry, I'm going', and he got up quietly and left the room. In a third condition, the stooge obediently passed all items on the scale. In the final condition the stooge protested again, but remained in his chair until the 'real' subject had finished.

The results showed that in the condition where the stooge had walked out of the room the susceptibility of the 'real' subjects was significantly lowered, in fact, six of the ten 'real' subjects failed to pass any more items after the departure of the stooge. When the stooge completed all the items this raised susceptibility slightly but not significantly. Subjects in the condition where the stooge walked out said afterwards that they regarded his behaviour as 'rude', and were not prepared to follow him out of the room. Hunt (1979) concludes that the results give some support for the idea that hypnosis may be influenced to a large extent by obeying the demands of authority in a legitimate situation, for when the authority of the hypnotist was threatened, responsivity to hypnotic suggestions was reduced.

The prestige of the hypnotist as reflected in his experience also seems to be an important determinant of hypnotic responsiveness. Coe and his associates (reported by Sarbin and Coe, 1972) found that, although the hypnotist administered the same induction procedure as someone who had hypnotised many people before, subjects' responsiveness scores were 30 per cent higher than if he told them he was just beginning to learn hypnotism and wanted to practise on them. This accords well with a compliance prediction that when the experimenter's expertise is questioned there is less obligation to comply; if the experimenter appears to be unsure of his ability to make the subject respond, the subject is committing less of an impropriety by not responding. Also, the motivation for not responding may be increased by fears of the consequences of hypnosis being wielded by a novice.

In this context it is interesting to note that subjects are also responsive to hypnotic suggestions if the induction is given on tape (Hilgard and Tart, 1966). However, in terms of compliance there is no a priori reason for assuming that taped induction will be any less effective. As long as the experimenter's expectations are explicitly or implicitly obvious, it should not really make much difference if he stands by a tape recorder and lets it do the work. The subject may still perceive his task as responding for the experimenter, rather than the tape recorder.

HYPNOSIS AND DEMAND CHARACTERISTICS

Orne's analysis of demand characteristics reveals that in most experimental situations, even when no obvious cues are given to subjects, they are nevertheless often very successful in picking the cues up and behaving appropriately. However, very often in the hypnotic situation the expectations of the hypnotist are very explicit, and could readily pressure the subject into exhibiting compliant behaviour. Sometimes the pressures to comply can be exerted in a rather unsophisticated fashion, as in the case of a student of mine who reported that her hypnotist's preliminary comments included, 'only unintelligent people and psychopaths cannot be hynotised'. As another instance, we can note the rather unsubtle tactics of a hypnotist described by Hall and Grant (1978), 'One hypnotist tried everything he knew to get the man on his couch to relax, but after three hours he was still lying their wide awake. In exasperation the hypnotist said suddenly "For Christ's sake go to sleep!" and the man immediately went into a deep trance' (p.51). Usually the message is not quite so blatant, but the following statements from some standardised scales illustrate the extent to which compliant behaviour may be encouraged.

1. Your ability to be hypnotised depends on your willingness to cooperate and partly on your ability to concentrate upon the target and upon my words. . . . You can be hypnotised only if you are willing. . . . If you pay

close attention to what I tell you to think about, you can easily experience what it is like to be hypnotised. . . . Probably all people can be
hypnotised. (SHSS:A)

2. You have already shown your willingness by coming here again today,
   so I am assuming that your presence here means you want to experience
   all that you can. You can be hypnotised only if you want to be. There
   would be no point in participating if you were resisting being hypnotised. (SHSS:C)

3. As for your willpower — if you want to, you can pay no attention to me
   and remain awake all the time. In that case, you might make me seem
   silly, but you are only wasting time. (BSS)

An important feature of most hypnotic suggestions is that they are issued
as directives; as such it may be embarrassing for a subject to fail to comply.
For example, the SHSS:A states: 'There will come a time . . . when your
eyes will be so tired, will feel so heavy, that you will be unable to keep them
open any longer, and they will close, perhaps quite involuntarily.' It is not
difficult to see how a refusal to carry out such directives could readily be
viewed by some subjects as a rejection of the hypnotist's claim to competence, resulting in the committing of a social impropriety. The subject may
find it very awkward just to sit there and do nothing.

In view of these conditions, rather than assuming that the hypnotic
situation is an unlikely source of compliance, it would seem ideally suited
for the purpose of demonstrating compliance. However, it is important to
emphasise that the intimidating characteristics of some hypnotic induction
procedures are not being put forward as *necessary* conditions for compliance, though for some subjects they may indeed be sufficient; they are
put forward as one contributing factor, and others may be equally or more
important. A person may initially respond to the experimenter's expectations not simply because of intimidation but because of a genuine attempt
to 'have a go' and to try to experience 'hypnosis'. In fact, according to
Barber, Spanos and Chaves (1974), it is chiefly the willingness to take part
and try to experience what is being suggested that distinguishes the 'good'
hypnotic subject. The good subject does not just sit in his chair waiting for
his eyes to close; he listens to the hypnotist, closely follows the suggestions,
thinking and imagining with them. Unfortunately, this desire to try to
experience what is suggested may result in compliance. Consider the following example. Supposing a 'keen' subject turns up to be 'hypnotised'. He
cooperates and listens intently to what the hypnotist says, so when given the
suggestion for eye closure he closes his eyes; after all there would be no
point if he did not close them, as he feels he would not stand an earthly
chance of falling into a trance with his eyes open. However, to his dismay he
finds he can still slightly open one when he tries, and concludes he is not in a
trance yet. What does he do? The interesting feature of this situation is that
this particular subject finds himself responding as if 'hypnotised', not

because he has been intimidated by the hypnotist's preamble, but because he is curious to 'try out' what the hypnotist is suggesting. The following is a verbatim case-report of a male student subject who found himself in exactly this position.

He [the hypnotist] asked for volunteers; I was dying to have a go, but at the same time a bit scared of what might happen. I'd heard that people can have pins stuck in them, and be made to act like children and animals, and I wasn't quite sure whether he was going to make me look a fool. Anyway, my curiosity overwhelmed me and I went up to the stage with about fifteen others. He told us just to concentrate on his voice and listen to nothing else. I thought to myself 'Right, here goes!' He told us to relax completely and kept repeating phrases telling us our bodies were limp. I listened to every word he said; I repeated the suggestions in my head and concentrated on making my body limp. Soon he started to tell us that our eyes were feeling tired, and we were sleepy, and that our eyelids would close. I concentrated hard on my eyes, telling myself they were heavy, very heavy. He kept on and on about them closing, so I gradually closed them. I thought to myself, 'Maybe they are a little bit tired'. I stood there with my eyes shut, knowing he must be looking at me. 'Is this it?' I thought. 'Am I in a trance?' It didn't feel like a trance; mind you he said it wouldn't feel particularly odd. I moved my right eyelid to see if I could still control it; it moved. I thought, 'I'm not in a trance yet!' I pulled myself together. I was determined that I was not going to miss out; if I kept concentrating surely I'd eventually lapse into a trance. He told us to concentrate on our right arms. He said it would feel lighter, and lighter, and eventually start to rise in the air of its own accord. I tried and tried. My own started to move; I wasn't sure whether I was controlling it or not. It moved slightly upwards from my side. He continued to say, 'It's rising, rising'. I wasn't so sure. It had moved about a foot, but he kept on and on, so I pushed it up in the air. I was a bit worried about whether I was pushing it up at the right speed, but he didn't seem to notice. At this point I was feeling sensations of anxiety and disappointment. I was disappointed that I had not become hypnotised, and anxious that an experienced hypnotist like himself would be sure to catch on and realise that I was not really hypnotised. I could hardly open my eyes and exclaim, 'Sorry, It's not working!' So I decided to keep going, and to keep trying to experience what he was asking me to in the hope that the trance would eventually overcome me. He gave us some more suggestions, like having our hands glued together, which I carried out. He also said that when we woke up we were to remain stuck to our chairs when he said the keyword 'alpha'. I repeated the word to myself a few times, so I would be sure not to forget it. When we were finally 'woken up' I was relieved to say the least; he hadn't found me out after all, but I remained disappointed that, unlike the others, I hadn't been really hypnotised.

To reiterate, the important factor in the behaviour of this particular subject was that his initial responsiveness was not apparently due to a feeling that he was being intimidated. He had volunteered and had positive motivations and expectancies but then somehow found himself 'pretending'. Only having committed himself of his own volition to carrying out the suggestions did he find that he had somewhat unwittingly placed himself in a situation where it would be very embarrassing for all if he did not obey.

The experience of this individual suggests the possibility that whether a subject ultimately complies or not in the hypnotic situation may be determined not so much by some generalised personality trait of obedience or conformity but by whether he decides to 'have a go' in the first place, thus placing himself in a situation where he is open to pressures for compliance. Another crucial feature of this individual's report is that he said he did *try* to experience the effects, he just did not succeed. Thus for some subjects compliance in hypnosis may not just be a case of a subject concluding the whole thing is a ridiculous waste of time and not worth *trying*. The hypnotic subject may try very hard to experience what is suggested to him. However, when he fails to experience the effect, pressures for compliance may lead him to fake the appropriate response. This kind of experience seems evident also in the following statement from another 'cooperative' subject, reported by Kidder: 'My conscious perception was that I was kind of going along with the thing all the way. I was kind of playing the game the way it's supposed to be. I was trying to achieve something which somehow felt different from just playing the game, and as far as I was consciously aware, I didn't succeed' (Kidder, 1973, p.2).

It should be noted, however, that the act of *trying* to experience, according to some theorists, is exactly what the hypnosis subject should *not* need to do in order to experience the suggested effects. According to Bowers (1976): 'Hypnotic subjects are not actively trying, in any ordinary sense, to behave purposely in accordance with the role requirements . . . demand characteristics, or hypnotic suggestions. Instead suggested events are experienced as *happening to them* [Bower's emphasis] in ways which would require active effort to resist' (p.108).

An even more dramatic example of a subject unwittingly becoming the victim of pressures for compliance has been brought to our attention by Sarbin and Coe (1972). The report concerns the experiences of Mark Twain. In his account Mark Twain, fired with enthusiasm and curiosity, visits a travelling 'mesmerist' and he notes: 'I was fourteen or fifteen years old, the age at which a boy is willing to endure all things, suffer all things short of death by fire, if thereby he may be conspicuous and show off before the public. . . . I had a burning desire to be a subject myself!' (Sarbin and Coe, 1972, p.11). Twain goes on to say that the first attempt to 'hypnotise' him was a failure. After a while though he became jealous of the attention that 'Hicks', a 'mesmerised' acquaintance of his, was receiving, so he finally succumbed and pretended to be sleepy. He then acted out a number of bizarre suggestions, including making love to imaginary girls and fishing from the platform. He says: 'I was cautious at first and watchful, being afraid the professor would discover that I was an imposter and drive me from the platform in disgrace; but as soon as I realised I was not in danger, I set myself the task of terminating Hick's usefulness as subject and of usurping his place' (p.12).

Twain's fears returned however when he found he was unable to imagine what the mesmerist was suggesting to him behind his back. He reported feeling 'ashamed and miserable', and believed that his 'hour of disgrace was come'. Fortunately, his honour was saved as he performed some spectacular feats, including an appearance of insensitivity to pins stuck into him, about which he commented:

> I didn't wince; I only suffered and shed tears on the inside. The miseries that a conceited boy will endure to keep up his 'reputation'. . . . That professor ought to have protected me and I often hoped he would, when the tests were unusually severe, but he didn't. It may be that he was deceived as well as the others, though I did not believe it nor think it possible. Those dear, good people . . . would stick a pin in my arm and bear on it until they drove it a third of its length in, and then be lost in wonder that by a mere exercise of willpower the professor could turn my arm to iron and make it insensible to pain. Whereas it was not insensible at all; I was suffering agonies of pain (pp.14–15).

A particularly salient feature of this report was that the first attempt to 'hypnotise' Twain was a failure. Again, this suggests that Twain's subsequent compliance was not the result of a general personality trait of susceptibility to social influence. If anything, his first failure would indicate he was somewhat insusceptible to social influence. However, in this case, by his own admission it was his conceit and desire to show off that led him into a situation where he had to tolerate 'agonies of pain' rather than commit a social impropriety. The motivation for participation in the hypnosis session was rather different for these two cases, but the resulting compliance was similar.

The fact that some subjects may feel the real pressures for compliance only after having commenced participation in induction, for example, after they have closed their eyes, seems very analogous to the foot-in-the-door phenomenon found in some social psychological studies of compliance. The foot-in-the-door technique is based on the salesperson's ruse of getting subjects to comply with a small demand, so that later they will accede to a larger demand. In this way subjects may be made to comply with quite ridiculous demands with initial *minimal pressure*. Freedman and Fraser (1966) investigated this possibility by telephoning people and asking them to answer a few innocuous questions about household products. They found that a group who had been contacted in this way was significantly more likely to then accede to a request that five or six men be allowed in their houses and have full freedom to cupboards and storage spaces in order to classify all the household products they had! In another part of the study subjects who had complied with a request to put a small sign in their windows, or sign a petition, were then far more likely to agree to have a large sign put in the front lawn of their houses, even though the sign was poorly lettered and they were led to believe it was big enough to completely conceal a doorway. It is as though once someone has committed himself to a situation, it then becomes far more difficult to 'pull out'. In the same way, a hypnotic subject who agrees to try and relax, who dutifully closes his eyes, then finds that he has placed himself in a situation where he is committed to continue responding irrespective of whether he genuinely experiences the suggested effects or not.

This kind of anecdotal and analogical evidence suggests that the a priori probability of compliance in hypnosis may be quite high, and we can now look at some more systematic studies relevant to this issue. It is important to note that compliance does not provide the *only* interpretation of the results of some of these studies, but for present purposes, it provides a very parsimonious interpretation.

PRECONCEPTIONS AND EXPECTATIONS

If the hypnotic subject is complying rather than eliciting involuntary responses like a zombie or robot, he should voluntarily respond according to how he thinks a hypnotic subject 'ought to' behave. It should be stressed again how different this emphasis is from that of Bowers (1976) that hypnotic subjects feel things 'happening to them' in an involuntary way, rather than deliberately trying to experience what they are told. Most people have preconceptions about hypnosis and, according to Orne (1959), many of the fixed qualities of hypnotic behaviour that are not provided from cues given by the hypnotists stem from reports from the mass media. He reports:

> In questioning well over 200 student subjects about their knowledge of hypnosis, the author failed to find one who did not have a very clear-cut notion about the nature of hypnosis, and who could not define the trance in a fashion similar to that found in dictionaries. . . . The normal subject population knows the meaning of the word hypnosis prior to taking part in any study (p.281).

However, to test the hypothesis that more specific prior conceptions concerning hypnosis can affect a subject's behaviour when 'hypnotised', Orne (1959) devised an experiment whereby half of a group of subjects, the experimental group, prior to being 'hypnotised', were given a lecture including the demonstration that catalepsy of the dominant hand was a characteristic hypnotic response (which it is not). The control group did not receive this particular demonstration. The results showed that during a subsequent hypnosis session five of the nine subjects in the experimental group showed catalepsy of the dominant hand, two showed catalepsy of both hands, and two showed no catalepsy. None of the control group showed catalepsy of the dominant hand, but three of the nine control subjects showed catalepsy of both hands. Orne comments that the fact that three of the control group manifested catalepsy of both hands is quite easily explained because the subjects had interpreted the repeated testing for catalepsy as a cue to manifest the behaviour. Of more interest is Orne's comment about the fact that two of the subjects in the experimental group failed to exhibit catalepsy; he says that it would be expected that not all subjects would manifest this behaviour, as some may have sufficient prior information to know that catalepsy is not a typical response. This comment explains a crucial feature of compliant behaviour in hypnosis; the manifested behaviour is an interaction between the preconceptions of the subject of how he is to behave and the directions and cues given by the hypnotist. Whether a subject will respond to any particular suggestion may partly be determined by his preconception of how suitable such a response is. For instance, if the subject believes that few hypnotic subjects exhibit auditory hallucinations, he could assume the hypnotist is also aware of this fact, and thus a failure to this particular suggestion would not necessarily be considered as a social impropriety or a questioning of the hypnotist's competence. Sometimes the contrary may operate, if the subject believes that it is unlikely that *any* subject would respond to a particular suggestion, failing to do so might be viewed as consistent with the hypnotist's expectations. The fact that some compliant subjects may not view their role as passing *all* the suggestions on hypnosis scales has an interesting parallel in the work on compliance and ingratiation (Jones, 1964; Jones and Gerard, 1967). In these studies Jones instructed individuals to ingratiate themselves with others. What the investigators found was that whilst the people so instructed agreed with many of the opinions of other, they did not agree with all of them, lest they appeared to be too obvious. In the same way, the compliant hypnotic subject may decide not to pass all the items for fear that his total compliance will give the game away.

It is also important to note that the probability that certain suggestions will be passed more readily than others can be predicted from subjects' expectations. For example, Wagstaff (1976b; 1977c) found that waking subjects could successfully predict the relative difficulty of passing items on the BSS, and could also predict the probability that subjects would pass an arm levitation suggestion when given various forms of imaginative instructions. Of interest in the first study was that although subjects were significantly consistent in their predictions there were nevertheless some discrepancies, i.e. subjects did show, now and again, some disagreement as to the relative ease of passing the items. This accords with actual performance on hypnosis scales; though subjects do significantly *tend* to pass some items consistently more readily than others, the consistency is not perfect, and individual discrepancies occur.

The fact that the subject's behaviour is influenced by a prior conception of what is expected is important in emphasising that hypnotic behaviours are not necessarily a consequence of some 'state' in which they will be spontaneously manifested. Some hypnotic behaviours, at least, do not appear to just 'happen' to the subject in some involuntary fashion when the hypnotist gives the command. This point is emphasised by two experiments showing that simply labelling a situation as 'hypnosis' is sufficient by itself to increase responsiveness to suggestions (Barber and Calverley, 1964e, 1965a). In both experiments two groups of subjects were treated identically, except that the subjects in one group were told beforehand that they were participating in a hypnosis experiment, and the other subjects that they were in a control treatment. In both experiments the subjects who thought they were participating in a hypnosis experiment showed a significant gain in suggestibility, as measured by the BSS, compared to those who were told they were control subjects. Barber, Spanos and Chaves (1974) conclude that his result occurred because, typically, present-day subjects construe the hypnosis situation as a special one in which they are expected to exhibit high responsiveness to suggestions and 'if they do not try to experience those things the hypnotist suggests, they will be considered poor and uncooperative and the hypnotist will be disappointed' (p.21).

Other evidence supports the conclusion that subjects may behave as they think they ought to behave. For example, if subjects are told that the experiment is a test of 'gullibility' rather than 'imagination' the number of subjects who score highly on the BSS drops dramatically from 41 to 6 per cent (Barber and Calverley, 1964b). This seems to be a very good example of the effects of evaluation apprehension (Weber and Cook, 1972). Although the hypnotist may be doing his best to make you comply, you might feel somewhat apprehensive about being evaluated by him as 'gullible', so compliance may be less. Of course, it could be argued that these experiments do not demonstrate that the subjects involved could not have achieved some kind of genuine hypnotic state if they had been induced to try. However, they do demonstrate that subjects' expectations as to what is expected of them, and what is 'socially desirable', can influence their responsiveness to hypnotic suggestions. These findings are what would be expected if compliance is an important factor in hypnotic behaviour.

SIMULATORS IN HYPNOSIS RESEARCH

Having established that subjects' preconceptions of hypnotic behaviour can influence their subsequent performance when 'hypnotised', Orne (1959) set out to determine whether the results of a well known hypnosis experiment could be accounted for in terms of demand characteristics. He replicated an experiment conducted by Ashley, Harper and Runyon (1951). In this study subjects were told, following hypnotic induction, that they were very poor; this was followed by an amnesia suggestion to forget they had been told this. Then, still 'under hypnosis', they were told that they were very rich, followed again by a suggestion of amnesia for this. Finally they were told they were themselves again. During these three 'states' each subject was required to make a series of estimates of the size of coins. The hypotheses tested by Orne were the same as those employed by Ashley, Harper and Runyon, that the subject in the 'poor state' would judge the coins as bigger than in the 'normal state', and that when in the 'rich state', he would judge the coins as smaller than in normal state. These hypotheses were derived from the concept that the perceiver's values alter his perception (Bruner and Goodman, 1947). However, Orne included a detailed enquiry after the experiment to determine how subjects had viewed the task. The results were in the direction predicted by the hypotheses and thus essentially identical to those found by Ashley, Harper and Runyon, but with the addition that all of Orne's subjects were subsequently able to describe correctly the purpose of the experiment and the hypotheses of the investigators who originally designed it. It should be noted that all of these subjects had previously been categorised as manifesting 'all deep trance phenomena including responsiveness to post-hypnotic suggestions and the ability to experience what appeared to be amnesia when this was suggested' (p.284).

In order to provide a more definitive demonstration that the results could have been attributable to demand characteristics, Orne (1959) employed an additional group of subjects instructed to 'play act' (p.286) being hypnotised. This group underwent exactly the same treatment as the 'real-trance' group except they were asked to fool the hypnotist that they were in a trance. It is important to note that these simulators were not told *how* they were to fool the hypnotist, it was up to them to decide which responses were appropriate. The experimenter was blind as to who were the seven 'real' subjects and who were the 'simulators'. The results showed that this 'faking' or simulating group responded almost identically to the 'real' group and the results were essentially the same as those found by Ashley, Harper and Runyon, i.e. the coin size judgments were larger in the poor state, and smaller in the rich state. A post-experimental enquiry revealed that of the twelve subjects whose results were in this direction, all perceived this to be the experimenter's hypothesis. Of the five who failed to differentiate their coin size judgments between the rich and poor state, four had failed to perceive the experimenter's hypothesis.

On the basis of this study Orne concludes:

> The implications seem very clear: demand characteristics may determine behaviour in hypnotic experiments. Before an effect can legitimately be attributed to hypnosis, it is necessary to demonstrate that it is not primarily a function of demand characteristics. *Such proof appears to require the use of blind techniques and adequate inquiry* (p.290; my emphasis).

Alas, Orne's stipulation that blind techniques should be used is sadly neglected in much research in the area of hypnosis.

Orne's finding that it was possible to fake certain hypnotic behaviours without any instruction on how this was to be done, and to deceive an experimenter experienced in hypnosis, contradicted a previous, widely held opinion that it was impossible to simulate hypnosis successfully (Jenness, 1944; Orne, 1959). This finding endorsed Orne's (1959) informal comment that he could recall having been successfully 'fooled' by some subjects on previous occasions who had subsequently owned up to faking, and that in his discussions with other hypnotists they could all recall similar instances. The finding also surprised a number of Orne's colleagues, who were experienced clinicians, who had insisted previously that simulators could be easily distinguished; Orne (1971) reports that using their clinical judgment they were unable to make an accurate and reliable differentiation. Nevertheless, certain conditions need to be satisfied if the simulators are to be successful (Orne, 1959). In particular, simulators must be aware that the hypnotist does not know beforehand that they are going to fake, otherwise the demand characteristics actually motivate the subject to give a half-hearted and unsuccessful performance, i.e. the subject may perceive that the purpose of the experiment is to establish that the hypnotist cannot be deceived. In this situation, when the experimenter knows beforehand who is faking, Orne noticed that there was a tendency for subjects to smile sometimes during the performance and ask, 'How am I doing?' at intervals.

The use of 'real' and simulating subjects in experiments on hypnosis has been termed the 'real-simulator' design. This design is useful, for then there is no difference in responding between the real and simulating groups; it enables the experimenter to conclude that it would have been possible for the 'real' subjects to have figured out the responses appropriate to the experimental task and to have complied accordingly. A failure to find a difference between real and simulating hypnotic subjects does not, of course, provide definitive evidence that the 'real subjects were publicly complying, rather it suggests that it is unnecessary to invoke a special feature of 'hypnosis' to explain their behaviour.

Although a simulating control group is useful in this respect, it has a number of limitations. For instance, it is important to note that subjects are usually selected to take the part of simulators on the basis that they have been shown to be insusceptible to hypnotic suggestions, i.e. they are subjects who for a variety of reasons have elected *not* to obey the hypnotist's commands. This presents a considerable problem, for if experimental procedures show a difference between the behaviours of hypnotic and simulating subjects, it is difficult to determine whether the differences are due to the hypnosis per se, or due to the fact that hypnotically insusceptible subjects possess certain characteristics which result in them viewing the task in a different way to hypnotically susceptible subjects.

Other experimenters have also noted that simply giving instructions to subjects to 'fake' 'hypnosis' alone is not as effective as when the instructions include items such as 'use all the cues you can in the task', 'the hypnotist knows some subjects are faking but doesn't know who they are', and 'intelligent subjects can handle the task differently' (Sheehan, 1973). The fact that the performance of simulators may be affected by the characteristics of the people selected for the simulating group, and the particular instructions they are given, makes it very difficult to compare across studies; some studies use hypnotically susceptible subjects as simulators, some issue extra motivating instructions and some do not, and often it is very difficult to know from reports which of these factors apply to a particular study (Sheehan and Perry, 1976). These factors are critical, so it has been assumed by some investigators that any differences between hypnotic subjects and simulators indicate that the hypnotic subjects are *not* complying. In the following chapters I hope to show that this logic can be very misleading, and whilst, as Orne says, no differences between 'real' and simulating subjects indicate that we cannot rule out demand characteristics and compliance, the converse does not necessarily apply; when there are differences, we cannot always conclude that demand characteristics and compliance cannot account for the behaviour of the 'real' subjects. To illustrate some of the methodological problems involved in attempting to assess the importance of compliance in hypnosis research, it may be useful to discuss some studies which have been interpreted as demonstrating that compliance does *not* significantly influence hypnotic behaviours.

COMPLIANCE AND HYPNOTIC SUSCEPTIBILITY

According to Orne (1966a) if compliance plays an important part in responsiveness to hypnotic suggestions then one might expect the kinds of people who are hypnotically susceptible to be demonstrably more compliant, in general, than insusceptible subjects. According to this rationale, if hypnotically susceptible subjects are shown to be no more compliant outside hypnosis than insusceptible subjects, then it is unlikely that compliance can account for their differential responsivity during hypnosis. Orne (1966a, 1970) provides some evidence which he suggests supports the view that susceptible subjects are not more compliant. For instance, he cites a study by London and Fuhrer (1961), which demonstrated that subjects who were not hypnotically susceptible actually performed better on a number of physical tasks than susceptible subjects. Evans and Orne (1965) replicated these studies and found no statistically significant difference between the susceptible and insusceptible subjects, though the results were in the same direction. In another study the hypnotic susceptibility of subjects was again established, but afterwards, when they were 'awake', they were given a large stack of postcards and asked to send them back to the laboratory every day. The rationale was that if hypnosis made subjects more compliant then the susceptible subjects should send back more postcards. Results indicated that there was essentially no relationship between hypnotic susceptibility and the number of postcards sent, and what little relationship there was suggested that the insusceptible subjects were more compliant.

On first consideration of this evidence it does appear that hypnotically susceptible subjects are not more compliant and we might therefore doubt the influence of compliance on hypnotic behaviours. However, if we look again outside the immediate domain of hypnosis we find the issue is somewhat more complex and alternative explanations are possible.

THE PROBLEM OF CONSISTENCY IN BEHAVIOUR

One of the greatest bugbears of personality research has been the repeated finding that people often do not seem to respond very consistently over a number of different situations which purport to measure the same characteristic (Mischel, 1968). Conformity behaviour appears to be no exception, and though a number of investigators have found a tendency for people who conform in one situation to conform in another (McGuire, 1968), the correlations are generally low and get lower the less similar the tasks become. The general consensus of opinion seems to be that although people may be very predictable in the same situation, different situations contain different factors which interact with any general trait. As Mischel (1968) says, it should be recognised that 'behaviour tends to change with alterations in the situation in which it occurs' (p.38).

Of course, if this is the case, one might argue that the studies of compliance reviewed in Chapter 2 are irrelevant to hypnosis. However, though in fact there are a few low positive correlations between responsiveness to hypnotic suggestions and some measures of conformity (Moore, 1964), it would not actually destroy the case for conformity in hypnotic behaviour if there were no significant relationships at all. Compliance will only operate maximally if a number of conditions are satisfied. For instance, if 'A' is convinced he is an expert judge of lines, other things being equal he will be less likely to yield in the Asch situation than 'B' who does not believe himself to be an expert (Asch, 1956). On the other hand, if 'B' is a member of the R.S.P.C.A. and 'A' is not, other things being equal, 'B' may be less likely to obey the experimenter and administer electric shocks to a puppy than 'A'. Such idiosyncratic factors may be more important determinants of behaviour than any general predisposition 'A' or 'B' might have to conform to social pressures.

When applied to hypnosis this is an extension of the argument proposed earlier in this chapter that whether a subject's attitudes and motivations lead to the decision to 'have a go' may be a far more important determinant of whether they end up complying than some generalised trait of obedience. For example, if 'A' yields in the Milgram situation, one might predict he should yield to the expectations of the hypnotist. But supposing he is scared to death of hypnosis, and thinks he is going to drift off into some state from which there is no return, or that the hypnotist is going to stick pins in him and he cannot stand pain. These fears or 'strain' factors might totally overcome any desire to please the hypnotist. There is evidence to suggest that such fears may indeed be important, as when subjects are assured that they will not lose control, or will not be asked to do anything embarrassing, then hypnotic responsiveness increases (Cronin, Spanos and Barber, 1971; Diamond, 1972). In another case, supposing 'B' stands up, denounces Milgram's experimenter as a sadist, and rushes in to save the innocent victim, yet would desperately like to be 'hypnotised' to see what it is like. Like the two cases discussed in the previous chapter, he might then initially follow the hypnotist's instructions, and upon finding out the trance is to elude him feel that his self-esteem will not allow him to admit to anyone that he has been complying.

The essential point of this argument is that the kinds of pressures exerted by the compliance studies in Chapter 2 and the hypnosis situation may be very similar, but whether or not an individual elects to yield to these pressures may depend on a number of other factors which may be idiosyncratic, such as his motivation towards the situation and his perception and experience of it. Behaviour in any context is the result of the interaction between trait and situation.

If we apply this kind of analysis to the studies cited by Orne at the beginning of this section, there seems to be a number of quite plausible reasons why insusceptible subjects ended up being equally if not more compliant than their susceptible counterparts. Ironically, one interpretation arises from a study by Orne (1970) in the same paper. He found that if subjects were given money to post the cards before actually posting them, they were more likely to post the cards than others who had not been paid for doing this, or who were paid after posting. This finding was supportive of his prediction that if subjects agreed to perform a task, and were paid in advance for so doing, *noncompliance would evoke guilt*. This result is in line with a number of other experiments in social psychology which indicate that when subjects are made to feel guilty they were subsequently more compliant. For instance, in a study by Wallace and Sadalla (1966), a situation was rigged so that it appeared to some subjects that they had ruined the experiment by blowing up the apparatus. Other subjects in a control group were led to believe that the 'accident' was not their fault. The experimenter then requested all the subjects to participate in an alternative study involving pain. Of the control group, only 15 per cent agreed to take part in the unpleasant substitute study. However, of those who admitted that they had blown up the apparatus, 69 per cent subsequently complied with the experimenter's request!

In the same way it seems plausible that those subjects in Orne's studies who had not complied with the hypnotist's expectations and had failed to respond to the hypnotic suggestions might also have felt some guilt that they had in some way ruined his experiment, or made a bit of a fool of him.

So to make amends they willingly carried out his request to post the cards. This could also explain why there was a slight tendency for the insusceptible subjects to be more compliant when sending back the cards. Again, this variable might totally swamp any general trait of obedience.

A number of other intervening variables could account for London and Fuhrer's (1961) finding that hypnotic subjects did not perform better on a number of physical tasks. Although maybe it is a little unfair to say the outcome of this study and Orne's replication argue *against* a compliance hypothesis. After all, most experiments on hypnosis and physical tasks have attempted to demonstrate a superiority of hypnotic subjects over 'unhyp-notised' controls (see Chapter 5) in order to support the notion of increased capacities under hypnosis, and accordingly provide evidence that hypnosis is more than compliance. It seems a bit of a heads I win tails you lose for compliance if a null result is *also* supportive of a special hypnotic ingredient. Nevertheless, there are a number of alternative interpretations which can be offered; in particular subjects who respond to hypnotic suggestions whether complying or not, could become relaxed if they follow the instruc-tions. On the other hand, the insusceptible subjects whether due to the exercise of iron will, stage fright, or inappropriate expectations may not become involved to as great an extent with the relaxation suggestions. It then follows that it might not be particularly surprising if sometimes a person in a state of relaxation shows an inferior performance on weight-holding endurance and strength of grip.

SUBJECTIVE REPORTS

One way of determining whether subjects' overt hypnotic behaviours are biased by compliance is to simply ask them. Most measures of hypnotic susceptibility use only the subjects' objective test scores as a measure of the extent to which he is 'hypnotised'; for example, they look at the number of inches his arm rises in response to an arm levitation suggestion, or whether he opens his eyes when challenged. Yet, as Orne has emphasised, these can only be classified as genuine 'hypnotic' effects if they are accompanied by an experience appropriate to the suggestion; thus, the arm should rise x inches *involuntarily,* or the subject should really feel he cannot open his eyes no matter how hard he tries.

In order to account for subjective experiences Barber (1969b) includes two sets of responses for the BSS, objective and subjective scores. After a subject's objective responses have been scored he is asked a series of questions such as, 'When I said that your left arm felt light and was rising, did your arm feel light or did you raise it deliberately in order to follow instructions or to please me?' Barber found that the subjective hypnosis scores were fractionally lower than the objective scores for seven of the eight items in the BSS; there was no difference for the other item. Neverthe-less, when analysed individually the differences between the objective and subjective scores for particular items did not prove statistically significant, i.e. the reductions were virtually negligible.

From this evidence it could be argued that compliance effects in the BSS are negligible, and if a subject scores highly, his overt responses genuinely reflect his private experiences. However, if the demand characteristics of this kind of study are analysed it does not seem surprising that the subjective scores are so like the objective scores. As mentioned before, the induction procedure provided for use with BSS includes classic statements such as: 'if you want to, you can pay no attention to me and remain awake all the time. In that case, you might make me seem silly, but you are only wasting time. On the other hand, if you pay close attention to what I say, and follow what I tell you, you can easily learn to fall into a hypnotic sleep' (p.251). Such statements do rather imply that the hypnotist would like the subject to become 'hypnotised', and the questions the subject is asked to answer as to genuineness of the responses seem somewhat rhetorical. If the subject is wasting time by not falling asleep, he is doubly wasting time if he goes through the whole procedure only to announce that he was pretending all along.

Another technique which has been applied to test the validity of subjects' verbal reports has been to specifically demand that subjects be honest in their reports. The application of demands for honesty of subjects' reports of hypnotically induced hallucinations has produced some interesting findings and highlighted some important methodological considerations. The innovation of demands for honesty was made by Bowers (1967) in a reappraisal of an earlier experiment by Barber and Calverley (1964a). In their experiment, Barber and Calverley employed a 'task-motivated control group'. Briefly, task-motivated subjects are given instructions to maximise motivation and compliance; for example, they are typically told that everyone is able to do the task if they try, as it is easy to do. The task-motivated group is then asked to carry out suggestions, but they are given no hypnotic induction procedure. When Barber and Calverley (1964a) applied the task-motivated paradigm to the investigation of suggested hallucinations they found that the hypnosis and task-motivated subjects did not differ in their ratings of the vividness of the suggested hallucinations. The implication of this finding was that it was not necessary to evoke some unique property of hypnosis to explain reports of hallucinatory experiences as they were readily replicated by 'unhypnotised' subjects. However, an important point left unanswered concerned whether the task-motivated and 'hypnotised' subjects genuinely experienced the hallucinations or whether they just exhibited compliance. In an attempt to answer this question, Bowers (1967) administered demands for honesty in reporting to a task-motivated group. Before reporting their hallucinatory experiences each subject was told that what was really wanted was for him to be honest in answering the questions, that he should not state that he saw and heard things simply because he thought it would please the experimenter, that if he did not see

the suggested object or hear the suggested sounds he should say so, and that previous statements by the experimenter were not strictly true. The results indicated that task-motivated subjects, when given these instructions, reported significantly less vivid hallucinatory experiences. However, Bowers did not employ a hypnotic condition, so it was impossible to determine whether 'hypnotised' subjects would also report less vivid experiences under similar conditions.

In order to determine whether this was so, Spanos and Barber (1968) repeated that experiment including the missing hypnosis group. The basic procedure involved firstly obtaining subjects' baseline responses to suggested visual and auditory hallucinations, i.e. responses without the administration of task-motivated instructions or hypnotic induction. One group of subjects was then given a hypnotic induction procedure, and another was given task-motivational instructions; subsequently, they were again asked to report if they could see or hear the hallucinations. When honesty reports were *not* demanded, the task-motivated instructions increased reports of vivid visual hallucinations above the baseline level. However, when honesty reports *were* demanded, they did *not* increase the reports above the baseline. Thus the task-motivated subjects, when asked to tell the truth, reported less vivid visual hallucinations. When the hypnosis group were *not* asked to give honest reports, they also increased their reports above their baseline; however, when they were asked for honest reports they *still* increased their reports above baseline. Thus the 'hypnotised' subjects, when asked to tell the truth, did not report less vivid visual hallucinations. The results for auditory hallucinations were difficult to interpret as the hypnotic induction procedure just failed to be effective in raising the reports above baseline even with no demands for honesty. The overall result has been interpreted by Bowers (1976) to mean that in the absence of honesty demands, the 'hypnotised' subjects' reports of visual hallucinations were genuine whereas those of task-motivated subjects were not. This conclusion appears to be supported by the fact that the retrospective reports of the hypnosis group as to how 'hypnotised' they were also seemed unaffected by demands for honesty. However, in view of the a priori probability of the operation of compliance in the hypnosis, the possibility also exists that the demands for honesty were only effective in reducing compliance for the task-motivated group. A closer examination of the instructions given to the two groups suggests how this might have occurred. In particular, the demands for honesty included a statement informing each subject that the experimenter might have lied to him: 'the experimenter might have told you a few minutes ago that everyone who really tried was able to hear the song and see the dog. This was not entirely true . . .' (p.147). Now this clearly would have different connotations for the two groups. According to the account given by Spanos and Barber, the subjects in the hypnosis group were *not* told initially that everyone could experience the hallucinations; thus the experimenter had not really misled them and their task was still to behave as if they had been 'hypnotised' and to report the hallucinations. On the other hand, for the task-motivated subjects, this statement was tantamount to saying 'forget the task-motivational instructions, the experimenter wasn't telling the truth'; in effect, the honesty instructions could have completely changed the task-motivated subjects' conception as to what was expected of them. The results of this experiment may thus have occurred not because the task-motivational group was complying and the hypnosis group was not, but because of the different ways the two groups perceived the demand characteristics of the situation.

The fact that requirements to tell the truth can be overruled by the instructions the subject may give himself is well-illustrated in a study by Levy (1967), and its relevance to hypnosis has been pointed out by Sarbin and Coe (1972) in their analysis of role-playing behaviour. Levy conducted his experiment on the role of awareness in learning. Specifically, he was concerned with the problem of whether subjects need to be consciously aware in order to learn, and the associated problem of the validity of subjects' verbal reports in this respect. Levy points out that in this kind of study the subject takes on the role of 'expert witness'. Levy had subjects do a task in which they were required to learn to begin sentences using the pronouns 'I' or 'We', rather than other pronouns. For the learning without awareness hypothesis to be confirmed it was necessary that the subjects complete the learning task successfully without being aware of what they had learned, i.e. they should start beginning the sentences with 'I' or 'We' but be unaware they had been conditioned to do this. However, Levy split the subjects into two groups. In the 'informed' group subjects were met before the actual learning experiment by a stooge briefed to tell the subject in a casual, *entre nous* fashion what the experiment was actually about, i.e. the stooge told the subject that the girl experimenter was doing the experiment as part of her doctoral thesis and the right thing to do was to catch on and begin the sentences with 'I' or 'We'. The other group, the 'uninformed' group, was not informed of these details. After the experiment such subject was given a standardised interview to determine whether they had been aware of what they had been learning, and each subject was also asked if he knew anything about the experiment before he participated in it. The results indicated that overall the interviewer was not able to detect the informed from the uninformed subjects; though, in fact, a larger number of questions was necessary to elicit reports of awareness from the informed subjects. As Levy puts it, 'as compared with the innocent subject, the beneficent (informed) subject appears less likely to give evidence, revealing awareness unless pressed for it' (p.367). Furthermore, *not one* informed subject spontaneously volunteered his knowledge to the experimenter during the experiment. On questioning, only one of the sixteen informed subjects reported he had been fully informed by the confederate, and 75 per cent of the informed group denied any prior knowledge of the experiment! In his summing up, Levy gives the following warning, 'to rely upon the subject as an expert witness would be to betray as much naiveté of the experimenter as that which he hopes exists in his subject; *without corroborative, independent data the subject's verbal testimony possesses no greater (or lesser) validity than does an unstandardised test*' (p.369, my emphasis). Relating these findings to hypnosis Sarbin and Coe (1972) conclude: 'If subjects operate under self-instructions to lie in a verbal learning experiment there is no reason to believe that the same kinds of self-instructions may not be activated in the hypnotic setting' (p.134).

A number of other studies supports the conclusion that reports of hallucinations may vary considerably according to whether the subject believes such reports are expected of him (Sidis, 1906; Goldiamond and Malpass, 1961). Working with non-hypnotic subjects Dobie (1959) found that nonverbal reinforcement procedures were effective in inducing people to say they had seen objects which were not actually present, and Murphy and Myers (1962) found that reports of hallucinations could be readily manipulated by giving subjects instructions that such reports were desirable or undesirable. Incidentally, in the Spanos and Barber (1968) study discussed in this Chapter, 48 per cent of the subjects said they had experienced an auditory hallucination and 27 per cent said they had experienced a visual hallucination, even *without* task-motivational or hypnotic induction procedures. It seems quite possible that when simple instructions such as 'I want you . . . to hear a phonograph record' and 'I want you . . . to see a cat' (Spanos and Barber 1968, p.139) are used alone, some subjects may still consider that they are supposed to report the hallucinations in accordance with the demand characteristics of the situation. A review of the literature on suggested hallucinations in Chapter 5 appears to indicate that evidence for 'genuine' suggested hallucinatory experiences is sparse indeed, and it seems reasonable to propose that even the non-hypnotic base-level responses of 48 and 27 per cent may have been inflated by compliance.

Some have argued that the task-motivational control group as used by Spanos and Barber (1968) is not really relevant to hypnotic phenomena (Bowers, 1976). Bowers (1976) says, 'No matter how similar the *outcome* of hypnosis and task-motivation . . . the behaviour of task-motivated subjects does not bear relevantly on a consideration phenomena, which is concerned with suggested (and unsuggested) alterations in *experience* as they may be revealed in overt behaviour and verbal report' (p.88). Unfortunately, this argument begs the question of what 'hypnotised' subjects are doing and experiencing. The rationale behind the use of a task-motivated group is similar to that behind the use of Orne's simulating group. If no differences occur between the control and hypnosis groups it remains to be demonstrated that the responses of the 'hypnotised' subjects reflect anything other than high motivation and compliance. A task-motivational control group is only irrelevant if you assume that hypnotised subjects are experiencing something uniquely 'hypnotic' and it is this which accounts for their responsiveness. Yet it is precisely this hypothesis which is in dispute. The principle is simple, if task-motivated subjects can do what 'hypnotised' subjects do, then we do not need a unique property of hypnosis to explain what the latter are doing. The burden of proof then lies on the credulous to demonstrate that the experiences and behaviours of 'hypnotised' subjects are qualitatively or quantitatively different from those of task-motivated subjects.

EXAMPLES OF COMPLIANCE IN HYPNOSIS RESEARCH

This discussion of methodology is unfortunately a foretaste of what has to come in the following chapters, but really regardless of how we rate these attempts to assess the influence of compliance on hypnotic behaviours there seem to remain many examples in the hypnosis literature of studies which the presence of compliance in some form would be difficult to deny. Some of the most infamous come from attempts by investigators to assess the role of hypnotic suggestions in the production of deafness, blindness, and age-regression, and a brief description of a few of these may help to elucidate further the problems that compliance may pose for the interpretation of hypnotic behaviours.

The production of 'deafness' by hypnotic suggestions would, at first, appear to be a dramatic phenomenon, but according to Barber, Spanos and Chaves (1974) it is sometimes not necessary to employ very sophisticated techniques to invalidate subjects' testimony of hypnotic deafness. For instance, if subjects who have been submitted to an induction procedure are given suggestions for deafness and the hypnotist then asks, 'Can you hear me?' some subjects will answer, 'No, I can't hear you'. Even those who do not fall for this can nevertheless be brought out of their 'hypnotic deafness' if the hypnotist states, 'Now you can hear again'. In a study by Pattie (1950) twelve selected subjects were exposed to a hypnotic induction procedure, and received a suggestion that they were deaf in one ear. Four of the subjects subsequently testified that they were deaf in one ear, saying that they could not hear a tone presented to this 'deaf' ear. However, he then went on to test them by presenting tones of different frequencies to each ear. The rationale for this was that it is known that when two tones differing in frequency are presented in this way, a person with normal hearing reports a fluctuating tone with beats, whereas a genuinely deaf person hears a single, steady tone. When this procedure was adopted, three of the four subjects reported a fluctuating tone with beats, thus indicating that their testimony that they were deaf was invalid. The fourth subject actually reported a steady tone, however, he stated after the experiment that he was majoring in physics and was aware of the nature of the test. Pattie concluded that as this subject knew the plan of the experiment he was reluctant to report the fluctuating tone and beats.

In another classic study (Pattie, 1935) a hypnotic induction procedure was again given to five carefully selected subjects, and a suggestion that they would be blind in one eye. Three subjects said that their vision had become blurred following the suggestions, and the other two reported that they experienced total blindness in one eye. A battery of visual tests was then administered to check the validity of this claim, upon which four of the subjects were found to have normal vision in both eyes. However, one female subject performed on this initial battery of tests as though she were actually blind in one eye. As a more stringent test she was subjected to a rather more complicated procedure which involved putting different col-oured filters over her eyes and requiring her to read coloured letters. This proved to be too much for her and it was demonstrated quite conclusively that she could see in both eyes. The post-experimental inquiry was very revealing. She said that she knew all the time she could see, but as the experimenter had said she could not, she acted as if she did not, i.e. she gave false testimony in accordance with the demands of the situation. Of particu-lar interest was the fact that for one test she had actually been practising being blind at home with a friend! Her statement to this effect was actually corroborated by the friend. However, these admissions were apparently accompanied by considerable distress and only after the woman had again been submitted to an induction procedure; as when questioned before induction, she said she could not remember faking. According to Bowers (1976) this 'amnesia' and the distress which accompanied her admissions may have been evidence for 'unconscious cooperation' with the hypnotist, rather than deliberate faking. Whilst this might be a charitable conclusion, it does seem somewhat unlikely that a person would go home and practise being blind with a friend, 'unconsciously'. Surely, it seems equally reason-able to suggest that the poor woman was acutely embarrassed at being found out, the amnesia would therefore be very convenient, and the distress at making the admissions very predictable. This case is possibly an impor-tant illustration of an ethical problem in hypnosis, and exemplified well the inadequacy of the assumption that anyone faking hypnosis has got to be some kind of unprincipled charlatan. The woman's extreme reluctance to admit to deception and the accompanying outburst of tears are testimony to the fact that she probably did not put on the performance as some kind of jolly jape. Most likely she found herself in an extremely awkward social situation in which she felt compelled to be a good subject, and to do what was expected of her. If this case is not exceptional then it seems that every effort should be taken by hypnotists to assure subject that they can release themselves from the contract at any time without compromising the hyp-notist or ruining his experiment.

In a study on hypnotic age-regression by Gidro-Frank and Bowersbuch (1948) six 'deep trance' subjects were given suggestions that they were four months old. The age was critical as a number of early textbooks stated that when a four-month-old infant is stimulated on the sole of the foot, his large toe reflexively moves backwards and his other toes spread out. This is called the Babinski reflex and is reputed to disappear when the infant reaches six months of age. After the age-regression suggestions three of the six subjects actually showed the Babinski response. The conclusion was that as these subjects had shown this rather specialised response the hypnotic induction had actually succeeded in sending them back psychophysiologically to the age of four months. However, Barber (1969b) has pointed out that this conclusion is invalid as there is much evidence to suggest that typically four-month-old infants do *not* show the Babinski result when systematically observed (Burr, 1921; Wolff, 1930) and thus the textbooks were inaccurate. Sarbin (1956) has suggested that the three subjects in the experiment by Gidro-Frank and Bowersbuch (1948) had performed the Babinski response voluntarily because they were aware of the purpose of the experiment. Unfortunately these subjects' prior information was inaccurate.

WHAT HAPPENS WHEN YOU CAN 'OWN UP'?

Although compliance seems implicated in the studies discussed in the previous section, one way of determining more conclusively its presence in hypnotic behaviours would be to try to assess the effects on hypnotic responsivity of removing pressures for compliance, i.e. if a particular hypnotic response is reduced or eliminated when pressures for compliance are removed, it would be reasonable to conclude that the response is normally biased, or completely accounted for, by compliance.

The following experiment (Wagstaff, 1977a) was an attempt to devise such a situation in relation to post-hypnotic amnesia. This seemed a particularly good candidate for investigation as it has been described as 'among the most striking and important phenomena of hypnosis' (Nace, Orne, and Hammer, 1974, p.257). Typically, the subject is submitted to a hypnotic induction procedure and it is suggested to him that he will have some difficulty remembering what has happened to him when he 'wakes up'. He is told that this loss of memory will continue until he hears a 'release' signal from the hypnotist, upon which his memory for the events during hypnosis will return. When investigated systematically the degree of post-hypnotic amnesia is usually estimated by getting subjects to perform a number of items on one of the standardised hypnosis scales, and determining the number of items recalled before and after an amnesia release signal (Hilgard, 1965; Cooper, 1972). This procedure was used in the following experiment with some rather important additional manipulations.

The subjects were fifty-four undergraduates, and all were naive as to the true nature of the experiment. The fact that it was their first experience of hypnosis was unlikely to have introduced any significant bias as, contrary to the belief of some, without specific training, hypnotic susceptibility does not necessarily improve with experience (Barber and Glass, 1962; Hilgard and Tart, 1966). The subjects were randomly assigned to two groups, A and B, which were tested separately. A standardised hypnosis scale (SHSS:A) was then administered to both groups and they were asked to perform ten items. To avoid the possibility of experimenter bias all the instructions were prerecorded on a master tape. The subjects' responses were recorded by an experimentally blind experimenter who was not aware of which group she was dealing with, and a different experimenter performed the subsequent treatments. One of the items they received was the suggestion for amnesia, i.e. when they 'woke up' they would find it difficult to remember anything that had happened until they heard the voice of the hypnotist say 'now you can remember everything' (i.e. the amnesia release signal). Both groups were subsequently given the instructions to wake up. So at this point they had both been treated identically. However, before receiving the recall instructions and the release signal, group B received the following statement:

> It has been shown experimentally that some subjects who have been given the particular induction scale that has just been administered to you do not really achieve any form of trance state; in fact, any 'odd' experiences that some have such as feeling very relaxed or drowsy are commonly reported by people who have simply been told to relax and keep their eyes closed for 10 minutes. Upon further questioning of these subjects it has been revealed that some of them had not *really* been hypnotised, but had been what is called 'role-playing'. Role-playing is not used in any derogatory sense; it just reflects the subjects' determined attempt to try to experience the hypnotic state. However, the subject is always aware that he or she has not achieved a *real* trance state. Now, will you please raise your hand if you feel you were not really hypnotised but were just role-playing.

This statement was designed to allow those subjects who had been compliant to 'own up' with the minimum of embarrassment, i.e. it was hoped that they could own up without feeling that they had been frauds, or had let the experimenter down. Following this statement group B received the following taped recall instruction: 'Please write down now in your own words everything that has happened to you since you began looking at the target'. After the subjects had finished writing down their responses the standard amnesia 'release' signal was administered: 'Now you can remember everything. Anything else now?' The procedure for group A was identical except that the role-playing statement was given *after* the instructions for recall and amnesia release. Thus group A was given no opportunity to own up to compliance until after they had carried out all the other instructions.

The results showed that scores for both groups on the hypnosis scale (excluding the amnesia item) were not significantly different, and that compared to available norms, an acceptable degree of hypnotic performance overall had been manifested by both groups. For purposes of comparison between the groups the measure used was the number of subjects who recalled extra items after the release signal, i.e. the number who displayed reversibility, which is assumed to be an important index of suggested amnesia (Hilgard, 1975). Ten subjects in group A displayed reversibility, thus showing the standard post-hypnotic amnesia effect. However, none of group B, the ones who had been allowed to own up, showed reversibility, indicating no evidence of amnesia. The difference between the groups in this respect was highly statistically significant (p < 0.001). One problem was whether group B had deliberately withheld recalling more items after the release signal. To check this a comparison was made between the overall number of items recalled by each group, including those recalled after the release signal. There was no statistically significant difference; thus at the end both groups had recalled a similar number of items.

As none of group B had displayed reversibility, yet to all intents and purposes they were as 'hypnotised' as group A, the implication seems to be that group B was faking amnesia; thus these data appear to strongly support the hypothesis that this measure of amnesia, at least, can be significantly biased by compliance. Another important feature of this study was that after *both* groups had been allowed to own up, only 17 per cent maintained that they had been 'hypnotised', although 80 per cent had manifested hypnotic behaviours of some kind.

Although this study was certainly modest in size and only begins to tackle the problem of determining the extent of compliance in post-hypnotic amnesia, it does seem to demonstrate two significant points. Firstly, one hypnotic behaviour, the reversal of post-hypnotic amnesia, was found to be non-existent when compliance was controlled for. This may be limited to the sample employed, but the validity of the phenomenon of post-hypnotic amnesia is brought into question, and will be discussed in further detail in Chapter 6. Secondly, although the controls did reduce the frequency of reports of being 'hypnotised', nevertheless 17 per cent of subjects still claimed to have experienced at least a 'light' state of hypnosis. Therefore, it seems that although compliance is very important, it is unlikely that it can account for *all* verbal reports of feeling 'hypnotised', i.e. not all subjects say they feel 'hypnotised' just to please the experimenter, to avoid committing a social impropriety, or to appear 'good'. In the amnesia study just mentioned it appeared that 17 per cent of the subjects who responded to the hypnotic suggestions may have genuinely believed themselves to have been in some kind of special state. Although this appears to conflict with the fact that post-hypnotic amnesia seemed to be absent when controls for compliance were used, a likely resolution would seem to be the possibility that compliance in hypnosis is not all-or-none. Just because a particular subject may feel himself to be in a hypnotic state this did not exclude the possibility that he may deliberately fake his post-hypnotic amnesia. Thus, emphasis should be placed again on the dangers of making gross generalisations across hypnotic phenomena. If *some* subjects appear to give genuine reports pertaining to some hypnotic phenomenon this does not mean that *all* subjects' reports of this phenomenon are genuine, or that subjects who give genuine reports in one instance must of necessity be giving accurate reports in another instance. After all, there seems to be no obvious reason why a person who believes himself to be 'hypnotised' should be immune from pressure for compliance when other behaviours are considered. This quite fundamental idea that hypnotic behaviours and experiences are multidetermined makes questions such as 'Is hypnotic behaviour faked?' fairly meaningless. The possibility exists that some hypnotic phenomena may be purely manifestations of compliance, some partly, and some impossible to simulate. Similarly, some subjects may never fake, some may fake some of the time, and some may fake all of the time.

AUTOHYPNOSIS

Before ending this part of the discussion it may be worth mentioning the alleged phenomenon of 'self-hypnosis' or 'autohypnosis', as it is sometimes called (Marcuse, 1976), where a subject is reputed to be able to hypnotise himself in the absence of a hypnotist. On first consideration the existence of such a phenomenon may appear to rule out the possibility of compliance (why should a subject comply in the absence of the hypnotist?). However, the problems concerning the interpretation of reports pertaining to self-hypnosis are manifold. Firstly, it seems difficult to reconcile the idea of a subject hypnotising himself with the idea that hypnotic responses are largely involuntary. There must be a very high degree of voluntary control (unless the instructions are issued on a tape-recorder) otherwise how could the subject 'wake himself up'? Secondly, in the applied literature 'autohypnosis' has largely been used for the treatment of clinical cases, and it is difficult to differentiate the techniques from some other procedures involving self-instructions for relaxation. This had led to a rather confusing situation in which procedures regarded as relaxation exercises by those involved, may be seen as a form of 'self-hypnosis' by some proponents of hypnosis. For example, Marcuse (1976) states, 'some form of self-suggestion or self-hypnosis may account for the success of many present-day "techniques of relaxing" ' (p.202). The problems of equating 'hypnosis' and 'relaxation' in some general way will be discussed in the next chapter. Thirdly, and most importantly in the present context, reports from subjects as to whether they have 'hypnotised' themselves are frequently *retrospective* and given to hypnotists or others. If the hypnotist says, 'go away and hypnotise yourself', the pressure still exists for the subject to report that he succeeded, if the subject perceives that success in 'autohypnosis' is the hypnotist's expectation. Thus, the subject's report that he 'hypnotised himself' is no less prone to problems of compliance than his reports given during a session with a hypnotist.

CONCLUSION

In this chapter examples have been given to illustrate the importance of compliance in determining hypnotic behaviours. However, as the final study seems to indicate, there appears to be more to certain reports by some subjects than compliance; it appears that *some* subjects may genuinely believe themselves to be, or to have been, in a special condition or state of 'hypnosis'. In the next chapter we shall consider how some subjects, when submitted to hypnotic induction, may come to believe they are or have been 'hypnotised'.

4. How Do I Know I'm 'Hypnotised'?

If some subjects decide to label themselves as 'hypnotised' how does this come about? One way of answering this question would be to say subjects know when they are 'hypnotised' because they actually fall into a unique trance state which is unmistakably hypnotic in quality. Unfortunately, people's reports of their experiences 'under hypnosis' sometimes differ; some report they completely blacked out and cannot remember a thing, and others may report awareness of what was going on but describe feelings like entering a cavern or a well (Sarbin and Coe, 1972). However, the fact that people do not always agree as to what it feels like to be 'hypnotised' does not necessarily mean that they are not in a unique state; after all, reports of other states such as being relaxed, or asleep, can differ from person to person, yet few would want to suggest that these states do not exist. Unfortunately, as discussed briefly in Chapter 1, our understanding does not seem particularly enhanced by the fact that investigators seem to differ in their conceptions of the utility of the term 'trance'. The problem remains that at our present state of knowledge saying a person feels 'hypnotised' because he is in a trance appears to explain nothing; especially if we accept Hilgard's (1975) proposal that words such as 'trance' and 'state' are only metaphors to describe subjects' experiences and behaviours. In view of the rather sterile nature of this trance debate, maybe a more useful insight into the problem may be gained from looking at some of the more general principles which govern the way in which people label their experiences and behaviours.

SELF-ATTRIBUTION AND HYPNOSIS

Bem (1965) has pointed out that society faces a unique problem in training the individual to make public statements describing internal experiences to which only he has direct access. According to Bem's self-perception analysis, the individual may make such statements by invoking the same processes that society uses to infer the inner states of others. Thus if a wife sees her husband eating brown bread in large quantities she may infer that he likes it; similarly, if the man is asked, 'Do you like brown bread?', his reply may also be determined by the same public events, i.e. 'I guess I do, I'm always eating it!' Accordingly we may come to possess knowledge of ourselves on a number of important characteristics only through social interactions with others; for example, we learn whether we are attractive or unattractive by listening to others' comments about us (Baron and Byrne, 1977). Investigators have pointed out that the less sure we are about our conceptions of ourselves, the more we rely on information from others to provide us with the knowledge we require; as Bem (1972) says, 'To the extent that internal cues are weak, ambiguous or uninterpretable, the individual is functionally in the same position as an outside observer, an observer who must necessarily rely upon those same external cues to infer the individual's inner states' (p.2). Also, Kelley (1972) has emphasised that a person will be more likely to accept information from external sources if his prior information is poor and ambiguous.

There is growing evidence to support the conclusion that our perceptions of our own ambiguous internal states may strongly be influenced by various external factors. For example, in an experiment by Valins (1966) male college students viewed slides of attractive nude female whilst being exposed to sounds described as an amplified version of their own heartbeats (in reality the heartbeats were bogus). On five of the slides, which were chosen at random, the experimenter either sharply increased or decreased the false heartrate feedback, whilst on the other slides it remained unchanged. Later, when asked to rate all ten slides, the students rated those that coincided with the apparent changes in heart rate as more attractive. Thus, the external cues regarding their level of arousal seemed to determine how much they liked the women, i.e. 'My heart rate has changed, I must like her!' In a further study Valins and Ray (1967) used subjects who were afraid of snakes. Some heard the bogus heart rate increase to an electric shock stimulus but not to pictures of snakes. A control group also received the snake pictures and shock stimuli but were not given the bogus information about the internal state. As predicted, the control subjects subsequently showed greater fear of snakes than the experimental subjects. The interpretation was that the later had external evidence that they were aroused by shock but not by snakes.[1] This work suggests that, particularly when we are unsure of how to interpret our real or apparent internal states, we may label these states according to external cues, or by looking at our own behaviour like an outside observer and making the appropriate attributional inferences. It is not difficult to see how some hypnotic subjects may be confronted with this exact situation. If a subject has followed the instructions in a typical induction procedure, he should generally be seated, feeling relaxed, with his eyes closed. He then has to ask himself, 'Am I hypnotised?' As we shall see, whether he believes he is or not may then depend partly on his preconceptions. If he has a fairly definite conception of hypnosis as a state of dreamy euphoria, unconsciousness, or a trip to Nirvana, he will not have to rely on external cues, and will probably decide that he is not 'hypnotised' as his internal cues unambiguously do not seem to match his expectations (though of course he may still comply to social expectations). On the other hand, if his preconceptions are not definite, if he finds the internal cues ambiguous, he may have to rely on external cues from which to label his state. Thus if the hypnotic subject is confronted with a number of novel internal experiences his only guide as to how to label these may come from the external situational cues of the hypnosis situation.

INFERENCES FROM BODILY CHANGES

Subjects who have been submitted to hypnotic induction often report sensations such as changes in the size or 'disappearance' of the body or body parts, changes in equilibrium such as giddiness or dizziness, experiences of feeling 'unreal', changes in temperature, and apparent changes in the distance of the hypnotist's voice (Gill and Brenman, 1959). It is difficult to determine the extent to which such reports are influenced by compliance, but interestingly, Barber and Calverley (1969) have reported that changes in the size of the body or body parts, equilibrium and experienced temperature are also reported by subjects who have simply been told to close their eyes. Subjects who have been trained to relax, without hypnosis, also report changes in body feelings such as floating and detachment. The possibility therefore exists that certain novel sensations which accrue from simply keeping the eyes closed and being relaxed may be interpreted by some subjects as evidence for being in a hypnotic 'state', and are reported as such. Indeed, Barber, Dalal and Calverley (1968) found that when questioning subjects about how they judged their level of hypnotic depth some subjects said they estimated it from the degree they felt relaxed and sleepy and others from changes in body feelings. In a relevant study Edmonston (1977) asked 191 fellows of the American Society of Clinical and Experimental Hypnosis to request that their 'three best hypnotic patients' respond to a number of questions about their experiences under hypnosis. In response to the item asking them to describe what the hypnotic state or trance was like, the overwhelming majority of patients mentioned relaxation, and virtually everyone mentioned either relaxation or feelings of being carefree, at peace, a loss of fear, and well-being. To an item asking them what was unique about hypnosis, the most common responses again were feelings of relaxation, accompanied by calmness and peace. When asked how they judged they were 'hypnotised', the most common response was the feeling of relaxation, and some reported also feelings of numbness, floating, and carefree peaceful sensations. Although, again, these data could be readily confounded by response bias, i.e. the patients responding as they thought they ought to; the preponderance of replies indicating feelings of being relaxed was very marked. Edmonston concludes that 'From the subjective standpoint of patients being treated in the context of hypnosis, the primary component is relaxation' (p.72). Of course, it could be argued that hypnosis *is* relaxation; however, the semantic problems associated with this relationship are well illustrated by the following statement from a paper by Cade and Woolley-Hart (1974):

In the hypnotic screening experiments which we undertook on behalf of the Society of Psychical Research (Cade, 1973), we made the quite unexpected discovery that, for a majority of subjects without previous hypnotic experience, the biofeedback from a skin resistance meter monitoring their state of arousal quickly produced a trancelike state of relaxation at which post-hypnotic suggestions were effective. This phenomenon we termed 'psychocybernetic hypnosis'; it is perhaps similar to what Dr. Donald Coulton terms *'non-hypnotic hypnosis'* (p.15, my emphasis).

In practice, the proposal that hypnosis is either relaxation, or at least similar to it, seems somewhat unfeasible in view of a number of considerations. For instance, there seems to be a vast discrepancy between a relaxed hypnotic subject sitting comfortably in his chair or on a couch, breathing deeply with his eyes closed, and a 'deep trance' subject performing human plank feats, behaving like a baby, throwing acid in the experimenter's face, lifting weights and performing complex cognitive tasks. To say subjects do these energetic tasks whilst in a drowsy state of 'deep relaxation' seems rather contradictory. This point has been clarified by Barber and his associates who note that induced relaxation usually disappears when suggestions are given that require the subject to be active (Barber and Coules, 1959). Even when relaxation is not present the subjects nevertheless tend to show a high level of responsiveness to suggestions (Barber, 1962a). Indeed, in one study by Banyai and Hilgard (1976), subjects were successfully 'hypnotised' whilst riding a bicycle ergometer under load, with eyes open, and receiving suggestions of alertness! These subjects subsequently performed no differently on eight tests from the SHSS-A and SHSS-B than when given the standard eye-fixation and relaxation induction; they also assumed a 'trancelike appearance' (p.223) in both active-alert and relaxation conditions. Moreover, performances in the two conditions were highly correlated, i.e. subjects who scored highly on hypnotic susceptibility after the active-alert induction also scored highly following the relaxation procedure. Barber, Spanos and Chaves (1974) point out that as long as it is made clear to subjects that they are in a special situation in which they are expected to respond to suggestions, the administration of suggestions for relaxation and sleep is unnecessary to elicit a high level of hypnotic responsiveness. They conclude that it is more likely that repeated suggestions for sleep and relaxation tend to result in responsiveness to hypnotic suggestions, not directly because they induce relaxation or a special state, but because they define the situation as 'truly hypnosis', i.e. a situation in which they are expected to respond to the suggestions.

However, as previously mentioned, the extent to which subjects might use relaxation experiences as evidence for a hypnotic state should depend partly on whether the experiences coincide with their beliefs and expectations of hypnosis. Barber and Calverley (1969) found that some subjects reported the changes in body feelings but did *not* consider themselves to be 'hypnotised' because they felt they were aware of what they were doing and did not experience complete amnesia. Most induction procedures actually try to counter such preconceptions with the result that a subject may find that what to him seem perfectly 'normal' experiences are being defined as 'hypnotic'. For instance, the SHSS:A says: 'The experience, while a little unusual, may not seem as far removed from ordinary experience as you have been led to expect' (p.9). Also, 'If you are unable to have an experience I suggest or to do something I ask you to do this does not mean that you are not hypnotised' (p.10). As a result of such statements the subject may find himself in a state of ambiguity; he may not really know what to make of his experiences.

Some good examples of the ambiguity of responses during hypnotic induction (with instructions for relaxation) are given by Kidder (1973) who reports on a hypnosis workshop attended by practising psychologists. He says that an almost unanimous feeling among the participants after the first induction was not what a new and different experience it was to be 'hypnotised' but rather 'what an ambiguous and vaguely defined experience it was, if it was indeed experienced at all' (p.2). The experience of hypnosis, for many, seems suspiciously like relaxation. Put in this position, the subject may then look to the hypnotist for cues on how to label his experiences; if the hypnotist says he (the subject) is 'hypnotised', then maybe the subject will believe he is.

Barber et al. (1968) have investigated what happens when the hypnotist's cues are taken to a logical extreme. Three groups of subjects were submitted to a hypnotic induction procedure, and all performed similarly. However, one group was then told by the hypnotist that he considered them to have been 'hypnotised'; a second group was told that the hypnotist did not believe them to have been 'hypnotised', and the third group was told nothing. The post-experimental depth reports revealed that the subjects tended to say they were or were not 'hypnotised' depending on whether the hypnotist said they were or were not 'hypnotised'. Although these results are probably as readily explicable in terms of compliance, i.e. the subjects' reports corresponded to what they thought they were expected to say, the possibility also remains that some may actually have used the hypnotist's statement as direct evidence: 'I wasn't sure at the time, but if he says I was hypnotised, then maybe I was'. This possibility is perhaps made more plausible by the reference to the conformity studies by Sherif (1935). Sherif's situation employed the autokinetic effect; this phenomenon occurs when one looks at a stationary light in an otherwise dark room and as the eyes have no other reference point the light appears to move. Sherif found that if subjects were tested in groups, individuals' reports of movement were highly influenced by the estimates of the other group members. Unlike the stimuli used in the Asch and Crutchfield studies discussed in Chapter 2, the stimulus in the autokinetic effect is particularly ambiguous and the estimates of the others provide an important source of information. The effect is particularly long-lasting (Bovard, 1948) and subjects often report that they are unaware that the responses of others influenced them (Hood and Sherif, 1962). In view of these considerations it has been suggested that Sherif's situation reflects both compliance and private acceptance (Wrightsman, 1972), i.e. some subjects may actually believe that the light is moving in the directions specified by the group. Jahoda (1970) has pointed out how when social pressures are present, some subjects may persuade themselves to 'see' what the rest of the group apparently sees, and how the pressure to fall in line will be more potent 'when the stimulus is not a straightforward one like the length of lines, but diffuse and ambiguous like the phenomena in the seance room, or the weird performances of cult-priest or magician' (p. 50). One might add 'the experiences of being submitted to hypnotic induction' to Jahoda's list as they could also be categorised as diffuse and ambiguous. Coffin (1941) too has pointed out that whether a subject accepts the propositions of an experimenter will depend to an important extent on how 'well-structured' the situation is. If the situation is not well-structured and possesses ambiguous stimulus characteristics, and some form of response is required of the subject, the more influenced he will be by the propositions of the experimenter.

The following dialogue (from Kidder, 1973) which actually occurred between a subject and two accredited hypnotists, illustrates well how comments sometimes made by hypnotists could actually pressure subjects to reinterpret perfectly ordinary experiences as 'hypnotic'.

> *Subject*: The question in my mind is, how do you know if you were in a trance or not? I mean, I know I did some things, but I think they were all under conscious voluntary control.
> *Hypnotist 1*: This is the one question that all patients will ask. . . . And they'll say, 'you see, it doesn't work'. I think you can tell if someone is in a trance by looking at them. . . . I thought you were, but maybe you didn't *think* you were.
> *Hypnotist 2*: You were actually the one that I thought went into trance the quickest . . . (p.2).

Kidder (1973) also points out that in training people to accept they have been 'hypnotised' it is often important for the hypnotist to tell the subject to expect less from 'hypnosis'. As an example he quotes an interview between a subject who had just been in a 'deep trance' and members of the group keen to know what it was like to be 'put under by an expert' and to experience the 'real thing'. In answer to how it felt, the subject replied, 'Just very good. Very, very relaxed . . . like being very tired . . . sort of hazy.' When asked what he thought it would be like the subject replied, 'Well, I thought you wouldn't be conscious. . . . And then when I was in it I felt like I could just come out any time I wanted to. *But I guess that's how you feel*. I thought it would be involuntary.' (p.7). This subject's experience was clearly at variance with the image of the hypnotic zombie and this kind of comment could easily result from subjects being told (as they were in the report of Kidder) by the hypnotist that, 'the idea that something is going to happen which will be unlike anything else you've experienced is a very common preconception (and it is wrong)' (p.7). It would probably be accurate to say that few modern hypnotists would dispute this, however, it should perhaps be noted that the subject's expectation that the experience should have been *involuntary* is, in fact, very much in line with the proposals of Orne (1966a) and Bowers (1976) that genuine hypnotic effects should indeed be experienced as involuntary.

The subject could actually do more than take the hypnotist's word for whether he was 'hypnotised'; he could also take cues from the particular way the hypnotist phrases his questions in order to interpret his own experience of being hypnotised. In the study by Barber, Dalal and Calverley (1968) subjects who had scored similarly on the SHSS responded differently to questions concerning their experiences depending on the wording of the question. For example, when asked, 'Did you experience the hypnotic state as basically similar to the waking state?', only 17 per cent reported that it was different. However, when asked, 'Did you experience the hypnotic state as basically different from the waking state?', 72 per cent reported that it was different. One obvious way of interpreting these data would be to suggest that subjects may have complied and responded with the answer implicitly demanded by the question in spite of contradictory private experiences. However, an additional possibility is that some may have actually used the implicit demands of the question to genuinely label ambiguous experiences. Although this interpretation at first seems rather unlikely, it becomes more credible in the light of a study by Loftus (1975) on the subject of eye-witness testimony. In this experiment subjects were shown a video tape of a car accident. Half of the subjects were then asked, 'How fast was the white sports car going when it passed the· barn while travelling along the country road?' The remaining subjects were asked, 'How fast was the white sports car going while travelling along the country road?' Subsequently all subjects were asked, 'Did you see the barn?' In fact, no barn existed. However, the subjects who hear the question presupposing the existence of a barn were over six times as likely to say they had seen one. According to Loftus these subjects genuinely believed they had seen a barn.

Looking to the hypnotist for cues can also perhaps be integrated within the conceptual framework of Festinger's (1954) theory of social comparison. According to this analysis, when objective means cannot be established to verify judgments we assess our judgments by comparison with those of others, especially if we trust their judgments as being authoritative. It seems reasonable to propose that a rather undecided hypnotic subject may decide the best judge of whether he is 'hypnotised' and what he has experienced is a hypnotist.

INFERENCES FROM RESPONSES TO SUGGESTIONS

In their study of hypnotic reports Barber et al. (1968) found that another common justification subjects gave for assuming they were 'hypnotised' was their observation of the degree to which they experienced the effects of specific items that were suggested. Unfortunately, it is difficult again to ascertain whether these reports are genuine, or whether they reflect subjects' attempts to comply with the hypnotist's expectations. If a subject has complied with the suggestions he may deem it socially desirable to state that he experienced the suggested effects. The general experiences of bodily feelings discussed in the previous section seem less subject to this criticism as they have been found to be spontaneously manifested in relaxed 'unhypnotised' subjects in situations where the pressures to report such effects are less obvious. However, there is certainly considerable evidence that subjects do not need to be submitted to a hypnotic induction in order to respond to at least some of the suggestions typically used to determine hypnotic responsiveness (Barber, 1969b; Barber, Spanos and Chaves, 1974). The term 'waking suggestibility' is frequently applied to this phenomenon and will be discussed in greater detail in Chapter 7, but for the moment a study I conducted at Liverpool University may be used to illustrate the point. The subjects were sixty-three non-undergraduate visitors to an open day in the Department of Psychology. All stated that they had had no previous personal experience of hypnosis. All were then instructed that they were to receive a number of suggestions, but that no attempt would be made to 'hypnotise' them. Four suggestions from the SHSS were then administered by tape. The items were: arm lowering, arm immobilisation, finger lock, and arm rigidity. No hypnotic induction procedure whatsoever was administered, but the subjects were told to close their eyes and concentrate. In this situation 68 per cent of the subjects responded to the arm lowering suggestion, and approximately 25 per cent to the other three suggestions. Although it may be possible that these results too were biased by compliance it was interesting to note that a small number of subjects spontaneously vocalised some surprise that they have genuinely experienced the suggested effects. If the testimony of these subjects is valid then the indication is that it may be necessary to be submitted to hypnotic induction in order to experience novel sensations appropriate to at least some suggestions, usually delivered within the context of hypnosis. Consequently, if the suggestions are preceded by a hypnotic induction procedure, any such novel experiences may be interpreted by the subject as being evidence that he is in a hypnotic state due, once again, to the untested assumption that he could not experience them in a 'waking' state.

This kind of rationale may be most clearly evident in situations where the subject is administered hypnotic suggestions not usually found in the standardised hypnosis scales. A good example of this concerns the reports of myopic (near sighted) individuals who are given instructions for relaxation of the eyes and are asked to view an optometric chart to test visual acuity. These subjects tend to report that when they fixate the chart, it appears to be 'crystal clear' for brief periods and then rapidly becomes blurred again (Graham and Leibowitz, 1972). Graham and Leibowitz (1972) found that when myopic subjects received the relaxation instructions in a waking condition they attributed these flashes of clear vision to eye relaxation; however, if subjects received the same relaxation instructions, but preceded by a hypnotic induction procedure, they tended to attribute the flashes to hypnosis. It is not difficult to see how a similar rationale could apply to suggestions for analgesia. People are often amazed by the fact that a hypnotised subject can appear to show no effects of pain when a steel pin is passed through his skin as it is assumed that such a procedure would normally be painful. However, there is evidence to suggest that for some subjects procedures for inducing relaxation and distraction can effectively reduce pain without any form of hypnotic induction (see Chapter 8). If a subject is given suitable instructions for relaxation and distraction in the context of hypnosis, but is unaware of the efficacy of these procedures without hypnotic induction, he may attribute any absence of pain to the presence of a hypnotic state; 'That didn't hurt very much, I must be hypnotised'. In fact, as far as the steel pin is concerned, relaxation and distraction may not always be necessary. It seems odd that we marvel at the 'hypnotised' individual tolerating the pin when a lot of us can take injections, give our blood and have our blood sampled without reeling in pain and bleeding copiously from the wound. Yet in this instance Bem's self-perception paradigm may again be very relevant; the hypnotic subject may be as surprised by his responses as we, the observers, are.

Barber (1972) gives an interesting personal report of how he considers a hypnotic subject may genuinely experience suggestions; this report differs somewhat from the previous reports of compliant subjects in Chapter 3, but even so, Barber's view is that it is unnecessary to postulate the existence of a special hypnotic state or trance to explain the following behaviours and experiences. Barber says that he approached the hypnotic situation willing to participate and believing that it was possible to experience certain suggested effects. This gave him a 'set' or predisposition to try not to think contrary to, and to try to imagine and visualise the things that were suggested. Thus when he was told his arm was 'rigid' like a piece of steel, he verbalised the thought continuously, and did not say to himself that he could bend it (though he realised he could, if he had wanted to). Thus, when challenged to bend it, by continuously telling himself it was rigid, he says he could not. The principle is fairly simple and the reader may wish to try it. Sit in a chair, and repeat to yourself continuously, 'I am glued in the chair, I cannot get up', and try to think *only of this*. After a while, some of you may feel that there is a sense in which you feel you cannot get up. However, what will be obvious to you is that if you stop thinking about being stuck, then getting up would be no problem; as such, whether it is really meaningful to term such a response 'involuntary' is a moot point.

Returning to Barber's experiences, when he was told to imagine that his hand was rubbery and numb he did so. Then when a weight, which was normally painful, was applied to the arm, he tried not to think of the stimulation as pain, but as 'sensations', for example, numbness, heat, pulsing, cutting and did not let himself think of the sensations as pain. Thus when asked if the stimulus was painful he reported that although he experienced sensations that would in other circumstances be labelled as 'pain' he did not label them as pain in this instance (as we shall see in Chapter 8, it may be possible that the active effort involved in 'imaginings' of this kind could exert an effect of reducing the experience of pain, by distracting the subject, or redirecting his attention). Barber goes on to report other experiences, for example, visualising a cat and trying to stop thoughts that the cat was only in his mind's eye; but all the experiences seemed to possess a common feature — they all involved a *voluntary* act of *trying* to imagine what was suggested whilst *actively trying* to suppress contradictory thoughts. The acts were conscious and deliberate; all the time the subject seemed to be aware that, should he desire, he could stop imagining. In this way, these kinds of experiences lack the 'automatic' quality that some assume are supposed to characterise hypnotic experiences, a point which will come up on a number of occasions in the ensuing discussions in other chapters.

Although there are at present no available estimates of how many subjects regarded as hypnotically susceptible actually engage in the imaginative activities described by Barber, or actually interpret their experiences the way he did, it does present a very interesting alternative way of conceptualising how *some* subjects might behave in hypnotic situations, and how they might interpret their experiences. The problem of hypnosis as imagination will be examined more thoroughly in Chapter 7, but for the purposes of the present discussion, the point is that if a person deliberately engages in these kinds of imaginative activities and is surprised about their results, he may label the experiences 'hypnotic'. Furthermore, it is important to emphasise Barber's view that the experiences he is describing represent a 'normal psychological phenomenon' conceptualised in terms of 'attitudes, motivations, expectancies' (p.120). There is nothing uniquely 'hypnotic' needed to experience the effects.

The psychologists in Kidder's (1973) report who were attending the hypnosis workshop, also reported that they were *trying* to experience the suggested effects. But using psychologists as subjects Kidder notes that the participants may have been more willing to criticise than naive participants, and this is why there testimony is particularly revealing. Kidder says that most of the subjects recognised in themselves the element of trying to be a good subject; but recognising this they doubted whether they could call themselves 'hypnotised' 'when they had tried so hard to cooperate and be good. It seemed that hypnosis should be something less voluntary, less dependent on such willing cooperation' (p.1). After a female subject had been brought out of a 'trance' in which the hypnotist had suggested she would feel sun shining on her face, an observer asked her if she had felt warm. She replied, 'Yes, kind of. But I think it was because I was *trying* to' (p.3).

Another way of looking at how some subjects may come to believe they have been 'hypnotised' has been proposed in a much neglected article by Skemp (1972). Skemp (1972) has argued that if subjects are surprised by their responses to suggestions, this may in turn increase the weight they attach to verbal information given by the hypnotist; and an important determinant of subjects' responses to suggestions is the hypnotist's ability to predict an event which the hypnotist *knows* will happen in an ordinary 'waking' state, but the subject believes is unlikely. In other words, if the hypnotist asks the subject to do something which then surprises the subject (but not the hypnotist), the subject may then be more likely to accept what the hypnotist says to him afterwards. In order to test this proposal, Skemp used the after-image phenomenon. He prepared a small card, half of which was coloured red and the other half white. Under normal circumstances, if a subject fixates the edge where the red and white halves meet, the edge of the red stripe appears to get darker, and the white edge becomes green. Skemp reasoned that if a subject were unaware of this 'normal' effect, but experienced it in the context of 'hypnosis', he would assume that the hypnotist had 'caused' its manifestation, and subsequently the subject be more responsive to further suggestions. Skemp has reported such a procedure can be useful for the successful induction of subjects who have been previously unresponsive. One could see how this kind of procedure might very well affect a non-compliant hypnotic subject who believes the whole thing is a silly waste of time or feels that it is pointless continuing as 'nothing is happening'. If the hypnotist can *make* 'something happen' which surprises the subject, this could increase the subject's motivation for continuing.

In the standardised hypnotic induction procedures Skemp argues that really the hypnotist is using a 'trick' (p.103). The hypnotist chooses events which he knows are probable in terms of perfectly ordinary processes, but the subject is unaware of this, so when the subject finds the prediction comes true he 'accepts the hypnotist's unspoken implication that the hypnotist is bringing them about' (p.103). Skemp gives the following example:

> In induction by eye gaze, for example, the subject is told to fixate an object slightly above his normal line of vision and told that his eyes are starting to blink, that the eyelids are getting heavy, wanting to close . . . etc. The hypnotist's words reinforce the sensations which the subject is experiencing anyway and so the subject believes him. Soon they do close for a moment — a long blink, perhaps, and the prediction is confirmed.

'They are closing more and more firmly . . .' is simply encouraging the subject along a path which, in a state of physical relaxation coupled with boredom at the monotonous repetitions of the hypnotist, he is likely to take anyhow. When the eyes do close however, the hypnotist had a successful prediction to his credit (p.103).

Skemp also makes it quite clear that his explanation is an attempt to integrate 'hypnotic phenomena with the other well-known processes and [it] explains them in the same terms as everyday waking behaviour' (p.106).

Kidder (1973) summarises the same kind of situations as follows: 'Making use of gravity and other physiological realities helps to eliminate the volitional aspect — it relieves subjects of the feeling that they were faking it or just playing the game. They can thus attribute their behaviour to something else, and if obvious coercion is ruled out (and the forces of gravity are not made salient), there remains only the "trance" ' (p.6). If some subjects believe they are 'hypnotised' because of the way they perceive their own responses to suggestions, it is interesting to postulate what would happen should the hypnotist take those suggestions away. Gill and Brenman (1959) have documented the effect:

> First we would induce hypnosis in someone previously established as a 'good' subject; then we would ask him how he knew he was in hypnosis. . . . He might reply that he felt relaxed. Now we would suggest that the relaxation would disappear *but he would remain in hypnosis*. Then we would ask again how he knew he was in hypnosis. He might say because his arm 'feels numb' — so again, we would suggest the disappearance of this sensation. We continued in this way until finally we obtained the reply, 'I know I am in hypnosis because I *know* I will do what you tell me'. This was repeated with several subjects, with the same results (p.36).

This result appears to indicate that when the suggestions are taken away, all that is left is pure compliance. The subject is wide awake and saying, 'I *know* I will do what you tell me'. He does not appear to be drowsy, relaxed, somnambulistic, or on a profoundly altered state of consciousness. The act of doing what the hypnotist wants has been described by Kidder (1973) as the 'contract' which may involve a process of placing the locus of responsibility on the subject. As one subject commented, 'You make it sound as if it's the patient's fault instead of yours if he doesn't go into a trance' (p.4).

BEHAVIOURS AND BELIEFS

There is another way, somewhat ironical, in which subjects may come to label their experiences as 'hypnosis' by virtue of the fact that they have been complying. Indeed, interesting areas of grey may exist between knowing one is telling a lie and knowing one is telling the truth, as there is a strong theoretical and empirical basis for the proposition that, in certain circumstances, overtly playing a role can lead to an acceptance of private attitudes appropriate to the role, i.e. behavioural compliance can lead to private acceptance.

One of the main theoretical bases of this idea is cognitive dissonance theory (Festinger, 1957, 1962; Brehm and Cohen, 1962). The basic units of the theory are cognitions, which are bits of knowledge one has about oneself and one's world, for example, 'I smoke cigarettes', 'I believe that people should not lie'. If any two cognitions imply the opposite of each other they are said to be dissonant, for example, 'I smoke cigarettes', 'I believe smoking causes lung cancer'. Such dissonance is experienced as an unpleasant state of tension which one is motivated to reduce. The magnitude of the dissonance depends primarily on the number and importance to the person of the dissonant elements involved, so it can be reduced in a number of ways. For example, the importance of one or more of the elements may be reduced, thus the smoker might convince himself that dying of lung cancer is not particularly important as we all have to go sometime. Another way of reducing dissonance is to add consonant elements, or consistent elements, such as 'I don't smoke enough cigarettes to do me any harm', or 'Cigarettes help me relax and stop me becoming ill in other ways'. However, the most important way of reducing dissonance is to change one or both of the dissonant elements, for example, the smoker may convince himself that smoking is unlikely to cause lung cancer, or he can give up smoking.

It is now possible to see how dissonance theory might also predict that if a person acts in a way inconsistent with his private feelings or beliefs, this will produce dissonance which might result in him changing his attitudes or beliefs to be consistent with his previous actions. However, for this to happen an additional factor has to be present; the individual has to have some degree of choice as to whether to engage in the behaviour. There will be less dissonance if you engage in an attitude-discrepant behaviour because someone has got a gun in your back, than if you volunteered to engage in the behaviour. The importance of these factors is illustrated in a study by Calder, Ross and Insko (1973). In this experiment subjects were offered a small or a large reward for informing another person that some really dull, tedious tasks were actually very fascinating, i.e. they were paid to tell a lie and thus behave in a manner contrary to their private attitudes. In another condition they were told that they had a choice of whether to do this, and were led to believe, after they had told the lies, that important consequences had resulted. Finally, they were asked to rate how enjoyable they thought the tasks had been. The results in this condition were in accordance with dissonance theory. Those who had been given a *small* reward rated the tasks as *more* enjoyable than those who had been offered a large reward. The rationale was that those offered the small reward felt they had performed an attitude-discrepant behaviour, i.e. told a lie for no good reason. In order to reduce the dissonance they changed their attitudes to be consistent with the behaviour of telling the other person the tasks were interesting. They decided the tasks actually *were* interesting. On the other hand, there was less dissonance for the high reward group as they had ample reason for telling the lie, they were being generously rewarded for doing so.

Dissonance reduction of this kind may well be applicable to some subjects and some hypnosis situations, as in the case of a subject who complies with the hypnotist's expectations and spuriously reports that he felt as though he was in a hypnotic trance. However, suppose then that upon deliberation the subject is rather ashamed or embarrassed of this, and is confronted with a dilemma as he cannot really justify how he could have been so gullible or easily intimidated. One way of reducing the dissonance might be to actually believe that he really was in a hypnotic state. If the cues were sufficiently ambiguous this might seem to be the line of least resistance.

Cognitive dissonance may also account for why some subjects might come to believe they have passed particular suggestions when their senses have revealed nothing of the kind. If, as mentioned in the last section, a subject has been surprised by his reaction to the eye-closure suggestion, has attributed it to the hypnotist and is eagerly awaiting the hypnotist's commands, he may experience considerable dissonance when the hypnotist predicts something *contrary* to the evidence of the subject's own senses. For instance, if the hypnotist says, 'your arm is getting lighter!', and the subject's senses say, 'it isn't', the subject will be in a state of dissonance. He could resolve the dissonance by saying publicly or privately, 'No, it isn't', and act accordingly; however, this confronts him with a very awkward social situation and an admission of failure which may be equally intolerable. Alternatively, he could privately accept the evidence of his senses, and publically comply or 'fake' by moving his arm up appropriately; according to some of the arguments proposed in this book this would probably be the line of least resistance for a lot of subjects, but also to some it could still be an admission of disappointment, failure, and lead to feelings of guilt. The intriguing third possibility, suggested by Skemp (1972), is that some subjects may override the evidence of their senses, and believe the hypnotist instead. This would be a very interesting exercise in self-persuasion indeed, and intuitively plausible, but again it must be recognised that no special state of 'hypnosis' is being proposed as a feature of the argument. If some subjects do react in this way, then the extent of the belief would probably vary according to the strength of contradictory input from the senses. If the hypnotist suggests that, involuntarily, your arms are rising, one leg is bending, and your head is turning from side to side all at the same time, you will have a job overriding the barrage of contradictory evidence from the senses (though I have no doubt that some 'good', compliant, hypnotic subjects would overtly conduct the whole ridiculous exercise). On the other hand, it might not be so difficult to override input concerning a falling arm which is already tired, or the lack of input from an imaginary voice, as the possibility that subjects may actually override the initial evidence of their own senses in favour of the statements made by the hypnotist is more likely when the input is weak and ambiguous. There might be interesting parallels here between this kind of self-persuasion and the reports I have heard from Merseyside Police Detectives that some individuals, questioned as suspects, although subsequently cleared as totally innocent, admit that during interrogation their interrogators seemed so sure that they (the suspects) were guilty, that they began to doubt whether their memories were accurate, and became worried that they might have actually been guilty.

According to cognitive dissonance theory, the amount of dissonance depends on the extent to which attitude discrepant behaviour can be justified, and in most experimental hypnotic situations factors to justify why the subject should comply would probably be all too obvious, and little dissonance reduction would be necessary. Where the effect is most likely to be influential is in a clinical situation where the following basic elements are present. Firstly, the consequences of the actions are important, the patient wishes to be cured and might have paid for the privilege; secondly, the patient may choose to be treated by hypnosis, and even ask for it. The patient is thus confronted by a mass of elements which oppose the cognition, 'I am not hypnotised'. If you have paid £20 to a hypnotist to stop smoking and your health is bad, then the line of lease resistance would involve believing that the treatment is of some value. Other work on cognitive dissonance suggests that if people have invested a lot of effort or even suffered for some goal, the more they value the goal (Aronson and Mills, 1959; Gerard and Mathewson, 1966). Again, in the hypnosis situation one might predict the more traumatic the ordeal the more subjects might believe they have been 'hypnotised'.

Bem (1965, 1972) has put forward his self-perception theory as another way of interpreting changes in beliefs which might follow counter-attitudinal behaviour. Thus a person observes his behaviour of giving a report under ambiguous circumstances and responds to the report as though it were true. In an ingenious experiment Bem found that if subjects were put in a situation where they were used to observe themselves telling the truth, they were more likely to believe what they had been asked to say. Sarbin and Coe (1972) too point out that police manuals provide officers with hints for subtly establishing truth telling, then obtaining confessions, some of which are false, but the accused believe are true. They also note that Bem has found support for the hypothesis that if conditions for truth telling are replicated, the subject is more likely to believe a false confession that he has uttered. Thus, if the hypnosis situation is seen as one where the subject is expected to tell the truth, yet he also feels obliged to give false reports, he may come to believe these false reports.

Kidder (1973) suggests that hypnotic induction techniques will be most effective in actually inducing compliance and attitude change (i.e. getting the subject to firstly do what he is told, and end up believing he is 'hypnotised') if the technique is worded in a permissive manner. If external pressures are too great they may threaten the person's sense of autonomy, and the persuasive attempts may 'boomerang'. If the technique is too authoritarian there will be too much external justification and thus there will be no dissonance to reduce. The advantage of permissive suggestions is that they would tend to make the subject feel that he was in some way responsible for his behaviour and could have behaved otherwise.

It should be emphasised that the generality of these proposals is limited. No suggestion is being made that whenever a subject performs or behaves in a manner discrepant with his beliefs he will inevitably change his attitude to accord with his actions. However, the evidence suggests that in the appropriate circumstances, when the subject feels he has no good reason for acting the way he has acted, or when it is actually difficult for him to decide whether his statement or action is consistent or inconsistent with his private feelings, then the possibility of a corresponding change in attitude exists. Bandura (1977) has suggested that self-evaluations can be very important determinants of behaviours and attitudes when a person's behaviour is a source of self-criticism. Thus another possibility which may be predicted by dissonance theory is that if a subject has committed himself publicly to a belief in the power and efficacy of 'hypnosis' before induction, the very fact that induction *fails* to live up to his expectations may subsequently motivate him to hold a *more* salient belief in its efficacy than before. A fascinating report by Festinger, Reicken and Schacter (1956), entitled 'When prophecy fails', tells of a group of people who had committed themselves to the belief that the world would end at a specified time and they would be whisked off to safety by flying saucers. When the world was still there after the specified time, instead of giving up their beliefs they engaged in an active proselytising campaign. One interpretation was that as the cognition 'I believe' was so powerful, when this belief was disconfirmed, the appropriate way to reduce the dissonance was to actively seek social support to bolster convictions, with the consequence that the convictions were held more strongly than ever.[2] This might be an appropriate analogy in the case of a subject publicly dedicated to the conviction that hypnosis is a weird and wonderful state of consciousness. When this is disconfirmed, rather than face the disappointment, he proselytises for hypnosis instead; this may be a point to ponder when considering some anecdotal cases. For an individual who finds it difficult to tolerate self-criticism it may be easier to change his attitudes than to suffer not only the condemnation of others, but also self-condemnation.

In this respect it is interesting to speculate that unless pressures for compliance are removed, statements requesting the subject to give honest reports may actually reinforce his belief that he has been 'hypnotised', as the subject is presented with an even more dissonant cognition, 'I have continued to lie even when asked to tell the truth'. Of particular relevance to this discussion is a study by Ås (1963) concerned with non-hypnotic correlates of hypnotic susceptibility. Subjects were administered with a sixty item questionnaire, and their responses to each item were correlated with hypnotic susceptibility measured by a hypnosis scale. The item which proved to be the most highly correlated with hypnotic susceptibility concerned whether the subject had ever told a story with elaborations to make it sound better, but then had found that the elaborations seemed as real as the actual incidents. The susceptible subjects were more likely to reply in the affirmative to this question. Assuming their testimony is valid, this could indicate a propensity on behalf of some susceptible individuals not only to fake reports but also to come to believe them.

So far we have isolated two possible important factors in hypnosis, compliance and belief in the hypnotic state, and we can now return to the problem of whether these factors, either singly or in combination, are capable of explaining the overt responses to suggestions and the subjective reports of subjects submitted to hypnotic induction procedures.

NOTES

1. The studies by Valins et al. have received some criticism and a number of authors has failed to replicate the Valins' effect (Sushinsky and Bootzin, 1970; Gaupp, Stern, and Galbraith, 1972; Kent, Wilson and Nelson, 1972). However, other investigators have suggested that failures of replication may have been due to the confounding of results by a behavioural pre-test, and by a failure to provide sufficient incentives to the subjects. When these factors are controlled it is claimed the effect can be replicated (Borkovec, 1973).

2. The followers of the prophecy were actually divided into two groups, the Lake City group which met at the home of the leader, Mrs Keech, and another group which met at a nearby town, Collegeville. On the day of reckoning only those who were gathered together around Mrs Keech, and met the disconfirmation of the prophecy with social support, actually engaged in proselytism. Those of the Collegeville group, who were dispersed to their homes and received no social support, relinquished their faith. These results were in accordance with the predictions of the dissonance theorists. In the same way, it could be predicted that dissonance would be the greatest for those hypnotic subjects who have to continue to interact with the hypnotist and fellow hypnotic subjects, rather than those who submit to induction as a 'one-off' event. However, this hypothesis awaits empirical verification.

5. Some Hypnotic 'Feats'

In this chapter consideration will be given to the proposition that hypnotic suggestions enable susceptible subjects to transcend their waking capacities. It is perhaps important to emphasise that some hypnotists and other proponents of the use of hypnotic techniques might not necessarily wish to make this claim; for example, those more interested in the experiences of hypnotic subjects might deem it unnecessary to assume 'superhuman' hypnotic powers to justify the use of hypnotic techniques. Nevertheless, frequent claims *are* made for the transcendence of waking capacities using hypnosis and a considerable amount of research has been conducted to either support or reject such claims; thus the analysis in this book would be incomplete if these investigations were ignored.

If the factors previously outlined are responsible for hypnotic effects, then an important prediction can be made; there should be nothing essentially unique about the capacities of subjects to perform various 'feats' following hypnotic suggestions, and such feats should be repeatable by waking subjects who are either highly motivated to do a task or who believe they are capable of responding in a certain way.

As an illustration let us consider an example of increased muscular performance under hypnosis. Supposing we find that when tested under normal conditions Mr. X lifts 150 lbs. over his head. He is then submitted to a hypnotic induction procedure and, to the surprise of all, lifts 180 lbs. over his head. To test for the possibility of order effects we might 'wake' him and re-test his capacity, which returns to 150 lbs. When 're-hypnotised' he again achieves 180 lbs. We might view this increase in strength as a product of a unique feature of hypnosis, possibly due to some fascinating chemical or electrical effect on his physiology contingent upon the production of a trance, and presumably incapable of repetition without the induction of a trance. However, supposing the same Mr. X were offered £50 if he could lift 180 lbs. or were told that he would ruin the experiment if he failed to lift 180 lbs. This might motivate him to try a little harder, and possibly without any hypnotic induction he might be capable of exceeding his normal performance, and lifting the heavier weight. Now, such demonstrations would certainly not prove that Mr. X was not in a special hypnotic state when he first lifted the 180 lbs., but they would demonstrate that he *could* have just been highly motivated, and this alone would be effective in producing his increased muscular capacity, i.e. it would be unnecessary to invoke the concept of a unique altered state of consciousness to explain his increased strength.

Alternatively, the same situation could be analysed in terms of the effects of belief. Supposing Mr. X really believed he was in a special state of 'hypnosis' which enabled him to exceed his normal capacities, but it was only his confidence in this belief, not a unique hypnotic state per se, which enabled him to reduce the increase in performance. If this were the case then any situation which inspired him with an equal amount of confidence might also be capable of producing the same effect. For instance, if we gave him a sugar pill and told him it would give him superhuman strength, and he believed this, then maybe again he might be able to lift 180 lbs. His belief might enable him to produce just that little extra effort in the same way as an athlete's belief that it is his 'lucky day' might spur him to produce a better performance. If all hypnotic behaviours could be interpreted in this way, this would certainly not discredit the remarkable 'powers' of hypnotic induction, but it might take away some of the more baffling mystique of hypnosis, and suggest some alternative ways of explaining how hypnotic suggestions may exert their effects.

Mr. X's performance and experiences may be interesting in another respect. He could have been complying completely; he may have been firmly convinced that he was not 'hypnotised', but felt obliged to produce the desired performance. However, he could alternatively have decided he was 'hypnotised', but was still aware that he was obliged to fulfill the demand characteristics of the experiment; in either case he could have voluntarily produced an inferior 'normal waking' performance. The latter case would be illustrative of an interaction between belief and compliance, and would suggest the possibility suggested at the end of Chapter 3 that compliance may not be an all-or-none phenomenon in hypnosis. Maybe some behaviours can only be manifested when the subject believes he is in a special state, and these effects cannot be simulated by subjects briefed to 'fake'; maybe other behaviours can and are produced because some subjects are being compliant, and some believe they are in a special state, and perhaps other behaviours are, in their entirety, the result of compliance. In relation to the last example it could be speculated that if it were possible to find subjects who believed they were in a hypnotic state, but did not respond to pressures for compliance, they might *never* show some effects usually attributed to hypnosis. Before dismissing this particular speculation as ridiculous those who are supportive of hypnosis as a unique special state might consider the status of alleged reincarnation under hypnosis. Iverson (1976) has carefully documented the remarkable tapes of Arnall Bloxham, a hypnotist who has reputedly regressed a number of hypnotic subjects from all spheres of life back through previous lives. According to Iverson, the incredible detail with which some of these subjects recall their 'past lives' in conclusive evidence for reincarnation. As subjects do not usually go round reading ancient tomes and forgetting they have done this, one is left in the position of seriously considering the possibility of reincarnation, or dismissing their testimony, at least partly, as a premeditated intent to deceive. Of course it could be argued that at the actual time of the hypnosis session they did actually believe they were being regressed, but the historical detail is so often authentic that if one does not accept reincarnation, then one has to admit that a lot of homework must have been done previous to the sessions by the subjects involved.

The tendency for some of those interested in maintaining the academic respectability of hypnosis has been to adopt a sceptical attitude towards these reports of hypnotic reincarnation and to conveniently dismiss them as having nothing to do with 'real' hypnosis, or to ignore the embarrassment completely. Yet this is a rather strange attitude when Bloxham has been reported as having regressed over four hundred people. Could this attitude be determined by the fact that to dismiss the Bloxham tapes as a hoax is an admission of the powerful influence of compliance and sham behaviour in hypnosis? If over four hundred people were prepared to read up on history and then lie about it, what other hypnotic phenomena might also be the result of faking? If one rejects the plausibility of reincarnation then Bloxham's subjects present a severe source of embarrassment to those convinced of the honesty of hypnotic subjects. One result of academic scepticism about Bloxham's hypnotic regressions has been that investigations have been left to television reporters, journalists and historians. Whilst such investigators may have excellent credentials and expertise in their own areas, many have failed to realise the methodological difficulties involved in such a task. Apart from the glaring inaccuracies and inconsistencies that paradoxically appear alongside the incredibly detailed reports of some of Bloxham's subjects, and total absence of 'detective work', such as the checking of subjects' passports, library cards and home bookshelves, the evidence has no sound experimental basis. Some of the subjects may 'look good' but we do not know whether these same people could produce the same performance in a motivated waking state. Whether reincarnation exists or not is not within the scope of this book; however, the essential point here is that we do not know whether hypnotic induction is either necessary or responsible for these performances.

Nevertheless, reincarnation apart, there is still a variety of hypnotic 'marvels' which are deemed academically respectable by some, and since the early days of hypnosis some of the spectacular feats of the 'hypnotised' subject have been put forward as evidence that there is something essentially unique about hypnosis which enables an individual to transcend his normal capacities. This kind of statement is indicative of one of many semantic problems in hypnosis, for when a subject is submitted to hypnotic induction, there is a very real sense in which we can do some things which he 'normally' would not do. People do not 'normally' engage in many of the bizarre behaviours attributed to hypnosis, and sometimes cannot 'normally' perform various feats manifested in the hypnotic situation. The point at issue is whether there is any unique 'hypnotic' property which makes it impossible to replicate these performances when the subject is given appropriate motivational instructions when he is not 'hypnotised'. The appropriate parallel in compliant behaviour is that subjects do not 'normally' go round giving dangerous electric shocks to people or judging eight inch lines as ten inches long, as they are not 'normally' under such strong pressures for compliance. Thus, if the subject is being compliant in the hypnosis situation we might expect him to perform 'unusually'. However, to reiterate, if *all* hypnotic behaviours could be replicated by individuals who were not 'hypnotised' this could never lead us to conclude that a unique hypnotic agent does not exist, but it would indicate that the same factors operating in the 'waking' situations which resulted in the behaviour could also have determined the behaviour in the hypnosis situation, and we would not have to postulate that something 'additional' or uniquely hypnotic was necessary to explain hypnotic performances.

It is this rationale which underlies the studies to be discussed in the rest of this chapter.

HYPNOSIS AND MUSCULAR PERFORMANCE

Some of the claims for increased muscular performance appear to be fairly dramatic on first consideration, but on closer examination points arise which epitomise more of the methodological difficulties encountered in studies of hypnosis. Let us consider first a popular stage demonstration, the human plank feat. There seem to be two versions of this. In one, the 'hypnotised' subject is suspended between two chairs, one beneath his head, and one beneath his ankles, and he remains suspended for a short while, as if a 'human plank'. In the other, the subject is again suspended between two chairs, but this time one is beneath the shoulders, and the other beneath the calves. In this position the 'hypnotised' individual can support the weight of a person on his chest. These versions of the human plank feat seem to impress some observers who assume that the subject is able to accomplish the feat because he is in some kind of unique hypnotic state. However, the impressive nature of the performance rests on another assumption, that subjects could not perform the feat if they were not in a hypnotic state. When this assumption is actually put to the test it appears to be false. Investigators have found that unselected 'unhypnotised' subjects are able to perform these feats just as well as 'hypnotised' subjects (Barber, 1969b).

The lesson is that no matter how unusual or superhuman the behaviour of a 'hypnotised' subject may appear, it cannot be deemed a unique property of hypnosis unless it is tested against a control, 'unhypnotised' condition. This is clearly the most common failing of anecdotal reports of hypnotic feats of all kinds; it is simply assumed that no person could do such things if not in a hypnotic state, yet this assumption is untested. However, even when studies have employed control procedures, in many cases the controls are far from adequate. A reasonable way of proceeding might be to test subjects' muscular performance in a waking state, and then to test them again when 'hypnotised', to see if hypnosis produces any increment in performance. The problem with this 'same-subjects' design is that mentioned earlier in this chapter regarding our hypothetical 'Mr. X'; if the subjects catch on to what is expected of them, i.e. the demand characteristics of the situation, they may deliberately distort or suppress their performance in the 'waking' condition, so as to produce a spurious boost to their performance in the hypnosis condition. Morgan (1972) suggests this may have been a significant artifact in a study by Eskridge (1969) which purported to demonstrate that post-hypnotic suggestions for increased performance in a psychomotor task (reaction-time) effectively increased performance to a level above that achieved in a waking condition. What is suspicious is that this enhanced performance persisted for some weeks in the absence of further hypnosis, practice and suggestion.

Another major problem in this area of research is what Morgan (1972) refers to as the confusion between 'state' and 'suggestion'. There is some evidence that waking suggestions alone, without hypnotic induction, can effectively increase or decrease muscular performance. For instance, if subjects are told that they are squeezing a 'hard' resistance they can show an increment in performance above that when they are told it is an 'easy' or 'medium' resistance. This has important implications for studies employing an independent 'waking' control group. A comparison of two independent groups of subjects, some in a hypnotic condition and the others in a waking condition, is of little value unless the waking group is given appropriate instructions, which are equivalent except for the hypnotic induction procedure. Another important factor, allied to this, concerns the respective motivation in the hypnotic and waking control conditions. The view has been put forward that hypnotic induction procedures, followed by suggestions, oblige the subject to behave in the direction desired by the experimenter, i.e. 'hypnotised' subjects may have a high degree of motivation. It would therefore be misleading to compare a 'hypnotised' group with an uncommitted unmotivated waking control group.

Keeping these methodological problems in mind we can now have a further look at the relevant evidence. Certainly most of the early attempts to demonstrate the increased muscular endurance of 'hypnotised' subjects suffer from the problems associated with using same subjects design with very small numbers of subjects, even though great claims were made for the efficacy of endurance tests for diagnosing fakers. Some good examples of the problem of possible distortion in the waking control condition are given by Gibson (1977). In one experiment by Nicholson (1920) seven subjects were required to lift a three-kilogramme weight up and down every two seconds. The results indicated that in a waking control condition subjects appeared to be exhausted and unable to continue after ten minutes, whereas when 'hypnotised' they continued for far longer. The result was, however, challenged by Williams (1929) who increased the weight to four-and-a-half kilogrammes and found that a subject in a 'normal unhypnotised' state was able to lift the weight up and down for half an hour and said he could keep it up all night! Nicholson also found that if a subject appears to be fatigued, he may be revived by hypnosis, but as Gibson (1977) has pointed out, there is much evidence to suggest that whatever you do in an encouraging way to a person working at a boring task will banish fatigue for a time. As Gibson says, 'We must not, therefore, confuse the effects of hypnosis with what is generally known as encouragement' (p.99). In another study by Hadfield (1924) the hand-grip power of three men in a waking state was tested on a dynamometer and their average grip was found to be 101 pounds. When 'hypnotised' their average grip increased to 142 pounds. However, Young (1925) in a much larger study found that the average grip in the hypnotic condition was no different from that in the waking condition. A study by Evans reported by Morgan (1972) also indicated increased performance with hypnosis, but Evans reports that the susceptible subjects 'appear to depress waking performance rather than increase hypnotic performance, presumably to protect the integrity of their own hypnotic experiences' (p.215).

Other investigators have also found that provided the non-hypnotic control group is given suitable motivating instructions weight-holding endurance is no better in hypnotic subjects (Rosenhan and London, 1963; London and Fuhrer, 1961; Evans and Orne, 1965). One exception was a study by Slotnik, Liebert and Hilgard (1965). However, Slotnik et al. report that most of their subjects were aware of the comparison between the hypnotic and waking sessions. Also the experimenters were not experimentally blind, thus the results could have been confounded by both subject and experimenter effects.

Some studies have actually demonstrated that subjects' waking performances are *superior* to their hypnotic performances. For example, Orne (1959) found that if subjects were motivated by a monetary reward they held a weight up longer in this task-motivated condition than in the hypnotic condition. However, the task-motivated condition always followed the hypnotic condition, so again the result may have been due to a 'warm-up' effect. In another study Barber and Calverley (1964f) found that whereas task-motivating instructions in the hypnotic and non-hypnotic conditions increased weight-holding endurance, the hypnotic induction procedure per se depressed weight-holding endurance. Morgan (1972) concludes that this result implies the ergogenic aid may be motivating suggestions, rather than hypnosis.

In conclusion, it is probably accurate to say that the methodological difficulties covered in this section apply to most of the studies that have purported to demonstrate the superior performance of hypnotic subjects. In a very comprehensive review of the literature concerning hypnotic performance and muscular strength and endurance, psychomotor behaviour and athletic performance, Morgan (1972) concludes, 'a review of the experimental literature does not justify the view that performance in the hypnotic or post-hypnotic states will necessarily surpass performance in the motivated waking state' (p.193). Other writers have come to a similar general conclusion. For example, Orne (1971) writes, 'Studies with stimulating subjects, as well as other recent research . . . have demonstrated that hypnosis does not magically increase capacities beyond those available in a motivated waking condition' (p.206).

DEAFNESS

Mention has already been made of the fact that some 'hypnotically' deaf subjects when asked if they can hear the experimenter, say 'No, I can't'. Nevertheless, claims have been made that some hypnotic subjects when given suggestions for deafness appear to manifest a condition indistinguishable from neurological deafness. In one study Erickson (1938a) found that six out of thirty hypnotic subjects categorised as 'able to enter a profound trance' failed to be startled when presented with unexpected sounds, failed to raise their voices when reading aloud accompanied by loud noises, and failed to show any response to embarrassing remarks. Unfortunately, no waking control group was used, a problem which should by now appear to be all too familiar. The results of this study seem particularly inconclusive as Dynes (1932) found that three 'hypnotised' subjects who had received suggestions of deafness showed no startle responses when a pistol was fired unexpectedly, whereas they all testified afterwards that they had heard the shot. In another study by Erickson (1938b) two good subjects underwent a conditioning procedure so that they would withdraw their hands when they heard a sound that had previously been paired with electric shock. However, when the subjects underwent hypnotic induction with suggestions for deafness, they did not withdraw their hands. Erickson concluded that 'under hypnosis' the subjects were unconscious of the sound. However, Lundholm (1928) found that in a similar situation a subject who also failed to withdraw his hand after the induction of 'hypnotic deafness' subsequently testified that he had heard the sound but had resisted the impulse to withdraw the hand.

Using electronic monitoring Malmo, Boag and Raginsky (1954) found that one subject exhibited significantly reduced startle reactions to a tone stimulus, when in a 'hypnotically deaf' treatment, compared to a non-hypnotic treatment. However, this subject acted as his own control and thus the experiment suffered the problems with the same-subjects design discussed earlier, i.e. the subject may have deliberately distorted his reactions in the non-hypnotic condition. Furthermore, Malmo et al. had already demonstrated that a patient with genuine organic middle-ear deafness failed to show any startle reaction at all to the same tone.

Other studies have used more sophisticated tests for deafness such as delayed auditory feedback. Delayed auditory feedback is a technique whereby a subject's ongoing speech is played back to him through earphones after a delay of a fraction of a second. Typically, a person who can hear will find this feedback impairs his speech, making him mispronounce and stutter. However, a deaf person will not suffer this impairment. In one study of this kind Kline, Guze and Haggerty (1954) found one subject who was judged to be 'genuinely deaf' following hypnotic suggestions for deafness, still stammered and slurred, but not as much as when he was in a 'waking' state. Again, this utilised a same-subjects design with the corresponding difficulties for interpretation. Barber, Spanos and Chaves (1974) conclude that when studies employing delayed auditory feedback are considered the results clearly indicate 'that hypnotic subjects who are supposedly deaf are able to hear' (p.69). Hypnotic subjects stammer and slur, even when they insist that they cannot hear, acting in a way unlike subjects who are organically deaf (Barber and Calverley, 1964c; Sutcliffe, 1961; Scheibe, Gray and Keim, 1968).

In summary, there is no definitive evidence that hypnotic suggestions for deafness are successful in inducing genuine deafness, or even partial deafness, in spite of subjects' testimony to the contrary. Moreover, contradictions between the subjects' reports of being deaf and the objective measures of deafness seem readily explicable in terms of compliance. In spite of these negative results some authors have claimed that despite the absence of behavioural criteria for deafness, the hypnotic subjects do not actually consciously perceive the sound, thus Malmot et al. (1954) claim that hypnotically induced deafness is 'the result of a defence mechanism which prevents sound from reaching consciousness' (p.315). Well, anything is possible, but all that can really be asked in answer to this kind of proposition is why should we accept this apparently irrefutable kind of reasoning when compliance provides a likely explanation? What Sutcliffe (1961) terms the 'puzzling discrepancy' between the subjects' reports and their objective behaviour is only a 'puzzle' if we do not accept the influence of compliance.

HYPNOTIC BLINDNESS

The possible influence of compliance on responses to hypnotic suggestions for blindness has been well illustrated in Chapter 3 with Pattie's work on testing subjects with sophisticated optical tests, and a number of other studies support the view that, in spite of the subjects' testimony to the contrary, they can actually see (Barber, 1970). However, there is some evidence that some hypnotic subjects may try not to see by crossing their eyes, staring at one point in space or unfocussing their eyes (Barber, Spanos and Chaves, 1974). This conclusion is derived from studies employing EEG brain wave measures. When a patient is organically blind there is a tendency for him *not* to display a phenomenon called 'alpha blocking' in the EEG patterning in response to visual stimulation, whereas non-blind individuals will typically display this response. In a study by Loomis, Harvey and Hobart (1936) one subject who had been given hypnotic suggestions for blindness actually failed to produce alpha blocking in response to visual stimulation. However, the same subject also failed to display alpha blocking when he was given instructions in a non-hypnotic condition to make no attempt to see, and he did not focus on the stimulation. Other investigators have also shown that non-hypnotic subjects can fail to display alpha blocking when they try to ignore visual stimuli. This emphasises again other important features of the behaviour of some hypnotic subjects. When a compliant subject is told he is blind, he may pretend he is totally blind. If he knows he is to be tested, the best way he can respond to what is expected of him is to at least try to be blind, by voluntarily trying to blur his vision or by staring at one spot, but of course, if this is the case, he will still not succeed in achieving blindness.

Using the Ishihara test for colour blindness, Erickson (1939) purported to demonstrate that some hypnotic subjects, who had been given suggestions for colour blindness, did appear to be colour blind. However, when Harriman (1942) repeated Erickson's procedure, but employing the 'malingering card' he found that seven of the ten hypnotic subjects gave the malingering response, i.e. they said that they could not see a number which colour-blind individuals were able to see. Furthermore, a number of other investigators have found that non-hypnotic subjects who are simply asked to act as if they are colour-blind are able to give as many colour-blind responses as hypnotic subjects (Barber and Deeley, 1961; Barber, 1969b). It can be noted, yet again, that the appropriate non-hypnotic control procedure was absent in the original study.

VISUAL ACUITY

Not only has hypnosis been claimed to produce blindness, it has also been claimed to increase visual acuity in near-sited subjects. However, most of the early work on this topic lacked the necessary controls, such as the provision of a task-motivated non-hypnotic control group. When the appropriate controls are applied the evidence suggests that relaxation suggestions for improvements in visual acuity are as effective when given in a waking condition as when given in a hypnotic condition (Barber, Spanos and Chaves, 1974).

Furthermore, an investigation by Graham and Leibowitz (1972), using a laser technique, failed to reveal any physical changes in the eye which could account for visual enhancement resulting from relaxation suggestions. Thus, if suggestions for relaxation do actually improve acuity and the improvement is not due to physical changes in the eye, the mechanism responsible seems as yet undetermined. Graham and Leibowitz (1972) propose that myopic subjects become over-dependent on spectacles and set their internal standard of daily visual performance lower than possible.

NEGATIVE HALLUCINATIONS

It has also been claimed that 'under hypnosis' subjects may be able to selectively eliminate parts of their visual input; such elimination is called a negative hallucination. One study by Gray, Bowers and Fenz (1970) has been reported as evidence that hypnotic subjects can genuinely experience these negative hallucinations (Bowers, 1976). In this study *four* red dots were projected on a wall, and subjects were instructed that they would only see *three* dots when they opened their eyes. A comparison was made of the heart rates of a group of hypnotic subjects, and a group of non-hypnotic simulators doing this task. All subjects reported seeing three dots, but there were differences between the heart rate responses of the two groups. The heart rate of the simulators tended to go down whilst that of the hypnotic subjects went up. Bowers (1976) interprets this in terms of Lacey's (1967) work on heart rate. Lacey suggests that if the subject is looking out for environmental cues his heart rate will decelerate; on the other hand, if he is trying to filter out or reject information his heart rate should increase. According to Bowers this rationale accords with the idea that the hypnotic subject is trying to reject material, whilst the simulator is on the lookout for cues which will help him fool the hypnotist.

Unfortunately, it is difficult to see how this result can substantiate the validity of the subjects' reports. The fact that the hypnotic subject may *try* to reject the fourth dot says nothing about whether he actually succeeds in doing so. He might try to reject the information and show a heart rate acceleration and still be lying when he reports only three dots. The compliant subjects in Chapter 3 also tried very hard to experience what they were being told but ended up giving rather inaccurate reports. It should be remembered that it is not the simulator's job to try to experience the effects; he is instructed to fool the hypnotist. On the other hand, if the preceding analysis is accurate, the hypnotic group will be made up of some feeling distraught and distinctly 'unhypnotised', but still desperately trying to experience the effect, and some feeling 'hypnotised', trying hard to experience the suggested effects, but possibly having some difficulty in experiencing the suggestion. The simple cognitive act of trying hard, and the stress that may be evoked from *not* succeeding might be quite sufficient to account for the acceleration in the hypnotic subjects. Indeed, studies have shown that stress alone may result in heart rate acceleration (for example, Lazarus, Speisman, and Mordkoff, 1963). Moreover, even Lacey's (1967) hypothesis to which Gray et al.'s findings have been allied, has been criticised (Elliot, 1972). It appears that heart rate acceleration and deceleration may accompany a number of tasks according to whether the subject is interested in the task (Adamowicz and Gibson, 1970), whether he is supposed to do something rather than just passively sit and receive information (Turskey, Schwartz and Crider, 1970), or even whether he moves around a little (Elliot, 1972). Any of these factors could have influenced Gray et al.'s result, without postulating that the hypnotic subjects genuinely experienced the negative hallucination.

It may be worth emphasising again that a number of differences between hypnotic groups and waking controls could occur because the hypnotic subjects are *trying* to experience the effects, whereas the waking controls, especially if they are 'insusceptible' simulators instructed to fool the hypnotist, may not be trying to experience the effects, but instead attempting to give an overt display for the hypnotist's benefit. However, as stated in Chapter 3, there is a number of reasons why a subject who has been submitted to induction may feel he wants to try but may actually end up complying because he is 'having a go', without experiencing any kind of special state, and why other subjects (categorised as 'insusceptible') might not do this; but far more importantly, as has also been mentioned previously, according to state or trance theorists 'trying' is not a valid index of hypnotic susceptibility; hypnotic subjects are not 'actively trying, in any ordinary sense to behave purposely or in accordance with . . . hypnotic suggestions. Instead, suggested events are experienced as *happening to them* in ways which would require active effort to resist' (Bowers, 1976, p.108).

An experiment on negative hallucinations which seems somewhat more conclusive was conducted by Underwood (1960). He used two optical illusions in which the illusion appears when a pattern of lines distorts a superimposed figure, for example, in one a superimposed square is presented with a pattern of lines making the square look wider at the top. Twelve carefully selected hypnotic subjects were then presented with the figures superimposed on the patterns, and given suggestions that they could not see the patterns. It was argued that the subjects should not see distorted figures if they genuinely had negatively hallucinated the line patterns. However, although nine of the twelve hypnotic subjects reported they could not see the patterns, they all showed the expected degree of distortion on the optical illusions that is normally produced by the patterns. Using this less analogical kind of procedure it seems quite apparent that even if subjects try to negatively hallucinate, they do not succeed in doing so, and heart rates apart, their verbal testimony may be somewhat suspect.

The enthusiasm that some authors proffer for the validity of negative hallucinations is probably a very good example of how, if hypnosis is accepted as a unitary phenomenon, and if its effects are seen as genuine, any number of almost incredible effects can be accepted as valid without further consideration of their anomalous nature. For instance, no attempt has been made to elucidate the mechanism by which a 'hypnotised' individual can selectively block out part of his visual field. Even work on subliminal perception, whereby stimuli of which we are unaware may influence our behaviour, indicates that subjects cannot selectively attenuate areas in the same visual field. For instance, some experiments on perceptual defence and vigilance appear to demonstrate that stimuli presented outside awareness, if they are emotional, can result in the emphasis or attenuation of a visual stimulus (Wagstaff, 1974; 1977b). However, the effect seems to apply to the whole visual field, not just part of it (Dixon, 1971). Also, whilst one may view a picture, for instance, and 'miss' a detail, this is rather different from standing in Trafalgar Square and negatively hallucinating Nelson's Column, which we might expect some 'deep trance', 'hypnotised', subjects to succeed in doing according to some reports.

POSITIVE HALLUCINATIONS

Suggestions for positive hallucinations occur in most of the hypnosis scales, but whether subjects actually experience the suggested hallucinations or not is usually determined by the subjects' verbal reports. However, as we have seen, the validity of subjects' verbal reports may be highly questionable, and we cannot assume that the fact that some hypnotic subjects report hallucinations in spite of demands for honesty is conclusive evidence that they have genuinely experienced the reported hallucinations. As this is the case, it would be useful if some other index of hallucinatory experience could be used, and investigators have attempted a variety of methodologies to try to gain more objective evidence. Unfortunately, the interpretation of reports of hypnotic hallucinations is again confounded by problems of a semantic nature. For example, if a subject says he 'sees' a suggested object, is he using 'see' literally or figuratively? To avoid getting too involved in this problem it is probably reasonable to suggest that if a subject genuinely 'hallucinates' an object, then the object to some extent is as vivid as objects *actually* present. Most of us are quite capable of imagining objects, in 'our mind's eye' as it were, and although this is an interesting problem for cognitive psychologists, it is certainly not an unusual event. Thus, if all that is meant by a hypnotic hallucination is that a 'hypnotised' subject imagines an object in 'his mind's eye', in the same way that we can close our eyes and imagine pleasant scenes, this hardly constitutes the term 'hallucination', as applied to the experiences of certain psychotic patients and alcoholics suffering with delirium tremens. Thus, for the term 'hypnotic hallucination' to warrant any special attention it would seem necessary to demonstrate that the hypnotic subject is perceiving an object, to some extent, as vividly as actual objects in his visual field (a similar analysis could of course be applied to auditory hallucinations; to warrant the term 'hallucination' the suggested sound would have to be to some extent as 'real' as actual sounds). In practice, the distinction may sometimes be difficult to make, as vividness may vary between extremes, and some individuals may be capable of experiencing near hallucinatory images in a 'normal' state; nevertheless, most people are probably sufficiently capable of distinguishing between the two classes of events to make a distinction meaningful.

Sutcliffe (1961) used the delayed auditory feedback method discussed earlier in this chapter in an attempt to assess the validity of auditory hallucinations. Sutcliffe reasoned that if hypnotic subjects were given suggestions to hallucinate the feedback from their own voices, they should experience speech disturbances similar to subjects who were actually exposed to feedback of their voices. The results showed that although hypnotic subjects testified that they actually heard the delayed feedback, they failed to show usually speech disturbances, and did not perform like subjects who were actually receiving voice feedback. Lundholm (1932) tried to induce the usual response of pupillary contraction, which occurs when the eye is stimulated by light, by giving hypnotic subjects suggestions that they were being stimulated by light. Again, although the subjects testified they saw the light, they failed to show the corresponding pupillary dilation.

Another way of testing for hallucinatory experiences has utilised the negative afterimage. For example, if a subject fixates on a red surface and then looks at a grey or white surface he is supposed to see a green afterimage; if he fixates on blue he will see yellow on the neutral surface. Some hypnotic subjects have claimed that when hypnotically hallucinated colours give rise to afterimages (Erickson and Erickson, 1938; Rosenthal and Mele, 1952). However, other studies have found that hypnotically hallucinated colours did not give rise to negative afterimages (Dorcus, 1937; Sidis, 1906). How can these discrepancies be reconciled? A very probable explanation comes from the work of Hibler (1940) who found that reports of hypnotic subjects varied according to their preconceptions of the afterimage effect; if they thought beforehand that the afterimage of blue was orange or blue, rather than yellow, this is what they reported they had seen. Barber (1969b) comments that hypnotic subjects' reports given in the experiments of Erickson and Rosenthal and Mele were *too* consistent with textbook descriptions. The textbooks give the impression that the same afterimage will always be seen, for example, the afterimage of red is always green. However, Elsea (reported by Barber, 1969b) found that subjects under non-hypnotic conditions who were presented with real colours reported a variety of colours of afterimages other than those reported in the textbooks, with the exception of the colour *blue*, the afterimage of which was almost always described as yellow. This is of course important in that it indicates that Hibler's subjects were still not reporting as they should have if they were actually hallucinating blue. The fact that hypnotic subjects' reports of afterimages seem to correspond to their preconceptions of what should happen can now be reconciled with the finding by Sidis (1906) of a failure to find reports of negative afterimages, for Sidis' hypnotic subjects were actually unacquainted with the afterimage effect. It is tempting to view the afterimage saga as a repeat of the Babinski reflex story told in Chapter 3; hypnotic subjects can sometimes give remarkable demonstrations of effects which the credulous would state they would be 'unlikely to know about'. However, the demonstrations backfire somewhat when the evidence which they are 'unlikely to know about' happens to be inaccurate.

Brady and Levitt (1966) reported that a few carefully selected hypnotic subjects showed optokinetic nystagmus (a condition where the eyes move quickly from side to side) when they were given suggestions to hallucinate a black and white rotating drum. This could possibly be a genuine hallucinatory effect as optokinetic nystagmus is prevalent when non-hypnotic subjects are asked to gaze at a real rotating drum which contains vertical black and white lines. However, Hahn and Barber (1966) found a similar small proportion of unselected individuals also showed optokinetic nystagmus in a non-hypnotic condition where they were simply asked to try to visualise the rotating black and white drum. However, as interesting as this finding may be, it does not really allow us to draw conclusions about the vividness of the imagery. Whilst a person may be able to conjure up a mental image sufficient to affect some appropriate physiological responses, the resulting image may be far from a vivid hallucinatory effect; thus whilst some of us may be able to produce a vivid mental picture of a relative or loved one, sufficient to evoke intense emotional feelings, this is not quite the same as projecting the image so that the person actually appears to be physically present in front of us. Furthermore, we might even question whether the results of Brady and Levitt (1966) conclusively demonstrated a vivid imagery experience, and evidence cited by Barber (1972) indicates that some subjects are able to produce optokinetic nystagmus quite consciously and voluntarily whilst 'awake'. The limitations of imagery are well demonstrated in a study by Miller, Lundy and Galbraith (1970) who devised a situation whereby, if subjects were able to successfully hallucinate the colour green, they should be able to identify a pale-green number of a red background. Although the ten subjects used in the investigation were highly hypnotically susceptible and trained to hallucinate colours, none of them was able to identify the number of the red background when asked to hallucinate green; though all were able to identify the number when an actual green filter was used.

In summary, the evidence that subjects can genuinely experience suggested hallucinations is very sparse, but even if a few can, hypnotic induction seems unnecessary. Motivating waking instructions seem equally effective by themselves.

HYPNOSIS AND DREAMING

A number of studies has indicated that if subjects are given hypnotic suggestions to dream on a suggested topic prior to going to bed, when they are woken up at various times during the night there is some tendency to report that they have been dreaming on the suggested topic (Tart, 1964; Tart and Dick, 1970). Only a few studies have used control subjects, i.e. subjects given the same suggestions, in a similar manner, but without hypnotic induction. A study by Stoyva (1961) showed that hypnotic subjects were more responsive in this way than control subjects, but in this study the hypnotic subjects were given the suggestions to dream in an emphatic way, whereas the control subjects were given the suggestions in a lackadaisical, 'by the way' manner and this different emphasis could have accounted for the results (Barber, Spanos and Chaves, 1974).

Another experiment by Mather and Degun (1975) attempted to assess the efficacy of post-hypnotic suggestions for dreaming with waking suggestions for dreaming given after relaxation. Each subject was given suggestions to dream on a stated topic both in a relaxation session and during a hypnosis session (i.e. a same-subjects design was used). It was also suggested to them that they were to waken following the dream, and to carry out a specified action. According to the authors more of the suggestions were carried out after hypnosis than relaxation. Unfortunately, this experiment is subject to some important criticisms (Wagstaff, 1976a), which can be summarised as follows. Firstly, the statistical analyses were inappropriate, so it is difficult to determine whether the one result they claimed reached significance really did so. Secondly, the same-subjects design was used, so the subjects may have differentially reported and carried out the suggestions in the two conditions, i.e. they may have voluntarily carried out more suggestions in the hypnotic condition as they thought this was expected of them. Furthermore, there was no difference between the groups waking at the correct time and heart rate, which are the only two measures which might be difficult to control voluntarily. Thirdly, the experimenter was not blind when the suggestions were given, so he could have consciously or unconsciously delivered cues, and changed the manner in which he gave the suggestions between the two sessions.

When the appropriate independent control groups have been applied and given non-hypnotic suggestions, in a similar tone of voice, the evidence suggests that waking suggestions to dream on a specific topic are at least as effective as suggestions given in a hypnotic condition. In fact, Barber and Hahn (1966) in one condition found that waking suggestions were *more* effective than post-hypnotic suggestion at eliciting dream reports. It is again impossible to determine how accurate these kinds of dream reports are; as yet there is no reliable index of dream experience and some subjects may have simply reported the suggested dream because they thought they 'ought' to. Nevertheless, according to Barber, Spanos and Chaves (1974) there are acceptable a priori reasons for assuming that instructions to dream on a topic may influence dream content. However, regardless of the validity of the reports, hypnotic induction does not seem to be a prerequisite or an aid to their occurrence.

Arkin, Hastey and Reiser (1966) report one subject who, following post-hypnotic suggestions, was supposedly able to 'talk-out' his dreams whilst they were occurring. However, there was no condition where he was given suggestions without hypnosis, his ability to do this lasted, on average, only sixteen seconds a night, and he was an habitual sleep-talker anyway (Hearne, 1978).

Tart (1970b) has presented data indicating that suggestions to awake at specified times during the night may be effective in getting subjects to actually awake at this time, and the evidence presented by Mather and Degun (1975) also supports this view. However, in the Mather and Degun study the data suggest that most, if not all, of the subjects managed to awake at a specified time under relaxation only (Wagstaff, 1976a).

In their paper, Mather and Degun (1975) suggest that one phenomenon in particular refutes the possibility that subjects may be deliberately fabricating dream reports. The phenomenon was first noted by Stoyva (1965) and refers to the decrease in REM (rapid eye movement) periods during sleep following post-hypnotic dream suggestion. Whilst some of Stoyva's (1965) subjects did indeed show decreases in REM periods after post-hypnotic suggestions to dream, he did not use a control group given 'waking' suggestions to dream on a selected topic. When the appropriate control group was applied, Wagstaff, Hearne and Jackson (1980) showed that REM reduction was equally present in subjects who were not given hypnotic induction. Wagstaff, Hearne and Jackson (1980) also speculated that whereas the concept of a hypnotic 'state' offered no explanation for the REM reduction effect, an explanation in terms of anxiety accruing from attempting to carry out the demand characteristics of the situation was possible.

Attempts have also been made to induce 'hypnotic dreams'. In these studies the subject does not actually go to sleep, but is given a hypnotic induction procedure followed by a suggestion that he will dream. In response to this suggestion some subjects will subsequently report that they have had an experience of dreaming. However, reviews of the literature concerning this topic indicate that methodological inadequacies of the studies make it impossible to ascertain whether the reports are just fabrications (Barber, 1962b; Tart, 1965).

In summary, though claims have been made that suggestions can influence dream content, wakening at specified times, and physiological sleep activity, there is no definitive evidence that hypnotic induction is either necessary or responsible for these effects. There is also insufficient evidence to conclude that 'hypnotic dreaming' is a valid phenomenon.

LEARNING AND MEMORY

Some studies have indicated that learning and memory can be improved by the administration of hypnotic induction procedures (for example, Sears, 1955). However, these earlier studies did not attempt to determine whether motivating instructions given without hypnosis were sufficient to produce an equivalent enhancement of performance (Barber, 1969b). Parker and Barber (1964) applied the necessary controls in a study of performance relating to memory for words, abstract reasoning and digit symbol substitution. They used three treatments; a task-motivated treatment (1) where subjects were told 'if you can try very hard, you will do better etc.', a task-motivated treatment with hypnosis (2), and a control condition without either hypnotic induction or task-motivational instructions (3). They found no difference between the groups on the memory and abstract reasoning tasks, but on the digit symbol task, which was lower in difficulty and complexity than the other tasks, subjects in treatments 1 and 2 performed better than those in treatment 3. However, treatments 1 and 2 did not differ in their effects, indicating that task-motivational instructions alone were as effective as task-motivation with hypnotic induction. This study again emphasises how important it is to compare the hypnotic group with an appropriate control group. Hypnotic treatments invariably include instructions to motivate the subject, and it is of little value to compare such a treatment with an unmotivated control treatment where the subjects are bored and uninterested. This is typified by an experiment by Sears (1955) which purported to demonstrate that hypnotic subjects made less errors learning Morse code than a group of subjects in a non-hypnotic treatment. However, in this study 44 per cent of the non-hypnotic group had dropped out of the experiment before the end, compared to 24 per cent in the hypnotic group. Moreover, Sears reports that the non-hypnotic group complained of boredom and loss of interest, whereas the hypnotic group were interested in knowing what effects hypnosis would have on the task. In view of Parker and Barber's findings it seems that these differences in motivation alone could have accounted for Sears' result rather than a special hypnotic agent.

In one particularly interesting study Krauss, Katzell and Krauss (1974) reported that 'hypnotised' subjects could recall as much material after three minutes of learning as waking subjects could with ten minutes of learning. This was accomplished by giving the hypnotic subjects special 'time-distorting' instructions so that three minutes of real-time would be experienced as ten minutes 'under hypnosis'. However, Wagstaff and Ovenden (1979) were unable to replicate this result; in fact, in Wagstaff and Ovenden's study the hypnotic subjects recalled *less* material in three minutes than the waking subjects did in three minutes. As Wagstaff and Ovenden used the same learning material as Krauss et al. some comparisons can be made between the two studies. Possibly of most significance is the fact that Wagstaff and Ovenden's waking group given *three* minutes to learn the material recalled as much as Krauss et al.'s waking groups given *ten* minutes to learn the material. This finding of Wagstaff and Ovenden was corroborated by the fact that the investigator who had originally devised the learning material (Bousfield, 1953) reports that his subjects (who were all 'waking'), given three minutes learning, recalled approximately the same amount of material as Wagstaff and Ovenden's three minute group, this again being far more than Krauss et al.'s three minute waking group, and similar to Krauss et al.'s waking group given *ten* minutes to learn the material. It seems possible, therefore, that Krauss et al.'s finding may have resulted from their waking control groups being undermotivated for some reason, rather than any genuine facilitation of learning due to hypnosis.

One of the most dramatic of all hypnotic effects is that of age regression, whereby hypnotic subjects are supposedly regressed to childhood and manifest childlike behaviours and report memories of amazing accuracy. However, the evidence concerning the Babinski reflex seems sufficient to sow some seed of doubt as to the validity of the age-regression effect, and when further evidence is examined this doubt certainly seems justified. True (1949) presented data which apparently indicated that some hypnotic subjects given suggestions for age regression managed to recall the day of the week on which their birthday or Christmas had fallen. True found that 81 per cent of the time the subjects were able to name the correct day of the week on which their birthday fell. However, this study lacked a number of important controls and has been criticised on a number of counts; for example, True knew which day the subjects were supposed to report, and he asked each subject in progression, 'Was it Sunday? Was it Monday? Was it Tuesday?' It therefore seems highly possible that his tone and inflections may have provided the subjects with the correct answer (O'Connell, Shor and Orne, 1970). Other possibilities are the subjects told each other a simple formula for computing dates (Barber, Spanos and Chaves, 1974), or some of them, hearing what they were going to be asked under hypnosis, cheated by looking up the calendar in advance (Gibson 1977). These criticisms seem very pertinent when it is considered that no less than *eight* subsequent sets of investigations have failed to confirm True's results (Barber, Spanos and Chaves, 1974). As Gibson (1977) says, 'Alas, so many wonderful things are under the suspicion of somebody cheating somewhere!' (p.104).

Another way of investigating hypnotic age regression has been to administer tests for intelligence, personality, etc. to see if the subjects regressed to a certain age perform as they would normally have done at that age. When regressed hypnotic subjects are given tests such as the Stanford-Binet I.Q. test, the Rorschach ink-blot test, and word-association and speech tests, they do not perform as a child of that age should perform or as they originally performed at the earlier age, but perform at a more mature level. What is more, the same kind of 'too mature' performance is also elicited by waking simulators (Barber, 1969b; Barber, Spanos and Chaves, 1974). As an example, Young (1940) gave the Stanford-Binet I.Q. test to nine hypnotic subjects who were regressed to age three, and seven non-hypnotic subjects who were asked to simulate age three. Young found that both the hypnotic and simulating group responded on the intelligence test as if they were about five-and-a-half to six years old rather than three years old.

Some investigators have proposed that a number of hypnotically regressed subjects fail to show hand withdrawal or conditioned eye-blink responses when regressed to a time before these responses were established

(Edmonston, 1960; McCranie and Crasilneck, 1955). However, other investigations have shown these responses can be inhibited voluntarily (Hilgard and Marquis, 1940) and the evidence suggests that the subjects could have performed in a similar way without hypnotic age regression (Barber, 1969b).

A study by Reiff and Scheerer (1959) purported to demonstrate that five hypnotic subjects gave more convincing and accurate performances of age regression than three simulating subjects, but this study again has received severe criticism (O'Connell, Shor and Orne, 1970). Of particular importance was the fact that the three simulators knew they were acting as controls and only play-acting, and they knew the experimenter was aware of this. As mentioned in Chapter 3, Orne (1959) has reported that under these conditions simulators will give strikingly unconvincing performances. Only when the simulator is told that the experimenter does not know whether he is actually 'hypnotised', and is told that it is possible for him to fool the hypnotist, will he be sufficiently motivated to give a convincing performance. The fact that simulators may benefit from the reassurance that they can fool the experimenter demonstrates the possible importance of subjects' apprehensions concerning their ability to role-play. In a study by Troffer (1966) subjects who were previously judged to be susceptible or insucceptible to hypnotic suggestions, were asked to simulate age regression in a waking condition. One of the findings was that the hypnotically susceptible subjects tended to give more convincing performances of child-like behaviour in this waking condition than the insusceptible subjects. A possible explanation of this difference might be that the insusceptible subjects doubted their ability to role-play and maybe thought the whole 'game' was a waste of time and never really got into the act; and it may very well have been the case that similar factors contributed to their lack of participation and involvement in the hypnotic suggestion procedures previously administered to them, which had resulted in them being classified as 'insusceptible'.

Troffer also found that more convincing childlike responses were given by both hypnotic subjects and waking-simulators when the experimenter treated the subjects like children by speaking in a friendly and supportive way. This result indicates how important experimenter effects are in the hypnosis situation. If Reiff and Scheerer had treated their hypnotic subjects like children, but had not spoken to the simulators in the same way, this alone could have accounted for some of the more convincing, childlike displays given by the 'hypnotised' subjects. It is not surprising that if the hypnotist treats the subject like a child a more lifelike performance will be given, as this would indicate to the subject that the hypnotist too is playing the game, which is a good signal for playing the whole thing with a bit more gusto and abandon. When the study of Reiff and Scheerer (1959) was repeated with the application of the appropriate controls, O'Connell et al. (1970) found that waking simulators performed just as well as the hypnotic subjects, and no evidence for the transcendence during hypnosis of waking role-playing behaviour was found. Other investigators have also found that the convincing childlike performances of some hypnotically regressed subjects can be produced equally as well by non-hypnotic control subjects who are asked to play the role of a child (Barber, Spanos and Chaves, 1974).

However, two studies do appear to stand out as apparently supporting the view that some hypnotic age-regressed behaviours cannot be replicated by non-hypnotic subjects. The first is an experiment by Parrish, Lundy and Leibowitz (1969) which utilised two visual illusions, the Ponzo and the Poggendorff illusions. They argued that, when normal populations are concerned, subjects' responses to these illusions differ according to their ages. Specifically, the extent of distortion in the Ponzo illusion *increases* as subjects get older, whereas distortion in the Poggendorff illusion *decreases* with age. As it seems highly unlikely that the subjects participating in hypnosis experiments would be aware of these different developmental trends, any signs of these trends in the responses of hypnotically age-regressed subjects would appear to provide fairly definitive proof that hypnotic age regression can reinstate early childhood responses in a remarkable way. So, in the study by Parrish et al., hypnotic subjects were 'regressed' to ages nine and five, and their responses to these illusions were compared with those of non-hypnotic subjects asked to simulate the responses of a child of nine and five. The findings indicated that the responses of the hypnotic subjects did indeed accord with the developmental trends of the illusions, i.e. they show less distortions in the Ponzo, and more distortions in the Poggendorff when regressed to the earlier ages. However, the simulators failed to show the different trends. This result seems amazing indeed, but unfortunately possibilities exist that the hypnotic subjects somehow did know how they were supposed to respond, as four subsequent carefully conducted studies have failed to replicate the results, two by Ascher, Barber and Spanos (1972), one by Porter, Woodward, Bisbee and Fenker (1971), and one by Perry and Chisholm (1973). Each of these studies has demonstrated that subjects 'hypnotically regressed' to ages nine and five perceive the two visual illusions in the same way as adults. These failures to replicate appear to cast some doubt on the validity and generality of the effect claimed by Parrish et al.

A second, perhaps even more remarkable effect, has been claimed by Walker, Garratt and Wallace (1976) in respect of the restoration of eidetic imagery in age-regressed hypnotic subjects. Eidetic imagery, or 'photographic memory', is a process whereby an image can be 'stored' in accurate detail after the actual stimulus has been removed. Thus an 'eidetiker' can examine a picture and later project an exact duplicate of it onto a blank surface (Haber and Haber, 1964). This ability has been found to exist, to a limited extent, in about 8 per cent of children (Haber and Haber, 1964). However, according to most investigators, only one instance has been found in adults (Stromeyer and Psotka, 1970). Walker et al. argued that as eidetic imagery is virtually non-existent in adults, but found in some children, then if adult subjects who were age-regressed with hypnosis could demonstrate this phenomenon, it would provide a very strong case for the validity of hypnotic age regression. In their study they used twenty adult psychology students who were chosen solely because they scored highly on a hypnosis scale, i.e. they were not chosen because of their imagery abilities. These subjects were then required to attempt three 10,000 dot stereograms under these conditions. A 10,000 dot stereogram consists of two separate patterns of 10,000 dots; when viewed by themselves they are formless, but when one is superimposed on the other a picture, such as a triangle, emerges. Eidetic imagery is thus tested by getting a subject to view one pattern, which is then removed, and to then try to superimpose his remembered image of that pattern on the other pattern. If he sees the appropriate image, such as the triangle, he is then judged to be a successful eidetiker. None of the subjects was able to identify the correct image when tested in a non-hypnotic condition, or when tested with hypnotic induction alone; however, two subjects correctly identified the image in all three stereograms when they were given hypnotic induction plus suggestions for regression to age seven. Walker et al. point out that the success of two subjects (10 per cent) was in line with the results of Haber and Haber (1964) who found 8 per cent of their sample of children to be eidetikers.

This result certainly seems to point to the conclusion that hypnotic age regression really does reinstate childhood responses with incredible accuracy. However, there seem to be two main difficulties in the interpretation of this finding. The first is methodological, in that the investigators failed to test non-hypnotic subjects with either task motivation or simulating instructions to age-regress. But this is not the only important problem. Although Haber and Haber (1964) found 8 per cent of children to have eidetic imagery, these children were *not* tested with 10,000 dot stereograms, but with less complex measures. Furthermore, a review of the literature reveals not one bona fide case of a child having successfully performed a 10,000 dot stereogram; the only report of such a case appeared in a popular newspaper but when this child was tested in the laboratory by Braddick, she failed to repeat her achievement (personal communication with Dr. O.T. Braddick, University of Cambridge). In a study by Gummerman, Gray and Wilson (1972) not one of a large sample of children was able to correctly identify the figures in the stereograms. In other words, Walker et al. have apparently not only succeeded in regressing their subjects to childhood; they have managed to get them to perform a task which, as far as we can determine, no child can do! It is perhaps not surprising therefore that a replication study by Spanos, Ansari and Stam (1979), using sixty highly hypnotically susceptible subjects, failed to reveal one instance of a subject, age-regressed or otherwise, who was able to correctly report the figure for any 10,000 dot stereogram test either before or after hypnotic induction. In an attempt to explain the success of the subjects in Walker et al.'s study

Spanos et al. suggest that, as the same subjects were tested in different sessions, some may have tracked down the relevant stereograms and appropriate responses in the intervening period. They mention that some introductory psychology books contain the necessary information leading to the references about the particular stereograms used in the study. Spanos et al. conclude, 'The hypnosis literature (for example, Pattie, 1935) contains documented cases of who have carried out such clandestine "homework" between sessions in order to comply with experimental demands. Although such a hypothesis may seem farfetched, our data and those of Gummerman et al. (1972) suggest that it is at least as parsimonious as assuming that age-regression procedures enabled subjects to form accurate images of 10,000 random dots' (p.91).

In another study, Fellows and Creamer (1978) looked at the role of hypnotic induction, and also hypnotic susceptibility in the production of age regression. In this experiment high and low hypnotic susceptibility subjects were assigned to hypnotic and non-hypnotic conditions. In the non-hypnotic conditions the subjects were given special motivating waking instructions to try to imagine hard what was suggested. They were then given appropriate hypnotic or waking suggestions for age regression to the age of seven. They were then given a drawing test (from the Goodenough-Harris Drawing Test), and afterwards asked how real they felt the experience was. The results of the drawing test were compared with the results of ten children who actually were seven years old. The results showed that the hypnotically susceptible subjects rated the experience as more real than in any of the other conditions, but of course this result would be predicted by a theory of behavioural compliance (it was implicitly assumed that subjects were 'supposed' to say it is more real in the induction procedure). On the drawing test, the high susceptibility subjects scored significantly lower overall than the low susceptibility subjects (i.e. the drawing scores of the high susceptibility subjects were 'younger'). Also *overall* the hypnotic induction produced lower scores, but the high susceptibility subjects did not actually do significantly better in the hypnotic induction condition than they did in the waking condition (though there was a trend in this direction). The results are difficult to interpret but Fellows and Creamer (1978) suggest that they can be interpreted in terms of both 'state' and 'non-state' theories of hypnosis. For the purposes of the present discussion, the non-state interpretation seems appropriate:

> Initially, we selected subjects who were either particularly adept or particularly poor at imagining certain unusual things . . . such as, going back in time and becoming a child again. The main effect of the hypnotic induction procedure was to prepare them for the imaginative task by defining the situation as one involving 'hypnosis' with all the expectations and demands that this brings with it, by establishing positive attitudes towards the forthcoming task and by setting up an effective

rapport between subject and experimenter. The motivational instructions also did some of these things, though less effectively than the induction procedure (p.169).

What was certain was that none of the subject groups was able to reproduce the drawing behaviours of the actual seven year olds. Of particular interest in this study was the surprising inability of the low susceptibility subjects to produce a drawing in any way like that of a child, with either the hypnotic or task-motivating instructions. Whereas the high susceptibility subjects were able to reduce their scores from approximately 55 to *38* with the age-regression instructions, the low susceptibility subjects could only reduce their scores from approximately 54 to 51 (the scores of the seven-year-old children averaged around 29). This finding seems significant in view of the fact that when I informally asked a number of people to simply 'draw a man like a seven-year-old would', and scored it according to the criteria provided by Harris for the Goodenough-Harris test, the average score was an interesting 38. Although this was not a formal study the results do accord with Fellows and Creamer's non-state explanation that the apparent higher scores of the low susceptibility subjects may have been more a consequence of motivational factors (they may have had more negative attitudes towards the task), rather than an inability to produce scores of 38 or so in a waking condition. These possibilities would seem worthy of some further systematic investigation.

Though, with the exception of some equivocal results, the evidence suggests that performances of hypnotically age-regressed subjects can be replicated by subjects in a non-hypnotic condition who are encouraged to play the role of an age-regressed individual, the question remains as to whether any hypnotic subjects actually believe that they have become the age that has been suggested to them. One could argue that even though the behaviour of a hypnotically age-regressed subject is no different from that of a simulator, only he believes that he is three or four years old, and this will only occur with hypnotic induction. An interesting study by Barber and Calverley (1966a) may shed some light on this issue. Hypnotic and waking subjects were given suggestions for age regression. However, the subjects in the non-hypnotic control group were *not* told to simulate or 'pretend', they were just given the suggestions that they were going back in time, but were, of course, not given any hypnotic induction procedure. Barber and Calverley found that all of the hypnotic subjects, and 70 per cent of the control group, testified that they were in another place at an earlier time. Barber (1969b) points out that the non-hypnotic control group was not given task-motivational instructions, and if it had would probably have been as responsive as the hypnotic group. However, post-experimentally only about 10 per cent of the subjects in each of the groups testified they had 'thoroughly felt' and 'thoroughly believed' they had returned to the past. Barber and Calverley interpret the discrepancies between the subjects' testimony during and after experiment in terms of the greater pressures from compliance during the experimental session. The important question is, did the 10 per cent of subjects 'really' believe they were in an earlier time? Unfortunately, we do not know. Maybe these subjects still felt some pressures to comply, maybe according to the dissonance reduction processes discussed in Chapter 4 some had eventually succeeded in convincing themselves, after the event, that they had experienced an earlier time. What is significant though, is that as many of the non-hypnotic control group made these belief reports as the hypnotic subjects, and we should remember that these non-hypnotic control subjects were not asked to pretend, and were given no additional, and possibly intimidating, task-motivational instructions. Thus if some people are capable of carrying out a prescribed regressed role with such vividness that they come to believe it, either at the time or afterwards, then hypnotic induction may be neither necessary to produce the effect, nor responsible for it.

HYPNOSIS IN POLICE INVESTIGATION

Recently some claims have been made that hypnosis has been useful in police investigations in improving the memory of witnesses and complainants. On the basis of an evaluation of forty cases Kleinhauz, Horowitz and Tobin (1977) conclude, 'hypnosis may be a potential tool to elicit essential information from cooperative subjects' (p.77). However, the lack of evidence for significant general improvements in memory using hypnotic techniques might lead one to question, on a priori grounds, the probability that hypnotic techniques for improving the memory of witnesses should have any specific advantages in this respect over and above waking procedures. As with most of the evidence reviewed in this chapter, claims for the efficacy of using hypnosis to help the recall of witnesses can be examined in the context of two main questions; firstly, does the evidence attest for the existence of a special hypnotic agent, i.e. can the results be replicated using waking procedures, and explained without reference to a unique hypnotic agent, and secondly, regardless of whether we accept the notion of a special (non-metaphorical) trance state, or agent, can procedures involving hypnotic induction nevertheless be useful in improving the memories of witnesses, or may they produce misleading data?

   Unfortunately, there appear to be no data produced from systematic controlled studies to enable a definitive answer to either question. The report of Kleinhauz et al. (1977) illustrates well the now familiar problems involved. The cases they use come from the Scientific Interrogation Unit of the Israel Police and involve the memory of details concerning descriptions of suspects, vehicles, licence numbers, weapons, etc. from subjects 'under hypnosis', which the subjects were apparently not able to recall in the 'waking state'. The first problem is that no details are given in this report of the kinds of hypnotic induction procedures used, and the kinds of aids to memory that might have been involved; thus we do not know whether subjects were given instructions in the hypnotic situation which might have been absent from the waking situation, such as taking the subject carefully through the sequence of events prior to the incident, and asking him to imagine the situation or getting him to relax and concentrate. Thus it may well be that the 'routine police questioning' (p.78) was different from the questioning in the hypnotic situation in other ways besides the use of hypnotic induction, and these alone could have been the basis for the improvements in memory. The second problem is that it seems the hypnotic induction procedure always followed the routine questioning though, unfortunately, details of the intervals are not given. In terms of experimental design this design was thus confounded by *order*, i.e. we do not know whether the witnesses' memories might have improved anyway, after an interval, due to factors such as a decrease of shock or anxiety with time, and an opportunity to think carefully over the events. The time interval may be doubly critical in view of the fact that certain individuals display 'reminiscence' effects. Eysenck (1977) reports that individuals categorised as introverts recall material better after an interval of twenty-four hours than they do immediately after the presentation of the material, whereas extroverts show the opposite effect. This may be significant in that Kleinhauz et al. report that fourteen out of forty witnesses showed an accurate improvement in memory in the hypnotic situation and it could be the case that these individuals were introverts subject to the reminiscence effect. Of additional interest is the fact that Eysenck relates the reminiscence effect to the level of cortical arousal in the brain, the rationale being that introverts have a high level of cortical arousal (Eysenck provides independent evidence supportive of this view) and this initially interferes with the availability of material for recall due to the operation of the consolidation process in memory, i.e. the storage of material in chemical form. This happens as arousal seems to increase consolidation; however, when the consolidation work is finished, the material then becomes available for recall. Eysenck (1977) says that support for this theory comes from studies which indicate that similar results are found if arousal is artificially stimulated, for example, if a subject is stimulated by white noise he is more likely to show the reminiscence effect. Now, it might be reasonable to suggest that witnesses to a traumatic incident might also be initially in a state of high cortical arousal due to shock and anxiety, and if this subsides over the period between the initial routine interrogation and the interrogation 'under hypnosis' one might expect an improvement in memory during the latter session. Clearly what is needed is a properly controlled systematic trial, balanced for order and involving the appropriate controls for relaxation and equivalence of instructions, etc. Unfortunately I am not aware that any such trial has yet been conducted. Indeed, as the situation exists at the present, it may well be that the use of suitable waking instructions may facilitate the recall of witnesses better than procedures employing hypnotic induction in view of the possible dangers of the fabrication of reports due to the demand characteristics of hypnotic situations, and the reluctance of some witnesses to participate in 'hypnosis'. It is notable that Kleinhauz et al. report that in two cases the information gathered in the hypnotic situation was contradictory to other evidence and they state that there is 'a possibility of details being inaccurate or distorted' (p.79).

In summary, the use of hypnotic procedures to aid memory in police investigations is an area in which it may be worthwhile conducting some rigorous research, but at present the results are too equivocal to enable any firm conclusions to be drawn.

PHYSIOLOGICAL RESPONSES

A vast number of cases of apparently unusual physiological events has been reported in response to hypnotic suggestions. The question therefore again arises as to the extent to which it is necessary to postulate some uniquely 'hypnotic' agent to account for these results.

Although some studies have reported that some 'hypnotised' individuals are able to show heart rate acceleration (Solovey and Milechin, 1957; Van Pelt, 1948), these studies have neglected to use waking controls given similar instructions to try to accelerate the heart. This is significant as a number of other studies have showed that some waking individuals are able to voluntarily accelerate the heart (Barber, 1961b). In one study by Klemme (reported by Barber, 1969b) subjects showed a non-significant trend to be able to control heart rate more successfully in a waking condition. Klemme suggested that the alterations in heart rate may have been indirectly produced by variations in respiration. Other studies have also shown that inhalation and exhalation produce cardiac acceleration and deceleration respectively, and that waking suggestions are effective in producing changes in peripheral blood flow and blood clotting time (Barber, Spanos and Chaves, 1974).

The use of hypnosis for curing skin diseases of one kind or another is another popular subject which some put forward as evidence for some magic 'hypnotic' ingredient. However, when controlled studies are conducted it seems that other explanations are applicable. In a study of Ikemi and Nakagawa (1962), reported by Barber (1969b), thirteen subjects were selected, all showing allergic dermatitis when exposed to an allergy-producing tree found in Japan. Five were submitted to hypnotic induction and told that at allergy-producing tree was being applied to the left arm (in fact, leaves from a common chestnut tree were applied). Next they were told that chestnut leaves were being applied to the right arm (though, actually leaves from an allergy-producing tree were applied). The other subjects were not submitted to hypnotic induction, but were blind-folded and given the same instructions. *All* hypnotic subjects and *all* waking subjects showed allergic responses to the chestnut leaves (i.e. flushing, erythemia, papules). Four of the five hypnotic subjects and seven of the eight waking subjects did not show allergic responses to the actual allergy-producing tree. Thus the hypnotic induction seemed irrelevant; all that was necessary was the suggestion that they were being exposed to an allergy-producing leaf, and the study attests to the power of the placebo effect to either produce or eliminate allergic responses if the subject *believes* that the suggestion will exert an effect. (The placebo effect will be defined in more detail in Chapter 8, but the term 'placebo' is applied to any procedure or inert or innocuous substance that may produce therapeutic benefits because the patient believes it will work, such as sugar pills). The power of the placebo effect is also evident in studies which show that waking suggestions of various kinds can result in the disappearance of warts. In one such study by Memmescheimer and Eisenlohr (1931) the application of an innocuous dye substance (a placebo 'ointment') resulted in the acceleration of the disappearance of warts in 24–28 per cent of a sample of seventy children (Barber, 1969b).

Of course one important point is that suggestions for the removal of warts or anything else might be effective only if the subjects actually 'believe' they will be effective. If subjects are complying during hypnotic induction then one might not expect them to privately accept the suggestions. It could thus be postulated that only subjects who believe they have been 'hypnotised' will respond to the suggestions, and accordingly, not all subjects who *appear* to respond to hypnotic induction will benefit from the suggestions. This appears to be the case (Sinclair-Gieben and Chalmers, 1959). However, the issue is complicated as there is a possibility that warts may disappear spontaneously if no suggestions are given. Thus even the warts of compliant subjects disappear, in time, with the problem that the effect could be spuriously attributed to 'hypnosis'. Also a number of recent studies have failed to demonstrate that suggestions, hypnotic or otherwise, have an effect on warts (Barber, Spanos and Chaves, 1974). It should perhaps be pointed out that hypnotic and waking suggestions for the removal of warts do not exert an immediate effect; the warts do not disappear in a few hours! For example, in the study by Sinclair-Gieben and Chalmers (1959) hypnotic suggestions for wart disappearance took between five weeks and six months, a significant point as Memmescheimer and Eisenlohr found that a good proportion of waking subjects given no suggestions 'lost' their warts in six weeks to six months.

Although a few studies have claimed to have produced blisters on subjects who have been submitted to appropriate hypnotic suggestions, such as 'a red-hot poker is being applied to your arm' (Pattie, 1941; Barber, 1961b), none of these studies employed waking control groups. Furthermore, investigators have failed to produce blisters on subjects who were judged to be 'deeply hypnotised' (Barber, 1969b). Other relevant points noted by Barber (1969b) are that in at least two of the successful studies wheals (the beginnings of a blister) rather than blisters were formed. Such

wheals can be produced in a few waking subjects by asking them to remember certain experiences, and also by mild mechanical stimulation, such as a firm stroke of the skin. In fact Lewis (1927) found that, in a sample of eighty-four men, one stroke of the skin could produce a small swelling in 25 per cent of the sample, and 5 per cent showed a full wheal. This may be very relevant, as in most of the 'successful' hypnosis studies tactile stimulation was used to point to the area in which the effect was to occur. Also Barber (1969b) points out that the few highly selected subjects who manifested these reactions in the hypnosis studies were either diagnosed as hysterics, or had histories of localised skin reactions. Thus, at present there appears to be little evidence that hypnotic induction is necessary for the production of blisters and wheals, if and when they occur, and it may not even be necessary for the subject to believe he is 'hypnotised' to manifest the effect. A compliant subject could produce a wheal if he were *predisposed to do so* upon *trying* to imagine an experience, or upon mild tactile stimulation.

Related to the work on cardiovascular functioning is the finding that some hypnotic subjects can exercise control of skin temperature (Zimbardo, Maslach and Marshall, 1970), to the extent of lowering the temperature in one hand, whilst raising the temperature in the other. The effect is achieved by getting the subject to vividly imagine that one hand is cold, whilst the other is hot. Hadfield (1920) showed that it was possible to accomplish a raising and lowering of temperature in the hands using similar waking instructions. Ambellur and Barber (1973) propose that the feat is accomplished as imagining cold gives rise to vasoconstriction, which in turn results in a drop in temperature, whilst imagining warmth gives rise to vasodilation which results in a rise in skin temperature. However, hypnotic induction seems unnecessary to produce the effect, and Ambellur and Barber (1973) suggest that 'a substantial proportion of normal individuals might be able to produce localised changes in skin temperature' (p.505). Moreover, a capacity for absorbed imaginative attention seems unnecessary to produce the effect, and the ability to control skin temperature is unrelated to hypnotic susceptibility (Roberts, Schuler, Bacon, Zimmermann and Patterson, 1975).

Lewis and Sarbin (1943) reported that gastric hunger contractions could be modified in 'deeply hypnotised' subjects when instructed to eat a fictitious meal. However, subsequently it was revealed that the inhibition of the contractions followed certain actions such as lip smacking, tasting, and swallowing, and furthermore, silent arithmetic had a similar effect on the contractions (Sarbin and Coe, 1972)

Sarbin and Coe (1972) have pointed out that most of the literature purporting to demonstrate physiological correlates of being 'hypnotised' is in the form of single case reports supplied by physicians, or by poorly designed experiments. As an example they cite a study by Brady and Rosner (1966) which demonstrated that eye movements decrease during trance induction, the implication being that eye movements (REM) may serve as an independent criterion of the trance state. Although in this study independent experimental and control groups were used, they differed on the REM measure before the hypnotic induction, and different instructions given to the hypnotic and waking groups could have accounted for the effect (Sarbin and Coe, 1972). In another study Cade and Woolley-Hart (1974) suggested that there was a significant relationship between trance depth and an increase in skin resistance. They conclude, 'If during the attempted induction of hypnosis, autohypnosis, or other trance state, the skin resistance remains substantially unchanged, or it decreases then the subject is not in trance' (p.24). However, they also report that equivalent increases in skin resistance occurred with biofeedback, relaxation and meditation techniques. Other studies have shown that the physiological changes that often accompany hypnotic induction are common to other situations in which relaxation is involved, for example, decreased oxygen consumption, respiratory rate, increased EEG intensity of slow alpha waves and beta waves, and skin resistance (Edmonston, 1977). Comparing directly hypnotic and relaxation conditions, Peters and Stern (1973) found no difference between the conditions in measures of skin temperature or vasomotor responses, and they concluded that the changes in both meas-ures 'cannot be attributed to anything other than relaxation' (p.106). In Chapter 1 it was mentioned that the brain waves of the hypnotic subject as measured on the EEG are clearly distinguishable from those of a sleep-walker, however, there appears to be no evidence that there is anything unique in the EEG patterns of 'hypnotised' individuals which differentiates them from waking individuals given suitable instructions. For example, Edmonston and Grotevant (1975) found that hypnotic induction did give rise to an increase in EEG alpha waves, however there was no difference in alpha production between a hypnotic and relaxation group.

The studies discussed so far are fairly typical of research into the physiological correlates of hypnosis and it seems that, as yet, there is no accepted, reliable, discrete set of physiological indicators which correlate with 'being hypnotised' (Barber, 1969b; Barber, Spanos & Chaves, 1974; Hilgard, 1975; Sarbin and Slagle, 1972). Subjects who are said to be 'hypnotised' cannot be reliably differentiated from waking subjects on a variety of physiological measures including EEG, electroculogram, elec-tromyogram, cortical potentials, skin resistance, palmar potentials, respira-tion rate, heart rate, blood pressure, peripheral blood flow, blood clotting time, skin temperature and oral temperature (Barber & Hahn, 1963; Crasilneck & Hall, 1959; Deckert & West, 1963; Edmonston & Pessin, 1966; Gorton, 1949; Levitt & Brady, 1963; Sarbin & Slagle, 1972; Barber, Spanos & Chaves, 1974). Furthermore, subjects who have been given hypnotic induction procedures differ from each other on physiological measures as much as they do from subjects who are 'awake' (Barber, 1969b). However, it is important to emphasise that the failure to find physiological correlates of a hypnotic state does not mean that responses to physiological measures do not *change* with hypnotic induction. As has been noted already in this chapter, when subjects undergo hypnotic induction with suggestions for relaxation or to imagine various effects, changes in the above parameters can occur. However, at present, the available evidence suggests that equivalent physiological changes in these parameters may also be induced in waking subjects given instructions for relaxation, or waking suggestions to imagine various effects (Barber, Spanos and Chaves, 1974). Indeed it is sometimes the case that changes in these physiological parameters are more pronounced in waking control groups. For example, Paul (1969) compared the effects of hypnotic suggestion with brief relaxation training with regard to measures of heart rate, respiration rate, tonic muscle tension and skin conductance. Both hypnotic suggestion and relaxation resulted in significant physiological changes over a control group; the changes in heart rate and tonic muscle tension (both of which were decreased) were significantly more pronounced in the relaxation group. Paul concludes, 'progressive relaxation is more effective than hypnotic suggestion in producing desired physiological changes, whether considered in terms of efficiency, intensity, or extent' (pp. 434–5).

Research of this kind reveals how totally pointless it is to conduct studies investigating possible physiological correlates of hypnosis without adequate control groups. It may seem a breakthrough when your hypnotised subject suddenly shows an increase in alpha density as he does into his 'trance'; however, the enthusiasm may be somewhat dampened when it is revealed that this may simply be due to the fact that your subject has closed his eyes (Edmonston and Grotevant, 1975). It is important to emphasise that the above discussion does not refer to attempts to relate hypnotic susceptibility to physiological responding *outside* the hypnotic situation (i.e. patterns of physiological responses which characterise hypnotically susceptible subjects irrespective of whether or not these subjects have been given a hypnotic induction procedure). Studies of alleged physiological correlates of hypnotic susceptibility, rather than correlates of a hypnotic state, will be discussed in Chapter 7, as will attempts to train subjects to become susceptible to hypnotic induction using various physiological techniques.

However, with regard to attempts to find physiological correlates of a hypnotic 'trance' the negative state of affairs seems well summarised by Hilgard (1975) in his view of the area of hypnosis which he concludes: 'Numerous reviewers have come to the conclusion that no physiological indicator has been found to tell whether a person is hypnotised, but the search continues' (p.28).

COMMITTING ANTI-SOCIAL ACTS

The reported marvels of hypnosis have not been limited to beneficial abilities. Another common source of anecdotes concerns the committing of anti-social acts under the supposed influence of hypnosis. A recent book called *Operation Mind Control* (Bowart, 1978) tells of how 'Through hypnosis and drugs, ordinary citizens became CIA "zombies", human computers, spies, trained assassins, with no control over or consciousness of their actions'. We are told 'In the Manchurian Candidate it was fiction — here it is chilling fact'! In spite of the vast amount of experimental research, in the media and popular press the concept of the somnabulistic zombie lives on, programmed to commit deadly deeds by the unscrupulous hypnotist.

The more systematic evidence tells a somewhat different story. In a notorious experiment by Young (1948), 'deeply hypnotised' subjects were asked to throw nitric acid at an assistant and also to pick up what looked to be a poisonous snake. The subjects duly performed these tasks, but resisted the identical suggestions given in the 'waking' state. However, Orne and Evans (1965) found that both hypnotic subjects *and* 'waking' simulators carried out the same tasks following emphatic suggestions to do so. The post-experimental interviews conducted by Orne and Evans seemed to reveal what had really been going on, as *all* subjects subsequently admitted that they were quite convinced that no-one would be harmed because the contest was an experimental one, presumably being conducted by responsible experimenters. However, it may not always be the case that the subjects believe what they are doing is really harmless. In the Milgram (1974) studies discussed in Chapter 2 a large number of subjects seemed capable of administering the shocks to an innocent victim even though behavioural indices such as twitching, uttering and sweating, indicated that some apparently did believe they were giving the shocks. Similarly in the Sheridan and King (1972) study subjects actually gave real shocks to the puppy. Nevertheless, hypnotic induction was unnecessary in these cases.

In one study Calverley and Barber (1965) found evidence for both views, i.e. some subjects do not really believe it is harmful so they carry out the anti-social behaviour, and others though convinced it is harmful still feel obliged to carry it out due to their obligation to do what the experimenter says. In this study student subjects were asked to sign statements about their supervisors which were increasingly slanderous, for example, "Miss X is a poor administrator, unfair to the students and also disgustingly immoral". The subjects were then assigned to four conditions; in two conditions they were simply given an instruction to sign the statements, however some were asked to do this after hypnotic induction, and some were asked to sign it in a waking condition. In the first two conditions the suggestions to sign were given emphatically, for example, 'Please do exactly as you are instructed. . . . It's absolutely essential that you do as instructed'. The results showed that the hypnotic induction made no difference to how many people signed the statements. About half of the subjects subsequently admitted that they thought that the statements would not *really* be harmful, and thus they did not feel guilty. However, other subjects said they really believed that the statements would be harmful and most felt guilty. Of these subjects almost all signed the statements only when given emphatic suggestions, i.e. when the pressures for compliance were greatest. Taken together these results suggest that a large proportion of people will perform anti-social acts in experimental contexts, with no physical coercion or threats, either because they feel the acts will not *really* be harmful, or because due to the pressures for compliance, they feel strongly obliged to perform such acts to prevent, ironically, a social impropriety being committed.

But what about the 'real-life' examples? Barber (1961a; 1969b) discusses two cases. In one (Hammerschlag, 1957) a woman claimed that her lover had 'hypnotised' her telling her to kill her husband and herself. Evidence was presented suggesting that she had actually tried to kill herself, though her lover pleaded that he knew nothing about hypnosis and had never 'hypnotised' anyone. The other case (Reiter, 1958) concerned a man who robbed a bank and killed two bank employees. He alleged that he performed the deeds whilst under the influence of hypnosis, and that a close friend had performed the induction. However, the friend claimed he had never hypnotised anyone. Later the robber was committed to a mental institution where he changed his story, saying he had not been hypnotised. Barber (1961a) points out that it is not at all clear whether hypnotic induction played any role in these cases. In both a close relationship existed between the subjects and the alleged hypnotists, which suggests that complex emotional and motivational factors may have led to committing the acts. Thus, if hypnotic induction did play any part in these cases, it was just to provide the subject with a rationale for justifying his behaviour to himself and to others. Reiter (1958) also discusses the case of a genuine 'hypnotist' (someone who actually claims to know something about 'hypnosis' and that he 'hypnotises' people!) who induced a Danish school teacher to shoot himself in the arm and to engage in several criminal acts. However, as Wolberg (1972) points out in relation to this and other cases, one does not need 'hypnosis' to persuade people to carry out anti-social acts and 'we may suspect that when a criminal act is actually carried out, other factors besides hypnosis are involved' (p.276).

The concept of the somnambulistic zombie, unconscious, powerless to resist, is a marvellous 'cover-up' if you wish to deny responsibility for your actions. If people are motivated to commit lawless acts for various reasons, when caught, what better than to say, 'I did not know I was doing it' or 'I was powerless, because I was hypnotised'? It is conceivable that a person might commit a crime whilst believing himself to be in a special state of hypnosis. However, such self-persuasion would usually be confined to someone suffering from paranoid delusions, who if he could not use 'hypnosis' to justify his actions, would probably choose something else.

The evidence suggests that a 'normal' person will only commit anti-social acts following hypnotic induction to a point when what he is being asked to do conflicts with his values or jeopardises his safety (Wolberg, 1972). What is also important, however, as mentioned before, is that the subject may be faced with a conflict between disobeying the hypnotist and infringing one set of social values or norms, and infringing another set of norms or jeopardising his safety. Individual differences in responding to anti-social acts may then vary according to the subject's commitment to obeying one or other set of norms. If the subject feels very strongly that he does not want to upset the hypnotist, or appear to be a poor subject, he may be more likely to commit anti-social acts than someone who does not care less about what the hypnotist thinks of him. Conversely, a person who quite likes the idea of committing the acts might only need to make the tasks 'socially acceptable' by assigning the responsibility to the hypnotist, before going ahead, regardless of any desire to please the hypnotist.

The present situation regarding hypnosis and anti-social acts is probably best summed up by Wolberg (1972): 'Dr. Jacob H. Conn . . . read widely through one hundred and fifty years of medical literature and case histories and found no proof of a single violent crime committed under hypnosis . . . each subject could have committed the crime of which he was accused without the formality of hypnosis' (p.279).

SUMMARY

In this chapter a number of phenomena put forward by some as evidence for the existence of a special property of hypnosis has been discussed. One popular view has been that the overt behaviours accompanying these phenomena are limited to hypnosis, i.e. they *cannot* occur unless the subject has been submitted to a hypnotic induction of some kind. The evidence that has been reviewed clearly does not support this proposition. Another more conservative view is that some of the effects can only be subjectively experienced by hypnotic subjects. However, the evidence does not seem to conclusively support this proposal either. What seems more the case is that we have a number of very interesting phenomena, but many of which are possibly unrelated and require somewhat different kinds of explanations. However, it seems most important to emphasise that many of the effects, especially some of the physiological changes, nevertheless remain of considerable interest in their own right, regardless of the necessity of employing special hypnotic induction procedures. It would be very inaccurate and misleading to give the impression that as hypnosis may be ruled out as a *necessary* agent, all these effects have been 'explained' with any degree of adequacy, for example, exactly how various 'waking' suggestions exert their effects through a placebo mechanism remains a fascinating problem. However, maybe by removing some of the effects from the traditional concept of 'hypnosis', they may become less anathematic to the psychologists, clinicians and physiologists who may be capable of providing some more clues as to the nature of the mechanisms involved.

6. Further Characteristics of Hypnotic Performance

As far as the studies reviewed up to this point are concerned, there appears to be no definitive evidence that subjects who have been submitted to hypnotic induction can transcend their capacities in a motivated 'waking state'. We will reserve judgment for the present on other more clinical aspects of hypnosis such as analgesia, as these issues involve consideration of additional and rather complex phenomena. Instead, in this chapter a rather different question will be examined, and this concerns the extent to which performance after hypnotic induction just differs from waking performance rather than transcends it. It should be perhaps noted that the emphasis on the non-superhuman characteristics of hypnotic performance as evidence for some special property of hypnosis is rather a step-down from the popular claims that are often made; thus none of the studies reviewed in this chapter involves getting subjects to do strange superhuman things; all that happens is that hypnotic subjects behave differently from non-hypnotic controls in some rather subtle and less spectacular ways.

Much mention has been made in previous chapters of the considerable differences in overt behaviours and reports that can result from quite subtle changes in instructions, and differences in the attitudes and expectations of subjects as to the tasks they are to perform. Whilst it is comparatively easy to look, for instance, at how much weight a subject can lift, we have already seen what kinds of problems occur when we attempt to look at subjects' verbal reports of their experiences, and how convincingly they play the roles suggested to them. Unfortunately, these difficulties will become all too apparent in this chapter. I will begin the analysis with a consideration of post-hypnotic phenomena, as a number of experiments related to this have recently been put forward as a basis for the argument that hypnotic behaviours are not readily explicable in terms of compliance. Though, admittedly, not all devotees of the hypnotic state have argued that these effects completely rule out the possibility of compliance, it has been assumed nevertheless that post-hypnotic effects do demonstrate conclusively that there is something uniquely 'hypnotic' operating.

EARS, FOREHEADS AND PENCILS

The impetus for much of the research that follows was a study by Fisher (1954), who submitted thirteen subjects to hypnotic induction and gave them the post-hypnotic suggestion that when they 'awoke', whenever they heard the word 'psychology', they would scratch the right ear. The results showed that, in accordance with the suggestion, when they 'awoke' and heard the cue word 'psychology' they all dutifully scratched the right ear. Shortly afterwards, a colleague of Fisher entered the room and started to chat; the conversation was designed to give the impression that the experiment was over. During this chatting session, the word 'psychology' came up, but nine of the chosen subjects failed to respond. However, when the colleague left, and Fisher turned to the subjects implying that the experiment was still in progress, eleven of the thirteen subjects began scratching their ears again when the word 'psychology' was used. This result seems to indicate that, in accordance with a compliance hypothesis, the subjects simply voluntarily responded in the manner expected of them. In an attempt to dismiss this interpretation, Orne, Sheehan and Evans (1968) maintained that the subjects may have interpreted the suggestion to mean that they were to scratch their ears in response to the word only 'as long as the experiment [was] in progress' (p.190). Orne (1970) argues that it would seem extremely unlikely that the suggestion was taken to mean that 'henceforth and for the rest of his life' (p.216) the subject was to respond to the suggestion.

However, the first point to consider is whether there is any evidence to suggest that subjects would actually interpret the suggestion in the first of these ways. Subjects given post-hypnotic suggestions in other settings are not always told, 'you will respond for five minutes', or something similar. Typically, what seems to happen is that if subjects are not given a time limit, they do not stop responding immediately after the experiment, but show a gradual decline in response rate over time, sometimes over a matter of weeks (Kellogg, 1929; Patten, 1930). Thus, an equally likely interpretation a compliant subject might make would be, 'if he's going to test me over the next few weeks, obviously I'm not supposed to respond for ever, maybe my best strategy is to let the response fade away with each testing'. One interpretation of what happened in Fisher's study is that really the subjects were 'tricked'; they just did not realise that even though the words came up in casual conversation they really ought to have been responding. Perhaps only the three that responded were really 'on their toes'.

Anyway, no matter what the interpretation of Fisher's particular result, Orne, Sheehan and Evans (1968) set out to investigate the phenomenon using a somewhat different procedure. Each of their subjects was given a hypnotic induction procedure with the post-hypnotic suggestion that 'during the next 48 hours whenever he heard the word "experiment" his right hand would rise up and touch his forehead' (Orne et al. 1968, p.192). The induction and suggestion were administered to subjects who were highly hypnotically susceptible and subjects who were not hypnotically susceptible. The low-susceptibility subjects had previously been given instructions to simulate hypnosis and fool the hypnotist. After all subjects were given instructions to 'awaken' they left the laboratory and were met by the secretary who confirmed the time 'to come for the next experiment'. In fact the secretary mentioned the word 'experiment' three times. The results showed that whilst the hypnotically susceptible subjects responded to the word 'experiment' in this context by touching their foreheads 29.8 per cent of the time, the simulators responded only 7.7 per cent of the time. Orne (1970) has interpreted this result to mean that the post-hypnotic suggestion appears to set up a temporary compulsion for the subject to respond independently of whether the hypnotist is present or even aware of the response. Bowers (1976) has suggested that the hypnotic subjects in this experiment were 'responding unconsciously to the previously delivered post-hypnotic suggestions' (p.20). But is this the only interpretation? It has been argued that compliance may not be an all-or-none phenomenon in hypnosis. Though some of the subjects may have believed they were 'hypnotised', this alone does not allow us to discount the possibility that they still displayed compliance and voluntarily touched their foreheads in accordance with how they thought they ought to behave. The point at issue then is not whether the hypnotic subjects believed they were 'hypnotised' during the induction, but whether they really did feel an 'unconscious compulsion' to carry out the post-hypnotic suggestion.

To start with, an explanation in terms of compliance can be advanced. Put yourself in the place of a subject assigned to the simulating condition. You are initially found to be insusceptible to hypnosis, and are then told by experimenter 'A' to fool the hypnotist 'B'. You are aware, therefore, that 'A', who seems to be running the show, knows you are only simulating, and it is all right if 'B' eventually knows as long as he, personally, does not pick you out during the next forty-eight hours. You go along to 'B', do your best to fool him, touch your forehead as directed, and then today's experiment is finished. You are met by the secretary who says the word 'experiment' three times. Well, 'A' presumably does not expect you to respond any more, after all, you have done your bit and fooled the hypnotist, so whether the secretary knows what is going on or not, there is not much point in responding to her. Now put yourself in the place of a compliant hypnotic subject. You have been submitted to hypnotic induction administered by 'A'. You have muddled your way through, and whether you like it or not, you have been labelled as hypnotically susceptible. You go along to 'B', and dutifully give another apparently convincing performance, including touching your forehead as directed. You are then met by the secretary who says the word 'experiment' three times. Well, you have fooled 'A', and fooled 'B', but supposing somehow the secretary tells either of them that, unlike your behaviour in the experiment, you failed to respond? Not only will you be a liar but you will also have ruined the experiment. The reader may be able to think of even more ways in which the 'real' and simulating subjects may have viewed the demand characteristics of the task, but the critical difference seems to be that it is 'all right' for a simulator to stop performing outside the presence of the hypnotist, as that is not what he has been asked to do. On the other hand the poor compliant hypnotic subject is in the difficult situation of being on the look-out for anyone who might 'let on' to either 'A' or 'B'; and in this case, it is the secretary who might do this. In another part of the experiment of Orne et al. the subjects were surreptiously met by the hypnotist in the corridor. Orne et al. present data on this aspect which, they propose, indicates that the simulators were *more* responsive to the hypnotist in the corridor than the hypnotic subjects. Although the difference fails to reach statistical significance when the appropriate statistical test is applied, the trend seems to be an indication of the 'overplay' phenomenon some simulators display which will be discussed shortly.

So far, we have considered the possibility of compliance as a determinant of the post-hypnotic behaviour in this particular experiment, and it seems possible that this alone could have accounted for the post-hypnotic behaviour of at least some hypnotic subjects. Another possibility is that some of the subjects may actually have felt a genuine compulsion to touch their foreheads. However, the problem is that as the hypnotic subjects were hypnotically susceptible by other criteria, but the simulators were not, we do not know whether any differences between the groups were the result of the hypnotic induction procedure or the different characteristics of the groups which were evident *before* the experiment; it is possible that the two groups might have responded differently to waking suggestions for compulsive behaviour. The only conclusion that can really be drawn is that some subjects may have responded because of compliance, some others may have felt a genuine compulsion, but there is no evidence to suggest that hypnotic induction was either necessary or responsible for the behaviour.

In view of the quite frequent use of the design that involves subjects being surreptitiously tested outside the formal experiment, it may be useful at this stage to attempt to clarify the social interaction processes which could exist in this type of design with a hypothetical 'non-hypnotic' example. Supposing you turn up to do an experiment run by Mr. X and he tells you that if you can see the word 'rhubarb' on a screen this will mean his experiment has worked. You stare at the screen but there is absolutely no 'rhubarb' to be seen on any part of it. Somewhat embarrassed by this, you decide to a 'white' lie and say that you can definitely see 'rhubarb' bright and clear. Mr. X seems very pleased. You are then unfortunately asked by Mr. X if you will report to his secretary about your expenses. During your conversation with the secretary she asks, 'By the way, did you see "rhubarb" on Mr. X's screen?' You are now in a very awkward situation, for if you say. 'No, I didn't', you are admitting you are a liar, and if this ever got back to Mr. X, not only would you be branded as a liar, but you would also have messed up his experiment. Now, supposing you turn up to do the same experiment, but you are told by Mr. 'Y' you are to *pretend* that you can see 'rhubarb' on Mr. X's screen and that Mr. X knows that some people have been asked to pretend. You are then asked to report to the secretary, who casually asks, 'By the way, did you see "rhubarb" on Mr. X's screen?' In this situation a reasonable reply would be, 'No, I didn't, I was one of the people who was asked to pretend'. Orne (1970) himself has outlined the essential difficulty with studies of this kind, 'Unless it is possible for the investigator to ascertain in detail how the subject perceives the situation, it is impossible for him to know whether a given set of stimuli or a particular manipulation has produced the desired effect . . . the conditions must be specified not only as they are seen by the investigator but also as they are seen by the subject' (p.226).

In another study Nace and Orne (1970) submitted a group of paid subjects to hypnotic induction plus a post-hypnotic suggestion that 'when I take off my glasses you will feel a compelling urge to pick up a blue pencil and play with it' (p.280). The experimenter then observed whether the subjects carried out the suggestion. They were then 'awoken' and the experimenter left the room, leaving them with instructions to complete some questionnaires. In front of them was a well full of pencils of different colours. Through a one-way screen a research assistant then observed and recorded each subject's choice of writing instrument. The results indicated that after the induction, the subjects were more likely to pick the blue pencil to answer the questionnaires. Also, there was a tendency for some subjects to pick the blue pencil, even though they had failed to 'play with it' when this was first suggested to them, i.e. according to Nace and Orne (1970) they had completed an 'incomplete' suggestion. As this occurred whilst the subjects were supposedly oblivious to being observed, Nace and Orne (1970) proposed that the hypnotic subjects picked the blue pencil because the hypnotic procedures had induced an 'action tendency' (p.278), presumably to pick blue pencils. They noted that the tendency to pick blue pencils was greater for the more hypnotically susceptible subjects. A significant problem with this study is that no waking control group was used, so as Nace and Orne (1970) admit, it is not possible to rule out the influence of demand characteristics.

In a follow-up study by Coe (1973) the experiment was repeated; the hypnotist issued a post-hypnotic suggestion to play with a blue pencil, then walked out of the room leaving the subjects to fill out a form. However, a simulating control group was also used. The results indicated that waking simulators also tended to pick the blue pencil to fill out the form, but there appeared to be no relationship between hypnotic susceptibility and the tendency to pick the blue pencil, and *none* of the hypnotic subjects completed an incomplete suggestion by picking the pencil when they had *not* previously played with it. In fact the only subject who did this was a simulator!

In view of this study by Coe (1973) the results of the Nace and Orne (1970) experiment seem equivocal and readily explicable in terms of compliance. Though it has been established that hypnotic induction seems unnecessary to produce the effect of 'pencil picking', an alternative or additional possibility to compliance is that some subjects, 'waking' or otherwise, really did experience an 'action tendency' to pick the blue pencil. If this is plausible, it then becomes pertinent to ask why 'action tendencies' or 'unconscious compulsions' occur; simply attributing them to some unique feature of 'hypnosis' without further elaboration unfortunately explains nothing. If we look once again outside the area of hypnosis, however, maybe we can view the problem from a different perspective. In an experiment by Zajonc and Sales (1966) subjects were put in a situation whereby they were exposed to a number of nonsense words. However, the frequency with which each word was exposed was varied so that the subjects saw, heard, and said, some words more than others. In the second part of the experiment a situation was devised in which the subjects were required to select one of the words as a 'guess' to what was being presented on a screen (in fact, only black lines, not words, were presented on the screen). The overall tendency was for the subjects to select as a response the word they had seen and heard most. The rationale behind this finding is that when subjects do not know what response to choose, they tend to go for the dominant response, i.e. they select the response they have recently been most familiar with. A possible explanation of Nace and Orne's (1970) result, therefore, may be that when the subjects came to select a pencil at the end of the experiment they tended to pick the blue one, as this is the one they had heard about, and thought about most recently (i.e. the dominant response).

Other studies have shown that if subjects are given repeated exposure to previously neutral stimuli, they come to like them more, for example, repeated exposures have been found to increase positive responses to Turkish words (Zajonc and Rajaecki, 1969), Japanese ideographs (Moreland and Zajonc, 1976), public figures (Harrison, 1969), and photographs of strangers (Wilson and Nakajo, 1965). If repeated exposure increases a liking for these stimuli, then why not blue pencils? Repeated exposure may not simply be a case of the experimenter mentioning or presenting the stimulus objects, the subject can also 'repeat' or rehearse mentally; it is a well-established effect that the more people mentally rehearse response patterns, the less likely they are to forget them and the more likely they are to be influenced by them than if they never think about them (Bandura, 1977). We might hypothesise that this was exactly the case for the subjects who responded to the suggestions; they heard about a blue pencil, mentally rehearsed a blue pencil, i.e. thought about it, and in some cases they played with a blue pencil; so if they had to pick a coloured pencil— why not a blue one? We certainly do not need to postulate any unique feature of 'hypnosis' to explain this unless we want to propose that the subjects who picked the appropriate nonsense words, and preferred the appropriate Turkish words, ideographs, public figures and photographs, must have been 'hypnotised' when they did it.

Now it would seem reasonable to say that a 'preference' or a 'dominant response' is not exactly a 'compulsion'. If you are required by the experimenter to pick one alternative (a pencil of one colour) from a number of others, the fact that you pick the one you like the most hardly seems to justify the use of the term 'compulsion'. However, if Nace and Orne's subjects had all been picked up shortly afterwards by the police for shoplifting (blue pencils of course!), then there might be a better case for using the term 'compulsion'. Incidentally, Nace and Orne (1970) did not actually argue that the pencil picking was anything more than an 'action tendency', but I think the possibility of a 'compulsion' is worth discussing nevertheless. Compliance and the 'dominant response' hypothesis could take care of the pencil study, and compliance alone the forehead scratching study, but maybe it would be very unwise to dismiss the possibility that suggested compulsions may occur. Most of us, at one time or another, have come across instances of people yawning, coughing when others do, or feeling car-sick at the beginning of a long car trip but not a short one; and I imagine that some readers might actually have started scratching their heads at all this talk of scratching heads. The spread of coughing and yawning through a room is usually classified as an imitation phenomenon and in the terms of Social Learning Theory it is a 'response facilitation' effect (Bandura, 1973, 1974). The mere exposure of a person to another performing this kind of behaviour (a 'model') seems sufficient to evoke it without any obvious external rewards or punishments. However, it seems that similar responses may also occur if a subject simply imagines the response, even when others are not present. The term 'covert modelling' has been used to refer to the situation where a person imagines himself, or others, performing an appropriate response (Thoresen and Mahoney, 1974). In this way the imitation or response facilitation effect may occur in response to not only real models, but to imagined models as well. We may be able to take the concept of covert modelling a step further and consider again the forehead scratching phenomenon. If I tell you to think very hard about scratching your forehead, what probably happens is you do not feel a compulsion to raise your arm, but perhaps your head itches. Supposing then I say, 'When you hear the word "experiment" your head will itch', and I repeat this a number of times and you mentally rehearse it, what in fact may happen is that you would build up an association between the word 'experiment' and an itching head, i.e. you are being conditioned to respond to the word 'experiment' with an 'itch'. It is interesting to note how mentally rehearsing even an undesirable or dangerous act can sometimes result in a kind of compulsion to perform the act, for example, many people have experienced the sensation of almost 'wanting' to fall off a high place when perched on the edge. There is some similarity between this model of suggested compulsions and Hull's (1935) notion that suggestion involved habit; 'learning the ordinary habitual responses to language stimuli is an essential component of acquiring the tendency called suggestibility' (p.394). Individual differences in whether a subject would respond to the suggestion would presumably depend on his own degree of mental rehearsal, his ability or willingness to imagine the response, and his individual capacity for conditioning. Obviously, there are some very interesting phenomena involved in the notion of suggested compulsions which seem well worthy of further investigation. For instance, the relationship of suggestion to curiosity would seem worth looking at; H.B. Gibson at the Hatfield Polytechnic has noted how a suggestion to subjects that they will wish to see what is inside a box on his desk seems to make some intensely curious, to the extent of coming back days later to examine the contents of the box!

However, before we get too carried away with the implications of such a model, its extent would seem rather limited, as at least when gross body movements are concerned, it would be easy to voluntarily override. Whilst a person might scratch his head when he hears the word 'experiment', and this might indeed sometimes be 'unconscious', I doubt whether he would unconsciously take his trousers down when he hears a word, or unconsciously wave his arms around and jump up and down in a crowded shop when he hears the cash till ring. We must be very careful about generalising from suggested itches and pencil preferences, to suggestions of murder or rape. If you think about murdering someone for the next five minutes, the next time you see him you might think about it again, but I doubt whether you would do it (if I hear of people being murdered by readers of this book, I shall have to have a good rethink!). Clearly, in these situations strong inhibitions would override the performance of any newly conditioned response pattern.

To summarise, the post-hypnotic phenomena discussed so far could have been a consequence of compliance or 'genuine' effects such as the performance of dominant responses or even compulsions. It seems possible that all three could have contributed to some degree, but none of these effects requires the postulation of a unique hypnotic element to account for it; for example, if, through imitation, a number of people yawn in a classroom we do not usually classify them as 'hypnotised'.

As a finale to this particular discussion, the evidence from some studies suggests that if you really want people to perform certain behaviours, a more effective technique is simply to ask them to rather than going to all the bother of 'hypnotising' them and giving them post-hypnotic suggestions (Kellogg, 1929; Patten, 1930; Damaser, 1964).

THE CASE OF THE DISAPPEARING HYPNOTIST

The 'Case of the disappearing hypnotist' has become a classic in the hypnosis literature (Orne and Evans, 1966; Evans and Orne, 1971). The purpose behind the studies was to see what would happen if a hypnotist 'hypnotised' someone, and then disappeared without 'waking' them up. Some of the popular myths about hypnosis might have predicted that the poor subject would starve to death, but you will be relieved to know that investigations have not supported this proposal. Orne and Evans (1971) made some rather more reasonable predictions. They figured that if hypnotic or 'real' subjects genuinely experience some kind of hypnotic state, and the hypnotist leaves the room without 'wakening' them, they should remain in the state for at least some period. On the other hand, insusceptible simulators, asked to fool the hypnotist, should stop playing their role as soon as the hypnotist leaves the room. Of course an essential feature of any such study would have to be that the subjects did not feel they were still being observed after the hypnotist had left; so this would entail the hypnotist having a credible excuse for leaving the room. In order to test this hypothesis a group of hypnotically susceptible subjects and a group of insusceptible simulators were given a taped hypnotic induction procedure. At the time they also had electrodes attached to them. After the initial induction they were given hypnotic suggestions to: (a) keep their eyes tightly shut; (b) keep their right arm stuck fast to their chair; and (c) tap out the rhythms of hallucinated music with their foot. After the last suggestion had been administered, a rigged power failure occurred, the tape-recorder stopped, and the experimenter left the room mumbling something about a fuse. The first time the study was run by Orne and Evans (1966) they found that the simulators remained *more* 'hypnotised' than the 'real' subjects! They kept their eyes closed longer, their arms in position longer, and their feet tapping longer. The simulators subsequently pointed out that they thought the power failure had been contrived and that the hypnotist was still watching them. One important consideration was that the simulators had been suspicious of the one-way screen, so Orne and Evans (1971) changed this for their second experiment and a more subtle means of observation was used. To make the breakdown of the apparatus more realistic, two large physiological recording machines also stopped and all the lights went out when the apparent failure occurred. The results of the re-run of the experiment were rather different. It seemed that the simulators saw the situation as a genuine power failure, and five of the six opened their eyes when the experimenter left the room. On the other hand, the 'real' subjects continued to behave as if 'hypnotised' for longer before eventually 'coming round'. Also, when the experimenter returned forty minutes later, the simulators closed their eyes again and continued simulating, whereas the 'real' subjects remained 'awake'. It is important to note that the simulators did not completely stop simulating when the experimenter left the room (they continued to keep their arms in position and their feet tapping for a while after the experimenter had departed), nevertheless there appeared to be a difference between the groups when the experimenter returned (only the simulators resumed the hypnotic appearance).

One problem with interpreting this particular result is that the simulators were subjects classified as being of low hypnotic susceptibility, thus we do not know whether high susceptibility subjects given instructions to simulate would have behaved in the same way. A feature of hypnotically insusceptible subjects' behaviour, to be discussed shortly, is that they tend to play their role very enthusiastically when instructed to simulate and fool the hypnotist, often appearing to be more responsive than the 'real' susceptible subjects. It is thus conceivable that the simulators started to simulate again when the hypnotist returned because only they believed a 'good' hypnotic would remain 'hypnotised' for forty minutes. In a criticism of the Orne and Evans study, Barber (1972) has argued that a simulating control group, no matter what its composition, was inappropriate. He proposes that the appropriate comparison would have been one between a 'real' hypnotic group, and a control group simply told to relax. In fact, Barber (1972) cites Dorcus, Brintnall and Case (1941) as having already conducted the appropriate experiment. In this, twenty susceptible subjects were given an induction procedure which was interrupted by an assistant telling the hypnotist he was wanted on the 'phone, and the hypnotist and assistant left the room. The subjects were then observed through a peep-hole, and remained passive with their eyes closed for a mean time of twenty-eight minutes, which is a little longer than Evans and Orne's (1971) subjects. In the control group twenty-five waking subjects were simply asked to relax, and during the relaxation period the experimenter left the room on the same pretext. In this condition the waking subjects again remained passive with their eyes closed for, on average, twenty-three minutes, which was not significantly shorter than the hypnotic subjects, and again a little longer than Evans and Orne's 'real' subjects. On the basis of these findings it could be argued that the 'real' subjects in Orne and Evans' (1971) studies could have remained passive with their eyes closed simply because they had followed the relaxation instructions in the induction procedure. Relaxation would not seem to constitute the 'unspecified alternations in the subjects' state of consciousness' (p.295) which Orne and Evans (1971) suggest were responsible for their result.

Of course, if some of the subjects actually 'believed' they were 'hypnotised', as discussed in Chapter 4, this again could account for the effect. Some may have felt relaxed and drowsy and labelled this as 'hypnotised'; the foot tapping could still have been compliance, or alternatively they could have been quite happy tapping away to the music they were imagining. If you close your eyes, imagine a piece of lively music and tap away, it is quite enjoyable; but you do not need to be in a unique state to do it. If a few really 'believed' they were 'hypnotised', there would of course have been no point in opening their eyes when the experimenter left; they were relaxed and drowsy and quite content to wait. Bowers (1973) has remarked how the self-attribution paradigm (see Chapter 4) may be applied to the Orne and Evans (1971) study. If some of the real subjects self-attributed the label of hypnosis because they felt relaxed and drowsy, then their behaviour was not totally controlled by the demands of the experimenter so the behaviour continued when she left.

Sarbin and Coe (1972) have also criticised the study of Evans and Orne

(1971) on the basis that the different instructions to the groups created different expectations as to what role was appropriate. Their argument is similar to some of those already mentioned. The role of the simulator was to be alert to cues so as not to give himself away. When it all broke down he stopped playing the role, when the power was restored, he started again as instructed. On the other hand, the hypnotic subjects were relaxed and comfortable, so as Sarbin and Coe (1972) say, 'Why should they awaken when there was no strain, or incongruency, or discomfort, involved in remaining in the role?' (p.211). Once again, Sarbin and Coe (1972) suggest that it is quite unnecessary to postulate some unique trance experience to explain the effects.

To summarise, the results of the 'case of the disappearing hypnotist' seem readily explicable in terms of the 'ordinary' concepts such as role-demands and relaxation. These could have contributed either singly or in combination to varying extents in different subjects.

THE 'OVER-PLAY' EFFECT

One interesting facet of the behaviour of simulating subjects who are asked to fool the hypnotist that they are 'hypnotised', is that although 'experts' cannot tell them individually apart from hypnotic subjects (Orne, 1959; 1971), when groups of simulators are compared with groups of hypnotic subjects the simulators often perform *better* than hypnotic subjects, appearing to be more responsive (Orne and Evans, 1966; Orne, Sheehan and Evans, 1968). It could be argued that this 'over-play' phenomenon is an important difference between 'real' hypnotic subjects and simulators, and therefore suggests that the hypnotic subjects are in a unique state. However, this argument seems to be somewhat untenable when one considers that the subjects selected as simulators are usually selected because they are insusceptible to hypnotic suggestions. Thus by definition they differ from the 'real' subjects in terms of their preconceptions and possibly experiences of the hypnotic situation. It has already been mentioned that a possible reason why some subjects do not respond to hypnotic suggestions is that they may have unrealistic preconceptions about hypnosis; Kinney and Sachs (1974) have proposed that an important motivational component in hypnotic susceptibility is the 'fear of losing control' (p.233). Obviously, the high responsiveness of some simulators reflects their conception of how a 'good' hypnotic subject should behave; they clearly manifest in their behaviour the preconception that 'good' hypnotic subjects respond to most if not all suggestions; also, in spite of the hypnotist's assurances, they possibly continue to think that 'good' subjects 'lose control' and are maybe oblivious to their surroundings. The latter possibility is evident in the following statement by Evans and Orne (1971) referring to the behaviour of the simulators in 'The case of the disappearing hypnotist': 'Simulators apparently believed that truly hypnotised subjects would not notice the power failure, and, as indicated by their return to simulation when the power was restored, believed hypnotised subjects would remain 'hypnotised' for more than 40 minutes' (p.289).

It therefore seems hardly surprising that simulators are sometimes 'better' than hypnotic subjects, as it is precisely these different conceptions that may have accounted for them being categorised as insusceptible in the first place. They might not like the idea that a hypnotic subject loses control, loses his memory, remains in a trance indefinitely, and always responds to hypnotic suggestions that unconsciously make him do ridiculous things. Thus, when told to fake, this is exactly the role they try to play. Rather than '*over*-playing' all they are really doing is acting the role of an excellent hypnotic subject, as *they* see it. If this is the case then one might expect that if *high* susceptibility subjects are asked to act out the role of a hypnotic subject (i.e. to simulate), they might behave somewhat differently from low susceptibility subjects asked to simulate, and there is some evidence from studies of 'trance logic', to be discussed shortly, which could be used to support this view.

Sometimes, groups of subjects are not assigned to a simulating condition on the basis of being insusceptible (i.e. there are equal or approximately equal numbers of high and low susceptibility in the hypnotic and waking groups), but still the over-play effect occurs (Williamson, Johnson and Eriksen, 1965; Barber and Calverley, 1966b). Nevertheless, this effect can still be largely accounted for in terms of compliance. For instance, let us take an extreme example; supposing the hypnotic and waking groups each consist of ten very insusceptible subjects and ten highly susceptible subjects. The hypnotic group is given an induction procedure with a suggestion, for example, 'arm levitation'. The ten insusceptible subjects could think the whole thing is stupid or scarey or 'it doesn't work' and fail the item, and the ten susceptible subjects pressured by compliance, or in good form, fake and pass it, giving an average group score of 0.5. However, the subjects in the simulating group are told to *pretend* to be good hypnotic subjects, so they all do what they are told, and pass the item, giving an average group score of 1.0. The real difference between the hypnotic and simulating groups is that in the hypnotic condition the low susceptibility subjects who have problems of misconceptions, manifestations of will-power or who are less subject to intimidation and the host of other variables that prevent them from responding to all or most hypnotic suggestions, fail to pass the item. However, in the simulating condition, these same subjects behave as they think the 'others' would and pass the item. Thus the difference between the groups cannot possibly be taken as evidence that the subjects who passed the item in the hypnotic condition were not just complying.

In practice of course the problem is even more complicated. One of the views put forward in this book is that responsiveness to any particular suggestion may be determined by a complex interaction of compliance and belief. A subject may be compliant only part of the time, he may 'have a go' and try to experience what is suggested to him and for some suggestions he may actually attribute his response to hypnosis, for others he may not. Moreover, although the study by Wagstaff (1976b) mentioned in Chapter 3 indicates there is a good deal of consistency in subjects' 'waking' preconceptions as to whether they will pass or fail certain items, the consistency is not perfect, the agreement is not total. Thus, in an actual hypnosis situation whether a compliant person passes a particular item may depend on his idiosyncratic perception of the situation at the time, and on interaction between the pressures for compliance and the perceived 'ease' of passing the suggestion. To *be* compliant and to act *as if* compliant are not exactly the same thing, and it should not surprise us if the two situations produce subtle differences in behavioural patterns. A person who under self-instructions 'fakes', is not in the same situation as a person who is asked to 'fake', and the difference is most evident when an instruction is emphatic and pre-emptive. For instance, supposing you are a 'good' compliant subject, a little worried about what is going on. You have been submitted to an induction procedure, you have tried to experience the suggestions and compliantly passed most or all of them and then you are told 'You will forget everything that has happened to you!' You could compliantly pretend you have forgotten everything, or you feel that this is taking things a bit too far, and decide to recall a little, or maybe you might think that even some 'good' hypnotic subjects would not do this, and decide to recall everything. Now, supposing in a 'waking' condition you are told to *act* like someone who has forgotten everything, clearly your role is perceived somewhat differently; your job is quite clearly to pretend as though you have forgotten *everything*; if you do recall a little you are not playing your prescribed role properly. In hypnosis experiments this appears to be what actually happens; when simulators are specifically asked to act as though they have forgotten everything, they tend to recall nothing. However, when highly susceptible subjects are given hypnotic suggestions which pre-emptively tell them to forget, a few of them, nevertheless, recall some items (Williamson et al. 1965, Barber and Calverley, 1966b).

The 'over-play' phenomenon is a good example of the limitations of the real-simulator design. When there are no differences between 'real' and simulating groups this may allow us to conclude that the behaviour of the 'real' subjects *may* be explicable in terms of compliance, motivation and demand characteristics, but that is all; it does not provide definitive evidence for this. It also allows us to check whether hypnotic subjects really are superior in tasks such as muscular performance, and cognitive skills. However, to say that hypnotic phenomena are genuine because the simulators are 'better' than hypnotic subjects seems somewhat untenable when the groups are given different instructions and are in different situations. It should also be emphasised that the 'over-play' effect only occurs in *group* comparisons. An expert cannot pick out simulators from a group of mixed hypnotic and simulating subjects on the basis of 'over-play' as the behaviour of simulators is indistinguishable from that of some very responsive 'real' hypnotic subjects (Orne, 1959; 1971).

SPONTANEOUS AMNESIA

Spontaneous amnesia occurs when the subject reports that he has forgotten all, or virtually all, of that happened whilst he was 'hypnotised', even though he received no specific suggestion for amnesia, i.e. the subject 'automatically' or 'spontaneously' says he has forgotten. Cooper (1972) reports a study by London in 1961 which indicated that 74 per cent of a sample of subjects agreed with the statement that 'People usually forget what happened during the trance as soon as they wake up from it'; however, only 20 per cent of hypnotic subjects actually manifested 'spontaneous' amnesia. This finding could be interpreted to indicate that spontaneous amnesia is not predicted accurately from subjects' expectations, and therefore is not due to compliance. Unfortunately, there are a number of problems with this kind of interpretation. Firstly, although there clearly seems to be some evidence that subjects do have preconceptions about spontaneous amnesia, it is very difficult to quantify these expectancies. Thus while 74 per cent of London's sample agreed with the previous statement, 52 per cent also agreed with the *opposing* statement that 'After they come out of the trance, people will ordinarily *remember* what has happened . . .' (p.230). In another study reported by Cooper (1972) 67 per cent of subjects felt that 'if they were hypnotised, they would *remember* what had happened unless the hypnotist suggested they forget' (p.230). The second problem is a logical one, whether 23 or 74 per cent of people think a 'hypnotised' subject should exhibit spontaneous amnesia, it does not logically follow that the 20 per cent who actually exhibit the phenomenon are *not* complying; it seems just as reasonable to conclude that the 20 per cent who do show spontaneous amnesia are the *most* compliant. A non-compliant, less susceptible subject may be convinced that hypnotic subjects show spontaneous amnesia, but when actually given a hypnotic induction, if he has decided he is not going to behave like a 'good' hypnotic subject, he may fail to show amnesia. Thirdly, the number of subjects who actually manifest spontaneous amnesia varies considerably between samples; for instance, Evans and Thorn (1966) found in one sample that 26 per cent manifested spontaneous post-hypnotic amnesia according to the criterion of failing to recall more than two-thirds of a list of items, but they also found that 24 per cent of a waking control group also showed spontaneous amnesia according to this criterion. Whilst some of this failure to recall may be a consequence of normal forgetting, Evans and Thorn (1966) also suggest that some of the forgetting may be due to the demand characteristics of the situation.

POST-HYPNOTIC AMNESIA

In Chapter 3 I mentioned how some investigators have referred to 'suggested' (rather than spontaneous) post-hypnotic amnesia as 'among the most striking and important phenomena of hypnosis' (Nace, Orne and Hammer, 1974, p.257). It is suggested to hypnotic subjects that they will have difficulty remembering what has happened to them when they 'awake' until they hear the key words 'now you can remember everything'. They are then 'woken up', and they are asked how much they can remember. At this stage some 'good' hypnotic subjects report they can remember only a little of what happened when they were 'under hypnosis', and some claim they can remember nothing at all. Then they are given the 'release' words 'now you can remember everything', and it all comes flooding back. Suggested post-hypnotic amnesia possesses a number of attributes which are not incompatible with an explanation in terms of compliance. For example, it seems that the information is not permanently forgotten, as if it had never been learned. The evidence does not indicate that hypnotically susceptible subjects who exhibit the phenomenon have poorer memories, or have learned the information less well, as when the reversal signal 'Now you can remember everything' is given, they recall just as much information as non-amnesic low susceptibility subjects (Nace, Orne and Hammer, 1974). Of course, some of the information may be naturally forgotten (Cooper, 1972), but the important factor is that the amnesic subjects do not ultimately forget any more than the non-amnesic subjects.

The problem of what constitutes a genuine amnesic effect, and what constitutes an interpretation in terms of compliance or 'faking' presents some more semantic difficulties. Bowers (1976) has defined genuine amnesia as being *non-volitional* forgetting, and Nace, Orne and Hammer (1974) have suggested that post-hypnotic amnesia is similar to the psychoanalytic mechanism of repression. Repression is sometimes termed 'unconscious forgetting'; for various reasons a person may, without purposefully trying, find that he cannot remember something, and no matter how hard he tries, he still cannot remember. According to Bowers (1976) this is what is supposed to happen with post-hypnotic amnesia; the subject experiences a loss of memory which is 'involuntary and resistant to conscious and deliberate efforts to recover "X", the forgotten material' (p.42). Barber and his associates (Barber, 1969b; Barber, Spanos and Chaves, 1974) who have rejected the concepts of 'trance' and hypnosis as a unique state have argued that post-hypnotic amnesia is not an involuntary phenomenon, but may be more usefully conceptualised as a voluntary unwillingness to think back to events. Thus when asked to recall some information subjects may employ deliberate tactics to try to stop thinking about the information, for example, by not putting any effort into thinking back, or by thinking about other things. Barber et al. (1974) give the following example: 'If the reader tells himself emphatically that he does not remember what he was doing yesterday at 2.30 p.m., he will recall the events only if he purposefully makes the effort to think back. If he keeps his attention on the present and does not make the effort to think back, he can truthfully state and can have the feeling that he does not remember what he was doing yesterday at 2.30 p.m.' (pp.111–12). In this particular case, as Barber et al. note, the subject's testimony that he cannot remember may contain an element of truth, so it may be questionable as to whether we interpret this kind of forgetting as 'pretending' or 'faking'. However, whether there is an element of truth in this type of testimony or not, it could be argued that it is not very useful to suggest that Barber's conceptualisation of post-hypnotic amnesia indicates that it is a 'genuine' hypnotic phenomenon. If I ask you to try to remember all the letters of the alphabet and you deliberately decide to think about egg and chips or to count down from 100 in threes, to then say you have genuinely and truthfully 'forgotten' the alphabet seems a debateable point.

In actual hypnosis situations the capacity for 'truthfulness' of this kind may be somewhat limited anyway. If a subject has responded for the previous half-hour to a number of suggestions involving moving arms up and down and hallucinating various objects it seems doubtful whether the most delicious vision of egg and chips could make him fail to recall *anything* of what had happened, as some hypnotic subjects claim. When I informally asked a group of students to try really hard to suppress their memories of the number 'seven' they typically reported that whilst they were able to keep their minds off it for brief periods, the number periodically kept flashing back, and they would have to try again. In fact, deliberately trying to forget something seemed to be very difficult indeed, some reported that the very act of trying to forget some information seemed to have the effect of bringing the information to mind.

To summarise, it seems useful to conclude that post-hypnotic amnesia can only be assumed to be 'genuine' if the subject has, for a period of time, *involuntarily* forgotten information that can later be recalled on cue. If the subject voluntarily gives the impression that he cannot remember, either by straight lying or by using distractive strategies, then I feel there is a case for conceptualising such behaviour as compliance, or even 'pretending' or 'faking' in as much as the subject privately knows very well that he has some information that is either already, or potentially, available to consciousness, but he is *deliberately* withholding. I have decided to emphasise this distinction as it may be too easy for some devotees of the 'genuineness' of post-hypnotic amnesia to attempt to fob off the uninformed reader with a claim that post-hypnotic amnesia is 'genuine' because even if subjects *try* to forget they are still telling the 'truth'. If telling the 'truth' involves nothing more than a conscious and deliberate strategy to try *not* to remember, this hardly seems to warrant the term 'amnesia' and besides this is not how post-hypnotic amnesia has traditionally been viewed; as Cooper (1972, p.248) says, 'Amnesia, like any other post-hypnotic behaviour, has been traditionally viewed as being *outside of the subject's volitional control* and *carried out automatically*' (my emphasis). Gregg (1979) has also made a pertinent comment:

> There seems little use for hypnotic techniques in developing memory theory if they reveal merely that hypnotised subjects demonstrate the same obligatory characteristics as unhypnotised subjects and choose to employ the same optional processes (and these include deliberate withholding of responses), even if with somewhat different frequencies and in different circumstances. .... Clearly, there is little to be gained by memory theory if the use of hypnosis is only capable of demonstrating that subjects can be persuaded to withhold responses, or simply make little or no effort to perform the task (pp.11–12).

In Chapter 3 I also mentioned an experiment I conducted (Wagstaff, 1977a) which demonstrated that if subjects are given an opportunity to 'own up' to compliance *before* receiving the 'release' words, their post-hypnotic amnesia seems to disappear, and I proposed that this was fairly strong evidence for viewing post-hypnotic amnesia as a phenomenon significantly biased if not governed by compliance. One particularly interesting finding in this study was that even the subjects who claimed they were really 'hypnotised' displayed no amnesia at all when confronted by other people owning up to compliance; and this result led me to conclude that compliance was not all-or-none, as even subjects who believe they are 'hypnotised' may fake amnesia if they are not put in a position where they are allowed to 'own up' if they want to.

However, a number of experiments on post-hypnotic amnesia have, according to some, demonstrated that post-hypnotic amnesia is not just 'faked forgetting'. One phenomenon that has cropped up in a number of texts on hypnosis is 'source amnesia'. The basic situation is as follows: subjects are given a hypnotic induction procedure with some hypnotic suggestions and then they are asked some questions such as 'What is the mean diameter of the earth?'. As they usually do not know, they are told the answers. They are then 'woken up' and the questions are asked again. If the subject answers a question correctly he is then asked, 'How did you know that?' (Cooper, 1966, p.184). If the subject cannot remember how he learned the correct answers 'source amnesia' has supposedly occurred, i.e. the subject recalls the answers, but has amnesia for the source. According to some investigators source amnesia is a very important index of amnesia as simulators do not show it. Unfortunately, if the data for source amnesia are examined more closely, it is difficult to see how any firm conclusions can be drawn as to their validity. In a study by Evans reported in Sarbin and Coe (1972) ten of thirty-seven 'deeply hypnotised' individuals showed source amnesia, whereas all of the fourteen simulators showed *complete amnesia*, i.e. they remembered neither the answers nor the source. All this seems to indicate is that the simulators *played better at being amnesic* than some of the 'real' subjects, which is just another example of the 'over-play' phenomenon we have just discussed. However, no matter how this particular simulating study is interpreted the most significant finding in terms of the present discussion is that source amnesia is not actually limited to hypnotic subjects, as Evans has also reported that a few 'waking' subjects treated otherwise identically to hypnotic subjects also exhibit spontaneous source amnesia (Cooper, 1966). Cooper (1966) remarks that this finding 'suggests that the item is not entirely free from subtle cues of E or expectations of Ss' (p.181).

In another study of post-hypnotic amnesia by Bowers (1966) hypnotic subjects were given an induction procedure with post-hypnotic suggestions that when they 'woke up' they would begin each sentence they uttered with the pronouns 'he' or 'they', but they would be unaware they were doing this, and would be amnesic for the instructions, i.e. they would not remember they had been told to do this. A group of waking controls were told they were to pretend they had been 'hypnotised' and given the same suggestions. After the hypnotic subjects had 'woken up' both groups were asked a series of questions. As expected, both hypnotic and simulating subjects began their sentences with 'he' or 'they'. The experimenter then generally acted like the experiment was over, and the subjects were asked if they would like to help a graduate student with his dissertation plans. The student was in fact a confederate whose real purpose was to see whether the subjects were aware of the fact they had been using 'he' or 'they' at the beginning of each sentence during the earlier questioning. The results showed that all the thirteen simulating subjects said they could remember using 'he' and 'they' in generating sentences. However, eight of the fourteen 'real' subjects said they could not remember using 'he' and 'they'. Bowers (1976) has argued that this experiment 'should have put the notion of faked forgetting to rest' (p.48). Unfortunately, this conclusion would seem to be a little optimistic as the study suffers from exactly the same problem that occurred in the 'head scratching' study described earlier. An interpretation in terms of compliance rests upon the fact that the hypnotic subjects and waking controls would view the whole pattern of social interactions in different ways. The simulators had a contract with the experimenters to pretend as long as the experiment was in progress, there was no reason why they should continue to simulate in front of the graduate student when the formal experiment had ended. On the other hand, the 'real' subjects contract was *not* finished when the formal experiment was over. Not only did the experimenters obviously know the graduate student (one experimenter actually introduced the subjects to the student) but the student also asked some rather suspicious questions such as 'At the time you were actually doing the experiment did you realise you were starting all your sentences with "he" and "they"?' (p.46). If the hypnotic subjects had admitted that they were aware this would commit a severe social impropriety if it ever got back to the other experimenters.

Some other findings in the Bowers (1966) study support Orne's (1959) warning that deceiving subjects in an experiment is very difficult; Bowers (1966) reports that approximately 25 per cent of all the subjects subsequently admitted that they were aware the actual experiment was still in progress when the graduate student was questioning them. In view of the fact that subjects are usually very reluctant indeed to admit knowledge of this kind (Orne, 1959; Levy, 1967), getting 25 per cent to make such an admission indicates that it is highly probable that far more subjects were aware of the true purpose of the final stage of the study. As some of the simulators were actually aware that the confederate was part of the experiment, one could ask why they still did not continue to respond. The answer could lie in the interpretation of one crucial detail in the instructions to the two groups. Before answering the graduate student's questions, both groups were told, 'Be completely honest with him [the graduate] regardless of what I've said before' (p.45). Clearly, this simple instruction would have completely different connotations for the hypnotic and simulating groups. For the simulators it implied, 'Forget all the simulation, be honest'. So, honest they were. In experiments of this kind a simple instruction, or even a single word, can dramatically affect the results.

Although in the previous experiments discussed in this chapter there seems a possibility that some of the results may have a 'genuine' component for some subjects even though hypnotic induction is unnecessary to produce the effect (i.e. maybe some subjects do feel that their heads itch), the Bowers (1966) experiment is a good example again of why it may be misleading to view compliance in hypnosis as all or none. Bowers (1966) has concluded his results demonstrate that a subject can be given a hypnotic suggestion so that when he 'wakes up' he will, in this fully alert state, begin every sentence with the words 'he' or 'they' but he will not be conscious of doing this, and he will not remember he has been told to do it. This kind of proposal does seem to be in a rather different league to having an itching forehead, or picking a blue pencil. To begin every sentence one utters with 'he' or 'they', to be unaware one is doing it, and to be 'wide awake' at the time, seems a remarkable feat, but without more definitive evidence compliance surely provides a possible alternative explanation.

INDIRECT METHODS

As the usual recall measure of post-hypnotic amnesia is so easily subject to influence by compliance a variety of other indirect techniques which are less subject to voluntary control have also been used to test the validity of the proposed phenomenon. Indirect measures of post-hypnotic amnesia have included: relearning (Strickler, 1929), practice effects (Patten, 1932), conditioned reflex responses (Scott, 1930), autonomic responses (Bitterman and Marcuse, 1945), associative responses (Williamson, Johnson and Eriksen, 1965), and coloured patterns (Goldstein and Sipprelle, 1970), and the evidence overwhelmingly suggests that contrary to the verbal reports of many of the subjects, the amnesia is far from complete (Cooper, 1972), i.e. there is little or no evidence for amnesia when measures that are less amenable to voluntary control are employed. For instance, regarding the findings of Williamsen et al. (1965) on the influence of post-hypnotic amnesia on the use of 'primed' words in word association and recognition tasks, Gregg (1979) remarks, 'all . . . sets of results can be explained in terms of compliant withholding of responses rather than obligatory effects on common storage or retrieval mechanisms' (p.12).

Probably the most important and revealing studies of this kind have concerned testing for the functional ablation of post-hypnotic amnesia by looking at retroactive inhibition. According to a functional ablation hypothesis, suggestions for post-hypnotic amnesia result in a temporary removal of the memory of specific experiences and events so that they can no longer influence behaviour. In a standard non-hypnotic situation if subjects are asked to learn a list of words, and then later they are asked to learn a second list, the learning of the second list appears to interfere with or retroactively inhibit the recall of the first list. If functional ablation exists in post-hypnotic amnesia then it might be expected that if subjects are given post-hypnotic suggestions to forget the second list, then there should be no less interference in their recall of the first list. A number of studies have purported to demonstrate that there is a decrease in retroactive inhibition following suggestions for post-hypnotic amnesia (Messerschmidt, 1927; Mitchell, 1932; Nagge, 1935; Stevenson, Stoyva and Beach, 1962), but these studies have been severely criticised by Cooper (1972) on the grounds that most used very small samples (in some cases only two subjects), differing instructions, and failed to suggest amnesia. In three more carefully controlled replications of these studies no support has been found for a decrease in retroactive inhibition when hypnotic amnesia is suggested (Orne, 1966b; Graham and Patton, 1968; Coe, Basden, Basden and Graham, 1976). In fact, Coe et al. (1976) found evidence that suggestions for post-hypnotic amnesia actually *increased* interference for some subjects. However, Gregg (1979) has suggested this effect may be an artifact of the design of Coe et al.'s study. According to Gregg (1979) the subjects in Coe et al.'s study were in the same kind of situation used in list discrimination tasks (Hintzman and Waters, 1970).

> Since list 1 and list 2 used by Coe et al. were composed of words drawn from the same taxonomic categories, their amnesic group was required to perform what was essentially a list-discrimination task. Given the difficulty of discriminating the source of words, these subjects could only achieve the primary objective of not recalling words from List 2 by not recalling words whose source was doubtful. These would, of course, include words from list 1 (p.14).

In view of the failure of studies to support the notion that post-hypnotic amnesia evokes functional ablation or reduces interference, other investigators have looked at the manner in which hypnotic subjects retrieve material. In one investigation Evans and Kihlstrom (1973) purported to demonstrate that post-hypnotic amnesia disrupts the retrieval of information; thus hypnotically susceptible subjects given suggestions for post-hypnotic amnesia displayed a disorganised, random recall of items, whereas insusceptible subjects failed to show this. However, Wagstaff (1977d) has demonstrated that this result is readily explicable in terms of compliance, as waking subjects given a simple instruction to 'pretend' that they were amnesic showed a disorganised manner of recall similar to that manifested by Evans and Kihlstorm's hypnotically susceptible subjects.

The present state of affairs concerning post-hypnotic amnesia seems well summed up by Gregg (1979): 'applications of hypnotic techniques cannot contribute significantly to an understanding of memory unless they can operate on processes which the unhypnotised subject seems unable to manipulate . . . I am yet to be convinced that studies of post-hypnotic amnesia have contributed to the understanding of memory processes' (p.14).

TRANCE LOGIC

Another phenomenon which has been put forward as illustrating the difference between subjects in hypnotic and 'waking' states is 'trance logic' (Orne, 1959). If a 'deeply hypnotised' person is given suggestions to negatively hallucinate a chair which is actually in front of him he may report that the chair is not there. However, if he is given suggestions to walk around the room with his eyes open, he will not bump into the chair, even though he reports he cannot see it. In other instances, if a 'deeply hypnotised' person is given suggestions to hallucinate someone sitting in a chair he may acknowledge seeing the back of a chair through the hallucinated person; also if he can see an actual person standing in the room, and at the same time see an hallucination of the same person in another part of the room. According to Orne (1959) and Bowers (1976), such instances attest to the validity of hypnotic experiences as simulators do not behave in this way; for example, simulators bump into the chair, and thus hypnotic subjects are exercising some form of illogical reasoning called 'trance logic'. According to Bowers (1976) trance logic operates because the hypnotic subject registers reality at one level while remaining unaware of it at another.

One problem with the kind of evidence initially used to support 'trance logic' wat that most of it was purely anecdotal; no real estimates were given of how many hypnotic subjects showed this 'logic' and how many waking subjects showed it. The obvious problems encountered in interpreting studies comparing highly susceptible hypnotic subjects and insusceptible simulators on 'trance logic' are that the simulators are in general selected from a different population (low susceptibility) with possibly different preconceptions about hypnosis, and they are given different instructions. However, if simulators do, in fact, *not* show trance logic it may simply be a result of the over-play effect once again.

Only a few highly hypnotically susceptible subjects actually display 'trance logic', but it may be that the hypnotically responsive subjects who do *not* display trance logic are actually 'better' subjects in passing a suggestion in the criterion; for example, if a subject is supposed to hallucinate a person on a chair, but can still see the chair through the person (i.e. the transparency test) then his hallucinated person is obviously not sufficiently vivid to block out the chair!

Not surprisingly, the results of studies on trance logic have been equivocal. Contrary to initial reports, Johnson, Maher and Barber (1972) found evidence that non-hypnotic subjects gave the same kinds of 'trance logical' reports to the same extent as hypnotic subjects. This study was promptly criticised by Hilgard (1972) who was subsequently criticised by Johnson (1972) for a variety of reasons, including computational errors. Other reports have failed to show differences between hypnotic and simulating subjects on some measures of 'trance logic' (Sheehan and Perry, 1976).

A revealing study on the topic was conducted by Sheehan, Obstoj, and McConkey (1976). They tested hypnotic subjects and simulators on two measures of trance logic; the double hallucination index, where the subject hallucinates an object in one place whilst acknowledging its presence in another place; and the transparency index, where the subject sees an object through his 'hallucinated' object. The results showed that the simulators actually reported a double hallucination slightly more often than the 'real' hypnotic subjects (39 and 29 per cent respectively), though whereas nearly half of the 'real' subjects reported a transparency response, *none* of the simulators reported one. However, there was no relationship between a subject reporting the double hallucination and reporting transparency, i.e. the hypnotic subjects who reported the transparency were not necessarily the same ones who reported the double hallucination (incidentally *all* subjects in the experiment reported that they could actually hallucinate the object in the first place). The result is interesting as it adds credibility to the possibility that the lack of ability for simulators in some instances to display 'trance logic' may be due to an over-play effect. With the double hallucination it may be unclear exactly what the hypnotist expects the subject, hypnotic or simulator, to see. When one simulator was asked afterwards why he responded to the double hallucination he replied that the real object 'couldn't just disappear' (p.467). According to Sheehan et al. the simulators may have thus been unaware of the paradoxical nature of their behaviour, they just gave what they thought was a sensible answer. Thus, in the same way, a compliant hypnotic subject might give the same double hallucination response without any need to exercise some special form of logic. However, questioning of the simulators also revealed that they did not think that they were expected to show transparent hallucinations. In other words, they thought a 'good' hypnotic subject would see the object vividly enough to blot out what was behind it. It could thus be considered that all they were doing was responding to the suggestion 'better' than the hypnotic subjects who reported a transparent hallucination. Furthermore Sheehan et al. point out there is evidence that reports of transparency may be given in the 'complete absence of hypnosis'. Also a relevant question is, just as some subjects might be unaware that reports of double hallucinations were paradoxical, what real grounds have we for assuming that a 'transparent' hallucination is somehow 'illogical'? If you sit down and try hard to imagine an object and you think you can actually vaguely see it, why is it illogical to also admit that it is not vivid enough to blot out the background? In this way some of the reports of some hypnotic subjects may have a genuine element; they thought they really did see 'something' but it was not that vivid. However, there was no test to see whether these high susceptibility subjects might not have made similar reports in a waking situation.

Whether there are reliable differences between hypnotic and non-hypnotic individuals on even the transparency index of trance logic still seems to be a point of considerable debate; in the study by Johnson, Maher and Barber (1972) *none* of the high susceptibility hypnotic subjects reported transparency spontaneously. However, when questioned, i.e. if they were asked if the image was transparent, an interesting result occurred which seems in line with some of the previous reasoning. Johnson et al. (1972) included a group of non-hypnotic 'imagination' controls who were given no hypnotic induction or instructions to simulate hypnosis but were simply asked to imagine the suggested effects. The results showed that the hypnotic subjects and the imagination controls did not differ, a similar number in each group reported transparency (60–90 per cent). However, both groups differed significantly from the simulators, of whom only 30 per cent reported transparency. Moreover, reports of transparency were unrelated to hypnotic susceptibility. This result suggests that subjects asked to simulate may report less transparency not because they think transparency is illogical, but because of playing the role of a 'good' hypnotic subject, who would see the image so vividly it would blot out the background. In another phase of the study a group of exceptionally highly susceptible subjects failed to give significantly more reports of hallucinations than a group of *highly hypnotically susceptible* simulators (60 and 50 per cent respectively). This finding suggests that high susceptibility simulators may give more reports of transparency than low susceptibility subjects, which could be interpreted to mean that these high susceptibility subjects do not 'overplay', because they have different conceptions as to the role of a hypnotic subject; when asked to fool the hypnotist, they do not think it is necessary to report *everything* that is suggested. Some highly susceptible simulators may feel that a hypnotic subject, though able to vividly imagine the suggested object, would not necessarily be expected to report a total hallucination. This finding thus seems to fit with the earlier account of why low-susceptibility simulators 'over-play'. It is possible that low-susceptibility subjects have different ideas as to the hypnotic behaviours desired of them than high susceptibility subjects when both are 'pretending' to be 'hypnotised'.

As a variation on the theme of trance logic, Orne (1974) has proposed that other anomalous and paradoxical responses may characteristically define hypnosis. For instance, he cites the example of a subject who was regressed to the age of five, a time at which the subject spoke only German. Orne then proceeded to question him repeatedly in English. However, the subject denied in German his ability to understand English while clearly demonstrating his ability to do so. Orne considers that such errors are one which 'no play actor would be so stupid as not to recognise [the] obvious paradox' (Orne, 1974, p.6). In support of this proposition Perry and Walsh (1978) did find some evidence for more inconsistencies in the responses of a small sample of highly susceptible subjects to the extent that when given suggestions to regress to the age of five, the insusceptible simulators behaved *more* like five-year-old children than the hypnotically susceptible subjects (p.577). However, this result seems to be in line with those mentioned earlier regarding 'trance logic' in hallucinations. Hypnotically susceptible subjects may produce inconsistent responses, such as supplying the wrong year at the five-year-old level when asked what year it was, not because of some enigmatic factor which enables them to tolerate incongruity, but because, unlike the simulators, they are less likely to perceive their role as one in which they are supposed to act out completely the behaviours of a five-year-old. However, Perry and Walsh (1978) failed to find evidence for the kind of gross anomalous responding postulated by Orne as a defining characteristic of hypnosis, and two other studies (Peters, 1973; Sheehan, 1977) have also failed to find evidence substantiating Orne's proposal.

The only conclusion that investigators do now seem to agree on is that there is little justification for calling 'trance logic' a general characteristic of hypnosis (Hilgard, 1972; Sheehan, Obstoj and McConkey, 1976; Sheehan and Perry, 1976). Sheehan and Perry (1976) conclude: 'Data seem to show the contribution of hypnosis to tolerance of incongruity in deeply hypnotised subjects remains somewhat indistinct from the influence of the subject's expectations and prior knowledge about appropriate ways of responding' (p.202).

CONCLUSION

On the basis of the evidence reviewed in this chapter it seems that we do not need to postulate anything particularly weird and wonderful to account for alleged differences between subjects high and low on hypnotic susceptibility; the differences may arise through the perfectly 'normal' and rational responses of subjects to the instructions they are given, and their interpretations of the situations in which they are placed. In the next chapter more detailed attention will be given to the factors which determine why some subjects are more responsive to hypnotic suggestions than others, given the same instructions and situations.

7. Differences in Hypnotic Susceptibility

It has been well established in personality research that how a person will behave in a particular situation is determined by an interaction between the elements he brings to the situation, such as motivations, expectancies and personality traits, and the elements of the situation itself, such as the relative rewards and costs. Many of the factors considered so far in relation to hypnotic susceptibility have been situational; thus subjects may vary in their responsiveness to hypnotic suggestions according to elements in the situation, such as whether they are told it is a test of 'gullibility', whether they are told they can 'own up', or whether a fellow subject refuses to cooperate. However, although these factors clearly impart a considerable influence, subjects are not affected to the same extent by them. Even when most people are owning up, saying they are not 'hypnotised', a few stick to their guns and say they feel 'hypnotised', and even if they are told it is a test of gullibility some people still remain responsive to hypnotic suggestions. These individual differences in responding have led to many investigations to determine what kinds of people might be most responsive to hypnotic suggestions and whether they have any defining personality traits or characteristics which might give us some clues as to the nature of hypnosis.

WAKING SUGGESTIBILITY

In Chapter 1 it was noted that suggestibility is a global term referring to the tendency to accept uncritically the 'judgments, opinions, attitudes, or patterns of behaviour' of others (Eysenck, Arnold and Meili, 1975). As 'hypnosis' might have something to do with this, the hypnotist could suggest something, and the subject might believe it, then perhaps 'suggestible' people might make good hypnotic subjects. The first problem concerns whether suggestibility as a trait really exists. Although we might have a concept of what suggestibility is, this does not necessarily indicate that it is meaningful to label people as 'suggestible' in some general sense as people may differ in the degree of suggestibility they may show in different situations. A person may accept without question what the vicar says in the pulpit on Sunday morning, yet reject vehemently the statements made by a politician in a party political broadcast. In view of this investigators have tried to identify a number of different measures of suggestibility in order to determine the extent to which individuals will perform consistently or otherwise across the measures.

In an important study Eysenck and Furneaux (1945) looked at the intercorrelations between twelve measures of suggestibility. They reported that the twelve measures seemed to fall into two main groups, which they labelled tests of primary suggestibility and tests of secondary suggestibility. The tests of primary suggestibility involved the subject's responding to direct verbal suggestions of the occurrence of bodily or muscular movements, *supposedly* without his volitional participation. These included tests such as body sway (the subject is told he is falling forward, and the amount of actual body sway is measured) and the Chevreul pendulum test (the subject holds a bob on a thread over a ruler and is told that he will notice the bob swinging even though he does not actively move his hand and the swing of the pendulum is measured). These kinds of suggestions have been termed primarily 'ideomotor' suggestions. The tests of secondary suggestibility were supposed to measure what Evans (1967) refers to as 'a more elusive entity involving "indirection" and "gullibility" ' (p.114). Secondary suggestibility has been measured by, for example, the ink-blot test (the subject is given an ink-blot and is told what some other people thought it looked like; he is then given some inapplicable responses, and the measure is how many of the suggestions he accepts), and the odour test (the subject is presented with six bottles with the name of a different flavour on each and he is then presented with the bottles, one after another, and asked to identify the contents; the last three contain water but if the subject claims to detect an odour he is scored as suggestible on this test). Attempts to replicate Eysenck and Furneaux's results have met with mixed success. Bention and Bandura (1953) found low or insignificant correlations between the tests, but in an extensive study Stukát (1958) isolated primary suggestibility as a factor, and found a new, more general secondary suggestibility factor related to susceptibility to personal influence. Other studies have failed to conclusively isolate a secondary suggestibility factor (Evans, 1967).

Tests of primary suggestibility seem to be important as they correlate significantly with tests of hypnotic susceptibility. For example, in the Eysenck and Furneaux study (1945) the correlation between body sway and hypnotic susceptibility was 0.73, and the pendulum and hypnotic susceptibility was 0.07. It thus seems that there is a tendency for people who respond to some measures of 'waking' suggestibility to also be responsive to hypnotic suggestions. This could indicate a number of possibilities. Perhaps people who respond to waking suggestions genuinely experience the suggested effects, and thus when given the *same* tests in a hypnotic situation they experience the effects in the same way. Although the fact that they might genuinely experience the effects would then be interesting in its own right, hypnotic induction would then be unnecessary, along with its accompanying 'state' of 'trance' or whatever. In order to justify the continued use of the concept hypnosis as a special state, some investigators have proposed that although hypnosis might have something to do with waking primary suggestibility, it is not exactly the same thing, as it adds something 'extra'; as Bowers (1976) says, 'these two forms of suggestibility are related, but . . . they are by no means similar' (p.90). Typically, if similar suggestions are given in waking and hypnotic conditions they are higher in the hypnotic condition, a point to be considered shortly.

Unfortunately, the possible role of compliance and other social influence variables has been sadly neglected and at times misinterpreted in this relationship between waking suggestibility and hypnotic susceptibility. A popular interpretation of investigations of this topic has been to assume that conformity and consequently compliance are manifestations of secondary suggestibility, and are thus distinct from primary suggestibility and hypnotic susceptibility. The mainstay of this argument has been that tests of conformity do not correlate highly with measures of hypnotic susceptibility; the corresponding logic is that as tests of conformity do not correlate with hypnotic susceptibility, hypnotic susceptibility cannot be a form of conformity. Although this argument may seem sound, it is based on one crucial assumption, that conformity in one situation correlates highly with conformity in another. Work in the areas of intelligence and personality has taught educationalists and psychologists to be wary of making such generalised assumptions concerning personality traits. A classic example concerns the attempts in the 1960s to determine whether 'creativity' was conceptually distinct from intelligence. In one case (Getzels and Jackson, 1962) five measures of creativity and a test of I.Q. were administered to large samples of school children. The correlation between the tests and I.Q. was only 0.26, which appeared to indicate that creativity was not related highly to I.Q. However, the average correlation between the creativity tests themselves was only 0.28, so there was no evidence that the so-called creativity tests measured a trait of 'creativity' better than an I.Q. test (Mischel, 1968). In another series of studies investigators attempted to look for consistencies in moral conduct (Hartshorne and May, 1928; Hartshorne, May and Shuttleworth, 1930). In this extensive inquiry large numbers of children were exposed to various situations in which they could cheat, lie and steal in a number of settings, for example, in athletics, in the home, at party games. When the children were assessed by pencil and paper measures such as questionnaires the correlations between the pencil and paper tests were high. However, the correlations dropped when the same tests were given in different settings. Also, the more the situation changed the lower the correlations became; for instance, copying on one test correlated 0.70 with copying on another; falsely adding on scores on one test correlated with adding on scores on another test 0.44; however, copying from one test correlated only 0.29 with adding on scores. The average correlation between four classroom tests and two out-of-classroom tests (contests and stealing) was only 0.17. The lying test in the classroom correlated 0.23 with other classroom tests, but only 0.06 with the out-of-classroom deception tests. Even the slightest changes in the situation seemed to make a difference, 'even such slight changes in the situation as between crossing out A's and putting dots in squares are sufficient to alter the amount of deception both in individuals and in groups' (p.382). Thus, although there was some evidence of consistency over situations the correlations were typically very small and the most important factor seemed to be that the more the situation was changed, the progressively lower the correlations between the tests became. The fact that individuals were not highly consistent over the different situations seemed to indicate not that the situations were not measuring honesty or dishonesty, but that children were not consistently honest or dishonest. A person may cheat in situation X but not in situation Y, and vice versa for another person.

The implications for the 'situational specificity' of responses is important for an understanding of the possible role of compliance in both hypnotic and waking responsiveness to suggestions. An example was given in Chapter 3 of how one measure of compliance (sending postcards to the experimenter) did not correlate significantly with hypnotic susceptibility, and a number of reasons were suggested as to why subjects might be compliant in the hypnotic situation but not in sending postcards, and vice versa. In view of the problems of situational specificity it may make no more sense to say that hypnotic responsiveness is not compliance because it does not correlate with other measures of compliance, than to say a person who 'fiddles' his arithmetic test by looking up the answers is not cheating because he does not cheat on other tests. As mentioned in Chapter 3 the evidence for a common trait of conformity in non-hypnotic situations in equivocal. Although there is some evidence for a degree of consistency the correlations are generally low and sometimes negligible (Vaughan, 1964; Back and Davis, 1965; McGuire, 1968). Thus there is not a strong tendency for people who conform in one situation to conform in another. However, in as much as a conformity does appear to be consistent to a small degree across different measures, and compliance is a form of conformity (Kiesler and Kiesler, 1970), we should perhaps expect there to be at least some positive relationship between hypnotic susceptibility and conformity in other situations if conformity plays a part in hypnotic susceptibility.

Starting at measures well divorced from the hypnotic situation, Moore (1964) found no relationship between hypnotic susceptibility and the autokinetic effect and questionnaire test of 'persuasibility', i.e. a test to determine whether the subjects would change their attitudes having read a booklet. In another study by Stukát (1958) subjects were given false information about how other subjects had ranked a series of occupations according to various values; the measure of conformity was then how much the rankings were influenced by this false information. The correlation between this test and a test of body sway suggestibility was only 0.14. However, when subjects were asked a series of leading questions by the experimenter the number of responses given in the direction implied by the questions correlated 0.26 with body sway, negligibly with arm levitation, and 0.35 with the pendulum test. These suggest the beginnings of a positive relationship, and what may be significant is that the leading questions place more emphasis on involvement with the experimenter and accord with the proposal in other group conformity studies that involvement with the group is a key determinant of conformity (Kiesler and Kiesler, 1970). Other results have suggested that false peer group information tests may also be related to hypnotic and waking suggestibility. Moore (1964) correlated a test of 'influencibility', which involved judgments after false peer group norm feedback and items on the SHSS. The correlation between the influencibility test and the SHSS was low but statistically significant (0.21) and the individual correlations between influencibility and the SHSS postural sway, hands moving, arm rigidity and amnesia items were 0.66, 0.39, 0.37 and 0.33 respectively; all were statistically significant and actually better than the correlation between the SHSS postural sway and amnesia items, which was 0.24.

GENUINE RESPONSES

As some studies have revealed significant relationships between measures of conformity and some waking ideomotor items it would seem pertinent to ask to what extent are the ideomotor suggestions which constitute primary suggestibility capable of producing genuine involuntary effects. A major problem is that different studies have sometimes used different ideomotor suggestions, so some of the relationships can only be inferred by comparisons across studies; nevertheless, there is some empirical support for the conclusion that *some*, but not necessarily all, ideomotor suggestions are capable of producing apparently involuntary effects. The most conclusive evidence concerns the body sway item. A most convincing theory of how this and possibly some other ideomotor suggestions may work was put forward long ago by Hull (1933). It is significant that he saw his work on suggestibility as serving 'to divest hypnosis of the air of mystery which usually surrounds it, by showing it to be entirely of a piece with everyday human nature' (p.41). Hull began his analysis by noting how we all, at one time or another, have caught ourselves unintentionally performing actions whilst observing another performing these actions. Thus, for example, when watching someone straining we tend to automatically start to strain ourselves. When we watch a person trying to reach for something we vicariously seem to reach ourselves. These phenomena have been variously called unconscious imitation or mimicry, ideomotor action, and empathy. In order to qualify this effect Hull devised some ingenious situations which seem to rule out the possibility of bias by compliance (it should be noted all the following studies cited by Hull used no induction procedures, they were waking situations). As a first demonstration, a young experimentally naive male subject was asked to see how still he could stand with his eyes closed. Under the pretext of placing him in the right position, a pin with a hook on the end was tagged onto his collar, unbeknown to him. From the pin a thin thread ran backwards through a black screen to a recording apparatus. The situation was carefully devised so that the subject thought he had to wait whilst the experimenter tested another subject, a female, but he was cautioned *not* to move. Before his eyes the female proceeded to reach for the wall with all her might, making appropriate facial grimaces. The results showed that the unsuspecting male subject, in spite of the instruction not to move, swayed forwards and backwards, as the female subject strained forwards and backwards. In another demonstration the subject was told to imagine as vividly as possible that he was leaning forward, but he was specifically instructed *not* to lean forward. Again, the result showed that in spite of this instruction, the subject actually began to lean forward. What was interesting was that in spite of the fact that the subject had leaned forward a full four inches he reported that he definitely thought he had inhibited all tendency to fall forward. From these results, which were repeated on many other subjects, Hull concluded that imagination may result in the 'feeble execution of acts customarily performed in connection with the situation being imagined' (p.46). Hull in fact found that it was uncommon to find a subject who did not exhibit this reaction to at least some extent.

Hull's conclusions are interesting in that they appear to indicate that the 'normal' response to the body sway suggestion is positive; when subjects fail to respond it is not necessarily because they lack some physiological ability, but because they fail to imagine or actively resist what is being suggested to them. Hull found similar results for suggestions that subjects' arms would swing in a horizontal plane. In this situation subjects who tried to resist the suggestion manifested movements of as much as ten inches. There is a considerable similarity between this suggestion and the suggestions that the hands are moving apart or together, found in some scales of hypnotic susceptibility. Also, one might expect this arm movement to be the key factor in the Chevreul pendulum test described earlier.

Viewed in this way, the fact that tests of primary suggestibility, particularly body sway, predict hypnotic susceptibility, is hardly surprising, for what better tests are there for sorting out, in particular, those who will *not* respond to hypnotic suggestions? Any person who actively resists a simple suggestion or refuses to imagine what is suggested to him is hardly going to make a 'good' hypnotic subject, for not only will he be incapable of having any genuine experiences of the same items given with hypnotic induction, but he is also demonstrating that, in a situation *very similar to the hypnotic one, he is not compliant*. Tests of primary suggestibility such as body sway and arm lowering may correlate significantly with hypnotic susceptibility not simply because they possess the capacity to evoke genuine suggested experiences, but also because they are able to sort out the compliant subjects from the non-compliant subjects in a situation more similar to the hypnotic one than the diverse, little related, settings used to test for secondary suggestibility.

This argument features again the importance of rejecting the notion that compliance in responsiveness to hypnosis scale items is all or none. A compliant subject who potentially may 'fake' amnesia may 'fake' a body sway item, or genuinely experience the body sway item. However, if he is the kind of person who is not going to even bother attempting the body sway item, or actively resists it, he is hardly the person to bother 'faking' amnesia.

As I mentioned earlier, it has been reported that performance on some tests of waking suggestibility correlates significantly with performance on tests of hypnotic susceptibility. The main distinction between responsiveness in the two situations is that, when the same suggestions are given, hypnotic induction appears to increase responsiveness (Barber, 1969b; Bowers, 1976). In fact, according to Hull (1933) 'hypersuggestibility' was the sole justification for maintaining the continued use of the word 'hypnosis' rather than 'suggestibility'. But how can hypnotic induction increase responsiveness to suggestions? Exactly how hypnotic induction accomplishes this seems to have defied explanation. However, it may be that the pressures to comply may be far greater in the hypnotic situation than in the usual waking suggestibility situations, a fact possibly corroborated by Barber's (1969b) finding that intimidating instructions given in a waking condition increased subjects' suggestibility responses (i.e. they responded to more suggestions) to levels similar, or even greater, than those achieved by hypnotic subjects. One way of interpreting the difference between 'hypnosis' and 'suggestibility' may therefore be summarised by the simple equation, hypnotic responsiveness = responsiveness to waking suggestions + compliance.

It would be presumptuous to assume that compliance provides the *only* interpretation of the increased responsiveness to suggestions following hypnotic induction. In fact, another viable explanation, shortly to be described in more detail, is that the instructions for relaxation may create a general hypnotic 'atmosphere' in which subjects feel they will be more able to respond to suggestions. Nevertheless, these two explanations need not be mutually exclusive, each may contribute either singly or in combination in different subjects.

PERSONALITY CORRELATES

So far it has been indicated that a 'good' hypnotic subject is one who is likely to respond to waking suggestions as well. He is presumably the sort of person who tries *in this particular situation* to do what the experimenter tells him to, and responds, possibly regardless of whether the effect is experienced as involuntary or not. We have noted that some investigators have found small, but sometimes significant, correlations between hypnotic susceptibility and tests of 'influencibility' or conformity. Are there any other measures of personality which might be relevant?

In general, attempts to relate personality characteristics to hypnotic susceptibility have not been very successful, but as we have seen from the problems of situation specific responses, this may be not particularly surprising, if the personality measures involve different situations and procedures. A similar overall lack of success has been found in attempting to relate personality measures to tests of conformity. Goldberg and Rorer (1966) are among those who have contended that the demonstration of a relationship between personality and conformity in one situation does not in itself establish a general pattern across different situations.

As previously emphasised, compliance in hypnosis may be situation specific; a potentially compliant hypnotic subject does not have to be an easily intimidated weakling (though this could help). Informational conformity may be a key factor; the subject may go along with the hypnotist, and try out the suggestions because he seeks information, and he may also simply be a person with 'good manners' who does not wish to upset the hypnotist or ruin experiments. Nevertheless, some studies have shown small relationships between hypnotic susceptibility and personality measures. Gibson and Corcoran (1975) confirmed a previous finding by Gibson and Curran (1974) that 'stable extroverts' and 'neurotic introverts' tended to be most hypnotically susceptible and 'neurotic extroverts' and 'stable introverts' least susceptible, although different results were found by Hilgard and Bentler (1963). In a small sample Barber (1956) found positive correlations between hypnotic susceptibility and factors relating to sociability, emotional stability, an absence of restraint and inconspicuousness. The high susceptibility subjects tended to be sociable, friendly, unrestrained, unsuspicious and did not mind appearing conspicuous. Lang and Lazowik (1962) also found that, in experimental situations, hypnotically susceptible subjects tended to be more extroverted and stable.

Although most of these results represent only small and rather unreliable relationships they form an interesting picture of not only hypnotically susceptible subjects but also of certain insusceptible subjects. Some insusceptible persons appear to show a very slight tendency to be unsociable, unstable, suspicious individuals who possibly do not like people investigating their personality characteristics. This is an interesting picture as it may help to clarify the distinction between trait and situational influences on compliance in the hypnotic situation. It has been mentioned that some small relationships have been found between general measures of 'influencibility' and hypnotic susceptibility. However, we can now see that the hypnotic situation is vastly different from other measures in that situations concerning judgments of weights and lines will be far less anxiety provoking to a suspicious subject worrying about whether he is going to lapse into a trance and unwittingly divulge his innermost thoughts. An otherwise compliant subject may thus be overcome by a fear of losing control, or getting 'carried away' in the hypnotic situation. As a result he may not give himself an opportunity to feel the pressures for compliance after initial commitment, as he refuses to carry out what is suggested to him in the first place. This kind of motivation is apparent in the 'fear of losing control' factor which Kinney and Sachs (1974) have suggested may be important and is reflected in this comment by one of their subjects, 'Part of the problem of not complete hypnosis is due to fear— I don't completely trust my mind if I remove all controls'. The lower 'sociability' element of the insusceptible subject may reflect the subject's comparative lack of concern with disappointing the experimenter, or committing a social impropriety. The fact that some 'poor' hypnotic subjects may actually be frightened about attempting to respond to hypnotic suggestions is supported by evidence showing that a tranquilizer increased hypnotic susceptibility in *some* previously poorly responsive subjects (Gibson, Corcoran, and Curran, 1977). However, it seemed to decrease it in others, some of whom reported feeling 'swinging' or dizzy, which might have made them worried about 'losing control'. Fear of hypnosis as a characteristic of some insusceptible subjects has also been noticed at an informal level by myself and my colleagues. For example, I have had experience of subjects who will not carry out 'waking' suggestions for fear they will become 'hypnotised'.

A similar small amount of success has been found in relating some general measures of imaginative involvement, or absorption in imaginative experiences, to hypnotic susceptibility. The literature on this is now quite voluminous, but a few key studies should serve to illustrate the point. Barber and Glass (1962) found that highly susceptible subjects gave more 'yes' answers to questionnaire items such as 'You like to read true stories about love and romance' and 'You find daydreaming very enjoyable'. Studies reported by Barber, Spanos and Chaves (1974) indicate that highly responsive hypnotic subjects give more 'yes' answers to questions such as 'I find pure fantasy more enjoyable than fantasy utilising realism to give it structure' and 'I would like to get beyond the world of logic and reason, and experience something different'. Hilgard (1970) found that hypnotically susceptible subjects say they become more involved in reading novels, acting in plays, and listening to music, and like getting 'carried away' by their imaginings. Even so, the correlations between reports of imaginative activities and hypnotic susceptibility are still not very impressive. They are usually around 0.30 (Morgan, 1973) and with a few exceptions rarely exceed 0.40, even with subjects with very favourable attitudes towards hypnosis (Spanos and McPeake, 1973). Furthermore, they can be unreliable (As, 1963); sometimes they cannot be replicated at all (Barber and Calverley, 1965c; London, Cooper and Johnson, 1962), or only for one sex (Bowers, 1971). Also, other inconsistencies occur, for example, Shor, Orne and O'Connell (1962) found no significant correlation between hypnotic susceptibility and the frequency of hypnotic-like waking experiences, only with their intensity.

Furthermore, the validity of such measures may be questionable in that they may be contaminated by a response bias factor known as acquiesence response set, or yea-saying. This is a tendency by some acquiescent subjects to say 'yes' to questionnaire items regardless of the truthfulness of their answers. Gibson (1977) gives an appropriate example, 'If you were to ask a large group of seven-year-old children a number of questions about their experiences and capacities and included the question, "Do you ever jump six feet in the air when you are very pleased?" a certain percentage would probably reply in the affirmative' (pp.174–5). In a study by Lee-Teng (1965) a particularly high and significant correlation of 0.70 was found between affirmative questionnaire responses to 'trancelike' experience items such as 'When you dance, do you often feel that the music and mood are being expressed through your movements, while you yourself fade into the background?' and a generalised yea-saying tendency. Although Lee-Teng admits there is probably some genuine content in these responses, she does suggest that this stylistic tendency is so strong that within a pool of relevant items it is impossible at present to indicate what kinds of items are really most predictive of hypnotic susceptibility. Gibson (1977) has noted a number of factors which could lead to distortions in these inventories, including deliberate falsehood, a sense of the dramatic, a taste for exaggeration, an inventive memory and a tendency to guess wildly when memory fails. All these factors could of course make a 'good' hypnotic subject, i.e. a good actor with a wild imagination and prone to exaggeration.

Attempts have also been made to relate imaginative involvement to hypnotic susceptibility using non-questionnaire measures. Some of the most important of these have concerned relationships with brain activity. For instance, Bakan (1969) found that hypnotically susceptible subjects showed a tendency to move their eyes to the left when asked a question which required them to reflect. This finding is important as the movement of the eyes to the left has been alleged to relate to the influence of the right hemisphere of the brain, i.e. the hemisphere which is assumed to have more control over non-verbal functions such as spatial awareness, musical ability, and awareness of one's body, as opposed to the left hemisphere which is assumed to have more control over analytic logical thinking, especially in verbal and mathematical functions (Ornstein, 1972). In sum, a 'good' hypnotic subject may be so because he is dominated by the side of his brain concerned with less logical and more intuitive thinking. Ornstein (1972) has descriptively put the difference as between the verbal-logical grammarian, scientist, logican and mathematician who is committed to reason and 'correct' proof, versus the boatman, ungraceful and untutored in formal terms, the artist, the dreamer, the craftsman, the dancer, whose output is often unsatisfactory to the purely rational mind. Unfortunately, other studies have shown that the relationship between eye movement and hypnotic susceptibility is rather more complex and seems to occur primarily in right-handed males (Gur and Gur, 1974). In fact, the opposite appears to occur in females; left-handed females who move their eyes to the *right* are more likely to be hypnotically susceptible (the relationship is negligible for left-handed males and right-handed females). This is particularly confusing as there is a slight, but nevertheless consistent tendency for females to be more hypnotically susceptible than males (Gibson, 1977). Although it has been reported that the specialisation of the hemispheres is possibly less marked in females (McGlone and Davidson, 1973), there is little evidence that the specialisation of the hemispheres is actually *reversed* in females, as the findings of Gur and Gur (1974) might predict. Thus Gur and Gur (1974) conclude one possibility is that 'hypnotisability may have very little to do with lateralisation for females' (p.640).

Morgan, MacDonald and Hilgard (1974) have found that high susceptibility subjects show a tendency to have more alpha wave activity in their EEG brain wave recordings when recorded in the 'waking state'. The significance of this finding is that during states of high alpha activity some subjects report pleasant, relaxed feelings similar to those reported by subjects during and after hypnotic induction. Furthermore, Bakan and Svorad (1969) found that, in the waking state, the tendency to move eyes to the *right* (when asked a reflective question) was negatively correlated with the amount of alpha EEG (about -0.60). Thus, the more eye movements to the right, the less amount of EEG alpha. Unfortunately, the relationship between alpha production and hypnotic susceptibility seems far from substantiated, as some studies have failed to find differences in alpha production between hypnotically susceptible and insusceptible subjects (Travis, Kondo and Knott, 1974; Edmonston and Grotevant, 1975). Recording alpha from the right hemisphere Edmonston and Grotevant (1975) found that although alpha densities were not related to hypnotic susceptibility, they could be controlled quite readily by opening and closing the eyes, and they conclude, 'It would seem that the condition of the eyelids — not necessarily the position of the eyes — is more crucial to alpha production than the general state of the organism' (p.229). When the eyes are closed, alpha density is greater regardless of whether the subject is relaxed or submitted to hypnotic condition. This finding suggests that differences between high and low susceptibility subjects could sometimes occur due to the simple fact that the insusceptible subjects either take longer to close their eyes, or do not close them at all. In one experiment Edmonston and Grotevant found that a dramatic increase in alpha density occurred between ten and twelve minutes into the induction, which corresponded with the average time it took for subjects to close their eyes! It is also important to note that it is somewhat problematical anyway to apply EEG criteria as an estimate of the degree to which a subject is 'hypnotised' or of the 'depth of hypnosis' he has achieved, as the EEG patterns soon change from the relaxed patterns to alert ones as soon as the subject is suitably stimulated. For instance, Saletu, Saletu, Brown, Stern, Sletten and Ulett (1975) found that although hypnotic suggestions produced significant changes in EEG alpha activity in hypnotically susceptible subjects, the EEG changes disappeared during stimulation by electric shocks; they say, 'the EEG records analysed during . . . analgesia suggestion did not show any drowsiness or sleep-like patterns. As a matter of fact, there were no statistically significant EEG changes at all' (p.234). Nevertheless, these authors still assumed the subjects were 'hypnotised' even though they failed to show the appropriate EEG responses. In view of the inconsistencies and the uncertain nature of the factors which actually account for the relationship between eye movement and hypnotic susceptibility, it is not surprising that Gur and Gur (1974) conclude, 'the complications probably preclude the use of laterality tests as a measure of hypnotisability' (p.640). Furthermore, a number of other studies have failed to find a significant relationship between left-moving and a facility for engaging in nonanalytic modes of thought (Etaugh, 1972; Hiscock, 1977; Spanos, Rivers and Gottlieb, 1978).

Other non-questionnaire correlates of hypnotic susceptibility include a capacity for high susceptibility subjects, outside the hypnotic situation, to respond to cues given to them while they are asleep (Evans, Gustafson, O'Connell, Orne and Shor, 1966), a tendency to report greater effects in visual illusions (Miller, 1975; Wallace, Knight and Garratt, 1976), and a greater ability to generate random numbers (Graham and Evans, 1977). Some of these findings have been interpreted to indicate that not only does the hypnotically susceptible subject have a greater capacity to become absorbed in imaginative activities but he has a greater capacity to attend to 'informational cues' (Wallace, Knight and Garratt, 1976). However, the central question about all these findings recorded outside the hypnotic situation is do they tell us anything about what the susceptible subject *does* or experiences during a session of 'hypnosis'? The main findings of both questionnaire and non-questionnaire measures seem to describe the 'good' hypnotic subject as one who likes trying out new experiences, and attends to things he is told to attend to. Again, we may see these capacities shown outside the hypnotic situation as evidence that the main difference between susceptible and insusceptible subjects could be that the susceptible ones 'have a go' and report experiences whether they have them or not, and the totally insusceptible or low susceptibility subjects either do not *try* in the first place, or report *truthfully* when they actually fail to experience what is suggested to them. Thus, at this stage in our knowledge it may be dangerous for us to be 'carried away' by the possible relationship between absorption in imaginative activities outside the hypnotic situation and subjects' actual experiences during hypnosis sessions. Because subjects have vivid imaginations this cannot necessarily lead us to conclude that during hypnosis they actually 'believe' they are children, or genuinely experience 'hallucinations'.

To justify the existence of a special hypnotic agent it would be useful if it could be demonstrated that these everyday imaginative activities are made more vivid by hypnotic induction. However, Starker (1974) found that neither hypnotic induction nor task motivational instructions increased the imagery scores from a waking baseline condition. He concludes that these results are 'in agreement with a growing body of literature in failing to confirm the contribution of hypnotic induction to the enhancement of imagery' (p.433). Starker's conclusion is supported by findings indicating no systematic relationships between primary suggestibility and responsiveness to therapies which involve the use of vivid imagery (Marks, Gelder and Edwards, 1968; Paul, 1966).

In another significant study Zamansky (1977) looked at the importance of imagining and focussing of attention on hypnotic behaviour. Specifically, Zamansky examined Barber and De Moor's (1972) contention that subjects pass hypnotic suggestions to the extent that they vividly imagine the suggested effects whilst ignoring contradictory information; for example, when imagining their arms are rigid they are able to achieve a 'genuine' experience or rigidity as they ignore contradictory thoughts telling them they can bend them. In Zamansky's study subjects were given hypnotic suggestions such as arm catalepsy (they cannot bend the arm), and finger lock (the fingers are stuck together). However, at the same time the subjects were urged to imagine that they actually *could* perform the acts of bending their arms or separating their fingers. They were also urged to perform another competing suggestion such as bending the other arm. The results indicated that the subjects tended to perform the suggested effects, i.e. they did *not* bend their arms or separate their fingers, in spite of the conflicting images. However, what was most significant was that all subjects reported that, in spite of the suggestions to produce contradictory images, they believed the experimenter had expected them to carry out the target suggestions successfully; for example, they stated, 'I thought you wanted them [the hands] to stay together'. Zamansky (1977) thus concluded that 'The behaviour of most subjects was more closely related to their beliefs about how the experimenter had expected them to respond than to whether they engaged in incompatible cognitive activities' (p.346). This highly revealing study appears to emphasise a previous point. The ability to become involved in imaginations may merely create a 'set' or predisposition for the subject to participate in the session. It may not be a necessary feature of hypnotic responsiveness at all in some subjects, as when the crunch comes it is compliance which wins the day, as the responsive hypnotic subject will do what he thinks the experimenter wants him to do, *regardless of what he is actually imagining*. Imaginative as the subject may be outside the hypnotic situation, when he is in the kind of hypnotic situation described by Zamansky compliance becomes more important than the validity of his imaginings.

AGE DIFFERENCES

Another source of individual differences in hypnotic susceptibility is age. In a major study, Morgan and Hilgard (1973) tested 1232 subjects ranging from five to over forty years of age for hypnotic susceptibility on the SHSS: A. The results showed that the most susceptible subjects fell into the nine-to-twelve-year-old category. The least susceptible were in the forty-one years old and upwards category. Studies using waking suggestions have found a similar profile in responsiveness with age. Responsiveness to waking suggestions (as measured by the BSS) increases from ages nine to ten, drops from ten to fourteen, and remains relatively stable from fourteen to twenty-two (Barber, 1969b). Considering the nature of this profile, it may be of some significance that studies reviewed by Hartup (1970) indicate that conformity to social influence also peaks at middle-childhood, for example, Costanzo and Shaw (1966) showed that conformity increased from ages seven-to-nine to eleven-to-thirteen, with a continuous decrease thereafter through ages fifteen-to-seventeen and nineteen-to-twenty-one. In another study Hoving, Hamm and Galvin (1969) found that the issue was rather more complex, and this kind of relationship only held for tasks that were mildly ambiguous; in other tasks conformity could either increase or decrease with age. In spite of some other complex results (Allen and Newton, 1972) it therefore seems reasonable to say there is sufficient evidence to show that *some* studies of conformity show the same age profile as hypnotic susceptibility, and thus changes in conformity could, at least in part, account for the variations in hypnotic susceptibility and waking suggestibility with age. Why conformity varies with age has been a vexing question. Hoving, Hamm and Galvin (1969) suggest it reflects an interaction between two competing needs, the need for approval and the need to be correct, which increase with age. Assuming these needs develop at different rates, the relationship could thus be accounted for. The overall decrease in hypnotic susceptibility with age could also be accounted for by a possible loss of interpersonal trust with age (Bowers, 1976). If this is the case, then fears and suspicions which subjects may have about hypnosis could increase with age. However, our present knowledge concerning such possibilities is severely lacking, and all that can really be said is that changes in factors concerned with social interaction, such as rigidity, trust and compliance, may provide a plausible interpretation of age differences in hypnotic susceptibility.

HERITABILITY OF HYPNOTIC SUSCEPTIBILITY

Morgan (1973) has presented results which she suggests indicate a significant genetic component in responsiveness to hypnotic suggestions. The statistic employed in this research is called a heritability coefficient, and is calculated by comparing the results of identical twins with non-identical twins. The assumption behind this comparison is that as identical twins are genetically more similar than non-identical (fraternal) twins, and the environments of the twin pairs are the same, then any differences in the scores will be the result of genetic influences. Heritability coefficients for intelligence and other ability tests typically range from 0.70 to 0.90.

Looking at the correlations between 140 pairs of twins, Morgan found that the correlations between the hypnotic susceptibility scores (as measured by the SHSS:A) were 0.52 for the identical twins and only 0.17 for the fraternal twins. A heritability coefficient of 0.64 was then calculated which apparently indicated a significant genetic component. However, there are methodological problems with twin studies of this kind. The calculation of the heritability coefficient rests on the assumption that the environments of the identical twins are no more alike than those for the fraternal twins. According to Bronfenbrenner (1975) there is substantial evidence that this assumption is unjustified, as systematic studies of the environments of identical vs. fraternal twins indicate that the former are more often placed in similar situations and are consistently treated more similarly by their parents. It is thus possible that the higher correlations found for identical twins by Morgan could have reflected, at least in part, the more similar environments of the identical twins in which they may have learned the appropriate attitudes and expectancies about the hypnotic situation.

Unfortunately, there may be cause to doubt not only the interpretation of Morgan's result in terms of genetic factors in hypnotic susceptibility but the reliability of the results themselves, as Thorkelson (reported by Spanos and Barber, 1976) failed to replicate Morgan's findings. Thus until reliable data can be collected with regard to this particular issue it would seem unwise to speculate further.

ROLE SKILLS

Another related factor which appears to coincide with responsiveness to hypnotic suggestions is the subject's possible belief in his ability to 'act out' what is implied in the role of a hypnotic subject. If the subject really cannot see himself convincingly acting the part of the hypnotic subject this may put him off trying. Sarbin and Coe (1972) refer to this acting capacity as 'role-skills', and it does seem to be relevant to hypnotic susceptibility. Moreover, as would be predicted from the work on the situation specific behaviours mentioned earlier, the more one samples skills specific to the hypnotic role, the more likely they are to predict hypnotic performance. In a study by Madsen and London (1963) children were given a scale which measured general acting ability; the correlation between this measure and hypnotic responsiveness was positive but very low (0.13). According to Sarbin and Coe (1972) the reason for this was that the scale was based on the subjects' passive verbal report, and was well divorced from the hypnotic situation. In a situation a little closer, subjects were rated for their actual behavioural ability to act out a pantomine (Sarbin and Lim, 1963). This ability might be seen as more similar to the motoric responses required of the hypnotic subject and produced a higher correlation with hypnotic susceptibility of 0.42. A situation even closer required subjects to actually fake nine items of a hypnosis scale, without becoming involved; the resulting correlation with the hypnosis scale administered proper was 0.60. The importance of this correlation is even more evident in view of the fact that the correlation between two equivalent versions of the SHSS is only 0.85, and emphasises well the point made earlier, that correlations between different tests of certain dimensions such as influencibility, compliance, acting skills and hypnotic susceptibility will be low if the situations are discrepant from the hypnotic situation. However, when they become more like the hypnotic situation one can expect them to increase.

The view of Sarbin and his associates that the ability and desire to play the role of the hypnotic subject may be an important determinant of hypnotic susceptibility is supported by the finding of Troffer (1966) that in a *waking* situation hypnotically susceptible subjects gave more convincing performances of childlike behaviour (i.e. a simulation of age regression) than insusceptible subjects.

Another logically consistent hypothesis which could be postulated is that as these correlations between acting or 'faking' skills and hypnotic susceptibility are at least as good as those found between imaginative experiences and hypnotic responsiveness, the most important relationship could be between imaginative involvement and acting skills, i.e. imaginative involvement may be related more to whether a subject has the confidence and skills to 'fake' hypnotic responses than to whether he becomes imaginatively involved in the hypnotic situation. This hypothesis is supported by the finding of Ås and Lauer (1962) of a significant relationship between hypnotic susceptibility and affirmative responses to an item concerning whether the subject had experienced 'becoming a character in a play'; in fact this item was the best predictor. Sarbin and Coe (1972) point out that by using this item Ås and Lauer may have inadvertently selected those subjects who had had experience with acting, a significant factor in view of the finding by Coe and Sarbin that drama students are significantly more responsive hypnotic subjects. Although the most likely state of affairs is that these factors interact to determine hypnotic responsiveness, the possibility does exist that the person who states he becomes absorbed in imaginary experiences outside the hypnotic situation is also the best 'faker' within the hypnotic situation.

INCREASING HYPNOTIC SUSCEPTIBILITY

A variety of techniques has been employed to try to increase subjects' responsiveness to hypnotic suggestions. In one study Tart (1970a) tested the susceptibility of seven subjects before and after a residential programme, and found that the programme including sensitivity groups, gestalt therapy and biofeedback training increased responsiveness to hypnotic suggestions. However, Tart did not employ a control group, and it is possible that after the amount of time invested in them they felt obliged to be more responsive. As Bowers (1976) says, 'Perhaps a control group given a nine-month all-expense-paid tour of the world would have shown similar enhancement of susceptibility' (p.71). It seems we are up against the basic problem of compliance again, any hypnotic training technique which an experimenter may employ may make it quite clear to the subject that he is supposed to increase his susceptibility. Other features previously discussed determining initial responsiveness to suggestions may also be changed by training procedures. For instance, it has previously been suggested that subjects' fears of experiencing hypnosis may overrule any desire they may have to avoid committing a social impropriety. If these fears could be reduced, then a reticent subject may decide to 'have a go', only to find he is subject to pressures for compliance, as well as having possible 'genuine' experiences of items such as body sway and arm lowering. Relevant here may be a study by Shapiro and Diamond (1972) who found that twenty-six hours of encounter group experience emphasising interpersonal interactions increased hypnotic susceptibility scores. However, there are at least three possible interpretations of this result which could operate either singly or in combinations: a) the subjects knew they were supposed to improve; b) they became more trustful generally and felt more willing to succumb to another's will; or c) because the importance of interpersonal interactions had been emphasised it became more important not to upset the hypnotist.

Some success has been reported in increasing hypnotic susceptibility scores with feedback of alpha brain waves (subjects are given auditory or visual signals so they are aware of their brain activity). In one study by London, Cooper and Engstrom (1974) subjects receiving genuine alpha feedback were compared with control subjects receiving false feedback (they were given a pre-recorded tape of alpha activity from another subject). The results showed that those receiving genuine feedback improved their susceptibility scores more than the subjects who received false feedback. Unfortunately, Cooper et al. provide no explanation as to why the true alpha feedback produced this effect. Perhaps the genuine feedback resulted in the subjects feeling more relaxed concerning the whole procedure so they were more inclined to become involved in the hypnotic suggestions, or perhaps they realised that as they felt different this was supposed to influence their susceptibility scores. At present we cannot say, moreover other studies have failed to find differences in alpha production between genuine and false feedback training (Paskewitz and Orne, 1973; Lynch, Paskewitz and Orne, 1974) and investigators have disputed the relationship between hypnotic susceptibility and alpha production (Edmonston and Grotevant, 1975). In two studies using biofeedback procedures, Edmonston and Grotevant (1975) found that none of their subjects was able to increase their alpha density significantly beyond the limits set by original baseline measures to a statistically significant degree. They did however point out the eye closure artifact, mentioned earlier, which again could account for how some subjects might be able to voluntarily increase alpha density during training procedures. The situation is complicated even more by the finding of Marenina (1955) of *decreased* alpha density and amplitude during hypnotic induction. One can only conclude at this stage that there appears to be little conclusive evidence to systematically relate alpha production to either hypnotic induction or hypnotic susceptibility.

In another study Wickramasekera (1973) claimed that feedback of muscle tension (EMG) resulted in dramatic gains in hypnotic susceptibility from a pre-treatment average of 4.83 to a post-treatment average of 10.16 (out of a maximum of 12), whereas control subjects with false EMG feedback produced virtually no improvement. This dramatic increase with simple muscle tension feedback is again extraordinarily difficult to explain; though the possible relaxation produced by the decrease in muscle tension could have been significant it still seems rather unlikely that muscle relaxation per se, without any training relevant to changes in attitudes or involvement, is sufficient in itself to enable subjects to suddenly start vividly experiencing hallucinations, amnesia and age regression. For instance Barber and Calverley (1965a) found that, although hypnotic induction procedures employing relaxation instructions facilitated responsiveness to suggestions, it made no difference whether the relaxation instructions were given for one minute, five minutes, or ten minutes. Furthermore, as previously mentioned, a number of studies have shown it is unnecessary for subjects to be relaxed in order to show a high degree of responsiveness to hypnotic suggestions (Barber and Coules, 1959; Barber, 1961b; Barber, Spanos and Chaves, 1974). Wickramasekera's own explanation is that relaxation may reduce the 'noise' in the body, so the subject is more able to attend to the suggestions. He further suggests that the relaxation may allow the subject to 'let go' more, which may also relate to the experience of trust. If Wickramasekera's speculations are valid, then these results can be readily accommodated in terms of concepts previously discussed; by 'having a go', the subject may attempt more suggestions which previously he may have been afraid of, he might also feel more confident of his 'role skills' and these factors might result in him overtly carrying out the suggestions but would not necessarily result in him actually experiencing them.

Perhaps the proposal of Barber and associates (Barber, Spanos and Chaves, 1974) concerning the relationship between hypnotic susceptibility and relaxation is a key factor in these biofeedback studies, i.e. the relaxation induced by biofeedback does not necessarily act *directly* on physiological mechanisms responsible for responsiveness to suggestions, but instead acts *indirectly* to reinforce the subject's attitude that the situation is genuinely 'hypnotic', i.e. it corresponds to the stereotyped sleep-like state to be expected, and this, in turn, defines the situation as one in which responsiveness to suggestions is expected and desired, thus the subject 'has a go'. This line of reasoning could also account for claims that hypnotic susceptibility can be enchanced by experiences of sensory deprivation (Sanders and Reyher, 1969) and hallucinogenic drugs (Sjoberg and Hollister, 1965). Barber et al.'s proposition is interesting, not only in its relevance to the provisions of cues which a subject may use in order to come to 'believe' he is in a special hypnotic state (see Chapter 4), but also for its implications in terms of compliance. What might happen is that some subjects may unwittingly find themselves, after the feedback, in a situation whereby it appears they are at the first stage of hypnotic induction, i.e. relaxed and drowsy, and this might make it far more difficult for them to withdraw from the situation. It is somewhat like the foot-in-the-door phenomenon discussed in Chapter 3, only instead of the subject voluntarily closing his eyes and relaxing in response to the hypnotist's commands and finding himself committed to comply with further suggestions, he is what could be described as 'tricked' into a situation where he suddenly finds himself sitting in a state of relaxation 'as if' ready to respond to what the hypnotist expects. The appropriate analogy might be someone asking you outside a laboratory whether you would be prepared to deliver dangerous electric shocks to an innocent victim for the purposes of science, and actually finding yourself sitting in front of an electric shock generator with everyone expecting you to deliver the shocks. Initial commitment may lead to further compliance, irrespective of whether the commitment is voluntary or accidental.

Kinney and Sachs (1974) attempted to increase susceptibility scores by employing training procedures including allowing the subjects to 'work at' items they wanted to work with, and verbal encouragements from the experimenters. These subjects improved more than a control group given no training procedures. Kinney and Sachs (1974) suggest that their results were not solely due to compliance on the grounds of a few anecdotal comments such as subjects seemed surprised at times and that subjects often failed items where the role demands were explicit, and honesty reports were employed. Unfortunately, lacking in this study was a control group given training in waking suggestibility to see whether hypnosis was a significant element. As noted in Chapter 4, one of the ways in which people may come to believe they are 'hypnotised' is to reinterpret ordinary waking experiences as hypnotic simply because they are novel; yet this relies on the untested assumption that such experiences could not be accomplished in the waking state. If subjects had not experienced a sensation of involuntary arm lowering before, or hands moving apart, because previously they had thought it was all silly, or they were scared of trying, then the training procedures could have changed relevant attitudinal and motivational factors. In this way many of the features of this study may be similar to those of the study by Kidder (1973) discussed in Chapter 3 concerning the modification of experiencing 'hypnosis'; furthermore, the subjects may be totally unaware that some of the experiences they attribute to hypnosis may be just as easily accomplished in a waking situation.

Earlier in this chapter a discrepancy was noted between the large number of studies indicating a relationship between imaginative involvement outside the hypnotic situation and hypnotic susceptibility, and whether subjects actually needed their imaginative capacities to respond to suggestions *during* hypnotic sessions. A similar discrepancy appears to arise in training procedures, as Diamond, Steadman, Harada and Rosenthal (1975) found that a carefully prepared, programmed learning treatment involving active participation by the subjects in learning to be responsive to hypnotic suggestions was no more effective in enhancing hypnotic susceptibility on the SHSS:C than a 'passive' information treatment in which subjects were given a booklet on the historical development of hypnosis. However, both treatments were more effective than a control treatment in which subjects were requested to browse through some magazines. Diamond et al. point out that the possibility exists that a training procedure employing information may only be necessary 'to the extent that it motivates the subject to go along with suggestions both behaviourally and experientially' (p.112), and that at present it cannot be ascertained whether information given to subjects just encourages them to try their best to be 'hypnotised' rather than teaches them to modify their actual abilities to respond to hypnotic suggestions.

EYE ROLLING

As a final example of an attempt to find a correlate of hypnotic susceptibility it is worth mentioning that Spiegel (1972) has purported to demonstrate a significant correlation between hypnotic susceptibility and the ability of subjects to roll their eyes into their heads while closing their lids. However, Spiegel's methodology has been criticised for serious methodological flaws (Spanos and Barber, 1976) and three independent teams of investigators have failed to replicate Spiegel's results (Eliseo, 1974; Switras, 1974; Wheeler, Reis, Wolff, Grupsmith and Mordkoff, 1974).

CONCLUSION

The work on individual differences in hypnotic susceptibility and techniques in changing susceptibility is clearly complicated by a number of possible interacting factors, including compliance and related attitudes, differences in the procedures employed, and differences in the capacities to experience genuine sensations such as 'unconscious mimicry'. Some of the correlations between imaginative experiences, alpha production, eye movements and hypnotic susceptibility at first look impressive, but the relationships are complex and inconsistent; further, equally impressive are some of the correlations between acquiescence and imaginative experiences, influencibility and body sway suggestibility, and acting ability in 'faking' suggestions and hypnotic susceptibility. Until it is realised that all these factors may interact, it will be impossible to determine which are most responsible for individual differences and changes in scores of hypnotic susceptibility scales. The evidence suggests again that we may not be looking at a unitary phenomenon; different tests of hypnotic susceptibility may require different skills and be influenced by different personal factors in the subjects who perform them.

This rather confusing situation is symptomatic of a logical problem in correlational work on hypnotic susceptibility. Spanos and Barber (1976) have outlined the problem in the following hypothetical example: 'It is certainly possible that a generalised proclivity toward engaging in certain types of imaginative behaviour may well have a physiological correlate. If this were the case we might find a correlation between the physiological variable and hypnotic suggestibility because they are both correlated with a third variable (generalised proclivity toward imaginative behaviour)' (p.124). If we extend this hypothetical example further, it could even be suggested that people who have this proclivity toward imaginative behaviour might also (due to the degree of commitment) be more likely to comply in the hypnotic situation. It is thus possible that if a reliable physiological correlate of hypnotic susceptibility were to be found, it might be totally erroneous to conclude that it bears some direct relevance to what subjects actually do when submitted to hypnotic induction. Of course, the logic of this argument applies to any attempt to correlate a single variable with hypnotic susceptibility, and once again, there seems to be a strong case for multivariate research and analysis in this area.

Having considered many of the interacting factors which may determine differential responsiveness to different suggestions labelled as 'hypnotic', we can now turn to another enigma of hypnosis, its relationship with the experience of pain.

8.   Hypnosis and pain

Hypnotically induced insentivity to pain (analgesia) and general insensitivity (anaesthesia) have been considered, by many, to be the most dramatic of all hypnotic phenomena. When talking to others of the problems of compliance in hypnosis I have found that hypnotic analgesia and anaesthesia crop up frequently as effects which seem inexplicable in terms of compliance. As Marcuse (1976) says, 'The problem of shamming or conscious simulation is most clearly answered in this question of anaesthesia' (p.49). Although in this chapter I hope to show that techniques labelled as 'hypnotic' have achieved genuine success in the alleviation of pain in some clinical cases, I also think the evidence suggests that our enthusiasm over the efficacy of such techniques should be tempered with caution, as even this area may not be free of the ubiquitous presence of compliance.

THE HISTORY OF SURGERY WITH HYPNOSIS

One of the first reports of painless surgery with mesmerism, or as it was later to be called, hypnotism, concerned an operation by a French surgeon, Dr. Cloquet, in 1829 (Barber, Spanos and Chaves, 1974). The patient was a sixty-four-year-old woman with a malignant tumour of her right breast; the woman received no drugs, but was 'mesmerised' before the operation. During the procedure the woman conversed with the physician and, according to the report, showed no signs of experiencing pain. This case was treated with a certain degree of scepticism at the time as the woman had previously diagnosed herself, whilst mesmerised, as having a diseased liver. She died of pleurisy three weeks after the breast surgery, and an autopsy showed no evidence of a diseased liver, and as the woman had lied about her liver, the commission from the Academie de Medicine decided that she was capable of lying about feeling no pain. A report of a painless dental extraction using magnetism some years later by a physician called Oudet was treated with similar scepticism. At about the same time a Scottish surgeon called John Elliotson was practising surgical operations using mesmerism at University College Hospital, London, and he continued until 1838 when the Hospital committee was advised to prevent the practice of mesmerism within the hospital. Whether this was because Elliotson's 'painless' operations were not quite as painless as everyone would have liked, or whether the Council of University College was rather sceptical of the whole business is difficult to ascertain. However, Gibson (1977) remarks that Elliotson's writings are 'vague and rambling, and full of anecdotes which simply do not ring true in the ears of any reasonable man' (p.40). Elliotson believed mesmerism was a cure-all, and claimed to have had no failures; a rather unlikely claim by modern standards.

However, it is James Esdaile who must go down in history as the champion of hypnotic surgery. Esdaile graduated in medicine at Edinburgh in 1830 and went to work in India for the East India Company. He worked in a number of hospitals and between the years of 1845 and 1851 was reputed to have performed over 300 major operations, and numerous minor surgical procedures. Esdaile's speciality was the removal of scrotal tumours, sometimes weighing more than 50 lbs. Here is an account of one of these operations which Bowers (1976) uses as an example of the efficacy of Esdaile's procedures:

> Oct. 25 — Gooroochuan Shah, a shop-keeper, aged 40. He has got a 'monster tumour', which prevents him from moving; its great weight, and his having used it for a writing-desk for many years, has pressed it into its present shape. . . . He became insensible on the fourth day of mesmerising . . . two men held up the tumour on a sheet. . . . I removed it by circular incision . . . the rush of venous blood was great, but fortunately soon arrested; and, after tying the last vessel . . . he awoke. The loss of blood had been so great that he immediately fell into a fainting state. . . . On recovering he said that he awoke while the mattress was being pulled back, and that nothing had disturbed him (Esdaile, 1957, pp.221–222).

Significant features of this account of a 'successful' case include the facts that attempts had been made to 'mesmerise' the patient for *four* days, at the end the patient fainted, and the patient reported complete amnesia.

Esdaile too seemed to have some rather improbable notions concerning the powers of mesmerism. During his latter years in India he also stressed the cure-all powers of mesmerism as distinct from its more limited application as an analgesic agent. He also tells of how he mesmerised men in a law court, without their knowledge, making the passes *behind* them. Then by putting them in a somnambulistic trance, he made them walk away, forgetting what had happened (Gibson, 1977). If we are somewhat sceptical of this latter account, then possibly Esdaile's accounts of analgesia with mesmerism should also be treated with some caution, a point we shall consider later.

After Esdaile's work in India, and following the discovery of anaesthetic drugs, interest in mesmeric surgery declined rapidly. However, about fifty years later there was a revival of interest, and more recently, since around 1930, a number of clinical reports and books have been published on the subject (Coppolino, 1965; Marmer, 1959; Werbel, 1965), and some of the more recent cases will be examined shortly.

SEMANTIC PROBLEMS

One difficulty in determining which properties of hypnosis were responsible for the apparent analgesia manifested by some patients undergoing
surgery in these historical reports is that different surgeons have employed
different techniques at different times with different results. It is significant
to note, for example, that Cloquet's patient conversed with the surgeon
during the operation; on the other hand, Esdaile's patients were supposedly
induced into a state of insensitivity, a 'mesmeric trance' during which they
were aware of nothing, and recalled nothing afterwards. Moreover, rather
than using traditional 'European' methods of induction, Esdaile learned to
employ an Indian healing ritual practice called 'jar-phoonk', which his
native assistants used in mesmerising the patients, making rhythmical passes and breathing on them till they went into a 'trance' (Gibson, 1977).
Once again, semantic problems arise. To what extent can all reports of
hypnotic surgery be subsumed under one central concept of hypnosis?
Recently I saw a television programme in which a woman was undergoing
'natural childbirth' with 'hypnosis'. The woman was apparently wide
awake, in some pain, and was being instructed to breathe deeply and relax.
In another context this would have been called 'natural childbirth with
relaxation'. The problem seems to be that *any* 'psychological' technique
that can be used to alleviate pain could be labelled a 'hypnotic technique' if
we define a procedure inducing hypnotic analgesia as any technique which
can alleviate pain without drugs or other physical means. This overgeneral-
ised use of the term 'hypnosis' would seem to be of little value, and certainly
is contrary to its usage by many investigators who assume hypnosis involves
something 'else' besides waking suggestions and relaxation. Once again,
one way of avoiding this problem is to look instead at some more general
physchological aspects of pain to see how certain techniques, labelled as
'hypnotic' by various investigators, might produce their effects.

INDIVIDUAL SUSCEPTIBILITY TO PAIN

The evidence appears to refute the concept that the intensity of noxious
stimulation and the intensity of perceived pain have a one-to-one relationship. A stimulus may be painful in one situation and not in another and the
same injury can have different effects on different people or even on the
same person at different times. Writers such as Livingston (1943, 1953)
have argued against the classical conception that the intensity of pain is
always proportional to the stimulus. Livingston proposes instead that pain,
like all perceptions, is 'subjective, individual and modified by degrees of
attention, emotional states and the conditioning influence of past experience' (from Melzack, 1973, pp.47–8). Although this quote by Livingston
indicates that pain is a complex sensation, two components seem to have
been usefully isolated. The first may be termed the 'sensory' or 'primary

component' of pain and refers to the pain sensation itself and its discrimination. The lowest amount of noxious stimulation needed to result in the experience of pain is referred to as the subject's 'pain threshold'. However, a weak stimulus, although perceived as a pain stimulus, may not necessarily be experienced as uncomfortable, or evoke suffering. The 'secondary component' involves suffering, and reactions such as anxiety and corresponding emotional responses to pain. The secondary or 'reaction component' is probably responsible for the many changes in physiological activity, for example, heart rate and blood pressure changes, which normally accompany pain. The amount of pain that can be tolerated just as it becomes unbearable is the subject's 'tolerance threshold'. The tolerance threshold is thus determined to a considerable degree by the secondary or reactive component. The reactive component differs significantly from person to person and this is the first point of relevance to hypnotic surgery, for although there is little scientific information on base-line levels of pain experience by surgical patients who have not been anaesthetised it seems that in the days prior to the use of anaesthetics, some patients seemed able to tolerate major surgery without drugs or hypnosis; according to contemporary accounts some 'bravely made no signs of suffering at all' (Chaves and Barber, 1973). In one case described by Barber, Spanos, and Chaves (1974) a woman who had just had a breast removed for cancer, tolerated the surgery and 'without a word, and after being bandaged up, got up, made a curtsy, thanked the surgeon and walked out of the room' (p.80). Barber, Spanos and Chaves (1974) have also reported that a small proportion of the general population does not report pain when exposed to certain noxious stimuli. Although the proportion of the population which could undergo painless surgery without analgesia or anaesthetic drugs is probably only very small it is important to emphasise that the proportion of surgical patients selected for surgery with hypnosis is also very small, a fact which was recognised in some early reports. For example, Moll (1958) reports, 'a complete analgesia is extremely rare in hypnosis, although authors, copying from one another, assert that it is common' (p.105), and Bernheim (1957) notes, 'hypnotism only rarely succeeded as an anaesthetic' (p.116). The possibility therefore exists that the carefully selected patients who are given surgery with hypnotic suggestions may include members of the population who have a general capacity to psychologically control pain, a high pain tolerance level, or an insensitivity to pain, regardless of whether they are 'hypnotised'. According to Chaves and Barber (1976) although there is a consensus that the proportion of the general propulation which can be operated on using hypnotic procedures in major surgery is small, the size of the proportion remains a point of controversy. Wallace and Coppolino (1960) conclude, 'the 10 per cent estimate is an oft-repeated but unsubstantiated quantity and the true percentage of successful cases is much below that figure' (p.3265).

However, perhaps it could be argued that Esdaile's claim of having performed 300 major operations in six years was rather too large to be dismissed in this way (or, on the other hand, that his claims were too good to be true). Nevertheless, it may be significant that Esdaile was working with populations from a different culture. As Gibson (1977) says,

> They were mainly the poor of Bengal, living in conditions of abject poverty, hunger and disease. In such conditions people develop an entirely different orientation to pain. In our protected, well-fed and hygienic European lives we are highly intolerant of and sensitive to pain and seek immediate relief by medical means. However, in a society where pain and disease are an everyday reality, people develop other means of coping with the situation (p.111).

Many other investigators have noticed cultural differences in the way people perceive and respond to pain; thus situations which would appear to be highly painful to Europeans elicit rather different responses in other cultures. Chaves and Barber (1973) cite the eyewitness report of the British physician P.E. Brown who visited a children's hospital in China where five year olds were queuing up for tonsillectomies. Each child had his tonsils removed in less than one minute, and walked into the recovery room spitting blood into a gauze swab. The only anaesthetic used was a quick anaesthetic spray of the throat by a nurse before each child walked into the operating theatre unaccompanied. As another example, anthropologists have observed the practice of 'couvade' in cultures throughout the world, in which the women show virtually no distress during childbirth; often the women work in the fields until the child is just about to be born, and after the birth the mother almost immediately returns to work (Kroeber, 1948). Chaves and Barber (1973) remark in the case of the Chinese children that the patient is conditioned from early childhood to accept surgical interference with his body with the full knowledge that it is going to be successful and he will experience little or no discomfort. This cultural conditioning is an important factor in the determination of pain, thus making it difficult to generalise from Esdaile's large-scale claims to surgery in the Western world. If Esdaile really could successfully conduct major surgery on the Indians using only mesmerism, it cannot necessarily be assumed that the same technique would have been as efficacious elsewhere.

However, even allowing for the possible stoicism of some patients, how could a ritual, whether it be called mesmerism, jar-phoonk, or whatever, be successful in alleviating or preventing pain? In order to determine this a number of psychological factors need consideration, the first being the placebo effect.

THE PLACEBO EFFECT

The term 'placebo', from the Latin 'I shall please', refers to any procedure or substance which affects the patient, not because of its specific properties, but simply because the patient 'believes' it will do something. Shapiro (1973) defines the placebo effect as 'The psychological, physiological, or psychophysiological effect of any medication or procedure given with therapeutic intent, which is independent of or minimally related to the pharmacological effect of the medication or to the specific effects of the procedure and which operates through a psychological mechanism' (p.218). In most recent studies a 'double-blind' procedure has been used to evaluate the effectiveness of placebo medication. Patients receive either a placebo in the form of an innocuous pill or an injection of saline and the effects are compared with those of an analgesic drug such as morphine or asprin. The 'double-blind' procedure attempts to ensure that neither doctor nor patient knows whether the patient is receiving the placebo or the actual drug. It is of course more difficult to conduct a double-blind study to assess the placebo effectiveness of a procedure, as both doctor and patient will be more aware of procedural differences, for instance, whether the patient is receiving hypnotic induction or relaxation.

According to Shapiro (1973) until relatively recently it is highly probable that almost all medications were placebos, and an historical look at the placebo effect reveals a wealth of claims made for the analgesic properties of a variety of amazing substances and procedures. For instance, in 1794 Gerbi published a miraculous cure for toothache which involved crushing a worm between the thumb and forefingers of the right hand, and then touching the affected part. An investigation revealed that using this techni-que 431 out of 629 toothaches ceased immediately, and it was subsequently reported that 65–70 per cent of patients reported immediate pain relief when a ladybird was used. One English newspaper reported, 'Fill your mouth with milk, shake it till it becomes butter, in this way at least three out of four toothaches cease immediately'. This seems rather more agreeable than other remedies which were used such as eating a mouse once a month or using urine as an analgesic mouthwash (Shapiro, 1973), or as Haggard (1929) reports, using a seventeenth century remedy for stomach ache of imbibing the powder resulting from grinding up the sole of an old shoe 'worn by some man that walked much'.

In the nineteenth century William Osler was one of the most ardent proponents of the importance of 'faith' as a therapeutic agent. He cites Galen saying, 'he cures most in whom most are confident', and Paracelsus, 'have a good faith, a strong imagination, and they shall find the effects', and himself says 'Faith in the gods or in the saints cures one, faith in little pills another, hypnotic suggestion a third, faith in a plain common doctor. . . . Faith in us, faith in our drugs and methods . . . a most precious commodity, without which we should be very badly off' (Osler, 1892). However, the placebo effect is certainly not a phenomenon limited to the past; Dubois (1946) says, 'You cannot write a prescription without the element of the placebo. A prayer to Jupiter starts the prescription, and it carries the weight of two or three thousand years of medicine'. More recent reports have concluded that 35 per cent of patients report pain relief following the administration of a placebo in the form of an inactive substance (Beecher, 1959). Evans (1974a) reviewed eleven studies using double-blind techniques and found that placebo medication reduced severe pain in an average of 36 per cent of 909 patients. Evans (1974b) points out that in a typical clinical situation, three patients out of twelve will gain no relief from any medication, five will benefit from a powerful analgesic drug such as morphine but not a placebo; the remaining third will benefit equally well from both morphine and a placebo. After reviewing more studies Evans (1974a, b) found that a placebo is 56 per cent as effective as morphine. Interestingly, he also found that it was 54 per cent as effective as asprin, and 54 per cent as effective as Darvon (a mild analgesic), 'Thus the placebo's effectiveness is directly proportional to the apparent effectiveness of the active agent that doctor and patient think they are using'. This would seem to emphasise the potency of the social communication that goes on between doctor and patient; if the doctor thinks the drug is mild, so the patient will report less relief; when the doctor thinks the drug is powerful, then again, so will the patient. Barber (1959) has noted that the placebo response is not merely a response to the inert pill; it is a response to the total situation, the pill, the doctor's statements, and the patient's previous experiences with doctors and pills.

Investigators in the field consider that a major feature of the placebo effect in analgesia is the reduction of anxiety and fear. As Melzack says, 'the placebo may also decrease anxiety because it makes the patient believe that something is being done to relieve the pain', and Cattell (1943) reports,

> The intensity of the sensation produced by a painful stimulus is determined to a large extent by circumstances which determine the attitude towards it cause. If there is no worry or other distressing implications regarding its source, pain is comparatively well tolerated and during important occasions injuries ordinarily painful may escape notice. On the other hand, in the absence of distraction, particularly if there is anxiety, the patient becomes preoccupied with his condition, and pain is badly tolerated (from Barber, 1969b, pp.136–7).

These factors are well illustrated in the important observation by Beecher (1959) that during World War II when wounded men were carried from the battle-field only a third complained of pain sufficient to require morphine; the others either denied the pain or appeared to experience little pain, even with extensive wounds. According to Beecher they were not in a state of shock, and were capable of feeling pain, for example, they complained as much as anyone else about an inept vein puncture. After the war Beecher asked a number of civilians with similar wounds whether they wanted morphine to alleviate the pain; in response 80 per cent complained of severe pain and wanted a morphine injection. Beecher (1959) concludes,

The data state in numerical terms what is known to all thoughtful clinical observers: there is no simple direct relationship between the wound per se and the pain experienced. The pain is in very large part determined by other factors, and of great importance here is the significance of the wound. . . . In the wounded soldier (the response to injury) was relief, thankfulness at his escape alive from the battle-field, even euphoria; to the civilian, his major surgery was a depressing, calamitous event' (p.165).

Melzack (1973) gives examples of the importance of the situation in determining the amount of pain experienced: abdominal discomfort assumed to be gas cramps and ignored may be felt as severe pain after learning a friend or relative has stomach cancer; however, upon learning from the doctor that nothing is wrong it may vanish. He also points out the frequent observations by dentists that patients who have had terrible toothache report that it disappeared when they entered the dentist's surgery. Melzack says 'The presence or absence of pain in these patients is clearly a function of the meaning of the situation: the pain was unbearable when help was unavailable, and diminished or vanished when relief was at hand' (p.31). In accordance with this view, Hill, Kornetsky, Flanary and Wickler (1952) reported that if anxiety is reduced (by assuring the subject he has control over the pain-producing stimulus), a given level of electric shock or burning heat is perceived as less painful than when the pain-producing stimulus is given under conditions of high anxiety. They also showed that morphine diminishes pain if the anxiety level is high, but has no demonstrable effect if the subject's anxiety has been dispelled before the administration of the drug.

The importance of reassurance in dispelling anxiety has now been taken very seriously and applied to clinical situations. Egbert and his associates found that a five or ten minute preoperative visit by an anaesthesiologist had a greater calming effect on patients than the usual administration of pentobarbital sodium (Egbert, Battit, Turndorf, and Beecher, 1963; Egbert, Battit, Welch and Bartlett, 1964).

Returning to hypnotic procedures for pain relief, it can now be suggested that at least part of the apparent insensitivity to pain reported in some cases may have been due to the placebo effect, i.e. the patients were receiving a treatment which many believed was effective and this could have served to alleviate fear and anxiety, which in turn could have resulted in a reduction of pain.

SUGGESTION, DISTRACTION AND RELAXATION

A number of other features of hypnotic procedures could also be useful in the alleviation of pain, but none is unique to hypnotic procedures. The first involves the use of suggestions for removing pain sensitivity without hypno-

tic induction procedures; it should be noted that these suggestions constitute 'waking suggestions' in as much as no attempt is made to induce a
hypnotic 'state'. During World War II, two surgeons, Sampimon and
Woodruff (1946), were working in a prisoner-of-war hospital near Singa-
pore. As drugs were not available, hypnotic suggestions were used. Unfortunately, some patients could not be 'hypnotised', which presented a problem, so two such patients were operated upon with just 'the mere suggestion
of anaesthesia'. To the surprise of the surgeon the two patients were able to
undergo the surgery without complaint and with no noticeable signs of pain,
though the surgery involved an incision for exploration of an abscess cavity
and the extraction of a tooth. As a result Sampimon and Woodruff wrote:
'Two other patients were anaesthetised by suggestions only, without any
attempt to induce true hypnosis, and both had teeth removed painlessly'
(Barber, 1969b, p. 134). Other investigators have reported similar findings
indicating the effectiveness of direct suggestions for pain relief (Klopp,
1961; Wolfe, 1961), though a particularly dramatic case was presented by
Lozanov (1967) which concerned a surgical repair of a hernia in the groin of
a fifty-year-old man. This man actually offered to undergo surgery without
drugs, and without hypnotic induction as he was 'convinced of the anaes-
thetising power of suggestion alone' (Barber, Spanos and Chaves, 1974,
p.90). According to Lozanov the man only appeared to show pain for two
minutes of the fifty-minute operation.

An important feature of the use of analgesic suggestions is that they
frequently involve or include instructions to focus the patient's attention on
something other than the painful stimulus, for instance, the patient may be
instructed to imagine pleasant scenes, to imagine his body is numb, or to
concentrate on his breathing, or he may be asked to sing or to report the
scenes he has been asked to imagine. In one example a patient undergoing
surgery with hypnotic procedures was asked to imagine a television with her
favourite programme and to give an ongoing commentary describing her
imaginings (Chaves and Barber, 1976). That distraction can be an important element in the reduction of pain has been illustrated by Kanfer and
Goldfoot (1966), who reported that pain could be reduced by the use of
distractions such as looking at slides, self-pacing with a clock, or verbalising
the sensations aloud, and Barber and Cooper (1972) have demonstrated
that subjects report less pain when they are listening to a tape-recorded
story and adding numbers aloud. The role of distraction has also been
emphasised by Cattell (1943) in the quote cited earlier, and by Liebeault
(1885) who suggested that hypnotic suggestions are successful in alleviating
pain because they focus attention on thoughts and ideas other than those
involving pain; August (1961) concluded the same after an investigation of
1000 patients during childbirth.

At this point it may be useful to spell out again that 'waking' suggestions
to imagine a pleasant scene, or imagine the body is numb, are not usually
described as 'hypnosis'. If a doctor asks you to picture a pleasant scene or to

imagine that your arm is numb while he gives you an injection, it would not seem very meaningful to say that you are 'hypnotised' if you carry out his instructions. If such instructions are accepted, they could be termed 'waking' suggestions, but most investigators state quite firmly that hypnosis is not the same as waking suggestibility.

The possibility also exists that a suggestion, if accepted, may work by itself, independently of an effect through the alleviation of anxiety and fear, or through distraction. For instance, in one case reported by Dr. C. Lloyd Tuckey in 1889 it was necessary to administer ether to an hysterical girl who was about to be operated on for the removal of two sebaceous tumours from the scalp. Although the ether bottle was in fact *empty* the girl cried, 'Oh, I feel it; I am going off', and lapsed into unconsciousness and the operation was apparently painlessly completed (Chaves and Barber, 1973). The important factor here, once again, is that the patient 'believed' she was being given ether. This case points to the relationship between the concept of suggestibility and the placebo effect. In a sense, the patient who responds to placebo medication is accepting the 'suggestion' that he is receiving a valuable therapeutic agent; as Chaves and Barber (1973) say 'placebos are also a way of implanting mental suggestion', and Leslie (1954) actually defines a placebo as 'a medicine or preparation which has no inherent pertinent pharmacologic activity but which is effective only by virtue of the factor of suggestion attendant upon its administration'. It is interesting to note that in general studies have failed to find a significant relationship between suggestibility, hypnotic susceptibility and the placebo response (Evans, 1974b). However, in view of the problems involved in finding measures of suggestibility and hypnotic susceptibility, this discrepancy is not really surprising; if existing measures of suggestibility and hypnotic susceptibility are biased by compliance, whereas a placebo effect involves a genuine belief component, then one might expect there to be little relationship between placebo reactions and the other measures.

Another important element in hypnotic induction is the employment of instructions for relaxation. The semantic problems of differentiating hypnotic induction from relaxation have already been discussed so I will not dwell on this aspect further; suffice it to say that a person does not need to be relaxed in order to be labelled 'hypnotised' or 'hypnotically susceptible'. Relaxation methods may be useful in the alleviating of pain in a number of ways; for example, relaxation involves muscle relaxation, which in turn seems related to pain responsiveness, as evident in the fact that muscle-relaxants can be used to exert a powerful influence on pain (Beecher, 1959). Also, relaxation can be used as an agent in reducing fear and anxiety (Benson and Klipper, 1976) which, as we have seen, are inextricably linked with the pain response. An interesting feature of relaxation procedures discussed in Chapter 4 concerns the possible achievement by some subjects of a number of novel experiences accompanying relaxation which they may label as 'hypnosis', or might at least convince them that something quite unique is happening which could be of benefit in relieving pain. After all, one would probably be far more convinced of the therapeutic benefit of a procedure if it resulted in novel experiences which could be interpreted to indicate that 'something is happening'.

THE EXTENT OF SURGICAL PAIN

The possibility that even a few carefully selected individuals may endure surgical pain with little apparent distress due to the effects of placebos, distraction, and relaxation, may still seem somewhat unlikely to some readers who might wish to argue that such factors could not alone be responsible, without some extra 'hypnotic' element. In view of this it may be worth putting forward some evidence cited by Barber, Spanos and Chaves (1974) indicating that some surgical procedures may not actually be as painful as some might expect; in fact, in certain surgical procedures it may be the anxiety, fear and worry which make the major contribution to the perceived pain rather than the capacity of parts of the anatomy to evoke pain sensations. One striking finding is that there is no evidence for the common assumption that the deeper the surgeon cuts into the body tissues and organs the more pain is evoked; in fact, if anything, the opposite is true, as a most sensitive area of the body to knife cut is the *skin*, whilst the underlying tissues and organs can be insensitive to incision. Lewis (1942) lists a number of parts of the body which when cut are actually either almost or totally insensitive, including the subcutaneous tissue, compact bone, the articular surfaces of joints, the brain, the lungs and visceral pleura, the surface of the heart, the abdominal viscera, the oesophageal wall, the great omentum, the stomach, lower portions of the alimentary canal, the uterus and internal portions of the vagina. In fact, solid organs such as the spleen, liver, and kidney can be cut without the patient being aware of it. However, it is important to note that parts of the body are generally sensitive to pulling, traction and stretching rather than incision. The lack of sensitivity of these parts of the body is evident in the fact that early in this century cases were reported of patients who had undergone major surgical operations painlessly without general anaesthetics or 'hypnosis', using only a local anaesthetic to remove the sensitivity of the skin. These included abdominal operations, amputation of limbs, removal of thyroid glands, breast removal, appendectomy, cutting into and draining the gall bladder, suturing a hernia, excising glands in the groin, extensive dissection of the neck and cutting the bladder (Mitchell, 1907). The fact seems to be that in the absence of fear and anxiety, simple superficial surgery involving the skin may actually be more painful than surgery on other major and 'deeper' organs. According to Barber, Spanos and Chaves (1974) modern surgery is usually carried out with a general anaesthetic to alleviate fear and anxiety. A patient may feel pain at having a boil lanced, or his skin stitched, or a tooth pulled out, but he may tolerate the pain with little fear as he feels the surgery is minor. However, the grisly thought of someone hacking away inside one's abdomen sounds positively terrifying, though in fact the potential pain might actually be less. Thus another feature of hypnotic surgery may be that the patient's belief in the efficacy of the technique may mean he will actually *allow* the surgeons to operate without a general anaesthetic. The possibility exists that certain major operations conducted with hypnotic suggestions actually evoke little pain, not because of 'hypnosis' but because they would not be very painful *anyway*; the problem is that studies have not used control groups undergoing the same surgery without hypnotic induction, drugs, or suggestions for analgesia.

In spite of the fact that many parts of the body are insensitive to incision and although pain may be reduced by the alleviation of fear and anxiety, one might still expect patients to show signs of pain at some time during operations, especially when incisions of the skin occur. It is thus significant that in most recent cases hypnotic induction has not been used alone in surgery, but has been used together with analgesic drugs, the main effects of the drugs being to anaesthetise the skin. A good example is reported by Werbel (1967). In this instance a sixty-nine-year-old women was operated on for the removal of a tumour from the neck. Although the alleviation of pain was attributed to hypnosis, several cubic centimeters of procaine were injected in the area where the skin was cut, with the effect of numbing the skin. In another example, brain surgery (a temporal lobectomy) was conducted on a fourteen-year-old girl. Although the girl was given a hypnotic induction procedure with suggestions for analgesia, the line of incision on the scalp was injected with procaine (Crasilneck, McCranie and Jenkins, 1956). Although the patient appeared to be comfortable during the main part of the surgery which involved cutting through the bone of the scalp and the brain tissue (areas which are generally insensitive to incision anyway), the patient showed signs of pain when the dura mater was separated from the bone and when a blood vessel in the hippocampal region was being coagulated (procedures which one might expect to evoke pain). Before the surgery was completed the patient was given another drug. Barber, Spanos and Chaves (1974) cite a number of other examples of hypnotic surgery which involved the use of a number of drugs, including sedatives and local anaesthetics, involving operations on the lungs, abdomen, feet and neck. The drugs were either given before the surgery, or when the patient showed signs of pain, and typically, they were used to numb those areas which one would expect to be particularly painful.

One notable exception was an operation presented by Mason (1955). The operation involved surgery on the breasts of a twenty-four-year-old woman. Although the woman was given a drug medication the night before the operation she was given no further medication either before, during, or after the surgery. During the incision the patient only reported pain alone and her blood pressure was the same before and after the surgery. The whole procedure lasted seventy minutes, during which the patient chatted to the surgeon, and after the operation the patient said, 'Good show!', and asked to sit up. Chaves and Barber (1976) suggest that it seemed the hypnotic procedures did appear to markedly reduce anxiety and pain, only they point out one minor reservation, that previous surgery had left some degree of insensitivity in part of the breast area and it is difficult to know how much this could have contributed to the apparent lack of pain. However, in single cases like this it is of course impossible to determine whether waking suggestions for relaxation, distraction, etc. might not have been equally effective.

THE DOCTOR-PATIENT RELATIONSHIP

Obviously if any procedure is to remove fear and anxiety, and is to allow the patient to believe that he will feel little or no pain, i.e. to maximise a placebo response, it is essential that the patient trust those who are concerned with his treatment. As Marmer (1957) says, 'the realisation that the anaestheologist is willing to invest time, effort, warmth and understanding in an attempt of hypnosis will give most patients added security and trust in the physician and will result in decreased tension and anxiety'. This statement is supported by the observations of Egbert et al., mentioned earlier. In fact, the attention and reassurance given to the patient by the hypnotherapist may be a more important factor, in some cases, than any specific feature of hypnotic induction. For example, Butler (1954) used hypnotic induction with suggestions for pain relief on twelve 'good' hypnotic patients suffering from cancer. The patients received the hypnotic treatment, every day, and sometimes two to four times a day. The patients reported that their pain was reduced during the sessions and sometimes for a brief period afterwards. When the sessions were finished, the patients showed pain again; however, then the physician continued to give personal attention to each patient, but *without the hypnotic sessions*, the patients again showed pain relief. This personal attention to patients has been put forward as an important factor in the alleviation of pain concerned with pregnancy and childbirth; for instance, Winkelstein (1958) reports that if suggestions for pain relief are to be effective, much time and attention has to be given to each patient. He has suggested general factors such as the attitude of the patient toward pregnancy and delivery, the will to succeed, the confidence of the patient in the procedure and obstetrician and the relationship between the patient and obstetrician as being more important than the 'depth of trance'. Similarly Chlifer (1937) notes that labour pain may be effectively reduced by suggestions given to 'unhypnotised' patients, and that the success of the suggestions depends on the relationship between doctor and patient, and the patient's personality. The importance of the doctor-patient relationship in obstetrics has also been stressed by Kroger and Freed (1956).

A close interpersonal relationship may also provide an opportunity for the patient to be prepared and given details of the surgical procedures;

Chaves and Barber (1976) suggest this preoperative preparation may further help to reduce the patient's anxiety. Schultz (1954) provides a description of the kind of information commonly used to prepare patients for hypoanaesthesia. For instance, he says, 'Every patient during the pre-paratory hypnotic sessions must be led to experience the operation or the labour with all details . . . if a thyroidectomy were imminent . . . every detail (is) gone into. . . . For example: . . . "You feel the warm fluid: you know 'it is my blood', and remain absolutely calm, with no pain, no anxiety" ' (p.24). Such preparation may minimise surprise and help to reduce anxiety, and a number of studies not involving hypnosis have suggested that giving information to patients can be very efficacious. For example, Egbert et al. (1963, 1964) found that patients given information about what was to be expected during surgery, and post-surgically, required smaller doses of narcotics for post-surgical pain than uninformed control subjects, and were discharged from hospital sooner than controls. Ley (1977) also reports a number of studies which indicate that preoperative communication can effectively reduce the necessity of analgesic drugs, and reports by others, such as Chapman (1969), also attest to the utility of giving information of this kind. Chaves and Barber (1976) propose that as preoperative familiar-isation with the medical setting and procedures are often provided prior to hypnoanaesthesia, such preparation may play an important role in reducing pain with hypnotic procedures; this point is also emphasised by Lewenstein (1978) who remarks, 'Individualisation is the key to successful use of hypnosis. Hypnotic abilities vary with motivation, situation, and the rap-port established between the patient and the physician. These factors are assessed during the preoperative interview' (p.145).

The overall situation is well summarised by Findley (1953) who com-ments that the effectiveness of the placebo effect lies in the action, faith, ritual and enthusiasm on the part of both the doctor and patient, and concludes 'despite the scientific achievements of this century the physician himself is still the most important therapeutic agent' (Shapiro, 1973, p.221).

COULD COMPLIANCE ALSO BE OPERATING?

So far only those factors relevant to genuine reductions in pain have been considered, and it is now necessary to consider whether compliance could conceivably play a part in responsiveness to clinical pain following hypnotic procedures. At first, the proposal that patients would 'fake' an absence of pain seems absurd. However, on first consideration the possibility that subjects might give lethal doses of electric shock to an innocent victim without physical coercion also might seem absurd, and Barber (1970) has made a forceful statement concerning the possible motivation for denying pain in the clinical situation:

The motivation for denial of pain is present in the clinical hypnotic situation. The physician who has invested time and energy hypnotising the patient and suggesting that pain will be relieved expects and desires that his efforts will be successful, and by his words and manner communicates his desires to the patient. The patient in turn has often found a close relationship with the physician-hypnotist and would like to please him or at least not to disappoint him. Furthermore, the patient is aware that if he states that he suffered, he is implying that the physician's time and energy were wasted and his efforts futile. The situation is such that even though the patient may have suffered, it may be difficult or disturbing for him to state directly to the physician-hypnotist that he experienced pain and it may be less anxiety-provoking to say that he did not suffer (Barber, 1970, pp.211–12).

This statement may be particularly important when we consider that the factors discussed so far, although able to evoke possible genuine reductions in pain in some cases, may not necessarily achieve optimal success in all cases. Some operations involve more than incisions of organs; they may include, for instance, a certain amount of painful stretching of tissue and furthermore it might be rather overoptimistic to assume that all patients undergoing surgery with hypnosis do become anxiety-free, accept the suggestions, and believe totally in the effectiveness of the procedures. In practice these reservations seem well justified as examination of a number of cases suggests that hypnotic surgery may not be as painless as some popular reports might at first indicate. As we have seen, some reports state that at some stage during the surgery the patient 'broke trance' and had to be given analgesic drugs, and indeed Barber (1972) reports that 'Most "hypnotic trance" subjects who undergo minor or major surgery without drugs show signs of pain' (p.141). Other cases which have been assumed to have demonstrated 'satisfactory anaesthesia' include statements like 'there was considerable grimacing' (Cooper and Powles, 1945), the patient 'began to whimper softly at the incision of the scalpel' (Betcher, 1960). Schultze-Rhonhoff (cited by Chertok, 1959) reports that obstetric patients who had received extensive antenatal training in entering 'deep trance' showed signs of pain, such as groaning and crying, but subsequently denied suffering.

The fact that some patients do show signs of pain might then lead us to suspect in particular that some of Esdaile's multitude of 'successful' cases were not quite the conclusive evidence for the reality of hypnotic analgesic that some writers might have us believe, and when some of his cases are considered in more detail such fears seem to be substantiated to a certain degree. Esdaile (1957) himself reported instances of patient responses which seem somewhat like responses to pain; he wrote, 'She moved and moaned' (p.200), 'About the middle of the operation he gave a cry' (p.222), 'He awoke, and cried out before the operation was finished' (p.232). In 1846 a committee appointed by the governor of Bengal was sent to investigate Esdaile's claims (Braid, 1847). In response Esdaile carefully selected six patients and removed scrotal tumours from them after putting them in a 'mesmeric trance' by making passes over them for six to eight hours. Another three patients failed to respond to mesmerism in spite of repeated attempts extending up to eleven days, and were consequently not operated upon. The committee reported that during the surgery three of the six patients showed 'convulsive movements of the upper limbs, writhing of the body, distortions of the features, giving the face a hideous expression of suppressed agony; the respiration became heaving with deep sighs' (Barber, 1969b, p.129). Two of the other patients showed marked elevations in pulse rate. The evidence of these reports suggests that although a small number of Esdaile's patients may not have suffered, possibly for the reasons already considered, this certainly does not appear to be true of all of them. What is particularly significant for the present discussion is that, in spite of his own admission that many of his patients showed these apparent signs of suffering, Esdaile (1957) claimed such operations were nevertheless successful, as the patients remembered nothing. He says, 'the trance is sometimes completely broken by the knife, but it can occasionally be reproduced by continuing the process, and then the sleeper remembers nothing; he has only been disturbed by a nightmare, of which on waking he retains no recollection' (pp.145–6). It is notable in the report cited earlier of Esdaile's operation of Gooroochuan Shah that he says, 'On recovering he said that he awoke while the mattress was being pulled back, and that nothing had disturbed him'.

The fact that so many of Esdaile's successful cases remembered nothing seems rather suspicious when it is considered that a complete, spontaneous amnesia after hypnotic induction is so rare (see Chapter 6). Perhaps it might be reasonable to argue that at least part of the claim made by the patients that they had been asleep and remembered nothing constituted the patients' compliant response to Esdaile's rather outdated view of hypnosis as a sleep-like state of insensibility. However, if some of the patients' reports were false we have still to answer Esdaile's questions as to why people should continue to come to him for surgery. A number of possible factors, either singly or in combination, could account for this. Firstly, a few patients might have felt little pain because of the factors outlined previously, though perhaps some of the same patients could have tolerated the surgery anyway without mesmerism. Such reports may have been accepted more readily by those desperately in need of surgery. Secondly, there could have been a certain degree of bravado in the reports of some patients. It may have been difficult for some to admit, 'It was awful, I cried and moaned'. Thirdly, and this ties in with the first point, these patients were presented with little alternative. They either continued to be incapacitated with their dreadful tumours, or they provided themselves with an opportunity to be relieved of their burdens. After all, before the advent of modern equipment and simple injections people still used to visit the dentist, in spite of the torture they might have heard of or experienced themselves. Thus, although their friends may have experienced agony at Esdaile's hands, at least in the end they are free of their tumours, which might make the ordeal seem worthwhile. Another possibility is that although some patients might have reported that they felt nothing, when in fact they had been in considerable pain, the cognitive dissonance process described in Chapter 4 could have resulted in them subsequently 'believing' their own false testimony. Sarbin and Coe (1972) have outlined this possibility in reports of hypnotic analgesia. They suggest that the subject may be faced with the problem of reconciling two incompatible bits of personal knowledge, 'I felt the pain (privately)' and 'I publicly said that I felt no pain'. Having preserved the 'secret knowledge' of feeling pain by public denial, the subject may then become committed to a further line of action to confirm the nondisclosure. Sarbin and Coe's (1972) interpretation might fit well in the case of Esdaile's patients and with the followers of Marion Keech, mentioned in Chapter 4, who, having their prophecy disconfirmed, reduced the dissonance by proselytising for their cause. In the same way, some of Esdaile's patients, having admitted they felt nothing, might have reduced the dissonance by persuading themselves they felt nothing, and actually proselytising for the efficacy of Esdaile's procedures.

The point of this section is not to put forward the proposition that *all* of Esdaile's patients were in agony, and had suppressed it and lied about it, but to suggest that even cases of hypnotic surgery may not be free from the presence of compliance; thus whilst some patients may have experienced little pain, this may only be part of the story. It should be pointed out that Esdaile's patients probably did have a special admiration for him. As Gibson (1977) says, 'Esdaile did, after all, bring great benefits to them, using his influence to set up hospitals and working untiringly for them', and thus, 'It is quite understandable that the Indians — doctors, medical assistants and patients — played the game of having the white sahib take all the credit' (p.110). It is therefore, perhaps, not unreasonable to postulate that both patients and assistants felt some obligation to report to Esdaile what they felt he wanted to hear, that the patients had been asleep and remembered nothing.

In fact, generally, the same close interpersonal relationships and training sessions which precede hypnotic procedures in the clinical setting, as well as reducing anxiety may also have the undesirable effect of leading the patient to deny painful experiences. This aspect of medical treatment has received some support from the report by Mandy, Mandy, Farkas and Scher (1952) that some patients undergoing 'natural childbirth' reported to the physician that they were pleased with the methods, but then admitted to an independent observer that the procedure was more painful than they had expected. However, they failed to report this to the medical staff because they did not want to disappoint them.

ANIMAL HYPNOSIS

Gibson (1977) has proposed an extremely novel hypothesis concerning the way patients submitted to hypnotic induction may be able to tolerate surgery, based on the concept of 'animal hypnosis'.

The term 'animal hypnosis' has been applied to the finding that at times, when an animal is physically restrained, for example, by holding it down, or turning it upside down suddenly, and the restraint is terminated, the animal assumes an almost catatonic-like state of immobility. According to Gallup (1977) fear is implicated as an important antecedent of the response, and according to Klemm (1977) this is a reflexive response in which fear evoking stimuli activate the brainstem sending inhibitory influences to the motor nerve cells in the spinal cord. In animals the response has been assumed by some to have survival value, as would-be predators are less likely to attack motionless prey. However, some investigators have suggested that the assumption that this response is similar to human 'hypnosis' may have been misleading, for example, Gallup (1977) comments, 'In recent years most investigators have come to prefer *tonic immobility* as a label because it is more descriptive of the reaction, and the surplus meaning associated with the word "hypnosis" probably has served to retard research on the response' (p.41), and Carli (1978) remarks, 'Animal hypnosis is a very different phenomenon from human hypnosis, and any comparison between the two only leads to confusing speculation' (p.70).

It is not difficult to see why the analogy between tonic immobility and human hypnosis would seem to be inappropriate. Most writers on and investigators into hypnosis have emphasised the passive, relaxed, unaroused state that often is supposed to accompany hypnotic induction; however, subjects lifting weights, performing cognitive tasks, age regressing, hallucinating, throwing acid at the experimenter, and avoiding chairs, are hardly in a catatonic state of immobility. Nevertheless, one of the most important points that this book is attempting to demonstrate is that the phenomena subsumed by the concept of 'hypnosis' may not be unitary. There may therefore be isolated cases of certain phenomena, which have been labelled as 'hypnotic', but which are unrelated to other phenomena which have also been labelled 'hypnotic'. Bearing this in mind we can look at some aspects of Gibson's (1977) proposal that a tonic immobility response in humans may be relevant to certain 'hypnotic' surgical cases. Gibson notes that in the nineteenth century some hypnotists and mesmerists used deliberately authoritarian techniques which induced fear, and that this was especially likely when patients were being prepared for analgesia in surgery. These techniques, plus the obvious terror that might accrue from anticipating surgery without analgesics, could have evoked a tonic immobility response in some patients. Gibson quotes one of Esdaile's reports of a patient who whilst being 'entranced' manifested quivering eyelids and trembling hands, though subsequently appeared to tolerate a 'severe' operation; Gibson remarks that the quivering eyelids and trembling of extremities closely resemble the tonic immobility responses of some animals. However, it should be noted that according to almost all recent research on pain reducing methods this patient should have felt a maximum amount of pain. He was apparently frightened, anxious and tense, all factors which should have increased the sensation of pain. Of course, as we have seen, great caution should be exercised before accepting Esdaile's own observation of what constitutes a 'painless' operation, but nevertheless, it might be difficult to conceive of a situation more frightening than the prospect of a surgeon slicing you open. Thus perhaps Gibson's hypothesis is plausible, and *some* of Esdaile's patients, and those of other surgeons, might have been in a state of tonic immobility. As Gibson says, the literature on animal hypnosis contains over 600 reports dealing with over fifty species of animals, thus it might not seem reasonable to suggest that the response could occur in humans, should an individual be sufficiently frightened. Gallup (1975) also suggests that human psychotic catatonic states precipitated and accompanied by emotional stress and fear may be manifestations of the immobility response, as the classic responses of tremors, muscle rigidity, stuporous gaze, and occasional fatalities, may occur in such cases. In animals one of the characteristics of tonic immobility is a reduced responsiveness to external stimulation (Gallup, 1977), and there are some reports of surgery being performed on animals during tonic immobility without the interruption of immobility (Rapson and Jones, 1964). If a similar insensitivity occurs in a human this would accord with Gibson's proposal. However, whether a surgical patient paralysed with fear would actually 'feel' pain cannot be discerned at present. The following quote from Moll is quite interesting in this respect: 'I once hypnotised a patient in order to open a boil painlessly. I did not succeed in inducing analgesia, but the patient was almost unable to move, so that I could perform the little operation without difficulty' (Moll, 1958, p.220). More information is obviously needed, but unfortunately, in spite of some early claims by Hoagland (1928), recent attempts to induce tonic immobility in humans by tying subjects into chairs and tilting them at various angles have failed to induce immobility, though they did succeed in making some feel dizzy and faint. However, rather than being paralysed with fear many subjects reported that after a number of trials, the experiment was fun! (Crawford, 1977).

If Gibson's proposal has some validity, and if tonic immobility in humans results in decreased sensitivity to pain then an interesting relationship may exist between anxiety, arousal and responsiveness to pain. The suggestion would be that *very* low or *extremely* high levels of anxiety and arousal could result in decreased sensitivity to pain, with maximum sensitivity lying somewhere in between. The possibility of tonic immobility in humans might also account for odd clinical cases of 'paralysed' hypnotic subjects who might have been scared out of their wits by the prospect of falling into a trance, or disobeying an authoritarian hypnotist. These possibilities await investigation, however Gibson's proposal has received some further support from recent work on morphine-like substances in the brain. These developments will be discussed later in this chapter.

CLINICAL ANALGESIA AND HYPNOTIC SUSCEPTIBILITY

So far an attempt has been made to relate the phenomenon of hypnotic analgesia in the clinical field with other factors not usually assumed to be unique to hypnosis. However, although clinical hypnotic analgesia has been frequently taken as the most crucial evidence for the 'power' of hypnosis, work in this field reveals an irony. The ability to respond to suggestions for analgesia in the most dramatic clinical situations, such as those involving surgery or obstetrics, is sometimes unrelated to hypnotic susceptibility. For example, Cangello (1962) reports that some individuals in a 'light trance' might be capable of obtaining pain relief, and others in a 'deep trance' might not; similar observations were made by Michael (1952) and Von Dedenroth (1962). Lea, Ware and Monroe (1960) report, 'We assumed that our success would depend upon the depth of hypnosis, but, to our surprise, we found that this was not necessarily the case. As a matter of fact two of our best patients obtained only light to medium trances, and significant responses were noted in even the very lightest hypnoidal states'. Winkelstein (1958) notes that some women, only lightly hypnotised, managed their delivery successfully, while others, assumed to be deeply hypnotised, were unable to cope with the discomfort of labour. Even Esdaile presented cases of subjects supposedly in a 'deep mesmeric trance' who 'shrunk on the first incision' (Barber, 1969b, p.132). On a sample of twenty patients Mody (1960) noted that the 'depth of hypnosis' was not always correlated with the degree of pain experienced during childbirth. When relationships have been found between hypnotic susceptibility and clinical pain they are often small or statistically insignificant; for instance, Gottfredson (1973) found a correlation of only -0.39 between hypnotic susceptibility and reports of pain experience in routine dental procedures on twenty-five patients, and Rock, Shipley and Campbell (1969) found there was no statistically significant relationship between hypnotic susceptibility and reports of decreased pain in patients in labour, though there was a trend in this direction. Even allowing for the insignificant trend in Rock et al.'s study, six out of ten of the subjects who scored *lowest* in responsiveness to a short hypnotic scale were nevertheless scored as 'good' in their ability to reduce pain with hypnotic suggestions for analgesia.

The whole area of hypnosis and clinical pain seems to be confused by the absence of definitive evidence from clinical trials controlling for factors such as the placebo effect, anxiety, fear, distraction, the doctor-patient relationship, suggestions per se, base-line levels to pain, compliance and the absence of standardised hypnotic induction and assessment procedures. Clinical trials of this kind are expensive and those involved with patients in distress may care less about academic arguments concerning *how* hypnotic suggestions result in analgesia. But for the present what available evidence there is suggests that rather than clinical analgesia being the *pièce de résistance* of hypnosis it is in certain cases an embarrassment. In Chapter 7, a number of studies which have attempted to correlate various traits and dimensions with hypnotic susceptibility was reviewed. Included in the findings from these studies was that certain traits or dispositions such as 'gullibility' or 'influencibility' did not correlate highly with hypnotic susceptibility. Some have interpreted these results to suggest that 'hypnosis' and these factors are distinct, and such traits of susceptibility to social influence lie outside the 'domain' of hypnosis. Although this conclusion was questioned, it is interesting to note that if the correlation between some factor 'X' and a measure of hypnotic susceptibility or 'hypnotisibility' is the criterion by which it is decided whether or not 'X' lies within the 'domain of hypnosis', it could possibly be argued that suggested analgesia too lies outside the 'domain' of hypnosis. The facts that (a) only a very few patients can undergo surgery with 'hypnotic' techniques alone, and (b) in some cases this capacity may be unrelated to other criteria of hypnotic susceptibility also suggest that it is somewhat untenable to try to attest to the validity of hypnotic phenomena *in general* by referring to hypnotic analgesia and anaesthesia in the clinical situation.

EXPERIMENTAL STUDIES OF PAIN

In view of the anecdotal nature of much of the evidence for hypnotic analgesia in the clinical setting, and the resulting equivocal nature of many of the findings, investigators have attempted to examine hypnotic analgesia in the laboratory where more factors can be systematically controlled. However, studying pain in the laboratory brings with it its own problems. As Bowers (1976) notes, people in clinical pain come to the therapist for their own good reasons, whereas people coming to serve as subjects in experimental studies may come to the laboratory less for their own reasons than for the investigator's. Barber, Spanos and Chaves (1974) suggest that the pain produced by stimuli given in the laboratory may differ in quality, and may give rise to less anxiety and fear than pain in the clinical situation. This problem has been emphasised further by studies which indicate that although certain analgesic drugs such as morphine may be effective in reducing clinical pain, which is usually accompanied by anxiety, they fail to work for experimentally induced pain, which involves little anxiety (Weisenberg, 1977). Of course there are no hard and fast rules on this, anxiety may be present in some laboratory studies of pain (Chapman and Feather, 1973), but there is good reason to consider that it is considerably less than in most clinical situations. For example, in the laboratory the subject may be less worried about the implications for health of the pain and he can in theory withdraw from the situation, or terminate the pain at any time. These points may be crucial in view of the evidence cited earlier which indicates that when anxiety and fear are minimal, the effectiveness of placebo medication is considerably reduced (Hill, Kornetsky, Flanary and Wickler, 1952). If it is the case that laboratory induced pain is less distressing, then one might have more cause to doubt whether the placebo features of hypnotic procedures, which may effectively eliminate pain for some in the clinical setting, will do so to the same extent in the laboratory setting; thus when subjects appear to respond to various suggestions with reports of reductions in pain it might be well to be very cautious about always accepting such reports as 'genuine'.

For experiments on pain to produce valid results, not only is it necessary to use control groups, but, as discussed in the previous chapters, the control groups must be appropriately instructed in order to rule out the possibility of subjects complying with the experimenter's expectancies. Unfortunately, this has not always been the case, as is illustrated in a report by Sears (1932) which reputed to demonstrate the effectiveness of hypnotic analgesia. In this study seven 'good' hypnotic subjects were submitted to a hypnotic induction procedure and were given suggestions that their left legs were insensitive. The pain stimulus was a sharp steel point which was then pressed on the right and left leg. The 'hypnotised' subjects flinched when the steel point was pressed against the 'normal' right leg, but not when it was applied to the 'anaesthetised' leg. In a non-hypnotic condition the same subjects in the 'waking' state were given instructions to try to inhibit all pain responses when the steel pin was applied; however, they flinched in this 'waking' treatment. Sears concluded that 'voluntary inhibition of reaction to pain does not present a picture that even remotely resembles the reaction under true hypnotic anaesthesia'. Unfortunately this conclusion seems highly questionable as Sears had found that subjects (including those participating in this experiment) had previously easily been able to prevent themselves from flinching when the steel point has been applied. Hull (1933) has pointed out that as facial flinch can ordinarily be inhibited at will it appears the subjects were *not trying* to suppress the pain responses when asked to do so when 'awake'. In other words, the subjects had disobeyed the experimenter's explicit instructions to try not to flinch, in order to comply with this more important implicit demand that they should look 'better' in the hypnotic condition. This experiment again points out the flaw in the same-subjects design as discussed previously and also indicates that compliance is potentially a powerful element in experimental studies in pain.

MEASURING PAIN

One way of avoiding the problem of subjects falsifying their reports of pain would be to find some other index of pain which is not so amenable to voluntary control, such as a physiological response. Unfortunately, there is no one accepted physiological indicator that relates in a completely orderly way the presence or absence of pain. However, Sternbach (1968), after a review of the relevant literature, summarises what he terms certain 'trends' in physiological responses when pain producing stimuli are applied; these include an increase in oxygen consumption which occasionally may be associated with an increased respiration rate, an increase in muscle tension, an increase in pulse rate and stroke volume (p.58). In fact, the responses are similar to those an organism would make when activated to avoid, or escape from tissue damage, which also could account for why other indices of activation, such as skin resistance changes, have been shown by some to relate to the perception of pain. Researchers have presented evidence suggesting that a rise in blood pressure is a reasonably useful indicator of pain using a number of methods. One involves 'cold-pressor' pain which is produced by immersing the hand and forearm in cold water, usually for about forty seconds; subjects are then asked to rate on a scale from 0 (no pain) to 10 (severe pain) how powerful the stimulus is. Using the cold-pressor test, according to Hilgard (1969b), subjects' verbal reports of pain correlate with rises in blood pressure significantly ($r = 0.53$), i.e. the more painful the stimulus is reported to be, the higher the blood pressure. Similar results have been found by Tétreault, Panisset, and Gouger (1964). Another way of inducing pain is by placing a tourniquet just above the elbow and then asking the subject to squeeze a dynometer a standard number of times. After the subject stops working the pain mounts; this is called *ischemic pain*. Blood pressure also rises in an orderly fashion with verbal reports of ischemic pain (Hilgard, 1969b, pp.107–8). Thus, although there is no perfect physiological indicator of pain there is sufficient evidence to suggest that some physiological measures may provide at least a rough guide to a subject's perceived pain in an experimental situation, and a way of 'checking' on the validity of verbal reports of pain.

SOME EXPERIMENTAL STUDIES OF HYPNOTIC ANALGESIA

A number of experiments indicates that suggestions for analgesia given without hypnotic induction are as effective as hypnotic suggestions for analgesia (Barber, 1969a; Spanos, Barber and Lang, 1974; Evans and Paul, 1970). However, an important finding from these studies was although the hypnotic induction seemed irrelevant, both the hypnotic and waking groups often did better than groups given no suggestions for anaesthesia. This point is important as it indicates that the appropriate waking control group in studies of hypnotic analgesia is one that has been given suggestions for anaesthesia of some kind, such as 'your hand is numb and insensitive' or 'your hand has no feeling at all', rather than one given no instruction at all. Another significant feature of these studies was that the subjects were assigned to *different* groups; if the same subjects had been assigned to *both* a hypnotic and non-hypnotic condition the problems of the same-subjects design would have arisen again, with the possible result that hypnotic suggestions might have spuriously appeared to be more effective than the waking suggestions.

However, no matter what the design, if subjects are given suggestions of any kind, the clear implication is that the suggestions are given for some reason, i.e. they are supposed to be effective in reducing pain, so the results of studies using verbal reports could be biased by compliance. If you are told 'your hand is insensitive', it rather goes against the implied purpose of the experiment if you reply that 'it hurts!', regardless of whether you are 'hypnotised' or not. In spite of these considerations Bowers (1976) has argued that compliance is perhaps an unlikely explanation of the verbal reports of the absence of pain in these studies as 'neither the hypnotic nor the waking analgesia procedure was completely effective in eliminating pain', there was not a 'complete denial of pain . . . subjects who were hypnotically analgesic were willing to acknowledge discomfort'. He suggests that, 'If the subjects were only interested in pleasing the hypnotist, why wouldn't they simply deny feeling any pain whatsoever?' (p. 79). However, as has been argued previously, what a subject gives as a compliant response may depend on his preconceptions of what is expected of him, and what other cues he is offering the experimenter. One way of finding out these preconceptions would be to employ a simulating group who are asked to pretend to be 'hypnotised' whilst being given suggestions for analgesia. Hilgard, Macdonald, Morgan and Johnson (1978) used such a group in a study involving cold pressor pain. Although, due to the 'over-play' effect (discussed in Chapter 6), the insusceptible simulators predictably reported less pain than the 'real' subjects, still only five of the twelve simulators denied feeling *any pain at all*. Thus, in this case even when over-playing their role, the majority of subjects who were pretending to be 'hypnotised' did *not* feel that a 'real' subject would deny *all* pain. However, the evidence suggests that one cannot generalise; it seems individual studies vary according to the subjects selected and the instructions given, as contrary to Bowers' argument, a number of studies (Lenox, 1970; Sachs, 1970; Knox, Shum and McLaughlin, 1978) have reported that many hypnotically susceptible subjects *will* deny *all* pain in response to hypnotic suggestions for analgesia.

Some of the physiological evidence for hypnotic analgesia is equally equivocal. For instance, in a study by Barber and Hahn (1962), there was the usual finding of no difference between the verbal reports of cold-pressor pain for the hypnotic and waking groups given suggestions for analgesia (i.e. 'instructed'), though both reported less pain than an 'uninstructed' group given no suggestions for analgesia. In general physiological measures showed that the 'instructed' groups showed less change in muscle potential and respiratory irregularity than did the uninstructed subjects, but the changes in heart rate and skin resistance were virtually the same for all of these groups. If these physiological changes are related to pain, the results appeared to indicate that hypnotic and waking suggestions had an effect on pain for muscle potential and respiration, but not for skin resistance and heart rate. However, Barber and Hahn note that the two measures that appeared to relate an analgesic effect, the respiration and muscle potential, are more responsive to *voluntary control* than the other two measures. Thus the result could fairly easily be explicable in terms of the subjects voluntarily inhibiting the physiological reactions to the pain in order to comply with what was expected of them. Unfortunately, the other two measures could not be so readily controlled, and possibly 'gave the game away'.

As mentioned earlier, Hilgard and his associates have singled out blood pressure as one of the more reliable physiological correlates of pain, so it might seem impressive if subjects given suggestions for hypnotic analgesia would show little or no increase in blood pressure. In an attempt to determine whether this was the case, Lenox (1970) exposed eight selected highly susceptible subjects to ischemic pain under both waking relaxation and hypnotic analgesia conditions. The results indicated that in the waking relaxation condition the blood pressure and reports of pain increased with time, whereas during the analgesic condition six of the seven subjects reported *no pain at all*, and the other one only reported a scale score of 1 (on a scale from 0 to 10). Data on blood pressure showed that on average it was considerably less in the hypnotic analgesia condition than in the waking condition. Although these results first appear to be quite impressive this study suffers from a number of very serious methodological flaws. Firstly, in the waking relaxation condition the subjects were not given any suggestions for analgesia. If, as Barber and his associates propose, waking suggestions for analgesia can exert a genuine effect over and above compliance, then this was a crucial omission. However, the second and most significant flaw was that for each subject the waking relaxation condition occurred on day 1, and the hypnotic analgesia condition followed on day 2. The effect was thus contaminated by *order*, and as Bowers (1976) points out, 'the subjects had a good deal of practice on the ischemic task between the waking and the hypnotic analgesic test sessions. This last is not made entirely clear in Lenox's published account. Consequently, the impressive absence of blood pressure increases during the second (hypnotic) test session may be due as much to subjects' interim practice as to suggestions for analgesia per se' (p.33). The problem is exaggerated by the fact that physiological reactions to painful stimulation generally show an habituation or adaptation effect, and thus decrease over time (Barber, 1963). As a further criticism Knox, Morgan and Hilgard (1974) have pointed out that in the study by Lenox the non-hypnotic stress was continued until the subjects were actually writhing in pain, whereas they did not writhe during hypnotic anaesthesia, and they suggest that during the waking treatment 'much of the rise in blood pressure may have been secondary to semivoluntary expression of pain response' (p.846). Hilgard (1975) has also commented in respect of Lenox's study that 'Attempts to replicate his results in the same laboratory (unpublished) have met with only partial success' (p.30).

A number of other studies could be interpreted as supporting the hypothesis that hypnotic subjects distort their verbal reports of pain in order to appear in less pain than they really are. For instance, Hilgard (1969b) has reported that whilst hypnotic suggestions for analgesia result in a decrease of verbally reported pain, blood pressure may slightly *increase* with hypnotic suggestions; the blood pressure of subjects exposed to cold-pressor pain being *higher* in the hypnotic analgesic condition than in the waking condition! Not only is the blood pressure higher under hypnotic analgesia, but it starts to rise more for the high susceptibility subjects even *before* the hands are placed in the water, a finding confirmed by Hilgard, Macdonald, Marshall and Morgan (1974). Although these findings seem somewhat troublesome for those arguing for the 'genuine' nature of experimentally induced hypnotic anagesia, perhaps the results can be interpreted in terms of compliance along the following lines. Whereas in the waking or non-analgesic conditions the subjects might be a little worried about what is to happen, no conflict is evident; however, the compliant subjects in the analgesic condition are not only worried about the pain they will surely have to endure, but also that they have to tell lies about how much pain they are feeling. The problems of trying to discern what to say, and the conflict between succumbing to social pressures or 'telling the truth' may be sufficient to provoke anxiety, with a resulting rise in blood pressure, and possibly, as anxiety is increased, a *greater* 'real' perception of pain, than in the non-analgesic conditions. The possibility therefore exists that, at least in some experimental studies of hypnotic analgesia, some hypnotic subjects may actually be feeling *more* pain, due to the stress of trying to comply, though they may give inaccurate verbal reports to the contrary. In fact the experimental evidence for any unique hypnotic analgesic effect seems scarce indeed. A study by Saletu, Saletu, Brown, Stern, Sletten and Ulett (1975) purported to demonstrate that electric shock pain was reduced following hypnotic suggestions for analgesia, and that the amount of pain reduction correlated with the 'depth of hypnosis' and EEG changes recorded before the actual shock stimulation. However, these results too seem somewhat problematical in view of the following features: a) the report of the study does not indicate whether it was a double-blind trial; b) there were no control groups given waking suggestions for relaxation and analgesia; c) in the same experiment morphine produced no significant EEG changes, and ketamine (another analgesic drug) produced EEG changes in the *opposite direction* to those produced by hypnotic suggestions; d) even the EEG changes produced by hypnotic induction disappeared during the actual session of shock stimulation; and e) there may be some doubt as to how relevant in general this study was to our understanding of the nature of the analgesia as we are told, 'the stimuli were not really painful' (p.219) in the first place. Other studies by Shor (1962b) and Sutcliffe (1961) have failed to show any differences in the physiological responses of subjects given painful stimulation with and without suggestions of analgesia. Shor concluded that his data offered no support for the hypothesis that 'hypnotic analgesia has special effects on physiological responses to painful stimuli that are beyond the bounds of waking volitional control'. This finding is now supported by further work by Hilgard and his associates who conclude, 'The bulk of experimental evidence suggests that whereas hypnotically analgesic subjects report much less pain than in normal waking, and occasionally none at all, the cardiovascular concomitants of pain response continue as usual' (Hilgard, Morgan and Macdonald, 1975, p.280). This conclusion appears to apply when other measures besides blood pressure are used, such as heart rate (Hilgard, Morgan, Lange, Lenox, Macdonald, Marshall and Sachs, 1974).

So far these experiments on hypnotic analgesia have only been considered from the point of view of compliance, and the possibility does remain that with the experimental induction of pain at least, suggestions that relax the subject, reduce anxiety, and distract him may reduce pain. However, as we have seen, although these factors might be important in clinical pain, other than verbal reports, there is little conclusive evidence so far that they are effective in the reduction of experimental pain.

It might help if one could actually demonstrate that there were something 'different' about the verbal reports of hypnotic analgesic subjects, or if they overtly behaved in a different way. However, evidence from the study by Hilgard, Macdonald, Morgan and Johnson (1978) shows that in response to cold-pressor pain, simulators 'were remarkably successful in predicting and imitating the responses of highly hypnotisable subjects except for a tendency to overreact and exaggerate compliance with suggestions' (p.239); as mentioned before, one would expect the simulators, who were selected because they were insusceptible, to display the over-play effect. The only difference emerged when 'honesty reports' were demanded. Predictably the high susceptibility 'real' subjects continued to say they felt little pain when exposed to hypnotic suggestions for analgesia, whereas the simulators said the pain was as 'normal'. The problems of 'honesty reports' have already been discussed in Chapter 3, and these results are thus what would be expected if the 'real' subjects were complying. Whereas it would present no conflict for the simulator to tell the truth and to say he really felt the pain, even with demands for honesty, the 'real' subject is in a totally different situation and like those cases discussed in Chapter 3 the onus is on him to maintain his original statement, even if false.

An interesting finding in this study by Hilgard et al. (1978) was that although in this instance waking suggestions for analgesia were given, both the 'real' subjects and the simulators verbally reported less pain in the hypnotic analgesia than in the 'waking' condition. This is a rather different result from those cited earlier which indicated that waking suggestions for analgesia were as effective as hypnotic suggestions (Barber, 1969a; Spanos, Barber and Lang, 1974; Evans and Paul, 1970). However, the latter studies all used the independent-groups design, i.e. waking suggestions were given to one group of subjects, whilst hypnotic suggestions were given to another *different* group of subjects. As discussed previously the independent-groups design helps to minimise the problem of subjects distorting their performance to look 'better' when 'hypnotised'. In contrast, Hilgard et al. (1978) used the same-subjects design, with all subjects participating in *both* a hypnotic session and a waking session, with the result that the 'real' subjects could have biased their response to 'look better' in the hypnotic condition.

HYPNOTIC ANALGESIA AS DISSOCIATION

Although the discrepancy between verbal and physiological indices of the effectiveness of hypnosis is far more 'puzzling' if compliance is ruled out as a significant contributing factor, Hilgard and his associates have provided an intriguing alternative explanation in terms of 'dissociation', (Hilgard, 1973a). According to 'neo-dissociation' theory as Hilgard has termed it, under hypnosis, cognitive systems may become dissociated. Thus at one level a person may not be aware of pain, but at another cognitive level, that the first level is unaware of, the pain may be experienced. The way Hilgard and his associates have attempted to get at these different systems is by 'automatic' talking and writing. The basic procedure involves firstly submitting subjects to hypnotic induction. The awareness of the subject after this induction then represents the manifestation of one hypnotic cognitive level; however, whilst he is in the 'hypnotic state' the subject is told that the hypnotist will be able to talk to another part of the subject, of which the 'hypnotised' subject is not normally aware. The idea is probably best illustrated by giving some of the instructions that have been used. After the induction the subjects are told,

> When I place my hand on your shoulder, I shall be able to talk to a hidden part of you that knows things are going on in your body, things that are unknown to the part of you to which I am now talking. The part to which I am now talking will not know what you are telling me or even that you are talking. . . . You will remember that there is a part of you that knows many things that are going on that may be hidden from either your normal consciousness or the hypnotised part of you. After you are out of hypnosis, I shall say: 'Now you can remember everything about the hidden part of yourself, what you said when I had my hand on your shoulder and how you felt during the experiment when the events we talked about where taking place' (Knox, Morgan and Hilgard, 1974, p.842).

When subjects who had been instructed in this way were given hypnotic suggestions for analgesia and subjected to ischemic and cold-pressor pain, the results were rather fascinating. Whilst the 'ordinary' verbal reports during the hypnosis session showed characteristically little evidence of pain, the reports of the 'hidden part' or 'hidden observer' as it has been termed, which were evoked when the hypnotist put his hand on the subject's shoulder, revealed that the 'hidden observer' was feeling substantially more pain. In fact, when ischemic pain was considered the amount of pain experienced by the 'hidden observer' was little different from that experienced in a normal waking condition (Knox, Morgan and Hilgard, 1974; Hilgard, Morgan and Macdonald, 1975). When cold-pressor pain was used, although the 'hidden-observer' reported more pain than the subject in 'ordinary' hypnotic analgesia, the 'hidden-observer's' pain was reported as somewhat less than that experienced in a normal waking condition; however, Hilgard et al. conclude that this latter finding was 'not unreasonable in view of the quiescence of the hypnotised subject' (p.284). Presumably, this refers to the fact that because the subject was still and relaxed he might have been expected to report less pain anyway.

This overall result seems similar to that found by Kaplan (1960). Kaplan gives a report of a twenty-year-old student who performed 'automatic writing' whilst 'hypnotised'. In Kaplan's words the subject's right hand was able to 'write anything it wanted to, not subject to the control or restrictions of "conscious personality" ' (p.567). When hypnotic analgesia was suggested for the subject's left hand the subject appeared to feel no pain when subjected to pin-pricks; however, as soon as the pin-pricks were administered the subject's right hand began to write, 'Ouch, damn it, you're hurting me' (p.568).

Whilst these findings are indeed fascinating, one must surely seriously consider the possibility that rather than providing an explanation of the discrepancy between verbal and physiological indicators of pain during hypnotic analgesia, they attest quite forcefully for the role of compliance in experimental studies of hypnotic analgesia. Let us once again try and see the situation as it might be viewed by a compliant subject. The subject arrives at the laboratory and is submitted to hypnotic induction. He is then told that when the hypnotist touches his shoulder he will speak on behalf of that part of him that is hidden from the 'hypnotised' part. He immerses his hand in the water, and it gradually gets more painful, but he dutifully says he feels nothing, or very little. Now, by pretending that he can speak through a 'hidden observer' hidden from the hypnotised part, he can quite legitimately say what he *really* feels . . . it hurts like mad! In fact some of the reports given by the subjects after the experiment are most revealing, for instance, they include statements like (my emphasis in all cases), 'the hidden observer is more aware and *reported honestly* what was there', 'the hidden observer is *like the way things really are*', 'When the hidden observer was called up, the hypnotised part had to step back for a minute and let the hidden part *tell the truth*' (Knox et al. 1974, pp.845–6), 'I'm not sure if the hypnotised part may have known it was there but *didn't say it'* (Hilgard, Morgan, and Macdonald, 1975, p.286). To those sceptical of how 'hidden' the 'hidden observer' is, these comments look suspiciously like the attempts of some subjects to appease their consciences and tell the truth; they lied when they said they felt little or no pain.

It remains to be decided whether we see the 'hidden observer' as a genuine phenomenon, or whether we view the whole business as a rather elaborate game that some subjects feel obliged to play in order to give the hypnotist what he wants. Perhaps at our present stage of knowledge, genuine automatic talking, out of awareness, under hypnosis, could be viewed as no more likely on a priori grounds than an explanation of these results in terms of voluntary compliance on behalf of the subjects. It should perhaps be reiterated that an important feature of compliance put forward in this book is that it may not be all-or-none. These same subjects might feel genuinely that they are 'hypnotised', and maybe some of them can genuinely experience some hypnotic scale items, but this cannot be used as an argument that ipso facto their analgesia reports are genuine, or that all these subjects really can 'dissociate' the 'hypnotised' part from the hidden part so that neither is aware of the other.

Other studies have attempted to investigate the validity of dissociation in hypnosis in other contexts than analgesia and it may be useful to digress for a moment to consider some of these. One of the most interesting was conducted by Stevenson (1976) and concerned the effects of hypnotic dissociation on interfering tasks. Under normal circumstances if a subject performs two tasks at once it is often the case that the tasks interfere, so each is done less well than if the tasks had been done one at a time. According to the dissociation theory of those such as Prince (1929) and Janet (1920) if the two tasks can be dissociated under 'hypnosis', then the interference between the tasks should be significantly less than it would be if both tasks were performed in the waking state. Stevenson's method involved submitting subjects to a hypnotic induction procedure followed by the post-hypnotic suggestion that when they 'awoke' on the hypnotist's signal their writing hand would perform a task without them being aware of it. In order to achieve this the writing hand of each subject was placed inside a box and concealed from the subject's view. Subjects were also given the amnesia suggestion that they would not remember any of the suggestions, or even remember that they had been 'hypnotised'. The hypnotist's signal was quite specific; it was the word 'begin'. Thus if the experimenter used any other word, such as 'start', they would be aware that the hand was writing. Thus two conditions were created; in both when the subject 'awoke', he could not remember he had been 'hypnotised', but in the first, when the hypnotist said 'begin' the subject's writing hand would write away inside the box, automatically or 'subconsciously', unknown to the subject. However, for the second condition, when the hypnotist said 'start' the subject would be aware that he was performing a task with his writing hand.

This methodology enabled subjects to perform two tasks at the same time, for whilst they were writing they were also required, quite consciously, to perform a colour naming task. Thus, whilst they were performing the colour naming, the 'hand' could perform another task either consciously (when the hypnotist said 'start') or subconsciously (when the hypnotist said 'begin'). The design was complicated a little more by the fact than the writing hand performed two arithmetic tasks, an 'easy' task (counting) and a difficult task (addition). To summarise, after hypnosis, the subjects performed: 1. colour naming with a 'subconscious' easy task; 2. colour naming with a conscious easy task; 3. colour naming with a 'subconscious' difficult task; and 4. colour naming with a conscious difficult task. The subjects were selected high hypnotic susceptibility subjects, and low susceptibility simulators given the standard simulators' instructions to 'fool' the hypnotist.

According to the theory proposed by Janet and Prince, the colour naming task should interfere with the conscious arithmetic task performed 'in the box', but should interfere less or not at all with the arithmetic task performed inside the box 'subconsciously', i.e. the arithmetic tasks should be performed 'better' when they are 'subconscious' rather than conscious. The results showed no significant differences between the subconscious and conscious conditions for the 'easy' task for either the hypnotically susceptible subjects or the simulators. However, for the difficult task, the hypnotically susceptible subjects showed *more* interference when the task was performed 'subconsciously' than when it was performed consciously, i.e. the subconscious task was performed *worse*. Although the simulators too did slightly worse when the task was 'subconscious', the difference was not significant for them.

The first point to consider is how the differences between the hypnotically susceptible subjects and the simulators can be accounted for. The instructions may be the crucial factor as the simulators were given specific instructions beforehand as well as the normal simulating instructions, and these included the instruction that, even though simulating, 'It is important that you do not "hold back" at any time and that you do your best on each task'. Now this instruction would completely overrule any contrary preconception a simulator might have as to whether a 'real' subject would perform the task better or worse in the subconscious condition. Unlike in the usual instructions given to simulators, the simulators in Stevenson's experiment were told *how* they 'ought' to behave, in fact they were specifically told to do their best on all tasks. Although similar instructions were given to the hypnotic subjects, they would probably carry completely different connotations. An analogous situation might be if a simulator were instructed by 'A' as follows: 'I want you to fool 'B' you are hypnotised, but when he sticks pins in you, *tell the truth* if it hurts, O.K.?' Clearly, the simulator is disobeying this command and upsetting both 'A' and 'B' if he says it does not hurt, when it does. Now if the 'real' subject is told, 'When 'B' hypnotises you, and sticks pins in you, *tell the truth* if it hurts, O.K.', this 'real' subject is in the compliant subject's usual position of conflict; if he *does* tell the truth and says it hurts, he has ruined the experiment for both 'A' and 'B'. The crucial difference between the interpretation of an instruction to 'do your best' for 'real' subjects and simulators, is that for simulators it is a *direct command*, an explicit statement as to how to behave. However, to say to the 'real' subject, 'do your best' is really little more than a request for honesty, and as we have seen in Chapter 3 requests for honesty are not always effective in situations where they are overruled by the implicit requirements of the experimental situation. It is interesting to note that it looks as if simulators did exactly what they were told, overall they were better at the addition task than the real subjects in both the conscious or unconscious conditions. It is thus difficult to know what to make of these findings. Whilst it would have been impressive if the hypnotic subjects had shown little or no interference when the task was performed subconsciously, the fact that they performed *worse* does not seem half so dramatic somehow. Stevenson argues that the finding supports an alternative conception of dissociation theory; that cognitive effort is involved in trying to keep the task out of awareness, and thus this effort diverts attention away from the task. However, this interpretation can be viewed in two ways; one could say that this cognitive effort or attention goes on 'unconsciously' or automatically, or that it involves conscious deliberate efforts on the part of the subject to try not to think about the task. It has been argued a number of times in this book that hypnotic phenomena, if they are to be of any unique significance, should be 'automatic'. As Bowers (1976) says, 'effortful, actively directed attention seems to be precisely what the high-susceptible subjects do *not* engage in. Rather, they typically experience their attention as *effortless*, almost as if the hypnotist were doing their concentration for them' (p.138, his emphasis). Bowers cites Weitzenhoffer and Sjoberg (1961) in support of this proposal. However, if you consciously and deliberately try *not* to think about your writing hand doing a difficult task, it should not be surprising if you did the task rather badly, but there would hardly be anything of devastating significance in this discovery. If the cognitive effort was perceived as 'automatic' and not under voluntary control, it would indeed be an important finding.

Unfortunately, there is little in any of the studies of hypnotic 'dissociation' discussed so far that enables us to conclude that they are not explicable in terms of compliance or voluntary cognitive strategies. At this stage, one is left with a decision of parsimony; it has been proposed that a person can be 'hypnotised' and then be unaware that it has happened, and then whilst wide awake, be oblivious to the fact that his writing hand is performing a task, and that it writes 'unconsciously' when the experimenter says 'begin' but not when he says 'start'. Also, it has been proposed that a person can be submitted to an induction procedure, and when the experimenter holds the person's shoulder, he can talk 'automatically', and the next minute when the hand is released, be unaware he has been talking. These proposals, if valid, are very important, but I feel there is a fairly strong argument at present to suggest that parsimony may equally be on the side of an explanation in terms of behavioural compliance, i.e. subjects may feel obliged to give an overt display of these behaviours in response to the social demands of the experimental situation.

There are other problems with these dissociation studies. For instance, none of the studies discussed so far used a waking suggestion condition to see whether hypnotic induction was necessary to evoke the effects, and equally important, none of the 'hidden observer' pain studies used independent groups of waking controls of simulators to establish independent base-line levels and to assess the possible influence of demand characteristics. However, these comments seem secondary to the main problem of whether there is sufficient evidence to make dissociation a viable explanation of the discrepancies between verbal and physiological indicators in experimental studies on hypnotic analgesia. Certainly there are examples of such discrepancies from outside the experimental sphere. For instance, in 1846, when a dentist named Wells attempted to demonstrate the anaesthetic properties of nitrous oxide his patient groaned (Bowers, 1976). Similarly, Bowers and van der Meulen (reported by Bowers, 1976) found that heart rate increased and skin resistance changed during dental surgery, even when the patient had been given a chemical anaesthetic. Bowers (1976) has suggested these responses may have occurred because of the 'rather ominous sound of the drill' (p.27) which could also have affected these physiological changes. Such cases point to the fact that there are exceptions, and there is not a one-to-one relationship between pain and physiological indices such as heart rate and blood pressure; other factors besides pain can affect these responses. However, anecdotal reports of patients moaning or moving during chemical anaesthesia are often as difficult to interpret as patients showing behavioural signs of pain during hypnotic anaesthesia. For instance, unless precise details are recorded there may be no guarantee that some patients do not actually feel pain even after the administration of chemical analgesics. The simple administration of an analgesic drug does not guarantee that any particular individual will not experience a painful stimulus. Individuals may respond differentially to the same drug, some requiring higher dosages, and it is thus quite possible that Wells' subject moaned because he was actually in pain. Like any drug, analgesic drugs are not effective unless a sufficient dosage is given in a particular case. All drugs have a pharmacokinetic profile (Goodman and Gilman, 1970) which basically means they 'wear on and off'. A patient may thus show signs of pain because the drug is 'wearing off'. The problem is made more complex by the fact that tolerance for the drug may develop, so that it is no longer as effective even when the same dose is given. Consequently, in surgery, a trained anaesthetist aware of the properties of drugs, does not just give a drug at a certain dosage and assume it will be effective;

the patient is carefully monitored and if he does show pronounced rises in respiration, sweating, blood pressure and heart rate, the anaesthetist does not content himself that, 'it's O.K. I've given him X dosage, so this must be dissociation'. Instead, he takes these indices as evidence that the drug is 'wearing off', and that more needs to be administered. Furthermore, if these physiological responses were accompanied by moaning or 'convulsions' and 'hideous expressions of suppressed agony', the patient's condition would indeed be some cause for concern. Thus until more definitive evidence is available as to the validity of experimental hypnotic analgesia, it would appear rather dangerous to always assume that even if subjects and patients moan, groan, convulse and show dramatic increases in heart pressure and blood pressure, they feel nothing because they are 'hypnotised' and 'dissociated'. Under these circumstances it would seem that the subjects' testimony as to the amount of pain experienced must be given in a context that minimises the possibility of compliance. The possibility exists that, in the experimental situation at least, some experimenters may be unaware of the compliant subjects' real suffering.

HYPNOSIS AS A PLACEBO EFFECT

It has been argued that, at least in the clinical situation, the placebo effect may sometimes produce genuine reductions in the experience of pain intensity through factors such as the removal of anxiety and fear. It has also been suggested that if hypnotic analgesia does, in some cases, result in genuine reductions in pain it may also work to a large extent through its placebo component, i.e. because the subject 'believes' the procedure will reduce pain, a corresponding reduction in anxiety and fear may accrue. A most obvious comparison to make, therefore, would be one between the effectiveness of hypnotic analgesia and a placebo treatment. In an ingenious study McGlashan, Evans and Orne (1969) attempted to do this. As this study is frequently cited I have decided to discuss the procedure and results in some detail. However, the original paper is very complex, so even in the following analysis I will only mention what I consider the main findings and the associated problems. I will interpret the statistical results using the conventional criterion of accepting results as statistically significant when they achieve a probability level of <0.05; there are, in fact, a number of difficulties with the statistical interpretation in the original paper[1].

McGlashan et al. selected twelve highly hypnotically susceptible subjects, and twelve low susceptibility subjects and submitted them to ischemic pain. Ischemic pain was estimated by two measures, the amount of time spent pumping a rubber bulb, and the amount of water displaced by the bulb following the application of the tourniquet. The amount of water displaced was the critical measure, as this determined how much work was done by the subject when squeezing the bulb, (i.e. the force applied to the bulb). In the usual way, it was assumed that if a subject could apply more force to the bulb for longer, he must be experiencing less pain; for only be experiencing analgesia would he be able to perform a task that normally would be very painful. The high susceptibility subjects were tested under two conditions, one with hypnotic suggestions for analgesia, and one where they were given a placebo pill which they were told was an effective analgesic drug. The low susceptibility subjects were also given the placebo pill in one condition, but in the other condition they were spuriously led to believe that they could actually respond well to hypnotic suggestions for analgesia. This interesting variation was taken from an experimental design by London and Fuhrer (1961) and attempted to make an assessment of the placebo component in hypnotic suggestions, i.e. although it was assumed that these low susceptibility subjects would not really be 'hypnotised', they might nevertheless believe that the suggestions would be effective. An alternative view could be to call the suggestions given to the insusceptible subjects 'waking' suggestions. The administration of hypnotic suggestions to *low* susceptibility subjects thus was seen as constituting a placebo treatment. In effect, then, there were two placebo conditions, a pill, and a treatment involving the administration of suggestions to low susceptibility subjects.

The results showed that in the placebo pill condition, although both high and low susceptibility subjects pumped for longer and displaced more water than in an initial base-line control condition, the placebo pill was equally effective for both sets of subjects. In the treatment using hypnotic suggestions, although the hypnotically susceptible subjects pumped more water longer before they first *said* they felt any pain (i.e. their report of pain *threshold* was apparently higher), they could not increase their pain tolerance (i.e. the point at which it became unbearable) beyond that achieved by the low susceptibility subjects. Thus, according to McGlashan et al., 'The total work scores demonstrate that both groups pumped to the point of maximum endurance and displaced an equivalent amount of water' (p.238). In fact there was a slight non-significant tendency for the high susceptibility to do slightly *worse* than the low susceptibility subjects on this tolerance measure.

The table of overall statistical results (McGlashan et al., p.237) reveals that in terms of the amount of water pumped the hypnotic suggestions were more effective than the placebo pill overall, but this effect was not significantly different for the high and low susceptibility groups. In sum, there was a general tendency for the hypnotic suggestions to be more effective than the placebo pill in increasing pain tolerance as measured by the amount of water pumped; however, on the tolerance measures hypnotic suggestions given to the high susceptibility subjects were no more effective than the same suggestions given to the low susceptibility subjects. The overall finding that the suggestions were more effective than the pill could have been confounded by the fact that a same-subjects design was used to compare the placebo pill and suggestions treatments. Thus, in spite of a statement extolling the virtues of the pill, subjects may have still interpreted the situation as one in which they were 'supposed' to do a little better with the suggestions than the pill. Alternatively, or additionally, the induction procedure and suggestions may have been more effective in relaxing the subject and keeping his mind off the pain (by attending to the thought that the arm is 'numb') than the placebo pill. In fact, subjects were told that only half of them would receive the real drug, and some recognised the capsules and had to be given a false cover story that 'as the drug was still experimental and not available for commercial distribution, it had been packed in Darvon capsules for convenience' (p.234). Such factors could have limited the placebo impact of the pill.

It is difficult to know what other factors, besides the effectiveness of the suggestions, could have accounted for why both the high and low susceptibility groups managed to pump more water in the experimental conditions than they did in the pre-experimental base-line assessment. It could have partly been compliance as they knew they were expected to do better with the pill and the suggestions; for example, they were told, 'I am sure you won't experience anything near the amount of discomfort you experienced last time' (p.234); it could also have been adaptation and practice as the experimental trials (suggestions and pill) *always followed* the base-line estimates; or it could have been a combination of factors. These problems make it difficult to determine the extent to which the hypnotic suggestion and placebo pill treatments were comparable. The placebo pill was always given in the *last* session. It is therefore possible, for example, that subjects gained experience from the first base-line session, gave their 'all' in the second session, but were unable to keep it up in the third session. An interaction of factors such as adaptation and fatigue could have confounded the results as the experimental results did not balance for *order* effects.

On the basis of the results presented by McGlashan et al. the only result which seemed to clearly favour the high susceptibility group was that they appeared to pump more water for longer before they first *said* they felt signs of pain. There thus seems to be a discrepancy between this threshold measure, and their ability to tolerate pain (to reiterate, the susceptible subjects were *not* able to tolerate maximum pain better than the insusceptible subjects according to the tolerance measures). There is thus no definitive evidence to suggest that the threshold differences reflected anything more than greater compliance (i.e. biased reporting) on behalf of the high susceptibility subjects, for when it came to tolerance as measured by their maximum capacity to pump the bulb (i.e. a *non-verbal* measure) they were no better than the 'unhypnotised' subjects. The problem of interpreting this result is exacerbated by the fact that the subjects were selected from the upper and lower 5 per cent of scorers on various measures of hypnotic susceptibility, and thus the results could have been confounded by population differences in the two groups to be compared. This may be a salient criticism since the two groups of subjects did actually differ in their *baseline* pain estimates, and although McGlashan et al. attempted to correct for this factor in their subsequent analyses, they nevertheless admit the possibility that the two groups of subjects could have been using a different criterion of *threshold* even before the experimental treatments were administered (p.235). The situation is made rather more complicated by the fact that there seemed to be a tendency for the high susceptibility subjects to employ a different pumping strategy in the hypnotic treatment to the one they employed in the placebo pill treatment; this involved squeezing the bulb *more* often and thus for a longer time, but *less* hard in the hypnotic treatment. The low susceptibility subjects did not display this anomalous change of tactics between the two treatments.

Thus the results of McGlashan et al.'s study seem somewhat complex and equivocal. Although the suggestions were apparently more effective than the placebo pill, the result was confounded by problems of the same-subjects design, order effects and population differences. Also, significantly, if hypnotic suggestions given to low susceptibility subjects do, in fact, constitute a placebo treatment, then there is no conclusive evidence, on the basis of this study, that hypnotic suggestions are more effective in inducing analgesia than a placebo treatment of this kind; or an alternative conceptualisation could be that if hypnotic suggestions are genuinely effective, the effective agent is the placebo component in the suggestions rather than some unique 'hypnotic' element.

HYPNOSIS, ACUPUNCTURE AND ENDORPHINS

Another source of considerable debate in the field of pain has been acupuncture. This ancient Chinese method of therapy involves the insertion of thin needles into specific areas of the body, and it has been used more recently as an anaesthetic in surgery. In a number of reviews, Barber, Chaves and their associates have noted similarities between some of the processes which may be effective in producing acupuncture analgesia and those which may be responsible for hypnotic analgesia, for example, preoperative preparation, the reduction of anxiety and fear, confounding with chemical analgesics, and distraction (Barber, 1973; Chaves, 1972; Chaves and Barber, 1973; Barber, Spanos and Chaves, 1974). Although some reports have suggested that hypnotically susceptible subjects may benefit more from acupuncture analgesia than hypnotically insusceptible subjects, more recent results have been less conclusive (Knox, Shum and McLaughlin, 1978; Ulett, 1978). Knox et al. (1978) remark, 'the relationship between hypnotic susceptibility and response to acupuncture is, at best, weak' (p.107). However, more evidence has recently come to light suggesting that acupuncture does evoke a specific analgesic effect over and above the other non-specific suggestion effects (Stewart, Thomson and Oswald, 1977). This was a carefully executed, balanced, double-blind trial, unlike so many of the experiments conducted on hypnotic analgesia. Furthermore, a mechanism has been proposed to account for the specific analgesic effect of acupuncture. It has been suggested that stimulation by the needles results in the release of naturally occurring substances in the brain called 'endorphins' (Sjolund and Eriksen, 1976; Pomeranz and Chiu, 1976), which produce an analgesic effect.

'Endorphins' refer to the family of endogenous opioids whose actions resemble opiate alkaloids such as morphine and heroin (Hughes, 1975; Simon, 1976; Goldstein, 1976; Barchas, Akil, Elliott, Holman and Watson, 1978). Much impetus for the work on endorphins originated from the discovery of opioid receptors in the mammalian nervous system and the finding that electrical stimulation in the periaqueductal gray and other mesencephalic and diencephalic sites in the brain produced analgesia. The latter finding was significant in that these areas of the brain are where high densities of opiate receptors are to be found (Goldstein and Hilgard, 1975). Similarities were then found between the effects of morphine administration and analgesia induced by electrical stimulation of the brain, including the ability of naloxone (a specific opiate antagonist) to block both effects (Barchas et al., 1978). Consequently, the presence of endorphins has been inferred from the results of the administration of naloxone, i.e. if naloxone reverses the effects of a procedure it may be assumed that the procedure has been responsible for the release of endorphins. Support for the theory that acupuncture analgesia may be mediated by the release of endorphins comes from the finding that injections of naloxone counter the analgesic effect of acupuncture (Sjolund and Eriksen, 1976; Pomeranz and Chiu, 1976). It thus seems that acupuncture analgesia may at least partially result from the release of these endorphins. However, results are not conclusive at present, as some investigators have reported acupuncture analgesia, and analgesia induced by electrical stimulation of the brain is not completely abolished by naloxone. It has been suggested therefore that more than one pain-inhibiting pathway may exist (Marx, 1977).

However, in view of the partial 'success' story with endorphins and acupuncture, it may be tempting to propose that a similar process could operate in hypnotic analgesia. In an attempt to determine whether hypnotic analgesia resembles opiate analgesia Goldstein and Hilgard (1975) subjected three high hypnotic susceptibility individuals to ischemic pain. All three subjects had previously claimed an ability to eliminate pain and suffering under hypnosis. Following suggestions for hypnotic analgesia, all three verbally reported no pain at all during ischemia. However, intravenous doses of naloxone (0.4 mg and 1.0 mg) failed to produce any effects on the subjects' reports during hypnotic analgesia, including the reports of the alleged dissociated 'hidden-observer'. Goldstein and Hilgard therefore report that in spite of receiving a dosage of naloxone 'well established as producing immediate block, the effects of heroin or morphine administered at high dosage. . . . Both the overt and covert reports of pain and distress with hypnotic analgesia were unchanged throughout.' (p.2042). Goldstein and Hilgard (1975) conclude: 'All the data agree in supporting the interpretation that naloxone is having no noticeable effect . . . the explanation of hypnotic analgesia must be found elsewhere' (p.2043). It is perhaps worth noting, however, that this finding is totally compatible with the hypothesis that reports of the absence of pain by hypnotic subjects in experimental situations may be severely biased by compliance. If subjects were faking an absence of pain (note that all three subjects overtly reported a *total absence of pain*), then one would hardly expect naloxone to reverse the effect in a blind trial.

More recently, the issue has become rather more complex as work involving clinical pain has implicated endorphins in placebo analgesia. It seems that naloxone may block placebo analgesia (Levine, Gordon and Fields, 1978). Levine et al. worked with patients suffering from postoperative dental pain. There placebo group was divided into responders and non-responders. The nine responders were those whose pain ratings remained constant or decreased compared with their rating five minutes before they took the placebos administered, whereas the fourteen placebo non-responders (n = 14) were those whose pain was greater one hour after placebo administration. Following the placebo administration subjects were given naloxone. It was hypothesised that if endorphin activity accounts, at least in part, for placebo analgesia, then the naloxone should result in an increase in pain ratings for the placebo responders. Levine et al. report that their results do support the hypothesis that endorphin activity accounts for placebo analgesia as naloxone caused a significantly greater increase in pain ratings in placebo responders than in non-responders, and prior administration of naloxone reduced the probability of a positive placebo response. Furthermore, the placebo non-responders had almost the same post operative pain levels as those receiving naloxone. A further study by Levine et al. (1978) replicated this result, but only when high doses of naloxone (10 mg) were employed.

Consequently, if indeed endorphins are involved in placebo analgesia, and if genuine hypnotic analgesia may occur through the operation of the placebo effect, it could be hypothesised that in conditions of high anxiety, such as clinical situations, naloxone may block hypnotic analgesia through its effect on the placebo component. It is notable, in this context, that Goldstein and Hilgard (1975) investigated *experimental* pain whereas Levine et al. (1978) worked on *clinical* pain, and as stated earlier, placebo action may be less in experimental pain due to the reduced level of anxiety. Indeed, Levine et al. (1978) themselves note that naloxone did not affect pain reports in their previous experimental situations and suggest, 'Perhaps the prolonged duration of the pain or the added stress of the clinical situation accounts for this difference' (p.657). A study by Frid and Singer (1979) appears to support the proposal that in a stressful situation naloxone may indeed block hypnotic analgesia. Frid and Singer employed ten hypnotically susceptible subjects and subjected them to ischemic pain by the tourniquet method. Following suggestions for hypnotic analgesia some subjects were allocated to a stress condition which involved performing a competitive memory task, whilst others were not stressed but were given instructions to relax and imagine a pleasant scene. Finally, subjects were given either naloxone or a placebo. The results indicated that naloxone but not the placebo (administered double-blind) was successful in reversing the reports of analgesia evoked by hypnotic suggestions, but only for subjects in the stress condition. Unfortunately, Frid and Singer used no waking control groups to determine whether hypnotic induction was a necessary factor in producing reported analgesia. However, the results do seem to accord with the proposal that it is possible that genuine analgesia, mediated by endorphins, may occur in stressful situations following suggestions for hypnotic analgesia, due to the operation of the placebo effect.

Earlier in this chapter I mentioned the proposal by Gibson (1977) that a possible state of tonic immobility in humans could account for some early cases of apparent analgesia in patients undergoing surgery with hypnosis. Gibson's proposal would receive further credibility if it could be shown that apparent ability of tonic immobility to decrease sensitivity to pain could be reversed by naloxone. Carli (1978) has presented evidence that supports the proposal that a morphine-like mechanism is active during tonic immobility. Firstly, Carli notes the similarities between tonic immobility and the effects of morphine, for example, the depression of spinal reflexes, high voltage slow wave EEG, and the blocking of pain and immobility. Secondly, he reports that, in rabbits, the injection of naloxone significantly reduces the duration of tonic immobility. He concludes, 'it is suggested that a pain-suppressing mechanism is active during animal hypnosis, and that this mechanism exhibits effects similar to the analgesic mechanism of morphine' (p.75). Thus if, as Gibson (1977) proposes, it is reasonable to suggest that in the early days of hypnotic surgery a small number of patients may have been in a state of tonic immobility, then the research on animals supports the hypothesis that such patients may have experienced analgesia. In addition, Bloom, Segal, Ling and Guillemin (1976) found that the injection of one particular endorphin peptide, β endorphin, in rats, produced a prolonged muscular rigidity and immobility similar to a catatonic state, which could be counteracted by naloxone.

A number of investigators has suggested that work on endorphins may have implications for work in other clinical areas. For example, Bloom et al. (1976) have suggested that the state of immobility produced by a β endorphin injection may be akin to catatonic symptoms of mental illness. This proposal is interesting in the light of Gallup's (1975) remarks concerning the similarity of tonic immobility to symptoms of catatonic schizophrenia such as tremors, rigidity, waxy flexibility, no loss of consciousness, and the onset of the reaction being precipitated by emotional stress. However the work on endorphins in the clinical context is still in its infancy, and firm conclusions can only be drawn after more extensive research and replica-

tion on larger samples using double-blind procedures.

Although the work is very promising a number of important anomalies exist which certainly require clarification. For instance, much of the work using naloxone indicates that in order for endorphins to be released the organism needs to be *stressed* earlier; yet most of the work on humans reviewed earlier in this chapter suggests that maximum pain relief may be obtained if anxiety and stress are *reduced*. It may be the case, as I suggested earlier, that extremely high or extremely low levels of physiological arousal may accompany an insensitivity to pain.

However, there seems to be no evidence, at present, to suggest that hypnotic suggestions for analgesia have a special capacity to precipitate the release of endorphins.

CONCLUSION

McGlashan et al. have suggested that hypnotic suggestions may work partly through a process 'conceptualised as a distortion of perception *specifically* induced during deep hypnosis' (p.227, my emphasis). However, on the basis of the evidence reviewed in this chapter it appears there is no substantive case for saying that hypnotic suggestions for analgesia exert their effect through a unique hypnotic agent. In fact, the evidence suggests that not only is suggested analgesia possible in subjects who are not otherwise hypnotically susceptible, but proposed physiological correlates of hypnotic 'depth' such as cardiovascular and EEG changes are sometimes absent or even reversed during painful stimulation following hypnotic suggestions for analgesia. The issues are clearly complicated due to the discrepancies between results found in clinical and laboratory situations, failure to use double-blind trials, failures to use appropriate control groups, and possibly of most significance, failure to see the role of compliance in influencing verbal reports in some situations. Clearly, techniques that have been labelled 'hypnotic' have been remarkably successful in eliminating clinical pain in some cases, but their superiority over other psychological or non-pharmacological techniques seems somewhat more questionable.

Certainly there are again many questions left unanswered in this complex and puzzling area, particularly concerning the mechanisms by which psychological factors can effect pain, but perhaps the fact that pain can be controlled by factors such as relaxation, distraction, expectancy and generalised placebo effects is 'magic' enough, without postulating extra 'hypnotic' magic.

It is well known that hypnotic techniques have been applied in many other clinical contexts as well as pain removal, and it is to the more general clinical use of hypnosis that we now turn.

NOTES

1 There are three main difficulties concerning the original statistical interpretation. 1) The authors adopted the probability level of <0.10 as their criterion of statistical significance. 2) In some analyses they employed large batteries of non-parametric tests (the results of 116 of these tests are presented in Tables 4 and 5 alone). 3) Many of the tabled probability values are one-tailed. As this was not a replication study one might question whether there were sufficient a priori reasons for using such liberal criteria for significance. In some instances, using conventional two-tailed values, the authors were accepting a probability level of <0.20 as statistically significant, even when the results came from batteries of non-orthogonal tests. The extent of the problem is illustrated by reference to Table 5; using a conventional criterion of <0.05, two-tailed, only four of the results shown reach statistical significance, instead of fourteen as the authors claim.

9. Hypnotherapy

Apart from their use as an analgesic agent hypnotic suggestions have also been used clinically for symptom removal and the explorative and interpretive aims in psychotherapy and psychoanalysis. However, Frankel (1976) has commented that in spite of the availability of many clinical case reports praising the use of hypnosis, few include more than the therapist's clinical impression and unless systematic procedures are employed, it cannot necessarily be assumed that patients genuinely experience the suggested effects. As Frankel says 'He [the patient] may merely be very relaxed or be complying with what he considers to be the wishes of his therapist, and be doing so sincerely' (p.47). The central problem again concerns the extent to which it is necessary to infer any unique property of 'hypnosis' to account for any of the benefits of therapeutic techniques involving hypnotic induction.

SOME CONFOUNDING FACTORS

Hypnotic induction procedures employ techniques for relaxation, and as Frankel (1976) points out, relaxation alone may result in the alleviation of symptoms arising from general tension or localised spasm that occurs, for example, in asthma or hypertension. As an example Frankel cites the case of a thirty-nine-year-old man who had difficulty in controlling his bowel actions. Previous use of pharmacological relaxant and anti-diarrheal agents had been of little or no help, and the patient had refused psychotherapy. Although the patient was described as being of 'only average responsiveness . . . to the induction of hypnosis' he showed considerable improvement after instructions to place his hand on his abdomen to induce a sense of relaxation in order to dispel the urgent need for bowel movement. But as Frankel says, 'He would probably have responded to any relaxation technique, including religious meditation, had the circumstances and the interaction with his mentor been favourable, and in my opinion, regardless of whether he had been encouraged in calming and persuasively reassuring tones to enter "deep hypnosis" or merely "deep relaxation"' (p.49). Frankel has highlighted two important factors in this account. Firstly, hypnotic induction may exert its effect through perfectly 'normal' processes such as relaxation. Secondly, the characteristics of the therapist may be an essential element in the treatment regardless of whether hypnotic induction is being used; a warm, encouraging atmosphere and a confident and authoritative therapist can do wonders no matter what specific treatment is being used (Shapiro, 1973).

Whether hypnotic induction is a necessary antecedent to otherwise waking suggestions has been questioned on a number of occasions throughout this book, and it is certainly extremely difficult to determine whether hypnotic induction was necessary in most case reports and studies of hypnotic clinical treatments. Typical instances are cited by Bowers (1976). These include reports of the effective use of suggestions for the treatment of skin diseases (a patient might be told to *imagine* herself being sprayed by shimmering sunlit liquids to purify the skin), the control of bleeding (the patient is told to imagine his blood being 'turned off'), the treatment of migraine headaches (patients are told to visualise the arteries in their heads becoming smaller), and the control of asthma (patients are given suggestions for deep relaxation and confidence in their recovery). However, without control groups it is impossible to determine whether waking suggestions might not have been equally, if not more effective. In one study by Maher-Loughnan (1970) a hypnotic treatment for asthma involving suggestions for deep relaxation appeared to be effective in 59 per cent of patients, whereas relaxation alone was effective in only 43 per cent. However, the author also noted that 'with the introduction of autohypnosis there seemed to be no correlation between trance depth and clinical responses' (p.13). Thus although a hypnotic treatment appeared to be slightly more effective than a relaxation alone treatment, it is difficult to determine whether the subject's ability to respond to hypnotic induction was the crucial variable, rather than other factors such as the experimenter's greater enthusiasm with the hypnotic treatment and the confidence of the patients in its success. The importance of these 'non-specific' factors is also indicated in that some investigators have achieved equivalent success using contradictory suggestions. For instance, Clawson and Swade (1975) reported the successful treatment of warts using hypnotic suggestions to *restrict* blood supply, whereas Ewin (1974) reported equally dramatic results in the treatment of warts by giving hypnotic suggestions to *increase* blood supply. Such contradictions tempt one to speculate whether the actual ability to imagine the suggested effects had anything to do with recovery.

We must also not confuse the success of hypnotherapy with the success of 'any' therapy. A good example of this concerns the effects of various therapies on smoking. A recent study by Berkowitz, Ross-Townsend and Kohberger (1979) indicated a 25 per cent rate of abstinence from smoking in forty patients up to six months following a one hour hypnosis session, thus replicating a similar finding by Spiegel (1970). However, neither study employed a non-hypnotic control group. The inclusion of a control group is crucial in this kind of work, for as Rachman and Philips (1978) point our, distinct, but usually brief, reductions in cigarette consumption occur with almost *all* kinds of treatments.

Anti-smoking treatment clinics of various kinds tends to produce an immediate success rate of anything from 30 to 85 per cent but with few exceptions this is quickly followed by 'wholesale relapse'. Any treatment may motivate a subject to try to give up smoking simply because it is novel, or because he may 'believe' something has happened, or because those providing the treatment have given 'orders', or simply because the patient has to justify why he took time off to bother with the treatment in the first place. As mentioned previously, paying a hypnotist a sum of money may need justifying as well; if you really want to give up smoking, it would be rather a waste of money if you continued to smoke.

The efficacy of using novel techniques is known as the 'Hawthorne Effect', a term developed from an investigation of the Western Electric Company in the 1930s (Roethlisberger and Dickson, 1939). In this study the investigators were looking at the factors which might improve production. They found, for example, that by increasing the illumination, production went up. However, when they decreased the illumination, production continued to rise! Obviously the illumination was irrelevant, the main factor appeared to be that the attempts to change the working conditions introduced novelty and boosted morale. Further experiments on some, who were allocated a special work room, revealed that whilst increases in rest breaks, and free lunches, increased production, taking these privileges away also resulted in a continued rise in production. As Gibson (1977) says, 'If they had hypnotised the girls once a week (which no one thought of doing) then they might have come to the erroneous conclusion that it was the hypnosis that increased the working efficiency' (p.100). The Hawthorne Effect may exert similar effects in the clinical situation. To some patients 'hypnosis' may be seen as a novel procedure administered by an enthusiastic therapist, so much better than dreary old pills which may have long lost their own Hawthorne Effect. Possibly 'standing on one leg' therapy, or 'putting your fingers in your ears' therapy might be just as efficacious for some individuals.

COMPLIANCE AND CLINICAL EXPERIENCE

Throughout this book stress has been laid on the nature of compliance in hypnotic situations, in particular the pressures for compliance may result in the subject experiencing a degree of conflict and humiliation rather than joy at his ability to 'put one over' on the hypnotist. To some hypnotists in the clinical situation this possibility may conflict with their everyday experience in as much as some subjects may report that their feelings of relaxation following hypnotic induction are pleasant and anxiety-free. However, some of the evidence reviewed in this book indicates that perhaps we should not accept too readily the credence of such positive reports by subjects. This reservation seems well illustrated in a disturbing study by Shevrin (1972) who examined in detail the reports of female subjects following hypnotic procedures. Shevrin was struck by a notable inconsistency between subjects' verbal reports of feeling relaxed and pleasant, and their underlying attitudes as assessed by other more disguised techniques involving telling stories about figures on the 'hypnosis' card of a projective personality test (the TAT). He says, 'The stories were those of angry, disappointed, and frightened women. The pleasant goodbyes masked the injury these women felt they had suffered' (p.528). Shevrin suggests that by allowing his subjects to tell stories about the card, rather than relate their experiences directly to the hypnotist, they were able to relate features of their experiences which might otherwise have been 'too direct and guilt-provoking'. He comments, 'These women wished to convey in a way that could remain politely disguised that they were angered and disappointed by the hypnotic experience. They were as women scorned' (p.534). Althought this was not a systematic and formal study, it presents data which concord with some reports of the so-called 'hidden-observer' in the work of Hilgard and associates, discussed in Chapter 8, who reported that they really had felt pain when an indirect measure was used. Shevrin concludes that, 'Conflict and anxiety may generate an angry, disappointed reaction, which is neither beneficial for the subject nor for the future of research on hypnosis' (p.536). Of particular importance was the fact that these negative reports were given by subjects who were 'distinguished by the readiness and completeness with which they entered the hypnotic state . . . as a group, they were friendly, willing, and even dedicated' (p.529). Although these findings could be interpreted in a number of ways, for example, it could be proposed that their stories reflected unconscious or 'dissociated' feelings, it seems equally parsimonious to suggest that they could reflect admissions of the 'true' feelings of subjects following their humiliation at feeling pressured to comply.

The problem of compliance would seem particularly serious when the patient feels obliged to report recovery, or freedom from distress, when no or little recovery has occurred. Work on the hypnotic treatment of asthma seems to illustrate only too well the possibility of this unfortunate confounding effect. Although asthmatic attacks are certainly manifested in very physical symptoms, they can be influenced to a considerable extent by psychological factors. Indeed, quite specific psychological attitudes have been proposed as precursors to asthmatic symptoms (Grace and Graham, 1952); it is therefore not surprising that placebos can be effective in controlling asthma in certain patients. However, when the effects of hypnotic suggestions on asthmatic patients are considered the results seem reliable and disturbing. In a typical study White (1961) investigated the effects of a number of hypnosis treatments over a four to eleven month period in ten patients. The sessions involved suggestions for easier breathing, lessening of tension and bronchospasm, and increase in self-confidence. Both physical and verbal measures were taken and the most striking finding was the disparity between the objective physical measures of improvement and verbal reports of improvement. Whereas respiratory functioning was objectively improved in 19 per cent of the sessions, verbal statements of improvement were reported in 58 per cent of the sessions. In another study Maher-Loughnan, MacDonald, Mason and Fry (1962) assigned fifty-five asthmatic patients at random to a hypnosis and a control treatment. Measures taken two to six months after the start of the study indicated that although the hypnotic group verbally reported a greater improvement than the control group, objective measures (spatum, vital capacity, blood oesinophil counts, forced expiratory volume and peak flow) failed to reveal significant changes in either group. Edwards (1960) also found that some asthmatic patients receiving hypnotic treatments reported improvement verbally, but failed to show improvement on tests of respiratory function. The disparity between the verbal and objective measures in these studies seems reminiscent of the disparity between verbal and physiological indicators of pain in many of the studies of hypnotic analgesia discussed in Chapter 8. However, in the case of asthma the proposal of some kind of dissociative mechanism would seem to be even more difficult to entertain (the situation of a patient being unaware that he is experiencing difficulty breathing might have frightening repercussions). The implication of such findings would seem clear; enthusiasm with hypnotic procedures and the premature proposal of dissociative mechanisms as alternatives to more simple explanations in terms of compliance, may not only be scientifically misleading, but may also result in the overlooking or even dismissal of genuine suffering and distress. Such an interpretation would indicate that it may be important not only for our knowledge of the genuine effects of techniques employing hypnotic induction, but also for a consideration of the feelings of patients that pressures for compliance should be minimised. I have suggested earlier that honesty demands may not be enough. However, anonymous reporting (where possible) and explicit statements from the experimenter allowing subjects to 'own up' might help towards the achievement of this end.

BUT IT WORKS, DOESN'T IT?

It cannot really be emphasised enough that claims for the effectiveness of clinical 'hypnosis' can only be accepted when correct clinical trials have been applied; no matter how dramatic the recovery it cannot be attributed to a unique factor of hypnosis until we can assess the effects of compliance, the equivalent success of waking suggestions, whether the patient would have got better anyway, etc., all of which require appropriate control groups. Unfortunately, these are hard to come by in most claims made for 'medical hypnosis' as it is sometimes called. These problems have been illustrated in the use of hypnotic techniques for the treatment of skin disorders mentioned in Chapter 7. The application of systematic clinical trials is particularly important as such procedures may enable us to ascertain not only *if* hypnotic techniques work, but also *how* they work if they do. It is perhaps unfortunate that many may have failed to see these two questions are related. The clinician's main responsibility is to successfully treat his patient, and he may feel that his main duty is to use a successful treatment, regardless of any knowledge as to how it achieves its effect. In this context it may seem justifiable to conclude that it does not really matter 'how' hypnotic techniques exert their effects, whether it be by compliance or the induction of a special trance, by non-specific therapist effects, relaxation, or whatever; if they 'work' then it makes sense to use them. However, this conclusion may not be as sensible as it first may seem. In order to justify the use of hypnotic procedures, one would need to decide whether such procedures are the best available for treating patients, and it is in relation to this that a knowledgw of 'how' the procedures 'work' may be of prime importance. Firstly, if compliance is an important element in hypnotic responsiveness then it may also confound our assessment of the effectiveness of the treatment. The patient may say 'it has worked' to please the therapist. The study by Mandy et al. (1952) mentioned in Chapter 8 indicates, for example, that patients may tell their clinicians that they have experienced little pain, yet give conflicting reports to other people. Unfortunately few attempts to examine the efficacy of clinical hypnotic procedures systematically consider this possibility. Secondly, if a particular hypnotic technique exerts its effect through the use of relaxation, or directed suggestions and instructions, we might well ask if the specific treatment would have been more effective if these procedures alone had been used without the rigmarole of hypnotic induction. Cautela (1975) has pointed out two fairly obvious disadvantages of using hypnotic techniques when other procedures may be just as effective, in that some patients will not cooperate when told that a hypnotic induction procedures is going to be used (Taylor, 1964), and some patients are not sufficiently hypnotically susceptible. Such factors may be particularly important in cases involving suggestions for pain relief, in that as there is clinical evidence to suggest that the ability to respond to suggestions for pain relief in the clinical situation is often unrelated to hypnotic susceptibility as determined by other criteria, it seems pointless employing hypnotic induction as all this may do is decrease the number of patients who may be able to obtain some relief by waking suggestions for relaxation, and distraction, etc.

In this context it is important to know what alternative treatments might be *most* effective. For instance, Anderson, Basker and Dalton (1975) have reported that a hypnotic relaxation treatment was more effective in the treatment of migraine headaches than Stemetil, a relaxant drug. However, they also point out that it is difficult to know to what extent the result may have been due to therapist bias, in that the therapist 'may be more enthusiastic about his favoured therapy, and may convey this enthusiasm consciously or unconsciously to his patients' (p.56). Furthermore, they point out that patients may have been encouraged by receiving something different from the usual mere prescribing of tablets (i.e. the Hawthrone Effect again). They conclude 'a further trial comparing hypnosis with some other therapy which did not confine itself to the ingestion of tablets would be desirable' (p.56).

This conclusion points to another very important issue in the assessment of hypnotherapeutic procedures. Whilst it may be found that hypnotherapy is more successful than a drug treatment, this cannot necessarily lead us to conclude that hypnotic induction is necessary or that this is the most desirable non-drug treatment. Perhaps similar waking suggestions might have been *more* effective, and would enable more sufferers to benefit; furthermore, other non-drug muscle-relaxant treatments, such as biofeedback, have also been used to successfully treat headaches, and other social factors such as disregarding complaints, increased attention and social rewards for healthy activities unrelated with headaches may also be important in the alleviation of this problem (Rachman and Philips, 1978); it would seem useful to compare the efficacy of these waking treatments with hypnotic treatments.

The significance of knowing 'how' hypnotic procedures exert their effects is well illustrated by examining the relationship between the hypnotic treatment of phobias and a standard non-hypnotic technique called 'systematic disensitisation'. Systematic desensitisation is a procedure used for the treatment of fears and phobias (Wolpe, 1958, 1969). It employs three steps. Firstly, the patient organises his fears hierarchically starting from those situations which produce only mild anxiety to those that produce high degrees of anxiety or panic. Thus if the patient is afraid of going out, then putting his coat on may be mildly anxiety arousing, whilst standing at the bus-stop might produce panic. The second step involves teaching the patient to relax whilst imagining the fear arousing situation, starting at the least fearful. The patient then works progressively down the hierarchy, passing to the next situation as he manages to relax whilst imagining the preceding one. Patients who manage to complete the desensitisation sequence, i.e. they are able to imagine the most fearful situation whilst remaining relaxed, often overcome their fears. Barber, Spanos and Chaves (1974) have pointed out how the use of hypnotic procedures for the treatment of fears and phobias may employ similar procedures. For example, as with hypnotic treatments, systematic desensitisation is of little value unless patients have positive attitudes and motivations towards the situation (Spanos and Barber, 1976) and 'are not strongly averse to the method' (Lazarus, 1971, p.95). Studies have indicated that desensitisation procedures are far more effective if the patients are specifically told that the procedure will help them overcome their fears (Leitenberg, Agras, Barlow and Oliveau, 1969; Miller, 1972; Oliveau, Agras, Leitenberg, Moore and Wright, 1969). Thus, as in the hypnotic situation, expectations and motivations play a key role. Secondly, hypnotic suggestions or instructions typically ask the subject to imagine various themes whilst remaining in a state of relaxation. Thus, if a patient has a fear of snakes, he may be given hypnotic suggestions for relaxation and then he told, 'Imagine you are standing at one end of a long corridor. At the other end of the corridor is a large, non-poisonous, black snake. Now imagine yourself taking a step down the corridor toward the snake' (Barber, Spanos and Chaves, 1974, p.143). Similar commonalities between the treatment of phobias by 'hypnosis' and systematic desensitisation have been pointed out by Cautela (1966). The possibility therefore exists that if patients report alleviation of fear and anxiety after hypnotic treatments, it may be these factors which are shared with systematic desensitation that account for the 'success' rather than some unique property of hypnosis. Now comes the comment, 'so what, who cares whether it works by the same principles, it still works!' Unfortunately, this comment ignores the issue of whether the patients would be better off with a waking desensitisation procedure, which would not need to be related to hypnotic susceptibility and would not provoke undue worry amongst certain anxious patients concerning the 'dangers' of falling into a 'trance' and might be more effective in sceptics. A controlled trial by Marks, Gelder and Edwards (1968) on phobic patients indicated that systematic desensitisation was *more* effective than a hypnotic-relaxation treatment, a result also found by Lang, Lazowick and Reynolds (1965), and Melnick and Russell (1976) found that systematic desensitisation was more effective than a directed-experience hypnotic treatment.

According to Cautela (1975) hypnotic procedures have also applied the principles of covert conditioning to modify behaviours such as phobias, alcoholism, overeating and sexual deviations. The main assumption underlying covert conditioning is that stimuli presented in imagination via instructions affect covert and overt behaviour in a manner similar to stimuli presented externally. Thus if, for example, an alcoholic patient is asked to imagine an unpleasant stimulus such as feeling sick when imagining taking a drink, subsequently whenever the subject takes a drink or wants to take a drink he will feel sick and this will put him off drinking. Also, if he imagines something pleasant after imagining a particular response, then the subsequent probability of him actually performing that response will increase. Cautela (1975) reports that these non-hypnotic procedures of covert sensitisation (punishment) and covert positive reinforcement (reward) have been successful in reducing maladaptive behaviours, and that similar techniques have been applied in hypnotherapy. For instance, hypnotic suggestions given to alcoholics typically instruct them to imagine having a hangover, feeling sick, or to imagine poison if they are about to take a drink. Another version of covert conditioning Cautela (1975) terms 'covert negative reinforcement'. Here the patient is asked to imagine a response which will help him avoid a noxious stimulus, thus an agoraphobic patient might be asked to imagine walking down the street to avoid a rat in his room. Again, Cautela suggests that similar procedures have been used in hypnotherapy; for example, Abraham treated a patient with hysterical paralysis of the legs using 'hypnosis'. He had his 'hypnotised' patient imagine sitting on a beach in uncomfortably cold water, and that he could only escape the cold water (noxious stimulation) by lifting his legs out of it.

Cautela (1975) suggests that hypnotherapists might benefit by the systematic use of these covert conditioning procedures. However, whether a hypnotic induction would benefit covert conditioning procedures is somewhat more debateable. Apart from the problem that fewer patients might benefit because a situation labelled as a 'hypnotic' one might put them off in the first place, it is also possible that some compliant patients, shamming the whole show, might privately be convinced that as they are not 'really' in a 'trance' it is no use expecting the suggestions to work. Furthermore, in spite of all the work reviewed in Chapter 7 on the relationship of non-hypnotic imaginative activities and hypnotic susceptibility the evidence supports the conclusion that neither the hypnotic induction procedure, nor degree of suggestibility, increases the effectiveness of procedures which supposedly involve the manipulation of imagery and its clarity, such as desensitisation (Lang, Lazowik and Reynolds, 1965; Paul, 1966, 1969; Marks, Gelder and Edwards, 1968). This finding is in line with that of Starker (1974) who makes the following comments concerning his own study, 'Subjects in the hypnosis group of this study had a cognitive set of expecting to be hypnotised, the experience of an induction procedure, and many supported the subjective experience of hypnosis. Still, the hypnotic procedure yielded no significant increase in the ratings of vividness of imagery beyond that produced by the motivational or control conditions' (p.435). Starker (1974) further suggests that, 'The variables most relevant to the experience of vivid imagery may be tangential to hypnotic induction per se yet implicit in the total hypnotic situation, for example, body position, level of arousal, restriction of sensory input. The future investigation of hypnotic imagery may therefore also be profitably pursued by mainstream psychological research into the vicissitudes of imaginal thought' (p.436). Although hypnotic induction per se may be unnecessary to account for the effectiveness of hypnotherapeutic procedures involving imaginal devices, nevertheless if a patient specifically requests 'hypnosis', it may be more effective to give him hypnotic induction prior to covert conditioning or densensitisation, assuming the patient has realistic expectancies of what the experience of hypnotic induction with suggestions for relaxation will be like (i.e. a pleasant, relaxed state in which he is conscious, rather than a state of insensibility). Indeed, Lazarus (1973) has found that subjects who specifically request 'hypnosis' may respond more enthusiastically if the word 'hypnosis' is substituted for 'relaxation' in their treatment. However, it does not seem to be a general principle that hypnotic suggestions for relaxation are more effective than waking suggestions; Paul (1969) found that a relaxation treatment given in a waking situation was more effective than a hypnotic suggestion treatment for removing tension and stress.

In view of the drawbacks of employing hypnotic induction procedures Cautela (1975) concludes, 'I feel that unless there is some substantial evidence that hypnotic induction procedures would facilitate covert conditioning, then it is more parsimonious not to use them' (p.24).

HYPNOSIS AS A TOOL IN PSYCHOANALYSIS

I mentioned at the beginning of this chapter that hypnotic procedures have been used clinically with the aim of furthering the explorative and interpretive aims of psychoanalysis. This has been attempted by 'hypnotising' subjects so that 'unconscious' wishes and fears of the patient may be revealed 'under hypnosis'. Unfortunately, again 'hard' evidence from clinical trials seems difficult to come by and the problems of assessing the effectiveness of hypnotherapy in this particular context have long been realised. For example, it is clear from the reports of the 'father' of psychoanalysis, Sigmund Freud, that he was not convinced that hypnotic induction provided any particular therapeutic advantages. Freud (1977) reports, for example, that Bernheim 'preferred to practise suggestion in a waking state, which can achieve the same effects as suggestion under hypnosis' (p.501). Freud also reports

> It was hackwork and not a scientific activity, and it recalled magic, incantations and hocus-pocus . . . the procedure was not reliable in any respect. It could be used with one patient but not with another; it achieved a great deal with one patient but not with another, and one never knew why. Worse than the capriciousness of the procedure was the lack of permanence in its successes. If, after a short time, one had news of the patient once more, the old ailment was back again or its place had been taken by a new one. . . . After this one could scarcely avoid, whether one wanted to or not, investigating the question of *the nature of one's authority* in suggestive treatment (pp.502–3, my emphasis).

However, even if hypnotic techniques can help in revealing patients' 'innermost' wishes and conflicts, one nevertheless may not necessarily have to assume that anything uniquely hypnotic accounts for this.

According to the interpretation of Sarbin and Coe (1972) everybody has some secrets, some observations of self that he will disclose to no-one. According to traditional psychoanalytic theory these secrets are held in the unconscious, so when the subject is asked a question and replies, 'I don't know', then he has no choice in the matter, he consciously does not know. However, when the subject on another occasion remarks that he is aware of such feelings, the usual interpretation is that 'repression has been lifted', or the 'unconscious has been made conscious'. Sarbin and Coe (1972) propose an alternative view. They suggest that when the subject replies 'I don't know', he is *choosing not* to disclose certain secrets, but when, on another occasion, he reveals the secrets, it is because he is in a situation where it seems appropriate to disclose the secrets, so he *chooses* to reveal them.

Basically, Sarbin and Coe are stating that the subject may voluntarily withhold information until placed in a situation where it seems more appropriate to disclose it. In the case of psychoanalysis the patient may voluntarily withhold embarrassing 'secrets' until placed in a situation with a warm, trustworthy analyst, where it is safe to disclose the secrets. The hypnotic situation with a friendly therapist may evoke the same 'warm' atmosphere in which 'secrets' may be divulged, but it could also have another advantage, in that if the patient 'pretends' he is in a 'trance' it may be possible for him to divulge secret fantasies and memories of the most intimate kind, whilst enabling him to maintain afterwards that he remembers nothing of what he has said! In other words, the hypnotic situation may provide the appropriate social context for patients to disclaim responsibility for their actions and statements, in the same way that some individuals may use alcohol as an excuse to indulge their more anti-social whims; it may be very convenient to be able to retort innocently, 'did I really say (do) that?'

This kind of uninhibited response could be seen as akin to the social psychological concept of 'deindividuation' (Zimbardo, 1969). According to Zimbardo (1969) 'deindividuation' is a general term used to refer to the kind of unrestrained behaviour that may occur following a number of antecedent social conditions. These antecedent conditions include feelings of diffused responsibility, new situations, acting emotionally, and physical action, and may result in a lessening of controls based on guilt, fear, shame, etc., with subsequent effects on behaviour. The hypnotic situation could be seen as one where, in some subjects or patients, deindividuation could take place; the subject could experience lessening of responsibility (he may be in Milgram's 'agentic state', or realise that his subsequent actions can be justified as 'outside his control' if he says he is 'hypnotised') and he may emotionally and physically play the role of a 'hypnotised' subject according to his expectations and the hypnotist's suggestions. These antecedent conditions in the hypnotic situation could thus provide the social context for deindividuation to take place, (a similar process could also account for some of the rather unrestrained behaviour of supposedly introverted people in hypnosis stage shows).

PERSUASION AND ATTRIBUTION

In many cases where hypnotherapeutic techniques are employed, the aim of the therapy is to change some element in the patient's behaviour, for example, to stop him smoking or drinking or to make him approach situations without fear. One could view such techniques therefore as, at times, fulfilling a function of persuasion, i.e. persuading the patient to adopt different attitudes and behavioural patterns towards these situations. This may be significant in that there are some aspects of the hypnotherapeutic situation which share commonalities with those factors known to produce optimal persuasive manipulation. For instance, factors known to maximise the effects of persuasion include a high credibility source (Hovland and Weiss, 1951), a repeated message (Staats and Staats, 1958), an explicitly stated conclusion supported by arguments pointing out the benefits of change (Hovland and Mandell, 1952; Greenwald, 1965), overlearning by the audience (Cook and Wadsworth, 1972), face to face communication (Jecker, Maccoby, Breitrose and Rose, 1964), and active role playing or participation by the audience in the message (Janis and King, 1954). In the hypnotherapeutic situation a qualified clinician (hypnotist) could be viewed as a high credibility source, the suggestions (messages) are certainly repeated, the patient may be told frequently of what will happen (how much better he will be) following the treatment, the repeating of the suggestion over a number of sessions could result in overlearning, the communication is usually face to face, and the suggestions usually require the subject to actively participate in the message by relaxation and the active formation of images. In the last context it may be worth noting that in the form that suggestions are issued in many hypnotherapeutic situations, the subject is not simply told the benefits that will result from a change in attitude and behaviour, but he is usually asked to imagine himself actually performing the desired behaviours and experiencing the desired effective response. Thus, for example, an alcoholic patient is not simply told the views of drink, rather he may be told to imagine himself taking an alcoholic drink and feeling sick. In effect the patient is being asked to self-attribute, in this case, the label of a person who dislikes drinking alcohol. Miller, Brickman and Bolen (1975) found that attribution can be very effective in modifying behaviour in non-hypnotic situations, and it is therefore possible that if hypnotic patients are motivated to continue self-attribution outside the hypnotic situation, then some change in related attitudes and behaviour could occur. On the basis of this kind of analysis one might predict that a degree of attitude change, with a corresponding behavioural change, could be expected for some patients following hypnotherapeutic sessions because of the operation of these basic principles of attitude change.

HYPNOTIC SUSCEPTIBILITY AND HYPNOTHERAPEUTIC SUCCESS

In answer to the question 'do clinical "hypnotic" techniques work?' then the unequivocal answer must be 'yes' in some circumstances. But as we have seen if we look at 'how' they work, when they do, we may not necessarily need to postulate that it is some unique property of 'hypnosis' to account for the effectiveness. In fact, hypnotic induction per se may be irrelevant to therapeutic success, in that, as with analgesia, general therapeutic success with so-called 'hypnotic' treatments seems often unrelated to hypnotic susceptibility. This is a widely held view which, according to Frankel (1976), 'is representative of the opinions, and commands the respect of many psychoanalytically oriented therapists' (p.51), and Gill and Brenman

(1959) also conclude that there is no correlation between the depth of hypnosis obtained by a patient and the therapeutic result. These writers describe case histories in which 'poor' hypnotic subjects responded well to hypnotherapy, whereas some highly susceptible subjects did not benefit at all from the introduction of hypnotic induction into the treatment programme. Frankel (1976) also gives examples of cases illustrating the discrepancy between the therapeutic success of a hypnotic treatment and the hypnotic susceptibility of the patient. In one case a twenty-seven-year-old salesman was treated for a phobia of flying. On the SHSS he scored 11, indicating that he was a highly hypnotically susceptible subject. He was then subjected to a course of hypnotherapy which included a desensitisation procedure. However, the treatment was unsuccessful. In another case a mother aged twenty-five was treated for a fear of animals. She expressed an interest in 'hypnosis' and scored highly on a hypnosis scale (HIP) indicating a high degree of hypnotic susceptibility. She was also given hypnotherapy with a desensitisation procedure, with some initial success, followed by a relapse. At the other extreme Frankel (1976) reports the case of a businessman who was treated for writer's cramp. He was given hypnotic suggestions for relaxation of his arm with some success in the alleviation of his symptoms but he was virtually unresponsive to other measures of hypnotic susceptibility. What, however, was interesting was that the man said he did experience his arm as being light and relaxed, even though his response to an arm levitation suggestion was negligible. The most important element in the results of these cases appears to be the attitude towards relinquishing the symptoms, rather than the motivation to be 'hypnotised'. In relation to the first two cases Frankel (1976) comments, 'Although both patients were motivated to respond well to hypnosis, neither were strongly motivated to work toward ridding themselves of their symptoms or changing their life patterns', (p.133). In relation to the third case he says, 'he was clearly motivated to relinquish the symptom' (p.167). Again it seems that it was not 'hypnosis' which was the magic ingredient. It was a positive attitude towards the general therapeutic situation which seemed more important. In the case of writer's cramp the subject seemed to respond well to a hypnotic procedure which involved a number of components which have been used successfully outside the context of 'hypnosis' to treat writer's cramp, for example, muscle relaxation, re-education, supportive psychotherapy, and encouraging suggestions (Crisp and Moldofsky, 1965). As in the case of hypnotic analgesia, when positive relationships between suggestibility, hypnotic susceptibility and therapeutic success are apparent they are typically low. For example, in their study of hypnotherapy for phobics Marks et al. (1968) report,

> The rather small correlation between improvement with hypnosis and our measure of suggestibility ($r = 0.34$) might suggest that factors other than suggestion are at work in the hypnotic procedure, and the part

played by relaxation comes to mind. . . . Lang et al. also found the scores on the Stanford Hypnotic Susceptibility Scale had a low correlation with improvement in their hypnosis group. . . . We found the same two of our 18 patients who received hypnosis went into a deep trance. One of these patients made a sustained improvement and the other was unchanged after hypnosis was completed' (p.1271).

It seems that this kind of relationship warrants the same conclusion as that made regarding hypnotic susceptibility and suggested analgesia, i.e. if the correlation between a variable 'X' and a standardised measure of hypnotic susceptibility determines whether 'X' is judged to be within the domain of hypnosis, then it could be argued that therapeutic success through suggestion procedures lies outside the domain of hypnosis. Put another way, if suggested analgesia and related hypnotherapeutic procedures are judged to be relevant in defining the area of hypnosis, then many measures of what has been labelled secondary suggestibility, i.e. characteristics such as influencibility and conformity, are equally relevant.

CONCLUSION

One of the main difficulties of assessing the contribution of hypnotic induction to various therapeutic procedures is that the necessary double-blind clinical trials are invariably absent. Certainly hypnotherapeutic procedures can be effective, but surely it is pertinent also to ask whether certain elements of the procedures might be even *more* effective if they had not been given in the context of 'hypnosis'. For instance, in the case of covert conditioning and desensitisation there might be a case for scrapping hypnotic induction for most patients with the important exception of those who are totally convinced that hypnosis will work. Unfortunately, even here the issue is complicated by the fact that, no matter how motivated the subject is to be 'hypnotised', if he is disappointed because he feels he has not entered a trance, or if he feels obliged to comply, then the effectiveness of hypnotic induction may be limited. Conversely, it may actually be possible to use compliance. For instance, if a patient 'shams' hypnosis, but feels obliged to stop smoking, or engaging in some maladaptive behaviour, then in accordance with the self-perception and cognitive dissonance theories discussed in Chapter 4, he may eventually change his attitudes and habits to be consistent with the behaviours he feels obliged to display. Thus, apart from the problem of wasting his money, the whole social context of compliance could be important. It may be easier for a person to stop smoking than to tell his friends, colleagues, and the hypnotist that he 'faked' hypnosis.

In this chapter I have tried to demonstrate how meaningless it is to apply the blanket statement that 'hypnotherapy works' as evidence for the operation of a special hypnotic agent, and as an unqualified justification for the usage of hypnotic procedures. Instead we must ask how 'work' is to be evaluated, what are the appropriate control measures, and in what circumstances are treatments labelled as 'hypnotic' relatively advantageous or ineffective compared to other procedures. The fact that a treatment is efficacious, in itself, says nothing of the way in which the treatment produces its effects, unless the appropriate control procedures are employed. Dr. Perkins' metallic tractors seemed very efficacious, but one does not see papers extolling the therapeutic advantages of metal plates very often. It may well be that there is an important place for some techniques now labelled as 'hypnotic' in clinical treatment, but possibly only by admitting that we do know something about how they might produce their effects will we be able to receive any genuine benefits that may accrue from their selective employment.

10. The Nature of Hypnosis

The discussion in this book has been directed towards illustrating the fact that most of the phenomena subsumed under the heading of 'hypnosis' do not need to be surrounded by the mystique which has probably cut them off from mainstream psychology. Due to the problem of space many important studies have had to be excluded, but I hope that some of the principles mentioned may be readily generalised to these other investigations. However, now I have outlined the general area of investigation and the corresponding problems, it is probably safer to examine the question which has generated so much controversy, namely, is hypnosis a special state of trance as distinguished by an altered state of consciousness?

HYPNOSIS AS A 'TRANCE' OR SPECIAL STATE

Although the term 'altered state of consciousness' has been defined in many ways, possibly the most extensive interpretation has been offered by Tart (1975a, b; 1977). Tart firstly defines what we mean by an ordinary, 'awake' state of consciousness. He seems the constitutents of ordinary consciousness as governed by a cultural consensus. The 'consensus reality' consists of a number of structures which are connected by certain preferred pathways for psychological energy and awareness to flow. For example, whilst reading a novel the 'arithmetical skill structure' is latent, but when asked how much is two plus three, it is activated, so the answer 'five' appears in awareness. Other structures include language, body skill, and emotional reactions, all of which may be culturally determined. Tart has proposed that each individual has a unique 'discrete state of consciousness' (d–SoC), consisting of a system of psychological structures, with probable, preferred ways of psychological energy or attention flowing between them; each individual has a system, or pattern, of structures and energy pathways with a recognisable 'feel or shape'. In this way we may be able to say, for instance, 'I'm perfectly awake but more relaxed than I was', because the relationship between being awake and relaxed is familiar and recognisable. A d–SoC, according to Tart, maintains its overall pattern or stability in a number of ways. For instance, we usually attempt to keep our thoughts and feelings occupied within a prescribed range of experiences, keeping most or all of our attention and psychological energy is desired structures. Consequently, when we feel that our emotions are going beyond their prescribed range we may take tranquillizing drugs to limit them. Thus, in order to produce a 'discrete *altered* state of consciousness' (d–ASC) we need to induce strategies such as pushing the known psychological functions to their

limits by overloading them with stimuli, giving them anomalous stimuli or depriving them of essential stimuli. In brief, according to Tart, *altered* states of consciousness essentially concern a radical change in our normal preferred use and integration of psychological structures such as language, arithmetic, body skills and emotions. However, the problem then becomes how radical does the change have to be before it actually becomes classified as an 'altered state'? Hilgard (1965) has proposed that experiences following hypnotic suggestions qualify hypnosis as an altered state, and its primary features as an altered state include the following: the subject loses initiative and the willingness to act independently, his attention is redistributed, his perception becomes selective and he develops a heightened ability for fantasy production and for distortion of reality. However, as I have mentioned in earlier chapters, some investigators have rejected the concept of a trance or a special altered state of consciousness, suggesting it to be an inappropriate way of interpreting hypnotic performance and experience. Barber, Spanos and Chaves (1974) have suggested that the appropriate analogy for describing the experience of a deeply involved hypnotic subject is that of someone engrossed in reading a novel who may become genuinely happy or sad or angry as a result of his imaginings whilst suppressing contradictory thoughts such as 'this is only a novel' or 'this is only make-believe'. Another analogy would be that of a person viewing a film who becomes involved with the action, actually crying or laughing, and suppressing throughts such as 'these are only actors', or 'this is just a story that someone made up'. In the same way a hypnotic subject who becomes deeply involved in the suggestions may behave in a similar way, crying like a child, or imagining a suggested object, because he does not tell himself, 'I am not really a child', or 'the object is not really there'. According to Barber and his associates, it is no more meaningful to describe the hypnotic subject who becomes involved with various suggestions as in a hypnotic 'trance' or special 'state', than it is to describe a person involved in a book or a film as in a hypnotic 'trance' or 'state'. The differences in the experiences of reading a book, looking at a film, or responding to suggestions simply reflect the effects of different communications, rather than radically different states of consciousness. Barber, Spanos and Chaves (1974) also suggest that it is of little utility labelling a subject as in a hypnotic 'trance' because the subject believes or feels he is. Here they suggest the appropriate anology is that of a Shaman who believes he is possessed by a spirit. Such Shamans may adopt unusual postures, froth at the mouth, appear to be unaware of their surroundings, and talk in strange voices. However, Barber, Spanos and Chaves (1974) suggest that few anthropologists would subscribe to the view that a Shaman's report of being possessed by a spirit, although sincere, is a very useful way of explaining why he behaves as he does. Thus it may be of no more value to say that a hypnotic subject is in a 'trance' because he says he is, than to say a Shaman is possessed by a spirit because he says he is.

In another 'non-state' analysis Sarbin and Coe (1972) have proposed that hypnotic behaviours and experiences can be seen as lying along a dimension of role-taking; that is, the degree to which the subject may adopt the role of the hypnotised subject. The role dimension may range from total non-involvement, with no effort to imagine what is suggested, through casual role-enactment, ritual acting (such as sham effects, or compliance without much private involvement), engrossed acting, classic hypnotic role-taking (according to Sarbin and Coe here the subject engages actively in 'as if' behaviours, trying for example, to feel like a child in age regression, and working himself into the role), histrionic neurosis (the involvement is more prolonged), ecstacy (voluntary action is suspended, the subject may end up fatigued or exhausted), and finally to bewitchment (the subject may become so involved that the role may be irreversible and outside the hypnotic situation such involvement could result in a person becoming sick or even dying because he believes he has offended someone with magical powers). According to Sarbin and Coe (1972) this scale represents a dimension of 'organismic involvement', i.e. the amount of effort and physiological participation that a person puts into a role. Sarbin and Coe (1972) conclude that concepts such as 'as if' experiences and behaviours, and 'believed in imaginings' are more applicable to the experiences and behaviours of the hypnotic subject than a special 'state' of trance.

However, the concepts of imaginative and organismic involvement put forward by non-state theorists have resulted in problems of interpretation. Hilgard (1975) argues there is little difference between the view of 'hypnosis' as an altered state of 'trance', and hypnosis as a level of imaginative or organismic involvement, and Spanos and Barber (1974) have argued that there is relatively little disagreement between state and non-state theorists concerning the characteristics and limits of hypnotic behaviour. However, Spanos and Barber (1974) also point out that the main difference between the two viewpoints will continue to concern the methodologies that the respective theorists adopt. Thus if state theorists continue to assume that there is a hypnotic stage that differs fundamentally from the 'normal waking state' they will continue to look for a physiological basis for such a state and pursue research to demonstrate that hypnotic performance involves unique or highly unusual changes in perceptual functioning. On the other hand, non-state theorists will continue to look at commonalities between hypnotic performance and experiences and normal 'waking' performance and experiences.

Although many of the interpretations of hypnotic behaviours put forward in this book could possibly be conceptualised within the boundaries of either state or non-state theories, my own view is that the notion of hypnosis as *an* altered state of consciousness could be somewhat misleading, and the attempts by some to identify both schools of thought with the concept of imaginative or organismic involvement could be equally misleading if both oversimplify the diversity of processes which contribute to various hypnotic phenomena. The first problem is that it has not been conclusively demonstrated that all subjects who respond to hypnotic suggestions are experiencing a high degree of imaginative or organismic involvement, i.e. compliance can easily disappear by default in this kind of analysis. It may, for example, be possible that subjects can experience one or more levels of Sarbin and Coe's (1972) dimension of organismic involvement at once, or during a single session, for example, a subject may be deeply involved in the relaxation instructions and believe he is 'hypnotised' yet fake amnesia, and the latter would constitute a different level of role-taking. Thus where an individual lies on the dimension may shift depending on what he is asked to do. Secondly, the alliance of the concepts of 'trance', 'altered states' and imaginative involvement leads to a variety of other semantic problems. For instance, it seems likely that it will take some time before the notion of a 'hypnotic trance' being something other than a state of profound insensibility similar to sleep, is incorporated into our cultural definition of the term. It may thus be somewhat misleading, *at least to subjects or patients*, for investigators into hypnotic phenomena to continue to use the term 'trance' as an explanation or description of what happens as a result of hypnotic induction, whether the term 'trance' is used metaphorically or otherwise. It is very likely that many people who are not familiar with the academic literature on hypnosis, or who have not frequently attended sessions in which hypnotic induction procedures are used, still conceive of a hypnotic trance as a sleeplike state of insensibility in which the individual loses his volition and responds like an automaton to the commands of the hypnotist. The continued use of words like 'trance' and 'somnambulism' surely only aids the perpetuation of this concept.

Furthermore, to describe a hypnotic subject as in *an* 'altered state of consciousness', seems to suggest that he is in a single particular state. Here the problem of when a 'normal' state of consciousness becomes an 'altered' state of consciousness becomes more pertinent. Benson and Klipper (1976) put forward some general principles in support of the proposition that there is an altered state of consciousness associated with the relaxation response, and that this state may follow other procedures which employ instructions for relaxation, such as those used in Transcendental Meditation and Yoga. Benson and Klipper (1976) suggest that four basic elements underly the achievement of this altered state of consciousness, a quiet environment, an object to dwell upon, a passive attitude, and a comfortable position. If these conditions are fulfilled the subject can achieve a state of profound relaxation with accompanying feelings of well-being. If the altered state of consciousness contingent upon suggestions for relaxation is achieved following hypnotic induction, then in this case, the hypnotic subject would indeed be in an 'altered state of consciousness'. Furthermore, if we wish to label this state a 'trance', in the same way that meditators and yogis are said to be in 'trances', then the hypnotic subject could be accurately described as 'in a trance'. However, there is no real basis, at present, to suggest that the achieved state is relevant to general responsiveness to hypnotic suggestions. For a start, it presumably disappears when relaxation disappears, yet unrelaxed subjects can still be labelled as 'hypnotised', as has been mentioned on a number of occasions previously.

If any experience outside our normal experience is labelled as an 'altered state of consciousness' then perhaps we might label 'deep concentration' in this way. Thus if the hypnotic subject concentrates hard, and is not very aware of his surroundings, then this could also constitute a genuine 'altered state of consciousness'. However, by the same token anyone getting 'lost' in a book, or becoming 'riveted' to the television screen would also have to be labelled as 'hypnotised'. Indeed the term 'hypnotised' is sometimes used loosely to apply to such situations. Again, this is logically consistent, except that people who concentrate on reading books or watching the television are not always in a state of profound relaxation (at least they would be unlikely to have their eyes closed); so this would mean that we would have *two* hypnotic 'trances' or 'altered states', one for relaxation, and one for concentration. In addition, suppose we decide to include 'obedience' as an altered state of consciousness. Milgram, in the obedience studies discussed in Chapter 2, described his subjects as being in an 'agentic state' where subjects become agents to the will of others. There are many historical instances of people becoming 'carried away', blindly obeying others and committing atrocities, such as in the concentration camps in Nazi Germany, who could be deemed to be in this altered state of consciousness, and again, such 'agents' have been referred to, by some, as 'hypnotised' by those whom they obey. However, as such blind obedience need not necessarily require relaxation or concentration, we could postulate *three* altered states of consciousness which might apply to the hypnotic subject who responds to suggestions. The point that seems to arise from this discussion is that it may seem logical to say that a hypnotic subject may be in a number of altered states of consciousness or states of trance, if he is relaxed, or obedient or concentrating. If, however, we propose that the particular communications during hypnotic induction make the versions of these states *unique* to 'hypnosis', one presumably would then have to propose *unique* discrete altered states of awareness or 'trances' for Yoga meditation, Transcendental Meditation, obeying the Pope, obeying the boss, watching television, and so on, because each of these would have its own 'unique' system of communications. As people do not usually talk about 'television trances', 'film trances', 'book trances' or 'boss trances', one really cannot blame them for thinking that a hypnotic 'trance' must be more than just deeply relaxing, concentrating very hard on something and doing what someone says.

Although many standardised scales involve a preamble to try to divest hypnosis of much of its magic (for example, the SHSS:C informs subjects that something very much like hypnosis occurs 'when driving along a straight highway and you are oblivious to the land marks along the road'), the statements are rarely adequate and often contradicted by more exciting analogies (SHSS:C also informs subjects that 'Hypnosis is a little like sleepwalking'). However, if hypnosis is just a state of focussing of attention, or like driving alone a motorway oblivious to landmarks, then what is the term 'waking' supposed to apply to? Clearly, it is at this stage of the argument that we can see how redundant, or metaphorically inept, this term 'waking' is. If you do what your boss says, you are 'awake'; but if you do what the hypnotist says you are 'asleep' or 'somnambulistic'. I feel that no amount of claims that the terms 'trance', 'somnambulism' and 'waking' are only metaphorical can really justify their continued usage unless it is made abundantly clear to all subjects receiving suggestions that they *are* only metaphors, i.e. 'hypnosis' is *nothing like* sleep or sleepwalking. Furthermore, I am not convinced that many academics and clinicians who use the term 'trance' are only using it as a metaphor to label 'normal and natural' phenomena (to use terms from the SHSS:C). As Bowers (1966) has said, 'Most (present-day) investigators interested in hypnosis believe that there is an hypnotic state which fundamentally differs from the waking state' (p.42). This hardly seems to describe a 'normal and natural' state of concentration or relaxation.

Possibly all that can really be concluded is that whilst it may be inaccurate to say that 'hypnosis' is *an* altered state of consciousness, it may be logically consistent to say the phenomena that have been labelled as 'hypnotic' may be accompanied by altered *states* of consciousness, *if* we include altered states of consciousness which accompany obedience, compliance, relaxation, and concentration.

THE BIGGEST MYSTERY

Having discussed some of the many phenomena attributed to hypnosis, and the associated semantic jungle, it may be useful to look again at how the whole muddle of metaphors might have come into being. I am very fortunate in that my task may have already been done for me in an excellent book by Thornton (1976), *Hypnotism, Hysteria and Epilepsy*, which provides a compelling solution to what is probably the greatest mystery in hypnosis, that is, how did so many disparate phenomena become linked to the term 'hypnosis'? How did Mesmer's writhing, convulsing patients come to be classified alongside subjects responding to suggestions for body sway and arm levitation, lifting weights, experiencing hallucinations, committing anti-social acts, falling into a state of profound relaxation and so on? In all probability the connection is the result of a bizarre set of historical circumstances. The possibility exists that many of these phenomena are related by historical misjudgment and error, rather than by some central unique 'hypnotic' property. As Thornton so aptly puts it, the history of magnetism from which hypnosis arose 'is a comedy of errors' (p.43).

In Chapter 1 a brief overview of the history of hypnosis was given in which it was emphasised how different investigators managed to get their subjects to display a variety of behaviours which have now become integrated into our concept of hypnosis. However, it is not clear from most historical accounts whether the varieties of behaviours were just 'chanced upon' or whether they developed from some central source.

Thornton (1976) provides a most convincing case for the proposition that the source of the behaviours we now attribute to 'hypnosis' resulted from the misdiagnosis of an ancient malady, epilepsy.

Epilepsy itself is difficult to define, but, in terms of neurophysiology, it is a condition characterised by seizures stemming from excessive neuronal discharge within the nervous system which can be caused by a variety of lesions in the brain, including scar tissue, atrophy, tumour, and inflammation (Zax and Cowen, 1976). The first type of epilepsy to be noted was the 'grand mal' type, characterised by firstly a 'tonic' phase of tenseness and rigidity, followed by convulsions (a rapid alternation of contraction and relaxation), known as the 'clonic' state. During the later clonic state the opening and closing of the jaws may produce a frothy foam round the mouth. Another type of attack is the 'petit mal' seizure, involving a dimming of consciousness in which the patient becomes totally or largely unaware of what is happening around him. This is accompanied by immobility. Sometimes these seizures are so brief that the patient may not be aware they have occurred. Sometimes the seizures may be limited to certain parts of the body, but showing the same tonic and clonic phenomena; such attacks have been termed 'Jacksonian seizures'. In other instances, in 'twilight states', the patient may be quite still in a state of drowsiness or able to move about and talk without obvious sign of impairment, but he is either totally or partially unaware of his surroundings.

Thornton begins his analysis of hypnotism and epilepsy by carefully reviewing the reports of Mesmer's procedures and the responses that Mesmer's patients manifested. He was particularly interested firstly in the techniques that Mesmer employed; these included the use of music, the tactile manipulation of the patients' bodies and the use of lights in a dark room. According to Mesmer these factors were an essential feature of 'animal magnetism', about which he made comments such as, 'It is like light, increased and reflected by mirrors', 'it is communicated, propagated and increased by sound', and 'By its aid the physician . . . can provoke and direct salutary crises, so as to completely control them' (Thornton, 1976, p.6). Even the most sceptical of early observers were convinced that in some patients the effects of these procedures were 'real' and not feigned. The convulsive fits of some of Mesmer's patients were at times violent and characterised by 'precipitate and involuntary motions of all limbs of the body, by a contraction of the throat, by sudden affections of the hypochonders and epigastrium. . . .' (Thornton, 1976, p.8). In fact, it was often the very gruesome nature of these responses, which included becoming blue in the face and foaming at the mouth, which convinced the Commission investigating Mesmer's claims that their therapeutic value was negligible.

The report of the Commission included statements such as, 'How can we imagine that a man, be his disorder what it will, can need in order to his recovery the intervention of crises, in which the sight appears to be lost, the members stiffen, he strikes his breast with precipitate and involuntary motions, crises in a word that are terminated by an abundant spitting of viscous humours and even blood?' (Thornton, 1976, p. 10). These crises were also apparently preceded or followed by a comatose condition. Mesmer's aim was actually to produce these convulsions or crises, as he believed that having brought the disease to a head, recovery would take place, and his speciality was the treatment of diseases of the nervous system. Having examined these accounts Thornton came to the conclusion that in many cases the disease of the nervous system that Mesmer was supposedly treating was epilepsy. The relationship between the sound, touch and light stimuli (as used by Mesmer) and the production of convulsive fits is well known in cases of epilepsy. The precipitation of epileptic fits by music (musicogenic epilepsy) is well documented in modern literature, similarly the use of light (photogenic epilepsy) and touch (tactile precipitation). If we accept Thornton's conclusion that the convulsions of some of Mesmer's patients were manifestations of epilepsy, the next step is particularly interesting. In 1950 Lennox classified the symptoms of 414 epileptic patients into a number of groups (Thornton, 1976). The three main groups were psychomotor, automatic and subjective. Symptoms of the psychomotor subgroups included rigidity of the muscles with unconsciousness and amnesia, periods of excessive muscular activity, and periods of immobility with 'staring, stupor and sleep-like states'. Symptoms of the automatic subgroups included full consciousness but with confusion, impaired speech, and amnesia. Symptoms of the subjective seizures included dream states, feelings of unreality, illusions, hallucinations of sight, hearing, smell or taste, and although the patient might be aware of what is said or done he cannot participate or speak. These different seizure patterns might vary from time to time and from patient to patient; also one person might have more than one pattern. Other investigators have reported that certain patients if they have very slight seizures may perform whole series of actions in a state of apparent unconsciousness or delirium. Thornton also cites other remarkable cases of people who during attacks of temporal lobe epilepsy follow the instructions of others; this would seem somewhat akin to the notion of 'suggestibility'. Furthermore Thornton suggests that, 'A discharge from the temporal lobes to the nearby sensory cortex in the Rolandic area would bring about diminished bodily sensations, a feature of both temporal seizures and hypnotism' (p.38).

The similarity of all these symptoms with hypnotic phenomena hardly requires comment, and Thornton concludes, 'We can thus identify the condition they produced and which they called "somnambulism", which later generations named "hypnotism" or nervous sleep, as a psychomotor or temporal lobe epileptic seizure' (p.39). The 'comedy of errors' that followed the magnetisers then stemmed from the fact that temporal lobe epilepsy was not conclusively established until this century. It was not known to the earlier investigators who, perhaps not surprisingly, had concluded that somethimg particularly weird and wonderful was happening to these unhappy epileptic patients. It was thus from these beginnings that the myths of 'somnambulism' and 'hypnosis' grew. It a magnetiser could produce such dramatic, convulsive and trance-like results, perhaps he should be able to make his subjects perform paranormal feats of levitation, elongation of body, and mental telepathy. Nevertheless, in clinical situations the familiar comatose and convulsive states continued to be manifested in patients, and Thornton feels there is evidence to suggest that some of Charcot's patients who manifested hypnotic catalepsy were epileptic patients who had incorrectly been diagnosed as 'hysteric'. In fact, Thornton doubts whether the disease of 'hysteria' ever really existed, as even the earliest accounts of hysteria by the ancient Egyptians and Greeks make the symptoms appear very similar to forms of epilepsy. For instance, the 'wandering womb' disorder (hysteria comes from the Greek 'hystera', uterus or womb) was typified by convulsions in which the fits commenced in the abdomen, and were accompanied by apparent suffocation, foaming at the mouth, and followed by unconsciousness. According to Thornton neurosurgeons have confirmed that in temporal lobe epilepsy it is very common for a spasmodic sensation to travel from the low regions of the abdomen, up through the chest, into the throat and to be followed by unconsciousness or by psychomotor automatism. These symptoms correspond exactly with Charcot's 'boule hysterique', or 'globus hystericus'. According to Freud and Breur (1974) Charcot had isolated four main phases of a 'major' hysterical attack: 1. the 'epileptical' phase (convulsions); 2. the phase of large movements; 3. the phase of hallucinations; and 4. the phase of terminal delirium. Freud and Breur (1974) also noted 'hysterical' symptoms such as 'clonic spasms or cataleptic rigidity' (p.65), though they did admit that such convulsions could well be epileptic in nature. Other accounts of 'hysterical fits' include the following by Dr. John Fulton in the Lancet in 1953, 'Suddenly she announced that she felt a fit coming on and in a few seconds more she was in a convulsion. The hands were tightly clenched; the lips firmly pressed together; the eyes open and slightly turned up; the pupils dilating; the pulse much accelerated'. This fit was diagnosed as 'hysterical' because the patient had an 'approaching knowledge' of it (Thornton, 1976). According to Thornton epileptic fits are sometimes followed by a temporary neurological deficit, such as paralysis or weaknesses of limbs, numbness, blindness or aphasia. He thus suggests that physicians of the time diagnosed these deficits as 'hysterical' because due to their lack of knowledge of the nervous system they did not appreciate that these were genuine neurological deficits. For example, they would label blindness after a fit 'hysterical' because they did not realise that the pupillary reaction to light could be preserved because of the separate innervation of this reflex. Thornton notes how a variety of symptoms including aphasia, facial paralaysis, and double vision may have been misdiagnosed in this fashion. There are many rather undignified accounts of physicians shouting at, sticking pins in, pinching and slapping patients in an attempt to test 'hysterical' paralysis and anaesthesia that followed fits of varying degrees of severity. It seems that in the latter part of the eighteenth century diagnoses of hysteria were occurring in epidemic proportions. Charcot possibly had not helped, for by relating hysteria to the cerebral cortex this may have simply confirmed that the determinants were psychological. Papers appeared at the time, including reports of 'hysterical' symptoms simulating heart disease, peritonitis, tetanus, menigitis, pregnancy, toothache, dysmenorrhoea, coma, and even death (Thornton, 1976, p.132). The result, according to Thornton, was that the physicians of the time had only themselves to blame when 'by the laws of supply and demand' they eventually obtained what they were looking for; professionals entered the scene, and many of the patients at the Salpetriere were 'ex-filles de joie' from the music hall stage who were 'agile comedians and excellent imitators' (p.134). Thus, starting from a basic misdiagnosis of epileptic symptoms, the disease of 'hysteria' began to become exaggerated by overenthusiastic investigators and compliant exponents of dramatics. This resulted in the bizarre range of cataleptic, hallucinatory, and anaesthetic effects that Charcot and his associates seemed to be able to turn on and off, and the use of this misinterpretation by quacks and charlatans who realised their chance to 'earn a quick buck' by taking advantage of the compliance of their subjects, and the gullibility of an astounded public. In this way, the concept of hypnosis at the time of Charcot became inextricably linked with hysteria, the primary manifestations of which were originally epileptic symptoms resulting in the emergence of a range of more specialised hypnotic phenomena which have now been integrated into a cultural understanding of the term 'hypnosis'.

One possible result of this historical 'comedy of errors' is that we now have a term 'hypnosis' which relates to *mimicking* of these clinical symptoms, and the bizarre range of extrapolations and exaggerated effects that accompanied and developed from them, by *normal* people (i.e. nonsufferers from pathological illnesses such as epilepsy). In blunt terms, when 'normal' subjects are given modern hypnosis scales they are being asked to perform, to the best of their ability, what really amounts to a parody of epileptic symptoms. The contradictions of hypnotic phenomena could now become clearer. Supposing we take two epileptic symptoms, muscular rigidity, and a trance-like stuporific appearance. In the epileptic the two symptoms are not incompatible, they are accompanied or followed by an electrical discharge which is identifiable on EEG records. However, in a 'normal' person a stuporific trance-like appearance might best be produced if the subject is told to *relax* and appear to be sleepy. However, deep relaxation, which some confirmation in terms of an abundance of alpha waves, is incompatible with muscle tonicity which occurs when the normal subject has to try to hold his body or his arm rigid in a distinctly *unrelaxed* state. These contradictions may thus exist in hypnosis because different methods have to be employed to mimic different epileptic symptoms.

In this context it is not difficult to see why 'hypnosis' has been used to apply to a whole range of contradictory phenomena from relaxation with accompanying feelings of pleasure and even euphoria, to the most unpleasant manifestations of anxiety, convulsions, and the spitting of blood and saliva from the mouth. Of course, Thornton's arguments, at present, are historical and speculative in nature, and rather difficult to validate systematically for a number of reasons. Cases of 'hysteria' as reported by Charcot, Freud and Breur are now comparatively rare, possibly as the result of more accurate diagnostic classifications of epilepsy and organic pathology, and also possibly because of advances in experimental and clinical technology some may feel they are less likely to get away with malingering. There would certainly be a public outcry if Mesmerists continued to roam the country inducing convulsive fits, though it may be possible that a few cases of epileptic seizures of a 'petit mal' or Jacksonian type may still conceivably occur in a few hypnotic subjects in clinical situations. In order to substantiate Thornton's arguments it could be possible to embark on an exercise involving the physiological and behavioural monitoring of a large sample of subjects to determine the extent to which seizure-like episodes might occur with various types of hypnotic induction procedure. However, there might be considerable ethical as well as methodological problems with this kind of approach.

Nevertheless, in spite of the absence of systematic evidence for Thornton's analysis, it does seem to be a very plausible interpretation of the evolution of hypnotic phenomena, which possibly gives some insight into and support for the notion that the modern hypnotic subject, who has no abnormal organic pathology, rather than spontaneously lapsing into a unique state of consciousness, actively takes the role of the hypnotic subject. One way of viewing the situation would be to say that, in many respects, the modern hypnotic subject plays the 'game' of hypnosis, according to the rules laid down by the hypnotist, our cultural notion of 'hypnosis' and his individual attitudes and preconceptions. If he is a very good subject he will play very hard, but he will not know that what he is really doing is employing a variety of strategies in order to mimic, in many ways, the tragic condition of epilepsy. The epileptic may look in a trance, so the hypnotic subject relaxes and tries to mimic this; the epileptic may suffer spontaneous hallucinations, so the hypnotic subject tries his best to imagine things which are not present; the epileptic may suffer spontaneous amnesia, so the hypnotic subject 'pretends' he cannot remember, or engages in a number of strategies such as thinking about something else in order to mimic amnesia. Fortunately, the modern hypnotic subject no longer has to mimic the more violent and more distasteful aspects of a 'grand mal' seizure, such as convulsions and foaming at the mouth, but he may have to mimic behaviours appropriate to the myths that grew from the early misunderstandings of the nature of epilepsy, and the 'powers' of those who seemed able to evoke fits in others. Thus he may be required to transcend his 'normal' capacities, or commit some anti-social acts like a zombie, or regress to childhood with incredible accuracy.

However, the set of historical accidents, or the 'comedy of errors' which gave rise to modern concepts of hypnosis has also produced some interesting beneficient consequences. In playing this 'game' of hypnosis along the way both hypnotists and subjects have also chanced upon examples of the benefits of relaxation in the removal of anxiety and pain, covert conditioning in the treatment of maladaptive behaviours, and the importance of patient-therapist interaction.

A CONCLUSION

A common conclusion to many discussions of 'hypnosis' is that 'no one knows exactly what it is, or why it works, but it does'. I would suggest that *it* may not be a unitary entity but rather a collection of phenomena; that we know more than many are prepared to admit about how some of the associated hypnotic procedures might exert their effects; and that hypnotic procedures do not always 'work' as often or as effectively as is sometimes claimed. In providing this interpretation I have not found some magic solution to solve all the mysteries of 'hypnosis', but what I hope I may have done is to draw attention to a variety of important phenomena, not mystic, not supernatural, but nevertheless intriguing and ripe for investigation in a systematic and controlled manner.

Bibliography

The following are cited in abbreviated form in the Bibliography:
American Journal of Clinical Hypnosis
American Journal of Diseases of Children
American Journal of Medicine
American Journal of Obstetrics and Gynecology
American Journal of Psychiatry
American Journal of Psychology
American Psychologist
Anesthesia and Analgesia
Annual Review of Psychology
Archives of Environmental Health
Archives of General Psychiatry
Archives of Neurology and Psychiatry
Archives de Psychologie
Behavior Research and Therapy
Behavior Therapy
Biological Psychiatry
Brain Research
British Journal of Children's Diseases
British Journal of Clinical Hypnosis
British Journal of Medical Psychology
British Journal of Psychiatry
British Journal of Psychology
British Journal of Social and Clinical Psychology
British Medical Journal
Bulletin of the British Society of Experimental and Clinical Hypnosis
Bulletin of the Maritime Psychological Association
Canadian Journal of Psychology
Clinical Research
Cognitive Psychology
Development Psychology
Dissertation Abstracts International
Human Behavior
Human Relations
Indian Journal of Psychology
International Journal of Clinical and Experimental Hypnosis
International Journal of Psychiatry
Journal of Abnormal Psychology
Journal of Abnormal and Social Psychology

Journal of the American Medical Association
Journal of the American Society of Psychosomatic Dentistry and Medicine
Journal of Applied Psychology
Journal of Experimental and Clinical Psychopathology
Journal of Clinical Investigation
Journal of Clinical Psychology
Journal of Consulting and Clinical Psychology
Journal of Counseling Psychology
Journal of Experimental Psychology
Journal of Experimental Research in Personality
Journal of Experimental Social Psychology
Journal of the Forensic Science Society
Journal of General Psychology
Journal of Genetic Psychology
Journal of Nervous and Mental Disease
Journal of Obstetrics and Gynaecology of India
Journal of the Optical Society of America
Journal of Personality
Journal of Personality and Social Psychology
Journal of Psychology
Journal of Psychosomatic Research
Journal of the Society for Psychical Research
Journal for the Theory of Social Behaviour
Journal of Verbal Learning and Verbal Behavior
Kyushu Journal of Medical Science
Laboratory Animal Care
McGill Medical Journal
Medical Clinics of North America
Medical Journal of Australia
Medical Times
Neurochemical Research
New England Journal of Medicine
New York State Journal of Medicine
Nursing Research Report
Perceptual and Motor Skills
Proceedings of the National Academy of Sciences
Progress in Behaviour Modification
Psychiatric Quarterly
Psychological Bulletin
Psychological Record
Psychological Reports
Psychological Research
Psychological Review
Psychology Today
Psychosomatic Medicine

Public Opinion Quarterly
Quarterly Journal of Experimental Psychology
Research News
Scientific American
Social Behavior and Personality

Adamowicz, J.K., and Gibson, D. (1970) Cue screening, cognitive elaboration and heart-rate change. Can. J. Psychol., 24, 240–248.

Allen, V.L. (1965) Situational factors in conformity. In Berkowitz, L. (ed.), Advances in experimental social psychology. Vol. 2. New York: Academic Press, 133–170.

Allen, V.L., and Newton, D. (1972) Development of conformity and independence. J. Pers. Soc. Psychol., 222, 18–30.

Ambellur, N.D.E., and Barber, T.X. (1973) Yoga, hypnosis, and self-control of cardiovascular functions. In Miller, N.B., Barber, T.X., Dicara, L.V., Kamiya, J., Shapiro, D., and Stoyva, J. (eds.), Biofeedback and Self-Control. Chicago: Aldine, 503–507.

Anderson, J.A.D., Basker, M.A., Dalton, R. (1975) Migraine and hypnotherapy. Int. J. Clin. Exp. Hypn., 1, 48–58.

Arkin, A.M., Hastey, J.M., and Reiser, M.F. (1966) Post-hypnotically stimulated sleep-talking. J. Nerv. Ment. Dis., 142, 293–309.

Aronson, E. (1977) The Social Animal. San Francisco: Freeman.

Aronson, E., and Mills, J. (1959) The effect of severity of initiation on liking for a group. J. Abnorm. Soc. Psychol., 59, 177–181.

Ås, A. (1963) Hypnotisability as a function of non-hypnotic experiences. J. Abnorm. Soc. Psychol., 66, 142–150.

Ås, A., and Lauer, L. (1962) A factor analytic study of hypnotisability and related personal experiences. Int. J. Clin. Exp. Hypn., 10, 169–181.

Asch, S.E. (1951) Effects of group pressure upon the modification and distortion of judgments. In Guetzhow, H. (ed.), Groups, leadership, and men. Pittsburgh: Carnegie Press.

Asch., S.E. (1952) Social psychology. Englewood Cliffs, New Jersey: Prentice Hall.

Asch, S.E. (1956) Studies of independence and conformity: A minority of one against a unanimous majority. Psychol. Mono. 70, 9, whole no. 416.

Asch, S.E. (1958) Effects of group pressures upon modification and distortion of judgments. In Maccoby, E.E., Newcomb, T.M., and Hartley, E.L. (eds.), Readings in Social Psychology. (3rd ed.) Holt: New York, 174–183.

Ascher, L.M., Barber, T.X., and Spanos, N.P. (1972) Two attempts to replicate the Parrish-Lundy-Leibowitz experiment on hypnotic age regression. Amer. J. Clin. Hypn., 14, 178–185.

Ashley, W.R., Harper, R.S., and Runyon, D.L. (1951) The perceived size of coins in normal and hypnotically induced economic states. Amer. J. Psychol., 64, 564–572.

August, R.V. (1961) Hypnosis in Obstetrics. New York: McGraw-Hill.

Back, K.W., and Davis, K.E. (1965) Some personal and situational factors relevant to the consistency and prediction of conforming behaviour. Sociometry, 28, 227–240.

Bakan, P. (1969) Hypnotisability, laterality of eye movement and functional brain asymmetry. Percept. Mot. Skills, 28, 927–932.

Bakan, P., and Svorad, D. (1969) Resting EEG Alpha and asymmetry of reflective lateral eye movements. Nature, 223, 975–976.

Bandura, A. (1973) Aggression: A social learning analysis. Englewood Cliffs, New Jersey: Prentice Hall.

Bandura, A. (1974) Analysis of modelling processes. In Bandura, A. (ed.), Modelling: conflicting theories. New York: Lieber-Atherton.

Bandura, A. (1977) Social Learning Theory. Englewood Cliffs, New Jersey: Prentice Hall.

Banyai, E.I., and Hilgard, E.R. (1976) A comparison of active alert hypnotic induction and traditional relaxation induction. J. Abnorm. Psychol., 85, 218–224.

Barber, T.X. (1956) A note on hypnotisability and personality traits. Int. J. Clin. Exp. Hypn., 4, 109–114.

Barber, T.X. (1959) Toward a theory of pain: Relief of chronic pain by prefrontal leucotomy, opiates, placebos and hypnosis. Psychol. Bull., 56, 430–460.

Barber, T.X. (1961) Antisocial and criminal acts induced by 'hypnosis': A review of clinical and experimental findings. Arch. Gen. Psychiat., 5, 301–312 (a).

Barber, T.X. (1961) Physiological effects of 'hypnosis'. Psychol. Bull., 58, 390–419 (b).

Barber, T.X. (1962) Toward a theory of hypnosis: Post-hypnotic behaviour. Arch. Gen. Psychiat. 7, 321–342 (a).

Barber, T.X. (1962) Toward a theory of 'hypnotic' behaviour: the 'hypnotically-induced dream'. J. Nerv. Ment. Dis., 135, 206–221 (b).

Barber, T.X. (1963) The effects of 'hypnosis' on pain: A critical review of experimental and clinical findings. Psychosom. Med., 25, 303–333.

Barber, T.X. (1965) Physiological indices of 'neutral hypnosis': A critical evaluation. Harding, Mass. Medfield Found. (Mimeo). Cited by Barber, 1969b.

Barber, T.X. (1969) Effects of hypnotic induction, suggestions of anaesthesia, and distraction on subjective and physiological responses to pain. Paper presented at the annual meeting of the Eastern Psychological Association, Phil., April (a). Cited by Chaves and Barber, 1976.

Barber, T.X. (1969) Hypnosis: A scientific approach. New York: Van Nostrand (b).

Barber, T.X. (1970) L.S.D., marihuana, yoga and hypnosis. Chicago: Aldine-Atherton.

Barber, T.X. (1972) Suggested ('hypnotic') behaviour: the trance paradigm versus an alternative paradigm. In Fromm, E., and Shor, R.E. (eds.). Hypnosis: Research developments and perspectives. Chicago: Aldine-Atherton, 115–182.

Barber, T.X. (1973) Acupuncture anaesthesia in surgery: A scientific explanation. Paper presented at the 2nd Western Hemisphere Conference on Acupuncture, Kirlian photography and the Human Aura. New York, Feb. Cited by Barber, Spanos and Chaves, 1974.

Barber, T.X., and Calverley, D.S. (1964) An experimental study of 'hypnotic' (auditory and visual) hallucinations. J. Abnorm. Soc. Psychol., 68, 13–20 (a).

Barber, T.X., and Calverly, D.S. (1064) Empirical evidence for a theory of 'hypnotic' behaviour: Effects of pretest instructions on response to primary suggestions. Psychol. Rec. 14, 457–467 (b).

Barber, T.X., and Calverley, D.S. (1964) Experimental studies in 'hypnotic' behaviour: Suggested deafness by delayed auditory feedback. Brit. J. Psychol., 55, 439–446 (c).

Barber, T.X., and Calverley, D.S. (1964) The definition of the situation as a variable affecting 'hypnotic-like' suggestibility. J. Clin. Psychol., 20, 438–440 (d).

Barber, T.X., and Calverley, D.S. (1964) Toward a theory of hypnotic behaviour: Effects on suggestibility of defining the situation as hypnosis and defining responses to suggestions as easy. J. Abnorm. Soc. Psychol., 68, 585–592 (e).

Barber, T.X., and Calverley, D.S. (1964) Toward a theory of hypnotic behaviour: enhancement of strength and endurance. Can. J. Psychol., 18, 156–157 (f).

Barber, T.X., and Calverley, D.S. (1965) Empirical evidence for a theory of 'hypnotic' behaviour: Effects on suggestibility of five variables typically included in hypnotic induction procedures. J. Consult. Psychol. 29, 98–107 (a).

Barber, T.X., and Calverley, D.S. (1965) Empirical evidence for a theory of 'hypnotic' behaviour: The suggestibility-enhancing effects of motivational suggestions, relaxation-sleep suggestions, and suggestions that the subject will be effectively 'hypnotised'. J. Pers. 33, 256–270 (b).

Barber, T.X., and Calverley, D.S. (1965) Hypnotisability, suggestibility and personality: II. Assessment of previous imaginative fantasy experiences by the As, Barber-Glass and Shor questionnaires. J. Clin. Psychol., 21, 57–58 (c).

Barber, T.X., and Calverley, D.S. (1966) Effects on recall of hypnotic induction, motivational suggestions, and suggested regression: A methodological and experimental analysis. J. Abnorm. Psychol., 71, 169–180 (a).

Barber, T.X., and Calverley, D.S. (1966) Toward a theory of 'hypnotic' behaviour: Experimental analyses of suggested amnesia. J. Abnorm. Psychol., 71, 95–107 (b).

Barber, T.X., and Calverley, D.S. (1969) Multidimensional analysis of 'hypnotic' behaviour. J. Abnorm. Psychol., 74, 209–220.

Barber, T.X., and Cooper, B.J. (1972) Effects on pain of experimentally-induced and spontaneous distraction. Psychol. Rep., 31, 647–651.

Barber, T.X., and Coules, J. (1959) Electrical skin conductance and galvanic skin response during 'hypnosis'. Int. J. Clin. Exp. Hypn., 7, 79–92.

Barber, T.X., Dalal, A.S., and Calverley, D.S. (1968) The subjective reports of hypnotic subjects. Amer. J. Clin. Hypn. 11, 74–88.

Barber, T.X., and Deeley, D.C. (1961) Experimental evidence for a theory of hypnotic behaviour: I. 'Hypnotic' colour-blindness without 'hypnosis'. Int. J. Clin. Exp. Hypn., 9, 79–86.

Barber, T.X., and De Moor, W. (1972) A theory of hypnotic induction procedures. Amer. J. Clin. Hypn., 15, 112–135.

Barber, T.X., and Glass, L.B. (1962) Significant factors in hypnotic behaviour. J. Abnorm. Soc. Psychol., 64, 222–228.

Barber, T.X., and Hahn, K.W. (1962) Physiological and subjective responses to pain producing stimulation under hypnotically-suggested and waking-imagined 'analgesia'. J. Abnorm. Soc. Psychol., 65, 411–418.

Barber, T.X., and Hahn, K.W. (1963) Hypnotic induction and 'relaxation': An experimental study. Arch. Gen. Psychiat., 8, 295–300.

Barber, T.X., and Hahn, K.W. (1966) Suggested dreaming with and without hypnotic induction. Harding, Mass.: Medfield Foundation. (Mimeo.) Cited by Barber, 1969b.

Barber, T.X., Spanos, N.P., and Chaves, J.F. (1974) Hypnotism: Imagination and Human Potentialities. New York: Pergamon.

Barchas, J.D., Akil, H., Elliott, G.R., Holman R.B., and Watson, S.J. (1978) Behavioural neurochemistry: Neuroregulators and behavioural states. Science, 200, 964–973.

Baron, R.A., and Byrne, D. (1977) Social psychology: Understanding human interaction. (2nd ed.). Boston, Mass.: Allyn and Bacon.

Beecher, H.K. (1959) Measurement of subjective responses. New York: Oxford Univ. Press.

Beecher, H.K. (1960) Increased stress and effectiveness of placebos and 'active' drugs. Science, 132, 91–92.

Bem, D.J. (1965) An experimental analysis of self-persuasion. J. Exp. Soc. Psychol., 1, 199–218.

Bem, D.J.L. (1972) Self-Perception Theory. In Berkowitz, L. (ed.), Advances in experimental social psychology. Vol. 6. New York: Academic Press.

Benson, H., and Klipper, M.Z. (1976) The relaxation response. London: Collins. Benton, A.L., and Bandura, A. (1953) 'Primary' and 'secondary' suggestibility. J. Abnorm. Soc. Psychol., 48, 336–340.

Berkowitz, B., Ross-Townsend, A., and Kohberger, R. (1979) Hypnotic treatment of smoking: The single-treatment method revisited. Amer. J. Psychiat. 136, 83–85.

Bernheim, H.M. (1884) De la suggestion dans l'état hypnotique et dans l'état de veille. Paris: Doin.

Bernheim, H.M. (1886) De la suggestion et ses applications a la therapeutique Paris. English translation by Herter, C.A. (1890) Suggestive therapeutics: A treatise on the nature and uses of hypnotism. (2nd ed.) London: Pentland.

Bernheim, H. (1957) Suggestive therapeutics. Westport, Conn.: Associated Booksellers.

Betcher, A.M. (1960) Hypnosis as an adjunct in anaesthesiology. N.Y. State J. Med. 60, 816–822.

Bickman, L. (1974) Social roles and uniforms: Clothes make the person. Psychol. Today, April, 49–51.

Binet, A., and Féré, C. (1901) Animal Magnetism. New York: Appleton and Company.

Bitterman, M.E., and Marcuse, F.L. (1945) Autonomic response in post-hypnotic amnesia. J. Exp. Psychol., 35, 248–252.

Bloom, F., Segal, D., Ling, N., and Guillemin, R. (1976) Endorphins: Profound behavioural effects on rats suggest new etiological factors in mental illness. Science, 194, 630–632.

Bogdanoff, M.D., Klein, R.F., Estes, E.H., Shaw, P.H., and Back, K.W. (1961) The modifying effect of conforming behaviour upon lipid responses accompanying CNS arousal. Clin. Res., 9, 135.

Borkovec, T.D. (1973) The role of expectancy of physiological feedback in fear research: A review with special reference to subject characteristics. Beh. Ther. 4, 491–505.

Boucher, R.G., and Hilgard, E.R. (1962) Volunteer bias in hypnotic experimentation. Amer. J. Clin. Hypn., 5, 49–51.

Bousfield, W.A. (1953) The occurrence of clustering in the recall of randomly arranged associates. J. Gen. Psychol., 49, 229–240.

Bovard, E.W. (1948) Social norms and the individual. J. Abnorm. Soc. Psychol., 43, 62–69.

Bowart, W. (1978) Operation mind control. Glasgow: Fontana/Collins.

Bowers, K.S. (1966) Hypnotic behaviour: The differentiation of trance and demand characteristic variables. J. Abnorm. Psychol., 71, 42–51.

Bowers, K.S. (1967) The effects of demands for honesty on reports of visual and auditory hallucinations. Int. J. Clin. Exp. Hypn., 15, 31–36.

Bowers, K.S. (1971) Sex and susceptibility as moderator variables in the relationship of creativity and hypnotic susceptibility. J. Abnorm. Psychol., 78, 93–100.

Bowers, K.S. (1973) Hypnosis, attribution and demand characteristics. Int. J. Clin. Exp. Hypn, 21, 226–238.

Bowers, K.S. (1976) Hypnosis for the seriously curious. Monterey, California: Brooks/Cole.

Brady, J.P., and Levitt, E.E. (1966) Hypnotically induced visual hallucinations. Psychosom. Med., 28, 351–363.

Braid, J. (1847) Facts and observations as to the relative value of mesmeric and hypnotic coma, and ethereal narcotism, for the mitigation or entire prevention of pain during surgical operations. Med. Times, 15, 381–383.

Braid, J. (1899) Neurypnology: Or the Rationale of Nervous Sleep considered in relation to animal magnetism or mesmerism. Waite, J. (ed.) London: George Redway.

Brehm, J.W., and Cohen, A.P. (1962) Explorations in cognitive dissonance. New York: Wiley.

Bronfenbrenner, U. (1975) Is 80% of intelligence genetically determined? In Bronfenbrenner, U., and Mahoney, M.A. (eds.), Influences on human development. Hinsdale, Ill.: Dryden Press, 91–100.

Brown, R. (1965) Social Psychology. New York: The Free Press.

Bruner, J.S., and Goodman, C.C. (1947) Value and need as organising factors in perception. J. Abnorm. Soc. Psychol., 42, 33–44.

Buckout, R. (1974) Eye witness testimony. Scientific Amer. 231, 23–31.

Burr, C.W. (1921) The reflexes of early infancy. Brit. J. Child Dis. 18, 152–153.

Butler, B. (1954) The use of hypnosis in the care of the cancer patient. Cancer, 7, 1–14.

Cade, C.M. (1973) Psychical research experiments under hypnosis. J. Soc. Psychic. Res. 47, 31.

Cade, C.M., and Woolley-Hart, A. (1974) Psychophysiological studies of hypnotic phenomena. Brit. J. Clin. Hypn., 5, 14–25.

Calder, B.J., Ross, M., and Insko, C.A. (1973) Attitude change and attitude attribution: Effects of incentive, choice and consequences. J. Pers. Soc. Psychol., 25, 84–99.

Calverley, D.S., and Barber, T.X. (1965) 'Hypnosis' and antisocial behaviour: An experimental evaluation. Harding, Mass.: Medfield Foundation. (Mimeo.) Cited by Barber, 1969b.

Carli, G. (1978) Animal hypnosis and pain. In Frankel, F.H., and Zamansky, H.S. (eds.), Hypnosis at its bicentennial: Selected papers. New York: Plenum, 69–77.

Cangello, V.M. (1962) Hypnosis for the patient with cancer. Amer. J. Clin. Hypn., 4, 215–226.

Cattell, M. (1943) The action and use of analgesics. Proc. Assoc. Res. Nerv. Ment. Dis., 23, 365–372. Cited by Barber, 1969b.

Cautela, J.R. (1966) Desensitisation factors in the hypnotic treatment of phobias. J. Psychol., 64, 277–288.

Cautela, J.R. (1975) The use of covert conditioning in hypnotherapy. Int. J. Clin. Exp. Hypn., 23, 15–27.

Chapman, J.S. (1969) Effects of different nursing approaches upon psychological and physiological responses. Nursing Res. Rep., 5, 1–71.

Chapman, C.R., and Feather, B.W. (1973) Effects of diazepam on human pain tolerance and sensitivity. Psychosom. Med., 35, 330–340.

Chaves, J.F. (1972) Acupuncture analgesia: New data for psychology and psychophysiology. Paper presented at the annual meeting of the Mass. Psychology Association, Boston, May. Cited by Barber, Spanos and Chaves, 1974.

Chaves, J.F., and Barber, T.X. (1973) Needles and Knives: Behind the mystery of acupuncture and Chinese meridians. Human Behav., 2, 19–24.

Chaves, J.F., and Barber, T.X. (1976) Hypnotic procedures and surgery: A critical analysis with applications to 'acupuncture analgesia'. Amer. J. Clin. Hypn., 18, 4, 217–236.

Chertok, L. (1959) Psychosomatic methods in childbirth. New York: Pergamon.

Chlifer, R.I. (1937) Verbal analgesia in childbirth. Psychotherapia, 307–318.

Clawson, T.A., and Swade, R.H. (1975) The hypnotic control of blood flow and pain: The cure of warts and the potential for the use of hypnosis in the treatment of cancer. Amer. J. Clin. Hypn., 17, 160–169.

Coe, W.C. (1973) A further evaluation of responses to an uncompleted posthypnotic suggestion. Amer. J. Clin. Hypn. 15, 223–228.

Coe, W.C., Basden, B., Basden, D. and Graham, C. (1976) Posthypnotic amnesia: Suggestions of an active process in dissociative phenomena. J. Abnorm. Psychol., 85, 455–458.

Coffin, T.E. (1941) Some conditions of suggestion and suggestibility: Psychol., Monogr. No. 4, 53.

Conn, J.H., and Conn, R.N. (1967) Discussion of T.X. Barber's 'Hypnosis as a causal variable in present-day psychology: A critical analysis'. Int. J. Clin. Exp. Hypn., 15, 106–110.

Cook, T.D., and Wadsworth, A. (1972) Attitude change and the paired-associate learning of minimal cognitive elements. J. Pers. 40, 50–61.

Cooper, L.M. (1966) Spontaneous and suggested posthypnotic source amnesia. Int. J. Clin. Exp. Hypn., 14, 180–193.

Cooper, L.M. (1972) Hypnotic amnesia. In Fromm, E., and Shor, R.E. (eds.), Hypnosis: Research developments and perspectives. Chicago: Aldine-Atherton, 217–252.

Cooper, S.R., and Powles, W.E. (1945) The psychosomatic approach to medicine. McGill Med. J., 14, 415–438.

Coppolino, C.A. (1965) Practice of hypnosis in anaesthesiology. New York: Grune and Stratton.

Costanzo, P.R., and Shaw, M.E. (1966) Conformity as a function of age level. Child Development, 35, 1217–1231.

Crasilneck, H.B., and Hall, J.A. (1959) Physiological changes associated with hypnosis: A review of the literature since 1948. Int. J. Clin. Exp. Hypn., 7, 9–50.

Crasilneck, H.B., McCranie, E.J., and Jenkins, M.T. (1956) Special indications for hypnosis as a method of anaesthesia. J. Amer. Med. Assoc., 162, 1606–1608.

Crawford, F.T. (1977) Induction and duration of tonic immobility. Psychol. Rec., 1, 89–107.

Crisp, A.H., and Moldofsky, H. (1965) A psychosomatic study of writer's cramp. Brit. J. Psychiat., 111, 841–858.

Cronin, D.M., Spanos, N.P., and Barber, T.X. (1971) Augmenting hypnotic suggestibility by providing favourable information about hypnosis. Amer. J. Clin. Hypn., 13, 257–264.

Crutchfield, R.S. (1955) Conformity and character. Amer. Psychol., 10, 191–198.

Damaser, E.C. (1964) Experimental study of long-term post-hypnotic suggestion. Doctoral dissertation. Univ. Harvard. Cited by Orne, 1970.

Deckert, G.H., and West, L.J. (1963) Hypnosis and experimental psychopathology. Amer. J. Clin. Hypn., 5, 256–276.

Diamond, M.J. (1972) The use of observationally-presented information to modify hypnotic susceptibility. J. Abnorm. Psychol. 79, 174–180.

Diamond, M.J., Steadman, C., Harada, D., and Rosenthal, J. (1975) The use of direct instructions to modify hypnotic performance: The effects of programmed learning procedures, J. Abnorm. Psychol., 84, 109–113.

Dixon, N.F. (1971) Subliminal perception: The nature of a controversy. London: McGraw-Hill.

Dobie, S. (1959) Operant conditioning of verbal and hallucinatory responses with non verbal reinforcement. Paper presented to the Midwest Psychological Association, Chicago, May. Cited by Barber, 1969b.

Dorcus, R.M. (1937) Modification by suggestion of some vestibular and visual responses. Amer. J. Psychol., 49, 82–87.

Dorcus, R.M., Brintnall, A.K., and Case, H.W. (1941) Control experiments and their relation to theories of hypnotism. J. Gen. Psychol., 24, 217–221.

Dubois, E.F. (1946) Cornell conference on therapy. N.Y. State J. Med., 46, 1718.

Dynes, J.B. (1932) An experimental study of hypnotic anaesthesia. J. Abnorm. Soc. Psychol. 27, 79–88.

Eagly, A.H. (1978) Sex differences in influencibility. Psychol. Bull., 85, 86–116.

Edmonston, W.E. (1960) An experimental investigation of hypnotic age regression. Amer. J. Clin. Hypn., 3, 127–138.

Edmonston, W.E. (1977) Neutral hypnosis as relaxation. Amer. J. Clin. Hypn., 30, 69–75.

Edmonston, W.E., and Grotevant, W.R. (1975) Hypnosis and alpha density. Amer. J. Clin. Hypn., 17, 221–232.

Edmonston, W.E., and Pessin, M. (1966) Hypnosis as related to learning and electrodermal measures. Amer. J. Clin. Hypn., 9, 31–51.

Edwards, G. (1960) Hypnotic treatment of asthma: Real and illusory results. Brit. Med. J., 2, 492–497.

Egbert, L.D., Battit, G.E., Turndorf, H., and Beecher, H.K. (1963) J.

Amer. Med. Assoc., 185, 553–555.

Egbert, L.D., Battit, G.E., Welch, C.E., and Bartlett, M.K. (1964) Reduction of postoperative pain by encouragement and instruction of patients. New Eng. J. Med., 270, 825–827.

Eliseo, T.S. (1974) The hypnotic induction profile and hypnotic susceptibility. Int. J. Clin. Exp. Hypn., 22, 320–326.

Ellenberger, H.F. (1970) The Discovery of the Unconscious: The History and Evolution of Dynamic Psychiatry. New York: Basic Books.

Elliot, R. (1972) The significance of heart rate for behaviour: A critique of Lacey's hypothesis. J. Pers. Soc. Psychol., 3, 398–409.

Erickson, M.H. (1938) A study of clinical and experimental findings on hypnotic deafness. I. Clinical experimentation and findings. J. Gen. Psychol. 19, 127–150 (a).

Erickson, M.H. (1938) A study of clinical and experimental findings on hypnotic deafness: II. Experimental findings with a conditioned response technique, 19, J. Gen. Psychol., 19, 151–167 (b).

Erickson, M.H. (1939) The induction of colour blindness by a technique of hypnotic suggestion. J. Gen. Psychol., 20, 61–89.

Erickson, M.H., and Erickson, E.M. (1938) The hypnotic induction of hallucinatory colour vision followed by pseudo negative after images. J. Exp. Psychol., 22, 581–588.

Esdaile, J. (1957) Hypnosis in medicine and surgery. New York: Julian Press.

Eskridge, V.L. (1969) The effects of limited training in hypnosis upon reaction time. Master's thesis. Western Kentucky Univ., Bowling Green. Cited by Morgan, 1972.

Etaugh, C.F. (1972) Personality correlates of lateral eye movement and handedness. Percept. Mot. Skills, 34, 751–754.

Evans, F.J. (1967) Suggestibility in the normal waking state. Psychol. Bull., 67, 114–129.

Evans, F.J. (1974) The power of a sugar pill. Psychol. Today, April. 55–59 (a).

Evans, F.J. (1974) The placebo response in pain reduction. In DiCara, L.V., Barber, T.X., Kamiya, J., Miller, N.E., Shapiro, D., and Stoyva, J. (eds.), Biofeedback and self-control. Chicago; Aldine, 72–79 (b).

Evans, F.J., Gustafson, L.A., O'Connell, D.N., Orne, M.T., and Shor, R.E. (1966) Response during sleep with intervening waking amnesia. Science, 152, 666–667.

Evans, F.J., and Kihlstrom, J.F. (1973) Post-hypnotic amnesia as disrupted retrieval. J. Abnorm. Psychol., 82, 317–232.

Evans, F.J., and Orne, M.T. (1965) Motivation, performance and hypnosis. Int. J. Clin. Exp. Hypn., 13, 103–116.

Evans, F.J., and Orne, M.T. (1971) The disappearing hypnotist: The use of simulating subjects to evaluate how subjects perceive experimental procedures. Int. J. Clin. Exp. Hypn., 19, 277–296.

Evans, M.B., and Paul, G.L. (1970) Effects of hypnotically suggested analgesia on physiological and subjective responses to cold stress. J. Consult. Clin. Psychol., 35, 362–371.

Evans, F.J., and Thorn, W.A.F. (1966) Two types of post-hypnotic amnesia: Recall amnesia and source amnesia. Int. J. Clin. Exp. Hypn., 14, 162–179.

Ewin, D.M. (1974) Condyloma acumination: Successful treatment of four cases by hypnosis. Amer. J. Clin. Hypn., 17, 73–78.

Eysenck, H.J. (1977) Crime and personality. St. Albans, Herts.: Paladin Frogmore.

Eysenck, H.J., Arnold, W.J., and Meili, R. (1975) Encyclopedia of Psychology: Volume Two L–Z. Bungay, Suffolk: Fontana.

Eysenck, H.J., and Furneaux, W.D. (1945) Primary and secondary suggestibility. J. Exp. Psychol., 25, 485–503.

Faria, J.C. di, Abbé (1819) De la cause du sommeil lucide; ou étude sur la nature de l'homme. 2nd edition, D.G. Dalgado (ed.), Paris: Henri Jouve, 1906.

Fellows, B.J., and Creamer, M. (1978) An investigation of the role of 'hypnosis', hypnotic susceptibility and hypnotic induction in the production of age regression. Brit. J. Soc. Clin. Psychol., 17, 165–171.

Festinger, L. (1954) A theory of social comparison processes. Human Rel. 7, 117–140.

Festinger, L. (1957) A theory of cognitive dissonance. New York: Harper and Row.

Festinger, L. (1962) Cognitive dissonance. Sci. Amer. 107, 4 (Offprint 472).

Festinger, L., Reicken, H., and Schacter, S. (1956) When prophecy fails. Minneapolis, Minn.: Univ. Minnesota Press.

Findley, T. (1953) The placebo and the physician. Med. Clin. N. Amer., 37, 1821.

Fisher, S. (1954) The role of expectancy in the performance of post-hypnotic behaviour. J. Abnorm. Soc. Psychol., 49, 503–507.

Fisher, S. (1966) Body attention patterns and personality defences. Psychol. Bull. 80, 9, whole no. 67.

Fowler, W.L. (1961) Hypnosis and learning. Int. J. Clin. Exp. Hypn. 223–232.

Frank, D.P. (1944) Experimental studies of personal pressure and resistance: 1. Experimental production of resistance. J. Gen. Psychol. 30, 23–41.

Frankel, F.H. (1976) Hypnosis: Trance as a coping mechanism. New York: Plenum Medical.

Frankel, F.H., and Zamansky, H.S. (eds.) (1978) Hypnosis at its bicentennial: Selected papers. New York: Plenum.

Freedman, J.L. (1975) Crowding and behaviour. San Francisco: Freeman.

Freedman, J.L., and Fraser, S.C. (1966) Compliance without pressure: the foot-in-the-door technique. J. Pers. Soc. Psychol., 7, 117–124.

Freud, S. (1977) Introductory lectures on psychoanalysis. Harmondsworth, Middlesex: Penguin Books.

Freud, S., and Breur, J. (1974) Studies on Hysteria. Harmondsworth, Middlesex: Penguin Books.

Frid, M., and Singer, G. (1979) Hypnotic analgesia in conditions of stress in partially reversed by naloxone. Psychopharmacology, 63, 211–215.

Gallup, G. (1975) Hypnosis in animals. New Scientist. April. 68–70.

Gallup, G. (1977) Tonic immobility: the role of fear and predation. Psychol. Rec. 1, 41–61.

Gaupp, L.A., Stern, R.M., and Galbraith, G.G. (1972) False heart-rate feedback reciprocal inhibition by aversive relief in the treatment of snake avoidance behaviour. Behav. Ther. 3, 7–20.

Gerard, H.B., and Mathewson, G.C. (1966) The effects of severity of initiation on liking for a group: A replication. J. Exp. Soc. Psychol., 2, 278–287.

Getzels, J.W., and Jackson, P.W. (1962) Creativity and intelligence. New York: Wiley.

Gibson, H.B. (1977) Hypnosis: Its nature and therapeutic benefits. London: Peter Owen.

Gibson, H.B., and Corcoran, M.E. (1975) Personality and differential susceptibility to hypnosis: Further replication and sex differences. Brit. J. Psychol., 66, 513–520.

Gibson, H.B., Corcoran, M.E., and Curran, J.D. (1977) Hypnotic susceptibility and personality: The consequences of diazepam and the sex of the subjects. Brit. J. Psychol., 68, 52–59.

Gibson, H.B., and Curran, J.D. (1974) Hypnotic susceptibility and personality: A replication study. Brit. J. Psychol., 65, 283–291.

Gidro-Frank, L., and Bowersbuch, M.K. (1948) A study of the plantar response in hypnotic age regression. J. Nerv. Ment. Dis., 107, 443–458.

Gill, M.M., and Brenman, M. (1959) Hypnosis and related states. New York: International Universities Press.

Goffman, E. (1959) The presentation of self in everyday life. New York: Double-day Anchor Books.

Goldberg, L.R., and Rorer, L.G. (1966) Use of two different response modes and repeated testings. J. Abnorm. Soc. Psychol., 3, 28–37.

Goldiamond, I., and Malpass, L.F. (1961) Locus of hypnotically induced changes in colout vision responses. J. Opt. Soc. Amer. 51, 1117–1121.

Goldstein, A. (1976) Opioid peptides (Endorphins) in pituitary and brain. Science, 193, 1081–1086.

Goldstein, A., and Hilgard, E.R. (1975) Failure of the opiate antagonist naloxone to modify hypnotic analgesia. Proc. Nat. Acad. Sci., 72, 2041–2043.

Goldstein, M.S., and Sipprelle, C.N. (1970) Hypnotically induced amnesia versus ablation of memory. Int. J. Clin. Exp. Hypn., 18, 211–216.

Goodman, L.S., and Gilman, A. (1970) The pharmacological basis of therapeutics. (4th ed.). New York: Macmillan.

Gorton, B.E. (1949) The physiology of hypnosis. Psychiat. Quart., 23, 317–343 and 457–485.

Gottfredson, D.K. (1973) Hypnosis as an anaesthetic in dentistry. Doctoral dissertation, Brigham Young Univ. Diss. Abs. Int. 33, 7–B, 3303.

Grace, W.J., and Graham, D.T. (1952) Relationship of specific attitudes and emotions to certain bodily diseases. Psychosom. Med., 14, 243–251.

Graham, C., and Evans, F.J. (1977) Hypnotisability and the deployment of waking attention. J. Abnorm. Psychol., 86, 631–638.

Graham, C., and Leibowitz, H.W. (1972) The effect of suggestion on visual activity. Int. J. Clin. Exp. Hypn., 20, 169–186.

Graham, K.R., and Patton, A. (1968) Retroactive inhibition, hypnosis and hypnotic amnesia. Int. J. Clin. Exp. Hypn., 16, 68–74.

Gray, A.L., Bowers, K.S., and Fenz, W.D. (1970) Heart rate in anticipation of and during a negative visual hallucination. Int. J. Clin. Exp. Hypn., 18, 41–51.

Greenwald, A.G. (1965) Behaviour change following a persuasive communication. J. Pers., 33, 370–391.

Gregg, V. (1979) Post-hypnotic amnesia and general memory theory. Bull. Brit. Soc. Exp. Clin. Hypn., 2, 11–14.

Gummerman, K., Gray, C.F., and Wilson, J.M. (1972) An attempt to assess eidetic imagery objectively. Psychonomic. Sci. 28, 115–117.

Gunne, L.M., Lindstrom, L., and Terenius, L. (1977) Naloxone-induced reversal of schizophrenic hallucinations. Neural Transmission. 40, 13–19.

Gur, R.C., and Gur, R.E. (1974) Handedness, sex, and eyedness as moderating variables in the relation between hypnotic susceptibility and functional brain asymmetry. J. Abnorm. Psychol. 83, 635–643.

Gur, R., and Reyher, J. (1973) Relationship between style of hypnotic induction and direction of lateral eye movements. J. Abnorm. Psychol. 82, 499–505.

Haber, R.N., and Haber, R.B. (1964) Eidetic imagery: I. Frequency. Percept. Mot. Skills, 19, 131–138.

Hadfield, J.A. (1920) The influence of suggestion on body temperature. Lancet, 2, 68–69.

Hadfield, J.A. (1924) The Psychology of Power. London: Macmillan.

Haggard, H.W. (1929) Devils, drugs and doctors. New York: Harper and Bros.

Hahn, K.W., and Barber, T.X. (1966) Hallucinations with and without hypnotic induction: An extension of the Brady and Levitt study. Harding, Mass.: Medfield Foundation. (Mimeo.) Cited by Barber, 1969b.

Hall, T., and Grant, G. (1978) Superpsych: The power of hypnosis. London: Abacus.

Hammerschlag, H.E. (1957) Hypnotism and Crime. Hollywood, Calif.: Wilshire Book Co.

Hansel, C.E.M. (1966) ESP: A scientific evaluation. London: MacGibbon and Key.

Harriman, P.L. (1942) Hypnotic induction of colour vision anomalies: I. The use of Ishibara and Jensen tests to verify the acceptance of suggested colour blindness. J. Gen. Psychol., 26, 289–298.

Harrison, A.A. (1969) Exposure and popularity. J. Pers. 37, 359–377.

Hartshorne, H., and May, M.A. (1928) Studies in deceit. New York: Macmillan.

Hartshorne, H., May, M.A., and Shuttleworth, F.K. (1930) Studies in the organisation of character. New York: Macmillan.

Hartup, W.W. (1970) Peer interaction and social organisation. In P.H. Mussen (ed.), Manual of child psychology. New York: Wiley.

Hearne, K.M.T. (1978) Lucid dreams: An electro-physiological and psychological study. Doctoral dissertation. Univ. Liverpool.

Hibler, F.W. (1940) An experimental investigation of negative afterimages of hallucinated colours in hypnosis. J. Exp. Psychol., 27, 45–57.

Hilgard, E.R. (1965) Hypnotic susceptibility. New York: Harcourt Brace and World.

Hilgard, E.R. (1969) Altered states of awareness. J. Nerv. Ment. Dis. 149, 68–79 (a).

Hilgard, E.R. (1969) Pain as a puzzle for psychology and physiology. Amer. Psychol., 24, 103–113 (b).

Hilgard, J.R. (1970) Personality and hypnosis. Chicago: Univ. Chicago Press.

Hilgard, E.R. (1972) A critique of Johnson, Maher and Barber's 'Artifact in the 'essence of hypnosis''. An evaluation of trance logic', with a recomputation of their findings. J. Abnorm. Psychol., 79, 221–233.

Hilgard, E.R. (1973) A neo-dissociation theory of pain reduction in hypnosis. Psychol. Rev., 80, 366–411 (a).

Hilgard, E.R. (1973) The domain of hypnosis: With some comments on alternative paradigms. Amer. Psychol., 23, 972–982 (b).

Hilgard, E.R. (1975) Hypnosis. Ann. Rev. Psychol., 26, 19–44.

Hilgard, E.R., Atkinson, R.C., and Atkinson, R.L. (1971) Introduction to psychology. (5th ed.). New York: Harcourt Brace Jovanovich.

Hilgard, E.R., and Bentler, P.M. (1963) Predicting hypnotisability from the Maudsley Personality Inventory. Brit. J. Psychol., 54, 63–69.

Hilgard, E.R., Macdonald, H., Marshall, G., and Morgan, A.H. (1974) Anticipation of pain and pain control under hypnosis: Heartrate and blood pressure responses in the cold pressor test. J. Abnorm. Psychol., 38, 561–568.

Hilgard, E.R., Macdonald, H., Morgan, A.H., and Johnson, L.S. (1978) The reality of hypnotic analgesia: A comparison of highly hypnotisables with simulators. J. Abnorm. Psychol., 87, 239–246.

Hilgard, E.R., and Marquis, D.G. (1940) Conditioning and Learning. New York: Appleton-Century.

Hilgard, E.R., Morgan, A.H., Lange, A.F., Lenox, J.R., Macdonald, H., Marshall, G., and Sachs, L.B. (1974) Heart rate changes in pain and hypnosis. Psychophysiology, 11, 692–702.

Hilgard, E.R., Morgan, A.H., and Macdonald, H. (1975) Pain and dissociation in the cold pressor test: A study of hypnotic analgesia with 'hidden reports' through automatic key pressing and automatic talking. J. Abnorm. Psychol., 84, 280–289.

Hilgard, E.R., and Tart, C.T. (1966) Responsiveness to suggestions following waking and following induction of hypnosis. J. Abnorm. Psychol. 71, 196–208.

Hill, H.E., Kornetsky, C.H., Flanary, H.G., and Wickler, A. (1952) Effects of anxiety and morphine on discrimination intensities of painful stimuli. J. Clin. Invest. 31, 473–480 (a).

Hill, H.E., Kornetsky, C.H., Flanary, H.G., and Wickler, A. (1952) Studies on anxiety associated with anticipation of pain. I. Effects of morphine. Arch. Neurol. Psychiat., 67, 612–619 (b).

Hintzman, D.L., and Waters, R.M. (1970) Recency and frequency as factors in list discrimination. J. Verb. Learn. Verb. Behav., 9, 218–221.

Hiscock, M. (1977) Eye movement asymmetry and hemisphere functioning: An examination of individual differences. J. Psychol., 97, 49–52.

Hoagland, H. (1928) The mechanism of tonic immobility ('Animal hypnosis'). J. Gen. Psychol., 1, 426–447.

Hood, W.R., and Sherif, M. (1962) Verbal report and judgment of an unstructured stimulus. J. Psychol., 54, 121–130.

Horowitz, I.A., and Rothschild, B.H. (1970) Conformity as a function of deception and role playing. J. Pers. Soc. Psychol., 14, 224–226.

Hoving, K.L., Hamm, N., and Galvin, P. (1969) Social influence as a function of stimulus ambiguity at three age levels. Dev. Psychol., 1, 631–636.

Hovland, C.I., and Mandell, W. (1952) An experimental comparison of conclusion-drawing by the communicator and by the audience. J. Abnorm. Soc. Psychol., 581–588.

Hovland, C.I., and Weiss, W. (1951) The influence of source credibility on communication effectiveness. Publ. Opin. Quart. 15, 635–650.

Hughes, J. (1975) Isolation of an endogenous compound from the brain with properties similar to morphine. Brain Res., 88, 295–308.

Hull, C.L. (1933) Hypnosis and Suggestibility: An Experimental Approach. New York: Appleton-Century-Crofts.

Hunt, S.M. (1979) Hypnosis as obedience behaviour. Brit. J. Soc. Clin. Psychol., 18, 21–27.

Ikemi, Y., and Nakagawa, S.A. (1962) A psychosomatic study of contagious dermatitis. Kyushu J. Med. Sci., 13, 335–350.

Iverson, J. (1976) More lives than one? London: Pan Books.

Jahoda, G. (1970) The psychology of superstition. Harmondsworth, Middlesex: Penguin Books.

Janet, P. (1920) Major symptoms of hysteria. New York: Macmillan. Janis, I.L., and King, B.T. (1954) The influence of role-playing on opinion change. J. Abnorm. Soc. Psychol., 49, 211–218.

Jecker, J., Maccoby, N. Breitrose, H.S., and Rose, E.D. (1964) Teacher accuracy in assessing cognitive visual feedback from students. J. App. Psychol., 48, 393–397.

Jenness, A. (1944) Hypnotism. In Hunt, J. (ed.), Personality and behaviour disorders. New York: Ronald.

Johnson, R.F. (1972) Trance logic revisited: A reply to Hilgard's critique. J. Abnorm. Psychol., 79, 234–238.

Johnson, R.F., Maher, B.A., and Barber, T.X. (1972) Artifact in the 'essence of hypnosis': An evaluation of trance logic. J. Abnorm. Psychol., 79, 212–220.

Jones, E.E. (1964) Ingratiation. New York: Appleton-Century-Crofts.

Jones, E.E., and Gerard, H.B. (1967) Foundations of Social Psychology. New York: Wiley.

Kanfer, F.H., and Goldfoot, D.A. (1966) Self-control and tolerance of noxious stimulation. Psychol. Rep., 18, 79–85.

Kaplan, E.A. (1960) Hypnosis and pain. Arch. Gen. Psychiat., 2, 567–568.

Kazdin, A.R., and Wilcoxon, L.A. (1976) Systematic desensitisation and non-specific treatment effects. A methodological evaluation. Psychol. Bull., 83, 729–758.

Kelley, H.H. (1967) Attribution theory in Social Psychology. In Levine, D. (ed.), Nebraska Symposium on Motivation, Vol. 15. Lincoln: University of Nebraska Press, 192–238.

Kelley, H.H. (1972) Attribution in social interaction. In Jones, E.F., et al. (eds.), Attribution: Perceiving the causes of behaviour. Morristown, New Jersey: General Learning Press.

Kellogg, E.R. (1929) Duration and effects of post-hypnotic suggestions, J. Exp. Psychol., 12, 502–514.

Kent, R.N., Wilson, G.T., and Nelson, R. (1972) Effects of false heart-rate feedback on avoidance: An investigation of 'cognitive desensitisation'. Behav. Ther. 3, 1–6.

Kidder, L.H. (1973) On becoming hypnotised: how sceptics become convinced: A case of attitude change? Amer. J. Clin. Hypn., 16, 1–8.

Kiesler, C.A., and Kiesler, S.B. (1970) Conformity. Reading, Mass.: Addison-Wesley.

Kinney, J.M., and Sachs, L.B. (1974) Increasing hypnotic susceptibility. J. Abnorm. Psychol., 83, 145–150.

Kleinhauz, M., Horowitz, I., and Tobin, Y. (1977) The use of hypnosis in police investigation: A preliminary communication. J. Forens. Sci. Soc., 17, 77–80.

Klemm, W.R. (1977) Identity of sensory and motor systems that are critical to the immobility reflex ('Animal hypnosis'). Psychol. Rec., 1, 145–159.

Kline, M.V., Guze, H., and Haggerty, A.D. (1954) An experimental study of the nature of hypnotic deafness. Effects of delayed speech feedback. Int. J. Clin. Exp. Hypn., 2, 154–156.

Klopp, K.K. (1961) Production of local anaesthesia using waking suggestion with the child patient. Int. J. Clin. Exp. Hypn., 9, 59–62.

Knox, V.J., Morgan, A.H., and Hilgard, E.R. (1974) Pain and suffering in ischemia. Arch. Gen. Psychiat., 30, 840–847.

Knox, V.J., Shum, K., and McLaughlin, D.M. (1978) Hypnotic analgesia vs. acupuncture analgesia in high and low hypnotically susceptible subjects. In Frankel, F.H., and Zamansky, H.S. (eds.), Hypnosis at its bicentennial: Selected papers. New York: Plenum, 101–108.

Krauss, H.H., Katzell, R., and Krauss, B.J. (1974) Effect of hypnotic time distortion upon free-recall learning. J. Abnorm. Psychol. 83, 2, 140–144.

Kretch, D., Crutchfield, R.S., and Ballachey, E.L. (1962) Individual in Society. New York: McGraw-Hill.

Kroeber, A.L. (1948) Anthropology. New York: Harcourt.

Kroger, W.S., and Freed, S.C. (1956) Psychosomatic Gynecology. New York: Free Press.

Kusche, L.D. (1975) The Bermuda Triangle Mystery — Solved. London: New English Library.

Lacey, J.I. (1967) Somatic response patterning and stress: Some revisions of activation theory. In Appley, M.H., and Trumbell, R. (eds.), Psychological Stress. New York: International University Press, 161–196.

Lang, P.J., and Lazowik, A.D. (1962) Personality and hypnotic susceptibility. J. Consult. Psychol., 26, 317–233.

Lang, P.J., Lazowick, A.D., and Reynolds, D.J. (1965) Desensitisation, suggestibility and pseudotherapy. J. Abnorm. Psychol., 70, 395–402.

Lazarus, A.A. (1971) Behaviour therapy and beyond. New York: McGraw Hill.

Lazarus, A.A. (1973) 'Hypnosis' as a facilitator in behaviour therapy. Int. J. Clin. Exp. Hypn., 21, 25–31.

Lazarus, R.S., Speisman, J.C., and Mordkoff, A.M. (1963) The relationship between autonomic indicators of psychological stress: heart rate and skin conductance. Psychosom. Med., 25, 19–30.

Lea, P.A., Ware, P.D., and Monroe, R.R. (1960) The hypnotic control of intractable pain. Amer. J. Clin. Hypn., 3, 3–8.

Lee-Teng, E. (1965) Trance-susceptibility, induction susceptibility, and acquiesence as factors in hypnotic performance. J. Abnorm. Psychol., 70, 383–389.

Leitenberg, H., Agras, W.S., Barlow, D.H., and Oliveau, D.C. (1969) Contribution of selective positive reinforcement and therapeutic instructions to systematic desensitisation therapy. J. Abnorm. Psychol., 74, 113–118.

Lenox, J.R. (1970) Effect of hypnotic analgesia on verbal report and cardiovascular responses to ischemic pain. J. Abnorm. Psychol., 75, 199–206.

Leslie, A. (1954) Ethics and practice of placebo therapy. Amer. J. Med., 16, 854.

Levine, J.D., Gordon, N.C., and Fields, H.L. (1978) The mechanism of placebo analgesia. Lancet, Sept., 654–657.

Levitt, E.E., and Brady, J.P. (1963) Psychophysiology of hypnosis. In Schneck, J.M. (ed.), Hypnosis in modern medicine. (3rd ed.). Springfield, Ill.: C.C. Thomas. 314–362.

Levy, L.H. (1967) Awareness learning and the beneficient subject as expert witness. J. Pers. Soc. Psychol., 6, 365–370.

Lewenstein, L.N. (1978) Hypnosis as an anaesthetic in pediatric opthalmology. Anesthesiology, 49, 144–145.

Lewis, J.L., and Sarbin, T.R. (1943) Studies in psychosomatics: The influence of hypnotic stimulation on gastric hunger contractions. Psychosom. Med., 5, 125–131.

Lewis, T. (1927) The Blood Vessels of the Human Skin and their Responses. London: Shaw.

Lewis, T. (1942) Pain. New York: Macmillan.

Ley, P. (1977) Communicating with the patient. In Coleman, J.C. (ed.), Introductory psychology: A textbook for health students. 321–343.

Liebeault, A.A. (1885) Anesthesie par suggestion. J. Magnestisme, 64–67. Cited by Chertok, 1959.

Lindeman, C.A., and van Aernam, B. (1971) Nursing intervention with the pre-surgical patient: the effects of structured and unstructured pre-operative teaching. Nursing Res., 20, 319–332.

Livingston, W.K. (1943) Pain mechanisms. New York: Macmillan.

Livingston, W.K. (1953) What is pain. Sci. Amer., 196, 59.

Loftus, E.F. (1975) Leading questions and the eyewitness report, Cogn. Psychol., 7, 560–572.

London, P. (1961) Subject characteristics in hypnosis research. I. A Survey of experience, interest and opinion. Int. J. Clin. Exp. Hypn., 9, 151–161.

London, P., Cooper, L.M., and Engstrom, D.R. (1974) Increasing hypnotic susceptibility by brain wave feedback. J. Abnorm. Psychol., 83, 554–560.

London, P., Cooper, L.M., and Johnson, H.J. (1962) Subject characteristics in hypnosis research: II. Attitudes toward hypnosis, volunteer status, and personality measures. III. Some correlates of hypnotic susceptibility. Int. J. Clin. Exp. Hypn., 10, 13–21.

London, P., and Fuhrer, M. (1961) Hypnosis, motivation, and performance. J. Pers. 29, 321–333.

Longo, V.C. (1972) Neuropharmacology and behaviour. San Francisco: Freeman.

Loomis, A.L., Harvey, E.N., and Hobart, G. (1936) Electrical potentials of the human brain. J. Exp. Psychol., 19, 249–279.

Lozanov, G. (1967) Anaesthetisation through suggestion in a state of wakefulness. Proceedings of the 7th European Conference on Psychosomatic Research, Rome, 399–402. Cited by Barber, Spanos and Chaves, 1974.

Lundholm, H. (1928) An experimental study of functional anaesthesias as induced by suggestions in hypnosis. J. Abnorm. Soc. Psychol., 23, 337–355.

Lundholm, H. (1932) A hormic theory of hallucinations. Brit. J. Med. Psychol., 11, 269–282.

Lynch, J.J., and Fertziger, A.P. (1977) Drug addiction: Light at the end of the tunnel? J. Nerv. Ment. Dis. 164, 229–230.

Lynch, J.J., Paskewitz, D.A., and Orne, M.T. (1974) Some factors in the feedback control of human alpha rhythm. Psychosom. Med. 36, 399–410.

McCranie, E.J., and Crasilneck, H.B. (1955) The conditioned reflex in hypnotic age regression. J. Clin. Exp. Psychopath., 16, 120–123.

McGlashan, T.H., Evans, F.J., and Orne, M.T. (1969) The nature of hypnotic analgesia and placebo response to experimental pain. Psychosom. Med. 31, 227–246.

McGlone, J., and Davidson, W. (1973) The relation between cerebral speech laterality and spatial ability with special reference to sex and hand preference. Neuropsychologia, 11, 105–113.

McGuire, W.J. (1968) Personality and susceptibility to social influence. In Borgatta, E.F., and Lambert, W.W. (eds.), Handbook of Personality Theory and Research. Chicago: Rand McNally. 1130–1187.

Mackay, C. (1869) Memoirs of extraordinary popular delusions and the madness of crowds. London: Routledge.

Madsen, C.H., and London, P. (1966) Role playing and hypnotic susceptibility in children. J. Pers. Soc. Psychol., 3, 13–19.

Maher-Loughnan, G.P. (1970) Hypnosis and autohypnosis for the treatment of asthma. Int. J. Clin. Exp. Hypn., 18, 1–14.

Maher-Loughnan, G.P., MacDonald, N., Mason, A.A., and Fry, L. (1962) Controlled trial of hypnosis in the symptomatic treatment of asthma. Brit. Med. J., 2, 371–376.

Malmo, R.B., Boag, T.J., and Raginsky, B.B. (1954) Electro-myographic study of hypnotic deafness. J. Clin. Exp. Hypn., 2, 305–317.

Marcuse, F.L. (1976) Hypnosis: Fact and Fiction. Harmondsworth, Middlesex: Penguin Books.

Marenina, A. (1955) Further investigation of the dynamics of cerebral potentials in the various phases of hypnosis in man. Fiziologicheski

Zhurnal. Science, 163, 434–445. Cited by Edmonston and Grotevant, 1975.

Mandy, A.J., Mandy, T.E., Farkas, R., and Scher, E. (1952) Is natural childbirth natural? Psychosom. Med., 14, 431–438.

Marks, I.M., Gelder, M.G., and Edwards, G. (1968) Hypnosis and desensitisation for phobias: A controlled prospective trial. Brit. J. Psychiat., 114, 1263–1274.

Marmer, M.J. (1957) Hypnoanalgesics: The use of hypnosis in conjunction with chemical anaesthesia. Anesth. Analg. 36, 27–31.

Marmer, M.J. (1959) Hypnosis in anaesthesiology. Springfield, Ill.: C.C. Thomas.

Marx, J.L. (1977) Analgesia: How the body inhibits pain perception. Res. News. Feb. 471–195.

Mason, A.A. (1955) Surgery under hypnosis. Anesthesia, 10, 295–299.

Mather, M.D., and Degun, G.S. (1975) A comparative study of hypnosis and relaxation. Brit. J. Med. Psychol., 48, 55–63.

Melnick, J., and Russell, R.W. (1976) Hypnosis versus systematic desensitisation in the treatment of test anxiety. J. Counsel. Psychol. 23, 291–295.

Melzack, R. (1973) The puzzle of pain. Harmondsworth, Middlesex: Penguin Books.

Memmesheimer, A.M., and Eisenlohr, E. (1931) Untersuchungen über die suggestivebehandlung der Warzen. Dermatologie Zietshrift 62, 63–68. Cited by Barber, 1969b.

Messerschmidt, R.A. (1927) A quantitative investigation of the alleged independent operation of conscious and subconscious processes. J. Abnorm. Soc. Psychol., 22, 325–340.

Messerschmidt, R. (1933) Responses of boys between the ages of five to sixteen years to Hull's postural sway suggestion. J. Genet. Psychol., 43, 405–421.

Michael, A.M. (1952) Hypnosis in childbirth. Brit. Med. J., 1, 734–737.

Milgram, S. (1963) Behavioural study of obedience. J. Abnorm. Soc. Psychol., 67, 371–378.

Milgram, S. (1972) Interpreting Obedience: Error and Evidence: A reply to Orne and Holland. In Miller, A.G. (ed.), The social psychology of psychological research. New York: The Free Press.

Milgram, S. (1974) Obedience to Authority. London: Tavistock.

Miller, R.J. (1975) Response to the Ponzo illusion as a reflection of hypnotic susceptibility. Int. J. Clin. Exp. Hypn., 23, 148–157.

Miller, R.L., Brickman, P., and Bolen, D. (1975) Attribution vs. persuasion as a means of modifying behaviour. J. Pers. Soc. Psychol., 31, 430–441.

Miller, R.J., Lundy, R.N., and Galbraith, G.G. (1970) Effects of hypnotically induced hallucination of a colour filter. J. Abnorm. Psychol., 76, 316–319.

Miller, S.B. (1972) The contribution of therapeutic instructions to systematic desensitisation. Behav. Res. Ther. 10, 159–169.

Mischel, W. (1968) Personality and assessment. New York: Wiley.

Mitchell, J.F. (1907) Local anaesthesia in general surgery. J. Amer. Med. Assoc., 48, 198–201.

Mitchell, M.B. (1932) Retroactive inhibition and hypnosis. J. Gen. Psychol., 7, 343–359.

Mixon, P. (1972) Instead of deception. J. Theory Soc., Behav. 2, 145–177.

Mody, N.V. (1960) Report on twenty cases delivered under hypnotism. J. Obstet. Gynec. India, 10, 348–353.

Moll, A. (1958) The study of hypnosis. New York: Julian Press.

Moore, R.K. (1964) Susceptibility to hypnosis and susceptibility to social influence. J. Abnorm. Soc. Psychol., 68, 282–294.

Moreland, R.L., and Zajonc, R.B. (1976) A strong test of exposure effects. J. Exp. Soc. Psychol., 12, 170–179.

Morgan, A.H. (1973) The heritability of hypnotic susceptibility in twins. J. Abnorm. Psychol., 82, 55–61.

Morgan, A.H., and Hilgard, E.R. (1973) Age differences in susceptibility to hypnosis. Int. J. Clin. Exp. Hypn., 21, 78–85.

Morgan, A.H., Macdonald, H., and Hilgard, E.R. (1974) EEG alpha: Lateral asymmetry related to task and hypnotisability. Psychophysiology, 11, 275–282.

Morgan, A.H., McDonald, P.J., and Macdonald, H. (1971) Differences in bilateral activity as a function of experimental task, with a note on lateral eye movements and hypnotisability. Neuropsychologia, 9, 451–469.

Morgan, W.P. (1972) Ergogenic Aids and Muscular Performance. New York: Academic Press.

Murphy, D.B., and Myers, T.I. (1962) Occurrence, measurement and experimental manipulation of visual 'hallucinations'. Percept. Mot. Skills, 15, 47–54.

Nace, E.P., and Orne, M.T. (1970) Fate of an uncompleted post-hypnotic suggestion. J. Abnorm. Psychol., 75, 278–285.

Nace, E.P., Orne, M.T., and Hammer, A.G. (1974) Post-hypnotic amnesia as an active process: The reversibility of amnesia. Arch. Gen. Psychiat., 31, 257–260.

Nagge, J.W. (1935) An experimental test of the theory of associative interference. J. Exp. Psychol., 18, 663–682.

Nelson, R.A. (1965) A complete course in stage hypnotism. Columbus, Ohio: Nelson Enterprises.

Nicholson, N.C. (1920) Notes on muscular work during hypnosis. John Hopkins Hospital Bulletin, 31, 89.

O'Connell, D.N., Shor, R.E., and Orne, M.T. (1970) Hypnotic age regression: An empirical and methodological analysis. J. Abnorm. Psychol. Mono. Supp., 76, 3, Part 2, 1–32.

Oliveau, D.C., Agras, W.S. Leitenberg, H., Moore, R.C., and Wright, D.E.

(1969) Systematic desensitisation, therapeutically oriented instructions and selective positive reinforcement. Behav. Res. Ther. 7, 27–33.

Orne, M.T. (1959) The nature of hypnosis: Artifact and Essence. J. Abnorm. Psychol., 58, 277–299.

Orne, M.T. (1962) On the social psychology of the psychological experiment: With particular reference to demand characteristics and their implications. Amer. Psychol., 17, 776–783.

Orne, M.T. (1966) Hypnosis, motivation, and compliance. Amer. J. Psychiat. 122, 721–726 (a).

Orne, M.T. (1966) On the mechanisms of post-hypnotic amnesia. Int. J. Clin. Exp. Hypn., 14, 121–134 (b).

Orne, M.T. (1969) Demand characteristics and the concept of quasi-controls. In Rosenthal, R., and Rosnow, R.L. (eds.), Artifact in behavioural research. New York: Academic Press, 143–179.

Orne, M.T. (1970) Hypnosis, motivation and the ecological validity of the psychological experiment. In Arnold, W.J., and Page, M.M. (eds.), Nebraska Symposium on Motivation. Lincoln, Nebraska Univ. Nebraska Press, 187–265.

Orne, M.T. (1971) The simulation of hypnosis: Why, how, and what it means. Int. J. Clin. Exp. Hypn., 19, 183–210.

Orne, M.T. (1972) On the simulating subject as a quasi-control in hypnosis research: What, why and how? In Fromm, E., and Shor, R.E. (eds.), Hypnosis: Research developments and perspectives. Chicago: Aldine-Atherton, 399–443.

Orne, M.T. (1974) On the concept of hypnotic depth. Paper presented at the 18th Int. Cont. App. Psychol., Montreal, Canada. Cited by Perry and Walsh, 1978.

Orne, M.T., and Evans, F.J. (1965) Social control in the psychological experiment: Antisocial behaviour and hypnosis. J. Pers. Soc. Psychol., 1, 189–200.

Orne, M.T., and Evans, F.J. (1966) Inadvertent termination of hypnosis with hypnotised and simulating subjects. Int. J. Clin. Exp. Hypn., 14, 61–78.

Orne, M.T., and Holland, C.C. (1968) On the ecological validity of laboratory deceptions. Int. J. Psychiat., 6, 282–293.

Orne, M.T., and Scheibe, K.E. (1964) The contribution of nondeprivation factors in the production of sensory deprivation effects: The psychology of the 'panic button'. J. Abnorm. Soc. Psychol., 68, 3–12.

Orne, M.T., Sheehan, P.W., and Evans, F.J. (1968) Occurrence of post-hypnotic behaviour outside the experimental setting. J. Pers. Soc. Psychol., 9, 189–196.

Ornstein, R.E. (1972) The psychology of consciousness. San Francisco: Freeman.

Osler, W. (1892) The principles and practice of medicine. New York: Appleton & Co.

Parker, P.D., and Barber, T.X. (1964) Hypnosis, task-motivating instructions and learning performance. J. Abnorm. Soc. Psychol., 69, 499–504.

Parrish, M., Lundy, R.M., and Leibowitz, H.W. (1969) Effect of hypnotic age regression on the magnitude of the Ponzo and Poggendorff illusions. J. Abnorm. Psychol., 74, 693–698.

Paskewitz, D.A., and Orne, M.T. (1973) Visual effects on alpha feedback training. Science, 181, 360–363.

Patten, E.F. (1930) The duration of post-hypnotic suggestions. J. Abnorm. Soc. Psychol., 25, 319–334.

Patten, E.F. (1932) Does post-hypnotic amnesia apply to practice effects? J. Gen. Psychol., 7, 196–201.

Pattie, F.A. (1935) A report of attempts to produce uniocular blindness by hypnotic suggestion. Brit. J. Med. Psychol., 15, 230–241.

Pattie, F.A. (1941) The production of blisters by hypnotic suggestions: A review. J. Abnorm. Soc. Psychol., 36, 62–72.

Pattie, F.A. (1950) The genuineness of unilateral deafness produced by hypnosis. Amer. J. Psychol., 63, 84–86.

Paul, G.L. (1966) Insight vs. desensitisation in psychotherapy: An experiment in anxiety reduction. Stanford, Calif.: Stanford Univ. Press.

Paul, G.L. (1969) Inhibition of physiological response to stressful imagery by relaxation training and hypnotically suggested relaxation. Behav. Res. Ther. 7, 249–256.

Perry, C., and Chisholm, W. (1973) Hypnotic age regression and the Ponzo and Poggendorff illusions. Int. J. Clin. Exp. Hypn., 21, 192–204.

Perry, C., and Walsh, B. (1978) Inconsistencies and anomalies of response as a defining characteristic of hypnosis. J. Abnorm. Psychol., 87, 574–577.

Peters, J.E. (1973) Trance logic: Artifact or essence in hypnosis. Doctoral dissertation. Penn. State Univ. Cited by Perry and Walsh, 1978.

Peters, J.E., and Stern, R.M. (1973) Peripheral skin temperature and vasomotor responses during hypnotic induction. Int. J. Clin. Exp. Hypn., 21, 102–108.

Podmore, F. (1964) From Mesmer to Christian Science. A Short History of Mental Healing. New York: University Books.

Pomeranz, B., and Chiu, D. (1976) Naloxone blockade of acupuncture analgesia: Endorphin implicated. Life Sciences, 19, 1757–1762.

Porter, J.W., Woodward, J.A., Bisbee, T.C., and Fenker, R.M. (1976) Effect of hypnotic age regression on the magnitude of the Ponzo illusion. J. Abnorm. Psychol. 79, 189–194.

Prince, M. (1929) Clinical and experimental studies in personality. Cambridge: Sci-Art.

Rachman, S.J., and Philips, C. (1978) Psychology and medicine. Harmondsworth, Middlesex: Penguin Books.

Rapson, W.S., and Jones, T.C. (1964) Restraint of rabbits by hypnosis. Lab. Animal Care, 14, 131–133.

Reiff, R., and Scheerer, M. (1959) Memory and Hypnotic Age Regression. New York: International Universities Press.

Reiter, P.J. (1958) Antisocial or Criminal Acts and Hypnosis: A Case Study. Springfield, Ill.: C.C. Thomas.

Reyher, J. (1973) Can hypnotised subjects simulate waking behaviour? Amer. J. Clin. Hypn., 16, 31–36.

Roberts, A.H., Schuler, J., Bacon, J.G., Zimmermann, R.L., and Patterson, R. (1975) Individual differences and autonomic control: absorption, hypnotic susceptibility, and the unilateral control of skin temperature. J. Abnorm. Psychol., 84, 272–279.

Rock, N., Shipley, T., and Campbell, C. (1969) Hypnosis with untrained non-volunteer patients in labour. Int. J. Clin. Exp. Hyp., 17, 25–36.

Rock, N.L., and Shipley, T. (1961) Ability to 'fake' colour blindness in the waking state: A control for colour blindness under hypnosis. Philadelphia: Dept. of Psychiat. Temple Univ. Medical Centre. (Mimeo.) Cited by Barber, 1969b.

Roethlisberger, F.J., and Dickson, W.J. (1939) Management and the worker. Cambridge, Mass.: Harvard Univ. Press.

Rosenberg, M.J. (1969) The conditions and consequences of evaluation apprehension. In Rosenthal, R., and Rosnow, L. (eds.), Artifact in behavioural research. New York: Academic Press.

Rosenhan, D., and London, P. (1963) Hypnosis: Expectation, susceptibility and performance. J. Abnorm. Soc. Psychol., 66, 77–81.

Rosenthal, B.G., and Mele, H. (1952) The validity of hypnotically induced colour hallucinations. J. Abnorm. Soc. Psychol., 47, 700–704.

Sachs, L.B. (1970) Comparison of hypnotic analgesia and hypnotic relaxation during stimulation by a continuous pain source. J. Abnorm. Psychol., 76, 206–210.

Saletu, B., et al. (1975) Hypno-analgesia and acupuncture analgesia: A neurophysiological reality. Neuropsychobiology, 1, 218–242.

Sampimon. R.L.H., and Woodruff, M.F.A. (1946) Some observations concerning the use of hypnosis as a substitute for anaesthesia. Med. J. Australia, 1, 393–395.

Sanders, R.S., and Reyher, J. (1969) Sensory deprivation and the enhancement of hypnotic susceptibility. J. Abnorm. Psychol., 74, 375–381.

Sarbin, T.R. (1956) Physiological effects of hypnotic stimulation. In Dorcus, R.M. (ed.), Hypnosis and its therapeutic applications. New York: Academic Press, 333–354.

Sarbin, T.R., and Anderson, M.L. (1967) Role-theoretical analysis of hypnotic behaviour. In Gordon, J.E. (ed.), Handbook of Clinical and Experimental Hypnosis. New York. Crowell, Collier and Macmillan, 319–344.

Sarbin, T.R., and Coe, W.C. (1972) Hypnosis: A social Psychological Analysis of Influence Communication. New York: Holt, Rinehart and Winston.

Sarbin, T.R., and Lim, D.T. (1963) Some evidence in support of the role taking hypothesis in hypnosis. Int. J. Clin. Exp. Hypn., 11, 98–103.

Sarbin, T.R., and Slagle, R.W. (1972) Hypnosis and psychophysiological outcomes. In Fromm, E., and Short, R.E. (eds.), Hypnosis: Research developments and perspectives. Chicago: Aldine-Atherton. 185–214.

Scheibe, K.E., Gray, A.L., and Keim, C.S. (1968) Hypnotically induced deafness and delayed auditory feedback: A comparison of real and simulating subjects. Int. J. Exp. Clin. Hypn., 16, 158–164.

Schultz, J.H. (1954) Some remarks about the technique of hypnosis as an anaesthetic. Brit. J. Med. Hypn., 5, 23–25.

Scott, H.D. (1930) Hypnosis and the conditioned reflex. J. Gen. Psychol., 4, 113–130.

Sears, R.R. (1932) An experimental study of hypnotic anaesthesia. J. Exp. Psychol., 15, 1–22.

Sears, A.B. (1955) A comparison of hypnotic and waking learning of the International Morse Code. J. Clin. Exp. Hypn., 3, 215–221.

Shapiro, A.K. (1973) Contribution to a history of the placebo effect. In Miller, N.E., Barber, T.X., Dicara, L.V., Kamiya, J., Shapiro, D., and Stoyva, J. (eds.), Biofeedback and self-control. Chicago: Aldine, 217–243.

Shapiro, J.L., and Diamond, M.J. (1972) Increases in hypnotisability as a function of encounter group training. J. Abnorm. Psychol., 79–112–115.

Sheehan, P. (1969) Artificial induction of post-hypnotic conflict. J. Abnorm. Psychol., 74, 16–25.

Sheehan, P.W. (1973) Analysis of the heterogeneity of 'faking' and 'simulating' performance in the hypnotic setting. Int. J. Clin. Exp. Hypn., 21, 213–225.

Sheehan, P.W. (1977) Incongruity in trance behaviour: A defining property of hypnosis? Annals N.Y. Acad. Sci., 196, 194–207.

Sheehan, P.W., Obstoj, S.I., and McConkey, K. (1976) Trance logic and cue structure as supplied by the hypnotist. J. Abnorm. Psychol., 85, 459–472.

Sheehan, P.W., and Perry, C.W. (1976) Methodologies of hypnosis: A critical appraisal of contemporary paradigms of hypnosis. Hillsdale, New Jersey: Laurence Erlbaum.

Sheridan, C.L., and King, R.G. (1972) Obedience to authority with an authentic victim. Proceedings, 80th Annual Convention APA, 165–66.

Sherif, M. (1935) A study of some social factors in perception. Arch. Psychol., 27, no. 187.

Shevrin, H. (1972) The wish to cooperate and the temptation to submit: the hypnotised subject's dilemma. In Fromm, E., and Shor, R.E. (eds.), Hypnosis: Research developments and perspectives. Chicago: Aldine-Atherton. 527–536.

Shor, R.E. (1959) Explorations in hypnosis: A theoretical and experimental study. Doctoral dissertation. Univ. Brandeis. Cited by Barber, 1963.

Shor, R.E. (1962) Physiological effects of painful stimulation during hypnotic analgesia under conditions designed to minimise anxiety. Int. J. Clin. Exp. Hypn., 10, 183–202 (a).

Shor, R.E. (1962) Three dimensions of hypnotic depth. Int. J. Clin. Exp. Hypn., 10, 23–38 (b).

Shor, R.E. (1970) The three-factor theory of hypnosis as applied to the book-reading fantasy and the concept of suggestion. Int. J. Clin. Exp. Hypn., 18, 89–98.

Shore, R.E., and Orne, E.C. (1962) The Harvard Group Scale of Hypnotic Susceptibility, Form A. Palo Alto, California: Consulting Psychologists Press.

Shor, R.E., Orne, M.T., and O'Connell, D.N. (1962) Validation and cross-validation of a scale of self-reported personal experiences which predicts hypnotisability. J. Psychol., 53, 55–75 (c).

Sidis, B. (1906) Are there hypnotic hallucinations? Psychol. Rev., 13, 239–257.

Sigall, H., Aronson, E., and Van Hoose, T. (1970) The co-operative subject: myth or reality? J. Exp. Soc. Psychol., 6, 1–10.

Simon, E.J. (1976) The opiate receptors. Neurochem. Res., 1, 3–28.

Sinclair-Gieben, A.H.C., and Chalmers, D. (1959) Evaluation of treatment of warts by hypnosis. Lancet, 2, 480–482.

Sjoberg, B.M., and Hollister, L.F. (1965) The effects of psychotomimetic drugs on primary suggestibility. Psychopharmacologia, 8, 251–267.

Sjolund, B., and Eriksen, M. (1976) Electro-acupuncture and endogenous morphines. Lancet, Nov. 2, 1085.

Skemp, R.R. (1972) Hypnosis and hypnotherapy considered as cybernetic processes, Brit. J. of Clin. Hyp., 3, 97–107.

Slotnik, R.S., Liebert, R.M., and Hilgard, E.R. (1965) The enhancement of muscular performance through exhortation and involving instructions. J. Pers. 33, 37–45.

Solovey, G., and Milechin, A. (1957) Concerning the nature of hypnotic phenomena. J. Clin. Exp. Hypn., 5, 67–76.

Spanos, N.P., Ansari, F., and Stam, H.J. (1979) Hypnotic age regression and eidetic imagery: A failure to replicate. J. Abnorm. Psychol., 88, 88–91.

Spanos, N.P., and Barber, T.X. (1968) 'Hypnotic' experiences as inferred from auditory and visual hallucinations. J. Exp. Res. Pers., 3, 136–150.

Spanos, N.P., and Barber, T.X. (1974) Toward a convergence in hypnosis research. Amer. Psychol., 29, 500–511.

Spanos, N.P., and Barber, T.X. (1976) Behaviour modification and hypnosis. Prog. Behav. Mod., 3, 1–44.

Spanos, N.P., Barber, T.X., and Lang, G. (1974) Effects of hypnotic induction, suggestions of anaesthesia, and demands for honesty on subjective reports of pain. In Condon, H., and Nisbett, R.E. (eds.),

Thought and feeling: Cognitive alteration of feeling states. Chicago: Aldine.

Spanos, N.P., Ham, M.L., and Barber, T.X. (1973) Suggested ('hypnotic') visual hallucinations: Experimental and phenomenological data. J. Abnorm. Psychol., 81, 96–106.

Spanos, N.P., and McPeake, J.D. (1973) Effect of attitudes toward hypnosis on the relationship between involvement in everyday imaginative activities and hypnotic suggestibility. Medfield, Mass.: Medfield Foundation. (Mimeo.) Cited by Barber, Spanos and Chaves, 1974.

Spanos, N.P., Rivers, S.M., and Gottleib, J. (1978) Hypnotic responsivity, meditation, and laterality of eye movements. J. Abnorm. Psychol., 87, 566–569.

Spiegel, H. (1970) Termination of smoking by a single treatment. Arch. Environ. Health, 20, 736–742.

Spiegel, H. (1972) An eye-roll test for hypnotisability. Amer. J. Clin. Hypn., 15, 25–27.

Staats, A.W., and Staats, C.K. (1958) Attitudes established by classical conditioning. J. Abnorm. Soc. Psychol., 57, 37–40.

Starker, S. (1974) Effects of hypnotic induction upon visual imagery. J. Nerv. Ment. Dis., 159, 433–437.

Sternbach, R.A. (1968) Pain: A psychophysiological analysis. New York: Academic Press.

Stevenson, D.R., Stoyva, J., and Beach, H.D. (1962) Retroactive inhibition and hypnosis. Bull. Maritime Psychol. Assoc., 11, 11–15.

Stevenson, J.H. (1976) The effect of posthypnotic dissociation on the performance of interfering tasks. J. Abnorm. Psychol., 85.

Stewart, D., Thomson, J., and Oswald, I. (1977) Acupuncture analgesia: An experimental investigation. Brit. Med. J. 1, 67–70.

Stoyva, J. (1961) The effect of suggested dreams on the length of rapid eye movement periods. Doctoral dissertation, Univ. Chicago. Cited by Barber, Spanos, and Chaves, 1974.

Stoyva, J.M. (1965) Post-hypnotically suggested dreams and the sleep cycle. Archs. Gen. Psychiat. 12, 287–294.

Strickler, C.B. (1929) A quantitative study of post-hypnotic amnesia. J. Abnorm. Soc. Psychol., 24, 108–119.

Stromeyer, C.F. and Psotka, J. (1970) The detailed texture of eidetic imagery. Nature, 225, 346–349.

Stukát, K.G. (1958) Suggestibility: A factorial and experimental analysis. Stockholm: Almquist and Wiksell.

Sushinsky, L.W., and Bootzin, R.R. (1970) Cognitive desensitisation as a mode of systematic desensitisation. Behav. Res. Ther. 8, 29–34.

Sutcliffe, J.P. (1961) 'Credulous' and 'sceptical' views of hypnotic phenomena: Experiments in aesthesia, hallucination and delusion. J. Abnorm. Soc. Psychol., 62, 189–200.

Switras, J.E. (1974) A comparison of the eye-roll test for hypnotisability and the Stanford Hypnotic Susceptibility Scale. Amer. J. Clin. Hypn., 17, 54–55.

Tart, C.T. (1964) A comparison of suggested dreams occurring in hypnosis and sleep. Int. J. Clin. Exp. Hypn., 12, 263–289.

Tart, C.T. (1965) The hypnotic dream: Methodological problems and a review of the literature. Psychol. Bull., 63, 87–99.

Tart, C.T. (1970) Increases in hypnotisability resulting from a prolonged programme for enhancing personal growth. J. Abnorm. Psychol., 75, 260–266 (a).

Tart, C.T. (1970) Waking from sleep at a preselected time. J.Am. Soc. Psychosom. Dent. Med. 17, 3–16 (b).

Tart, C.T. (1975) Discrete states of consciousness. In Lee, P., Ornstein, R.E., Galvin, D., Deikman, A.J., and Tart, C.T. (eds.), Symposium on consciousness. New York: Viking Press. 89–175 (a).

Tart, C.T. (1975) States of consciousness. New York: Dutton (b).

Tart, C.T. (1977) Drug induced states of consciousness. In Wolman, B.B. (ed.), Handbook of parapsychology. New York: Van Nostrand Reinhold. 500–525.

Tart, C.T., and Dick, L. (1970) The conscious control of dreaming: 1. The post-hypnotic dream. J. Abnorm. Psychol., 76, 304–315.

Taylor, W.S. (1964) Psychotherapeutic methods with hypnosis. Amer. J. Clin. Hypn., 6, 322–325.

Tétreault, L., Panisset, A., and Gouger, P. (1964) Étude des facteurs, emotion et douleur dans la réponse tensionnelle au 'cold pressor test'. L'Union Médicale du Canada, 93, 177–180.

Thoresen, C.E., and Mahoney, M.J. (1974) Behavioural Self-Control. New York: Holt, Rinehart and Winston.

Thornton, E.M. (1976) Hypnotism, Hysteria and Epilepsy: An historical synthesis. London: Heinemann.

Travis, T.A., Kondo, C.Y., and Knott, J.R. (1974) Alpha conditioning: A controlled study. J. Nerv. Ment. Dis., 158, 162–173.

Troffer, S.A.H. (1966) Hypnotic age regression and cognitive functioning. Doctoral Dissertation. Univ. Stanford. Cited by Barber, 1969b.

True, R.M. (1949) Experimental control in hypnotic age regression states. Science, 110, 583–584.

Tuddenham, R.D., and Macbride, P. (1959) The yielding experiment from the subject's point of view. J. Pers. 27, 259–271.

Tursky, B., Schwartz, G.E., and Crider, A. (1970) Differential patterns of heart rate and skin resistance during a digit-transformation task. J. Exp. Psychol., 83, 451–457.

Ulett, G.A. (1978) Acupuncture: Pricking the bubble of scepticism. Biol. Psychiat., 13, 2, 159–161.

Underwood, H.W. (1960) The validity of hypnotically induced visual hallucinations. J. Abnorm. Soc. Psychol., 61, 39–46.

Valins, S. (1966) Cognitive effects of false heart-rate feedback. J. Pers. Soc.

Psychol., 4, 400–408.

Valins, S., and Ray, A.A. (1967) Effects of cognitive sensitisation of avoidance behaviour. J. Pers. Soc. Psychol. 7, 345–350.

Van Pelt, S.J. (1948) The control of heart rate by hypnotic suggestion. In Le Cron, L.M. (ed.), Experimental Hypnosis. New York: Macmillan, 268–275.

Vaughan, G.M. (1964) The trans-situational aspect of conformity behaviour. J. Pers. 32, 335–354.

Volavka, J., Mallya, A., Baig, S., and Perez-Cruet, J. (1977) Naloxone in chronic schizophrenia. Science, 196, 1227–1228.

Von Dedenroth, T.E.A. (1962) Trance depth: An independent variable in therapeutic results. Amer. J. Clin. Hypn., 4, 174–176.

Wagstaff, G.F. (1974) Perceptual vigilance: A review. Ind. J. Psychol., 49, 3, 181–186.

Wagstaff, G.F. (1976) A note on Mather and Degun's 'A comparative study of hypnosis and relaxation'. Brit. J. Med. Psychol., 49, 299–300 (a).

Wagstaff, G.F. (1976) Why are some hypnotic suggestions easier to pass than others? An explanation in terms of compliance. Dept. Psychol. Liverpool Univ. (Mimeo.) (b).

Wagstaff, G.F. (1977) An experimental study of compliance and post-hypnotic amnesia. Brit. J. Soc. Clin. Psychol., 16, 225–228 (a).

Wagstaff, G.F. (1977) Behavioural correlates of repression-sensitisation — a reconciliation of some conflicting findings. Ind. J. Psychol., 52, 195–202 (b).

Wagstaff, G.F. (1977) Goal-directed fantasy, the experience of non-volition and compliance. Soc. Beh. Person., 5, 389–93 (c).

Wagstaff, G.F. (1977) Post-hypnotic amnesia as disrupted retrieval: A role-playing paradigm. Quart. J. Exp. Psychol., 29, 499–504 (d).

Wagstaff, G.F. (1978) How do I know I'm hypnotised? Paper presented to the BPS, Social Psychology Section, Annual Conference. Sept.

Wagstaff, G.F. (1979) The problem of compliance in hypnosis: A social psychological viewpoint. Bull. Brit. Soc. Exp. Clin. Hypn., 2, 3–5.

Wagstaff, G.F., Hearne, K.M.T., and Jackson, B. (1980) Post-hypnotically suggested dreams and the sleep cycle. An experimental re-evaluation. IRCS J. Med. Science, 8, 240–241.

Wagstaff, G.F., and Ovenden, M. (1979) Hypnotic time distortion and free-recall learning — an attempted replication. Psychol. Res., 40, 291–298.

Wallace, B., Knight, T.A., and Garratt, J.B. (1976) Hypnotic susceptibility and frequency reports to illusory stimuli. J. Abnorm. Psychol., 85, 558–563.

Wallace, G., and Coppolino, C.A. (1960) Hypnosis in anaesthesiology. New York State. J. Medicine. 60, 3258–3273.

Wallace, J., and Sadalla, E. (1966) Behavioural consequences of transgression: 1. The effects of social recognition. J. Exp. Res. Pers. 1, 187–194.

Walker, N.S., Garratt, J.B., and Wallace, B. (1976) Restoration of eidetic imagery via hypnotic age regression: A preliminary report. J. Abnorm. Psychol., 85, 335–337.

Weber, S.J., and Cook, T.D. (1972) Subject effects in laboratory research: An examination of subject notes, demand characteristics, and valid inference. Psychol. Bull., 77, 273–295.

Weisenberg, M. (1977) Pain and pain control. Psychol. Bull., 84, 10081–044.

Weitzenhoffer, A.M., and Hilgard, E.R. (1959) Stanford Hypnotic Susceptibility Scale, Forms A and B. Palo Alto, Calif.: Consulting Psychologists Press.

Weitzenhoffer, A.M., and Hilgard, E.R. (1962) Stanford Hypnotic Susceptibility Scale, Form C. Palo Alto, Calif.: Consulting Psychologists Press.

Weitzenhoffer, A.M., and Sjoberg, B.M. (1961) Suggestibility with and without 'induction of hypnosis'. J. Nerv. Ment. Dis., 132, 205–220.

Werbel, E.W. (1965) One surgeon's experience with hypnosis. New York: Pageant Press.

Werbel, E.W. (1967) Hypnosis in serious surgical problems. Amer. J. Clin. Hypn., 10, 44–47.

Wheeler, L., Reis, H.T., Wolff, E., Grupsmith, E., and Mordkoff, A.M. (1974) Eye-roll and hypnotic susceptibility. Int. J. Clin. Exp. Hypn., 22, 327–334.

White, H.C. (1961) Hypnosis in bronchial asthma. J. Psychosom. Res., 5, 272–279.

White, R.W. (1941) A preface to the theory of hypnotism. J. Abnorm. Soc. Psychol., 36, 477–505.

Wickramasekera, I. (1973) Effects of electromyographic feedback on hypnotic susceptibility: More preliminary data. J. Abnorm. Psychol., 83, 74–77.

Williams, G.W. (1929) The effect of hypnosis on muscular fatigue. J. Abnorm. Soc. Psychol., 24, 318–329.

Williamsen, J.A., Johnson, H.J., and Eriksen, C.W. (1965) Some characteristics of post-hypnotic amnesia. J. Abnorm. Psychol., 70, 123–131.

Wilson, W., and Nakajo, H. (1965) Preference for photographs as a function of frequency of presentation. Psychonomic Science, 3, 577–578.

Winkelstein, L.B. (1958) Routine hypnosis for obstetrical delivery: An evaluation of hypnosuggestion in 200 consecutive cases. Amer. J. Obstet. Gynec. 76, 152–160.

Wolberg, L.R. (1972) Hypnosis: Is it for you? New York: Harcourt Brace Jovanovich.

Wolfe, L.S. (1961) Hypnosis in anaesthesiology. In Le Cron, L.M. (ed.), Techniques of hypnotherapy. New York: Julian Press, 188–212.

Wolff, L.V. (1930) The response to plantar stimulation in infancy. Amer. J. Dis. Child. 39, 1176–1185.

Wolpe, J. (1958) Psychotherapy by reciprocal inhibition. Stanford, Calif.: Stanford Univ. Press.

Wolpe, J. (1969) The practice of behaviour therapy. Oxford: Pergamon.

Wrightsman, L.S. (1972) Social psychology in the seventies. Belmont, California: Wadsworth.

Young, P.C. (1925) An experimental study of mental and physical functions in the normal and hypnotic states. Amer. J. Psychol., 36, 214–232.

Young, P.C. (1940) Hypnotic regression — fact or artifact? J. Abnorm. Soc. Psychol., 35, 273–278.

Young, P.C. (1948) Antisocial uses of hypnosis. In Le Cron, L.M. (ed.), Experimental Hypnosis. New York: MacMillan. 376–409.

Zajonc, B., and Rajaecki, D.W. (1969) Exposure and affect: A field experiment. Psychonomic Science, 17, 216–27.

Zajonc, R.B., and Sales, S.M. (1966) Social facilitation of dominant and subordinate responses. J. Exp. Soc. Psychol., 2, 160–168.

Zamansky, H.S. (1977) Suggestion and countersuggestion in hypnotic behaviour. J. Abnorm. Psychol., 86, 346–351.

Zax, M., and Cowen, E.L. (1976) Abnormal psychology: Changing conceptions. (2nd ed.). New York: Holt, Rinehart and Winston.

Zimbardo, P.G., Maslach, C., and Marshall, G. (1970) Hypnosis and the psychology of cognitive and behavioural control. Dept. Psychol., Stanford Univ. (Mimeo.) Cited by Barber, Spanos and chaves, 1974.

Zimbardo, P.G. (1969) The human choice: Individuation, reason, and order versus deindividuation, impulse and chaos. In Arnold, W.J., and Levine, D. (eds.), Nebraska Symposium in Motivation. Lincoln: Univ. Nebraska Press.

Subject Index

compliance and reports of, 35,
165–8, 175
culture and, 156
dissociation and, 179–81, 184–5
distraction effects of, 64, 159–60
doctor patient relationship and,
164–5
drugs and, 163, 184–5
endorphins and, 189–92
hypnotic susceptibility and, 171–2
information and, 165
ischemic, 174, 189–90
laboratory studies of, 172–9
measurement of, 173–4
physiological correlates of, 174–9
placebo effect and, 185–8
relaxation and, 64, 161–2, 176
suggestion and, 159–62
surgery and, 152–6, 160, 162–4,
166–8
susceptibility to, 154–6
tonic immobility and, 169–71, 191
Personality, *see* Susceptibility to
hypnosis
Persuasibility, 132–5
Phobias, *see* Hypnotherapy
Physiological responses, 98–102
Placebo effect, 99, 105, 156–9, 185–8
endorphins and, 190–1
naloxone and, 190
suggestion and, 185–8
Police use of hypnosis, 96–8
Post-hypnotic amnesia, *see* Amnesia
Post-hypnotic suggestions, 15, 106–13
Psychoanalysis, *see* Hypnotherapy

Rapid eye movements (REM), 100–1
Reincarnation, 74
Relaxation, 58–61, 64, 101–2, 115–16,
148–9, 154, 161–2, 194–5
pain and, *see* Pain
Role-enactment, 9–10, 52, 91, 211

Self-attribution, see Self-perception
Self-hypnosis, 54
Self-perception, 56–72, 204–5
Sham behaviour, 9–11, 17–28, 40,
49–50, 54, 72, 75, 120–1, 146, 207
Shaman, 210
Simulation, 38–41, 48, 90–2, 103,
107–10, 113–24, 126–9, 182
real-simulator design and, 40
Skin temperature, 100
Sleep, 3–7, 214
Smoking, *see* Hypnotherapy

Social comparison theory, 62
Somnambulism, 3, 5, 6, 212, 214,
216–17
Stage hypnosis, 19
Stanford Hypnotic Susceptibility Scale,
12, 30, 32, 51, 59, 62, 63, 135, 144,
150, 213–14
Stomach contractions, 100
Subjective experience of hypnosis, 8,
33–6, 48, 53, 56–72
inferences from bodily changes,
58–62
inferences from responses to
suggestions, 63–7
Suggestibility, 13, 131–5
comparison with hypnosis, 14, 137
habit and, 112
primary and secondary, 132–7
Subliminal perception, 83–4
Surgery, *see also* Pain, 11, 17
Susceptibility to hypnosis, 12, 15, 51, 91
94–5, 117, 131–51, 205–7
age differences and, 143–4
compliance and, 42–4
eye rolling and, 150
heritability of, 144–5
increasing, *see* training in hypnosis
lateralisation and, 140–2
personality and, 137–43
role skills and, 145–6
trance logic and, 128–9
Systematic desensitisation, *see*
Hypnotherapy

Task-motivational instructions, 45–8,
78, 88, 89
Time distortion, 89–90
Tonic immobility, 169–71
Training in hypnosis, 51, 146–50
biofeedback and, 148–50
Trance, *see* Hypnotic trance
Trance logic, 126–9
hypnotic susceptibility and, 128–9

Verbal reports (validity of), 18, 44–9,
120–1
Visual acuity, 81

Waking suggestibility, 131–5, 137
Waking suggestions, 15, 63, 86–7, 99
131–5, 137, 160–1
Warts, 99

Yoga, 212

Author Index